DOING
QUALITATIVE
RESEARCH

DOING QUALITATIVE RESEARCH

A COMPREHENSIVE GUIDE

DAVID SILVERMAN

Goldsmiths College, University of London, UK

AMIR MARVASTI

Penn State Altoona

SAGE Publications

Los Angeles • London • New Delhi • Singapore

For information:

Sage Publications, Inc.
2455 Teller Road
Thousand Oaks, California 91320
E-mail: order@sagepub.com

Sage Publications India Pvt. Ltd.
B 1/I 1 Mohan Cooperative
 Industrial Area
Mathura Road, New Delhi 110 044
India

Sage Publications Ltd.
1 Oliver's Yard
55 City Road
London EC1Y 1SP
United Kingdom

Sage Publications Asia-Pacific Pte. Ltd.
33 Pekin Street #02-01
Far East Square
Singapore 048763

Printed in the United States of America

Library of Congress Cataloging-in-Publication Data

Silverman, David.
Doing qualitative research: a comprehensive guide/David Silverman, Amir Marvasti.
   p. cm.
Includes bibliographical references and index.
ISBN 978-1-4129-2639-3 (pbk.: acid-free paper)
  1. Social sciences—Research—Methodology. 2. Qualitative research. I. Marvasti, Amir B., 1966- II. Title.

H62.S472 2008
300.72—dc22   2007046634

This book is printed on acid-free paper.

08   09   10   11   12   11   10   9   8   7   6   5   4   3   2   1

Acquisitions Editor:	Vicki Knight
Editorial Assistant:	Lauren Habib
Associate Editor	Sean Connelly
Production Editor:	Catherine M. Chilton
Copy Editor:	Brenda Weight
Typesetter:	C&M Digitals (P) Ltd.
Proofreader:	Doris Hus
Indexer:	Marilyn Augst
Cover Designer:	Candice Harman
Marketing Manager:	Stephanie Adams

Contents

Preface

This edition of *Doing Qualitative Research* has many revised chapters. Chapter 2 discusses what you can (and cannot) do with qualitative research, with an expanded discussion on the diversity of qualitative research. Chapter 3 is based on entirely different material, which comes from recent PhDs speaking about their experiences in graduate school and the job market. Other revised chapters are on

- Selecting a research topic (Chapter 6, with a new discussion on IRB considerations)

- Making good use of your supervisor (Chapter 18, with new material on how to select an "ideal" mentor and how to be an "ideal" protégé)

- Surviving the PhD examination (Chapter 25, with new examples from U.S. students)

- Getting published (Chapter 27, with an expanded discussion of different theoretical models of writing and representational strategies)

- Tailoring your writing for different audiences (Chapter 28, with a new discussion on writing as writer–audience interaction)

- Getting a job (Chapter 29, with a more comprehensive discussion of job search strategies from choosing a suitable graduate program to the dos and don'ts of a job interview)

All these revised chapters include new exercises and case studies that elaborate on the content of each chapter using personal accounts of triumph and struggle. These stories come from David, Amir, and other qualitative researchers who generously shared their experiences with us.

We have also tried to make this edition attend to the needs of the range of students from different disciplines who are involved with qualitative research projects. Each chapter also now begins with a list of objectives and ends with a set of key points. The glossary is greatly expanded and words that appear in it are listed in bold the first time they are used in each chapter.

With these changes, we hope this book will be equally accessible to students of qualitative methods across a wide range of disciplines. Although we cannot escape our own sociological background, we have tried throughout to provide helpful resources for students across the social sciences and throughout the world.

We hope that this book will be used as a basic primer for PhD students, combining "hands-on" guidance on completing a good qualitative research project with practical advice on the criteria used in oral examinations and in publication. We have also attempted to make the book useful and accessible to the many master's and bachelor's students who are interested in writing a qualitative research for their theses. Although such students will normally be expected to complete their research in months rather than years, they face the same problems of research design, execution, and writing discussed in this book. Even if they do not face an oral examination on their research, the best master's students should be thinking about publishing their work, and both bachelor's and master's students should be interested in how higher-level work is evaluated and the significance of "originality."

The content of this book derives from our biographies. For David, in addition to his numerous publications, his vast experience comes from supervising more than 20 successful PhD students and more than 20 years of teaching introductory workshops for research students at universities around the world, as well as the course "Concepts and Methods of Qualitative Research" for MA students. These courses have convinced him that the only way to learn the craft of qualitative research is to apply classroom knowledge about different methodologies to actual data (found here in the case studies and exercises provided in each chapter).

Amir's contributions to this new edition of an already successful book come from a different source. Although Amir has published several books and articles and has taught undergraduate courses in research methods, his contributions to this book reflect a novice researcher's perspective on an ever-growing field rather than expertise per se. In one form or another, Amir has had to grapple with many of the topics covered in this book. Thus, wherever appropriate, he has interjected his understanding of these various matters in the text more as one graduate student speaking to another rather than as an expert educating his peers. Straddling the world between a recent PhD and a position as junior professor at a small liberal arts college, Amir supplements David's decades of experience with a degree of empathy for the plight of struggling graduate students.

Our readers should be aware that no textbook offers a purely neutral treatment of the topics it covers. Much will depend on the material included (and excluded) and on the particular position of the author(s). We have our own particular "axes to grind" in this book. First, we argue that doing qualitative research is always a theoretically driven undertaking. This means that practical skills are not the whole of the story, particularly if such skills are (wrongly) seen as sets of arbitrary "recipes."

Second, as David has long argued, most dichotomies or polarities in social science are highly dangerous. At best, they are pedagogic devices for students to obtain a first grip on a difficult field—they help us to learn the jargon. At worst, they are excuses for not thinking, which assemble groups of researchers into armed camps, unwilling to learn from one another.

For instance, as a qualitative researcher, David has been open to using quantitative measures where appropriate. This is because, while recognizing the different **models** we often use, David shares quantitative researchers' aim to do a *science* (loosely defined as critical sifting of data, leading to cumulative generalizations that can always be later refuted).

There are pragmatic as well as intellectual reasons for taking this position. As the introduction to a book David recently coedited puts it,

> The great conversation that, in practice, is carried out in the world (what researchers like to call "common sense"), assumes that facts are "out there" and can be "collected" and therefore can constitute "evidence." A social research practice that does not go along with this view will, on the whole, fail to enter the world's conversation. (Seale, Gobo, Gubrium, & Silverman, 2004, p. 6)

This attention to practice, as reflected in the title of this book and displayed throughout the text, also implies that *learning* qualitative research is inseparable from *doing* qualitative research. No two qualitative studies are exactly alike. The setting, the players, the research question, or essentially everything is fluid in qualitative undertaking, to a large extent by design. Throughout this text, we provide scenarios, stories, and examples that both illustrate and reinforce this position. As noted earlier, our aim is not to provide research recipes. Such a formulaic approach is counter to the reflexive nature of qualitative research, as we understand it. Instead, we approach teaching, learning, and doing qualitative research as an ongoing process of "chance learning." Although the book serves its instructional purpose of providing outlines, models, and lists, it also urges students to relentlessly look for the undiscovered possibilities presented through their fieldwork, interviews, or other material. To use a metaphor, we aim to simply teach students to keep their eyes open but cannot possibly foretell the substance of what they will see.

In completing the revisions for this edition, we enjoyed the generous support of many colleagues and friends. We want to thank all those whose work is discussed throughout this book (Sylvia Ansay, Michael Arter, Craig Boylstein, Kirstin Bratt, Jennifer de Coste, Sara Crawley, Dean Dabney, Christopher Faircloth, Lara Foley, Nikitah Imani, John Linn, Karyn McKinney, Michelle Miller-Day, Eileen O'Brien, John Talmage, and Darin Weinberg). Our thanks are due to our editors at Sage (Sean Connelly, Lisa Cuevas, and Margo Crouppen). We are particularly grateful for Jay Gubrium's most helpful suggestions. Finally, Amir is indebted to David for the opportunity to contribute to this book.

Sage Publications would also like to thank the following reviewers:

Jeanne E. Bitterman, ED.D.
Teachers College, Columbia University, New York

Janet Ambrogne Sobczak, Ph.D., R.N., C.S.
Decker School of Nursing Binghamton University

Monika Ardelt
University of Florida

Kathryn Roulston
University of Georgia

David W. Scott
University of South Carolina, School of Journalism and Mass Communications

Deborah Kilgore
Iowa State University

Audrey J. Noble
University of Delaware

Enrique S. Pumar
William Paterson University

John Rinciari
William Paterson University

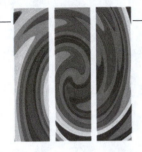

PART I

Introduction

Part I provides a context for thinking about doing qualitative research. A brief introduction to the themes of this book and how best to use it is provided in Chapter 1. Chapter 2 compares qualitative and quantitative research and raises questions about how to decide whether qualitative methods are appropriate for your research topic. Chapters 3 and 4 offer examples of early and late stages of research students' work and show what we can learn from their experiences and ideas. Finally, in Chapter 5, we address (and seek to demystify) the troubling concept of originality in research.

CHAPTER 1

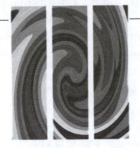

How to Use This Book

This is the fifth textbook on **methodology** David has written or edited since 1985. Everyone knows that research methods texts often sell well, but that is hardly an excuse to write yet another one. So, you may properly ask, what has this book to offer?

The brief answer is that, in our view, research students still lack a singly authored, hands-on, practical guide to the business of doing qualitative research, writing it up, and making use of it. This is what this book sets out to do. Much more than other methodology texts, it aims to teach the skills of qualitative research in the context of the practical problems that face the novice researcher. To this end, it combines telling examples of students' experiences in the **field**, case studies of relevant qualitative research, summaries of key skills, and exercises to test your knowledge.

In this short chapter, we outline the structure of this book and provide some suggestions about how to make optimum use of it.

Part I is aimed at the beginning research student. Part II assumes that you have overcome your initial doubts and now need to deal with the nitty-gritty issues that arise when you start to design a research study. Chapter 6 discusses how to select a topic. Chapters 7 and 8 deal with using **theories** and choosing a methodology. The tricky question of selecting which case(s) to study is discussed in Chapter 9. The final chapter in Part II considers how to write a research proposal.

Part III focuses on the period when you have begun to gather and analyze data. In Chapter 11, we outline what is to be gained by working early with data sets. Chapter 12 discusses how to develop your early analysis. The next two chapters consider the use of computer-aided qualitative data analysis and *validity* and *reliability*. Chapter 15 shows you how to apply what you have learned in Part III to evaluate qualitative research.

In Part IV, we address ways of keeping in touch with your data, with subjects in the field and with your university department. In four chapters, we discuss record keeping (including a research diary), relations in the field (including ethical issues), making good use of your supervisor, and how to get feedback about your research.

Alasuutari describes writing a thesis as rather like learning to ride a bicycle through gradually adjusting your balance:

> Writing is first and foremost analysing, revising and polishing the text. The idea that one can produce ready-made text right away is just about as senseless as the cyclist who has never had to restore his or her balance. (1995, p. 178)

Following Alasuutari's guidance, Part V is concerned with the "writing up" stage of research. Its five chapters address the following topics: how to begin your research report, how to write effective literature review and methodology chapters, and how to produce a lively concluding chapter.

For PhD students, the oral, or viva, is a crucial and much-feared part of the process. It also may seem to be shrouded in mystery, like some weird Masonic ritual! Part VI attempts to demystify the PhD examination. Whereas Part VI is only relevant to PhD students, Part VII offers all readers a discussion of effective qualitative research, which provides an overview of the main themes of this book.

The three chapters in Part VIII consider the aftermath of a finished piece of research. Depending on the level of your work, this may involve the possibility of getting your research published and, perhaps, getting a job. Whatever its level, a good research report always is designed for a particular audience.

From Part II onward, the order of this book very roughly follows the likely chronological sequence of doing a piece of research. However, we recognize that textbooks are not usually read in the same way as novels. For instance, although you may want to resist the temptation to skip to the final chapter of a whodunit, no such prohibitions are sensible when using a textbook. So, for example, you may want to consult Chapter 18 on making good use of your supervisor quite early on. Or, if you want a quick summary of the story this book offers, you may turn at once to Chapter 26. Each chapter is more or less self-contained and so there should be no problems in zigzagging through the book in this way, using the glossary provided where appropriate.

Zigzagging also makes sense because qualitative research rarely follows a smooth trajectory from hypothesis to findings. As we shall see, this is less a drawback than an opportunity to refocus your work as new ideas and opportunities arise in the field. Consequently, most readers will want to move backward and forward through the book as the occasion arises. Alternatively, you may find it useful to skim-read the book in advance and then work through certain chapters in greater detail to correspond with different stages of your research.

The examples and exercises in this book are designed to allow the novice to emerge with practical skills rather than simply the ability to write good examination answers. The exercises mostly rely on the stage of your research coinciding with the chapters where they are found. So when you are zigzagging through the book or skimming it, it will usually make sense to return to the exercises at a relevant stage of your work, using your supervisor for feedback and advice.

Ultimately, of course, no book can or should provide for how it will be read. Complete anarchy is nonetheless rarely very useful to anybody. In this spirit, the structure we have provided tries to give you an initial orientation. From then on, it is up to you. As the philosopher Ludwig Wittgenstein wrote, "All we want to do is to straighten you up on the track if your coach is crooked on the rails. Driving it afterwards we shall leave to you" (1980, p. 39e).

CHAPTER 2

What You Can (And Can't) Do With Qualitative Research

CHAPTER OBJECTIVES

By the end of this chapter you will be able to

1. Recognize that there is no simple distinction between qualitative and quantitative research

2. Understand the uses and limitations of both forms of research

3. Understand that *qualitative research* refers to a wide range of **models** and research practices

4. Work out whether qualitative methods are appropriate to your research topic

INTRODUCTION

This chapter offers practical help in answering three very concrete questions that you should consider before beginning a qualitative research study. Namely:

- Are qualitative methods always the best?

- Is qualitative research appropriate to the topic in which I am interested?

- If so, how should it influence the way I define my research problem?

Arguably, these are recurring concerns throughout this book, as they are relevant to all phases of the research process (e.g., data collection, analysis, writing, etc.).

In this chapter, however, we treat these questions as items in a "buyer's guide directory," so to speak. Our aim is to challenge some common misconceptions and help our readers assess the advantages and disadvantages of qualitative methods before committing to them for their thesis or dissertation. As in the rest of the book, we will set out our argument through examples of actual research studies.

ARE QUALITATIVE METHODS ALWAYS THE BEST?

The sociology department in which David used to work offered a degree in qualitative research. The offerings for this program included a course largely taught by ethnographers who themselves mainly used qualitative methods. However, such a title seemed to attract students more in terms of what it promised to avoid rather than by reason of what it offers.

Specializing in qualitative research sometimes implies avoidance or downplaying of statistical techniques and mechanical, quantitative methods used in survey research or demography. In fact, this was indeed the case in David's former sociology department—although students were expected to take a course in survey methods and to be aware of how the issues of validity and reliability so often posed by quantitative researchers are relevant to any kind of credible research (albeit in varying ways).

There is a potential danger in overemphasizing one's qualitative training or orientation. For some novice researchers, qualitative methods are embraced to the point of a dogmatic stand against all other methodological **paradigms**. It is particularly troubling to hear students speak of a fixed preference or predefined evaluation of what is "good" or at least "appropriate" (i.e., qualitative) and "bad" or "inappropriate" (i.e., quantitative) research. Any good researcher knows that your choice of method should not be predetermined. Rather, you should choose a method that is appropriate to what you are trying to find out (see Punch, 1998, p. 244).

For instance, if you want to learn about the demographic characteristics of Americans who favor the death penalty, a quantitative approach would do very nicely. In their article "Racial Prejudice and Support for the Death Penalty by Whites," Steven Barkan and Steven Cohn (1994) use General Social Survey (an opinion survey conducted annually in the United States) data to do exactly that. In particular, their study shows how **variables** like racial stereotyping, political conservatism, and antipathy toward blacks are associated with support for the death penalty. Table 2.1 represents some of the findings from this research.

As seen in Table 2.1, Barkan and Cohn use quantitative analysis of survey data to show that there is indeed a statistically significant relationship (as indicated by the starred correlation and regression coefficients) between respondents' political

Table 2.1   Correlations and Logistic Regression of Racial Stereotyping, Political Conservatism, and Antipathy Toward Blacks on Support for the Death Penalty

Independent Variables	r (Correlation Coefficient)	B (Regression Coefficient)
Racial stereotyping	.10	.08
Political conservatism	.18	.30
Antipathy toward Blacks	.17	.26

SOURCE: Adapted from Barkan and Cohn (1994).

NOTE: $p < .05$

and racial attitudes and their support for the death penalty. In this example, researchers' use of statistical techniques is quite appropriate. That is not to say that the research is beyond critique. On the contrary, one can raise legitimate questions about the validity of the dependent variable as measured by the question, "Do you support or oppose the death penalty for persons convicted of murder?" On its face, this question offers nothing about the circumstances and context of a death penalty case. For example, what if the offender was a minor, or what if the offender had been abused by the victim? In other words, serious questions can be posed about the extent to which the dependent variable in this study in fact measures what it claims. However, we should be careful not to throw away the proverbial baby with the bath water in our critique of quantitative methods. The findings here are significant, worthy of discussion and further analysis, and very appropriate for the research question and data at hand.

On the other hand, if you are concerned with exploring people's life histories or everyday behavior, then qualitative methods may be favored. Depending on the data and the research question, attitude toward the death penalty can also be investigated using qualitative techniques. For example, in their article "'I Hope Someone Murders Your Mother!': An Exploration of Extreme Support for the Death Penalty," Margaret Vandiver and her colleagues show how publicized executions engender hostility against the opponents of the death penalty. Using participant observations, newspaper accounts, and interviews, the researchers display the tumultuous and brutal attitudes of some of the supporters of the death penalty. Below are excerpts from this article based on letters sent to death penalty abolitionists in the state of Tennessee.

Since I can't be sure what if anything is going to happen to these murdering scumbags in the afterlife, I'll opt to fry them right now! If this is insensitive to weakling [sic] such as yourself, it's just too fucking bad! While people stand around executions with candles, I'm popping the cork on my bubbly and celebrating that another useless (that's right—useless) mother-fucker is gone. According to you, we should try to "understand what transformed a human being into a murderous monster." Guess what? Who the fuck cares? Get rid of them, end of story, period! I don't know what Bible you read but mine talks about "an eye for an eye" and that's EXACTLY what I want! (Vandiver, Giacopassi, & Gathje, 2002, p. 400)

Compared to Barkan and Cohn's quantitative article, Vandiver and her colleagues' research question and data focus on the nuances of pro–death penalty attitudes. The data and analysis in this case underscores how the themes of revenge and retribution are used as rhetorical justification for brutal punishment.

These two studies of attitudes toward the death penalty show how the questions and the data shape the research design and focus. In this book, we favor a purely pragmatic argument, according to which research problems define the most appropriate method. Research methods are not inherently right or wrong, they simply fulfill different purposes. On the one hand, an insistence that any research worth its salt should follow a purely quantitative logic would simply rule out the study of many interesting phenomena relating to what people actually do in their day-to-day lives, whether in homes, offices, or other public and private places. Similarly, an exclusive qualitative orientation excludes the possibility of understanding and appreciating social trends that are evinced in aggregate, numerical data. So, in choosing a method, everything depends on what we are trying to find out. No method of research, quantitative or qualitative, is intrinsically better than any other.

Moreover, as we shall see later, research problems are not neutral. How we frame a research problem will inevitably reflect a commitment (explicit or implicit) to a particular model of how the world works. And, in qualitative research, there are multiple, competing models. Simply declaring, "I am a qualitative researcher," in and of itself, explains little about your particular take on the diverse practices and languages of qualitative research. Our commitment to qualitative methods should accompany answers to the following questions:

- Exactly what methods do we have in mind (e.g., interviews, **focus groups**, observation, texts, audio or video recordings)?

- In what ways are these methods relevant to our research problem and to our model of how the world is put together?

In the next two sections, we show how you can begin to answer these questions.

SHOULD I USE QUALITATIVE METHODS?

Table 2.2 offers some general answers to this question.

Table 2.2   Should I Use Qualitative Research?

1. What exactly am I trying to find out? Different questions require different methods to answer them.

2. What kind of focus on my topic do I want to achieve? Do I want to study this phenomenon or situation in detail? Or am I mainly interested in making standardized and systematic comparisons and in accounting for variance?

3. How have other researchers dealt with this topic? To what extent do I wish to align my project with this literature?

4. What practical considerations should sway my choice? For instance, how long might my study take and do I have the resources to study it this way? Can I get access to the single case I want to study in depth? Are quantitative samples and data readily available?

5. Will we learn more about this topic using quantitative or qualitative methods? What will be the knowledge payoff of each method?

6. What seems to work best for me? Am I committed to a particular research model, which implies a particular methodology? Do I have a gut feeling about what a good piece of research looks like?

SOURCE: Adapted from Punch (1998), pp. 244–245.

This table shows that qualitative research is not always appropriate to every research problem. For example, following Item 2 of Table 2.2, if you are mainly interested in making systematic comparisons in order to account for the variance in some phenomenon (e.g., crime or suicide rates), then quantitative research is indicated. Equally, as a rule of thumb, if it turns out that published research on your topic is largely quantitative (Item 3), does it pay to swim against the tide? As we stress several times in this book, if you can align your work with a previous, classic study, this makes a lot of sense. The last thing you want to do is to try to reinvent the wheel!

Let us try to flesh out the broad guidelines provided in this table by using one example, which, we believe, shows the issues you need to think about when fitting your choice of methodology to your research problem. To concretize the discussion, we will use a research example to help us focus on Items 5 and 6 from Table 2.2.

A few months ago, when David was idly reading the job advertisements for university researchers, he came across an advertisement that caught his eye. This was the research question to be tackled: How is psychosocial adversity related to asthma morbidity and care? It was explained that this problem would be studied by means of qualitative interviews.

David's immediate question was, how can qualitative interviews help to address the topic at hand? The problem is not that people with asthma will be unable to answer questions about their past nor, of course, that they are likely to lie or mislead the interviewer. Rather, like all of us, when faced with an outcome (in this case, a chronic illness), they will document their past in a way that fits the present, highlighting certain features and downplaying others. In other words, the interviewer will be inviting a retrospective **rewriting of history** with an unknown bearing on the causal problem with which this research is concerned.

This is not to deny that valuable data may be gathered from such a qualitative study. Rather, it will address an altogether different issue—**narratives** of illness in which "causes" and "associations" work as rhetorical moves to establish a coherent present.

By contrast, a quantitative study would seem to be much more appropriate to the research question proposed. Quantitative surveys can be used on much larger **samples** than qualitative interviews, allowing inferences to be made to wider populations. Moreover, such surveys have standardized, reliable measures to ascertain the causal relationship and "facts" with which this study is concerned.

For that matter, why should a large-scale quantitative study be restricted to surveys or interviews? If we wanted reliable, generalizable knowledge about the relation between these two variables (psychosocial adversity and asthma morbidity), we would start by looking at hospital records.

This example illustrates the need to fit your research design to your research topic. But, of course, it overplays the opposition between qualitative and quantitative methods.

If resources allow, many research questions can be thoroughly addressed by combining different methods, using qualitative research to document the detail of, say, how people interact in one situation and using quantitative methods to identify variance (see Chapter 8). The fact that simple quantitative measures are a feature of some good qualitative research shows that the whole qualitative/quantitative dichotomy is open to question. In the context of this book, we view many such dichotomies or polarities in social science as highly dangerous. At best, they are pedagogic devices for students to obtain a first grip on a difficult field—they help us learn the jargon. At worst, they are excuses for not thinking, which assemble groups of researchers into "armed camps," unwilling to learn from one another.

As Table 2.2 (Point 6) suggests, such armchair debates are of less relevance than the simple test "what works for me." As Howard Becker comments about his use of qualitative data,

> It's the kind of research I've done, but that represents a practical rather than an ideological choice. It's what I knew how to do, and found personal enjoyment in, so I kept on doing it. (1998, p. 6)

However, Becker adds that his "choice" has not blinded him to the value of quantitative approaches:

> I've always been alive to the possibilities of other methods (so long as they weren't pressed on me as matters of religious conviction) and have found it particularly useful to think about what I did in terms that come from such other ways of working as survey research or mathematical modeling. (1998, p. 6)

Not only does it sometimes pay to think of qualitative research, as Becker suggests, in terms of quantitative frameworks, it can also be helpful occasionally to combine qualitative and quantitative methods. As we show in Chapter 14, simple tabulations can be a useful tool for identifying deviant cases.

In this section, we have used one example to show the importance of thinking through your research problem before committing yourself to a choice of method. But, as we have already hinted, the situation is rather more complicated than this.

UNDERSTANDING RESEARCH IN TERMS OF DIFFERENT MODELS

We can understand this complication better by returning to Point 6 of Table 2.2: namely, are we committed to a particular research model, which implies a particular methodology? Models provide an overall framework for viewing reality. They inform the **concepts** we use to define our research problem.

For instance, in the example we have been considering, the problem was defined in terms of the relation between an independent variable (psychosocial adversity) and two dependent variables (asthma morbidity and asthma care). These kinds of concepts appear to derive from a positivist model, which encourages us to chart the relation between variables that are operationally defined by the researcher.

Now, although **positivism** is the most common model used in quantitative research (i.e., the default option), it sits uneasily within most qualitative research designs. This is why David was puzzled by the choice of qualitative data in the design of the asthma study.

Qualitative research designs tend to work with a relatively small number of cases. Generally speaking, qualitative researchers are prepared to sacrifice scope for detail. Moreover, even what counts as detail tends to vary between qualitative and quantitative researchers. The latter typically seek detail in certain aspects of correlations between variables. By contrast, for qualitative researchers, detail is found in the precise particulars of such matters as people's understandings and interactions. This is because qualitative researchers tend to use a nonpositivist model of reality.

To underline the intellectual diversity of the field, in the next section we offer a brief summary of Gubrium and Holstein's analysis of four models of qualitative research.

THE DIFFERENT LANGUAGES OF QUALITATIVE RESEARCH

A thorough discussion of differences in method and theory among qualitative researchers is found in Gubrium and Holstein's *The New Language of Qualitative Method* (1997). This book classifies qualitative research in terms of various orientations on the **empirical** data under analysis. In particular, Gubrium and Holstein focus on how each qualitative approach uses a particular analytical language to emphasize a particular facet of social reality. As the authors put it,

> Our strategy for understanding the diversity of qualitative research is to treat each variant as an enterprise that develops, and is conducted in, a language or idiom of its own. Accordingly, each idiom represents a distinctive reality, virtually constituting its empirical horizon. (p. 5)

At the heart of this classification system is the division between substance and process, or between *what* is being studied and *how* it is constructed. Take the topic of nudity, for example. A qualitative researcher might ask the following: *What* are the deviant traits that characterize nudists and *what* practices are associated with a nudist? Another researcher studying the same topic could examine *how* nudity could be made normal or routine. In "The Nudist Management of Respectability," Martin Weinberg (1994) explores how nudist colonies achieve the "respectability" of the unclothed body through a set of locally defined and enforced norms like "no body contact" and "no accentuation of the body" (e.g., sitting with one's legs open). Weinberg's goal is to answer the question, "How can they see their behavior as morally appropriate?" (p. 392).

With this distinction between *how* (process of constructing reality) and *what* (reality as substantive truth), let us now look at the four models of qualitative research discussed in Gubrium and Holstein's book (i.e., **naturalism**, **emotionalism**, **ethnomethodology**, and **postmodernism**).

Naturalism

As a model of qualitative research, *naturalism* focuses on the factual characteristics of the object under study. Gubrium and Holstein cite William Whyte's *Street Corner Society* as a classic example of naturalism. In this urban ethnography from the 1940s, Whyte's goal is to describe what life is really like in an inner-city Italian neighborhood located in Boston. The observations and analysis are intended to objectively reflect *what* Whyte saw and heard in this real world of poverty. Naturalism's strength is its representational simplicity. A naturalistic **ethnography** is almost formulaically built around the following tasks: entering the setting, establishing rapport, recording observations with an eye toward sociological concepts (social status and group dynamics), and presenting the findings. The major shortcoming of this approach, according to Gubrium and Holstein, is this:

> Because they view the border [between the topic of study and the way in which it is socially constructed] as a mere *technical* hurdle that can be overcome through methodological skill and rigor, they lose sight of the border as a region where reality is constituted within representation. (1997, p. 106)

This criticism suggests that naturalists overlook *how* people create meaning in their lives. Respondents are treated as mere sources of data without any interpretive capacity of their own. In a naturalistic framework, the participants' "interpretive practice" (Gubrium & Holstein, 1997), or how they make sense of their own world, is irrelevant.

Emotionalism

Like naturalism, *emotionalism* takes for granted the reality of the topic under study. The difference between the two is that where naturalism searches for objective reality in physical places, emotionalism locates the real in the emotional life of the researcher and the respondents, or as Gubrium and Holstein put it, an emotionalist "virtually takes naturalism to heart" (1997, p. 59). Emotionalists are especially concerned with authenticity, which for our purposes can be defined as "deeper truths about the self." For emotionalists, alternative writing techniques can be used in qualitative research to better represent "true feelings." In the following extract, for example, Laurel Richardson describes why she chose poetry to represent her interview data:

> Writing poetry is emotionally preoccupying; it opens up unexpected, shadow places in my self. As a kind of time-saving/snaring-two-birds-with-one-net

strategy I decided to fashion material from an unmarried mother interview into a poem. (1992, p. 131)

For Richardson, transforming interview data into poetry enables the researcher to preserve the authenticity and breadth of her respondent's story—information that she feels would otherwise be lost in a traditional style of writing and analysis. As she puts it, "For sociological readers, the poem may seem to omit 'data' that they want to know. But this is Louisa May's [her interview respondent's] story not the sociologist's" (p. 126).

The problem with emotionalism, as Gubrium and Holstein note, is that "by peering so intently into subject's interior lives and inner realms, emotionalists can blind themselves to the ways that subjects shape these spheres by way of their own interpretive actions" (1997, p. 108). Under emotionalists' exclusive focus on inner feelings and self-reflective confessions, all substantive inquiries about social reality dissolve into self-explorative texts.

Ethnomethodology

The third qualitative approach reviewed by Gubrium and Holstein is *ethnomethodology*, which could roughly be translated into the study of people's methods of constructing reality in everyday life. Unlike the other two approaches, ethnomethodology is very much concerned with *how* social reality is constructed in everyday interaction. Ethnomethodologists' primary aim is to understand how people go about doing things in their everyday lives by creating meaningful categories for themselves and others. Thus, for example, an ethnomethodologist might ask seemingly curious questions like: What does it mean to be a "man"? The researcher would then *bracket* any prior knowledge about the topic (i.e., keep preconceived understandings from entering the analysis). In essence, bracketing means ontological detachment from the topic. Therefore, in representing the analysis, the word *man*, for example, would be placed in quotation marks to indicate its bracketed usage for the purpose of the study.

Harold Garfinkel, one of the founders of ethnomethodology, offers numerous examples of this qualitative approach in *Studies in Ethnomethodology*. Some of the studies cited in this book are labeled "breaching experiments," or small research projects deliberately designed to violate taken-for-granted social order in order to reveal the process of its construction. In one such study, college students were asked to "engage an acquaintance or a friend in an ordinary conversation and, without indicating that what the experimenter was asking was in any way unusual, to insist that the person clarify the sense of his commonplace remarks" (Garfinkel, 1967, p. 42). The goal of the study was to reveal "seen but unnoticed" (p. 42) norms used in everyday conversations. Here is an extract from the study (S = subject, E = experimenter):

The victim waved his hand cheerily.

S: How are you?

E: How am I in regard to what? My health, my finances, my school work, my peace of mind, my. . . ?

S: [Red in the face and suddenly out of control.] Look! I was just trying to be polite. Frankly, I don't give a damn how you are. (p. 44)

In this case, by problematizing conversational norms, the experimenter reveals how the question "How are you?" is used to achieve "politeness" in everyday encounters.

For Gubrium and Holstein, although analytically powerful, the problem with ethnomethodology is that it risks losing sight of the topic of analysis in the name of focusing on the process of its creation. As they put it, "As the substantively meaningful aspects of local culture are shunted aside in order to concentrate on constitutive interactional activity, the content of lived experience becomes almost incidental" (1997, p. 107).

While ethnomethodology's analytical rigor can free us of trite or stereotypic understandings of a research problem, it does, on the other hand, impose restrictions on substantive interests. For example, one cannot study poverty ethnomethodologically without bracketing its meaning, or placing it in quotation marks (i.e., "poverty"). In this way, poverty loses its significance as a global social problem and becomes a particular achievement at a particular place and time. As a whole, a strict ethnomethodological analysis trades the substance of everyday life for a rigorous understanding of the activities that define it.

Postmodernism

Although *postmodernism* refers to a vast body of literature, for the sake of simplicity and flow of discussion, let us assume the term encapsulates an analytical orientation that questions all the achievements of modernity (e.g., humanism, rationality, reason, science, and so on). One of the key contributions of postmodernism to qualitative analysis is its critique of the representational authority of the written text. In particular, postmodernists ask, Who owns the knowledge embedded in the text and what power or authority supports it?

Gubrium and Holstein assert that the common theme of postmodernism is how and through what cultural forces we come to understand and accept certain representations of reality as being "true," "legitimate," or "acceptable." Whereas ethnomethodologists study the processes through which **members** construct their reality, postmodernists question the power relations and the political rhetoric embedded in the representations and constructions of social reality. While some postmodernists call for experimenting with alternative modes of representing social reality, others fundamentally question all forms of representation to the point of nihilism by arguing that nothing can be known as "true" or "good" (for a discussion of the different branches of postmodernism, see Pauline Rosenau, 1992). Gubrium and Holstein's critique of postmodernism is best illustrated by these ominous words:

> Postmodernism in the guise of qualitative inquiry is very risky business. Rhetorical ubiquity notwithstanding, at the lived border, reality is always on the verge of collapsing into representation, taking with it the substantively distinct parameters of experience whose "qualities" are qualitative method's unique subject matter. Trying to capture that which is not there, or to describe the inexpressible, using mere rhetoric that begs its own deconstruction, is hazardous indeed. Qualitative inquiry is surely in peril as it gambles with empirical nihilism. (1997, p. 109)

Thus, while raising very important questions about the content of social reality and the methods of its production, in its extreme forms, postmodernism threatens the very need for scientific investigation and analysis. If, according to some postmodernists, we cannot and should not separate fact from fiction or truth from falsehood, then there is no point in spending precious resources to empirically study and analyze social reality—we could just as well write poems or a novel about our experiences. Nonetheless, it is possible to learn from the important insights of postmodernism without drowning in its whirlpool of intellectual nihilism. The most important of these insights is an emphasis on the rhetorical and constructive aspects of knowledge. That is, the realization that facts (social science facts included) are socially constructed to serve the interests of a particular group. In fact, this limited interpretation of the postmodern project is consistent with our own position in this book about qualitative research being a pragmatic enterprise that serves different interests.

It is worth noting that although these four models differ in how they emphasize the nature of social reality, they are not mutually exclusive. For example, the emotionalists and the postmodernists share a common concern with exploring alternative representational strategies. David discusses the emotionalist position further in Silverman, 2004, and the nature and purpose of models is examined in greater depth in Chapter 7. For the moment, we just want to leave you with the thought that qualitative research can mean many different things.

Table 2.3   Four Models Compared

	Naturalism	*Emotionalism*	*Ethnomethodology*	*Postmodernism*
Focus	Objective reality	Meaning, emotions, self	Practice in everyday life	Representation and power
Objective	Observing and reporting things as they really are	Revealing deeper, authentic truths about the self	Understanding how things become what they are	Relentless critique of all form of authority and all claims to "truth"

By now, this whole debate may have left you thoroughly confused. As a beginning researcher, you may rightly feel that the last thing you need is to sink into an intractable debate between warring camps. However, it helps if we treat this less as a war and more as a clarion call to be clear about the issues that animate our work and help define our research problem. As we argue in Chapter 6, purely theoretical debates are often less than helpful if we want to carry out effective research. The point is to select a model that makes sense to you (and, of course, there are more than the two models relevant to qualitative research—see Chapter 7). The strengths and weaknesses of any model will only be revealed in what you can do with it.

We will, therefore, conclude this chapter with a single case study that we believe is an inspiring example and that shows the value of using a clear-cut model and, thereby, demonstrates the particular explanatory power of qualitative research.

CASE STUDY: "POSITIVE THINKING"

Sue Wilkinson and Celia Kitzinger (2000) (henceforth WK) were interested in the way in which both laypeople and many medical staff assume that "positive thinking" helps you cope better with cancer. They point out that most of the evidence for this belief derives from questionnaires in which people tick a box or circle a number.

What alternative can we offer to this kind of quantitative research? The preferred qualitative route has been to analyze what people with cancer say in open-ended interviews. Deriving from what is referred to as the emotionalist model, such research has generally sought out patients' meanings and emotions and, as WK point out, has broadly supported the findings of quantitative studies.

However, there is a problem here, namely: "There is a widespread assumption in [both] these literatures that research participants are naïve subjects, intent primarily upon accurately reporting their cognitions to the researcher" (Wilkinson & Kitzinger, 2000, p. 801).

By contrast, WK prefer to treat statements about "thinking positive" as actions and to understand their functions in particular contexts of speaking. So, although they use similar data to the emotionalists (interviews and focus groups), the way they analyze that data is very different. Using an ethno-methodological model, WK place quotation marks around "positive thinking" (i.e., they bracket its meaning) to show when and how it is used.

Let us look at one data extract that they use from a focus group of women with breast cancer:

EXTRACT 1.1

Fiona: Life's too short to worry about whether you can afford or whether you can't afford, or whether you should spend the money or whether you shouldn't spend the money, you know, I think we, we're sort of thinking that towards the back end of next year, we're off on a holiday to Australia. I think you've got to feel like that. If you wanna do it, I think you've gotta go for it, because none of us, I mean, it's all very well, they say, "Oh yeah, you're fine now," you, you know, "Everything's gonna be okay," but none of us know what next week, or next month, or next year has in store. And I, so I think you, you have to be positive. (Wilkinson & Kitzinger, 2000, p. 805; see Appendix for transcript conventions)

Fiona ends her comments about spending money now because "life's too short" by saying "you have to be positive." But should we take this to mean that this shows she is a positive thinker?

First, as WK note, Fiona shows that the object of her positive thinking is vague and diverse. She is "thinking positively neither about the cancer and its effects, nor about [her] possible recovery, but about [her life] apart from the cancer" (2000, p. 805).

Second, if we inspect closely what Fiona says, we can notice that she uses a multiplicity of different voices to frame what she is saying. "You" expresses the voice of any reasonable person (e.g., "if you wanna do it" and "you have to be positive"). "They" occurs once to refer to other people who tell you things that may not turn out to be true. "I" is used to refer to someone who ponders about all this ("I think").

Like many of the women in these focus groups, Fiona frames her references to positive thinking in the voice of "you." Used in this way, as what "you have got to do," positive thinking is used as a kind of maxim.

The beauty of maxims is that, because they are supposed to reflect a shared world, their recipients can do little other than agree with them (Sacks, 1992, Vol. 1, pp. 23–25). So, if you say, "you have to be positive," you are likely to get agreement, in the same way as if you say, "many hands make light work." And, interestingly enough, WK report that Fiona's last comment does indeed elicit agreement.

What Fiona is saying turns out to be complex and skillful. A lot of the time we want to obtain the agreement of others and Fiona structures her talk to do just that—notice that she also invokes a maxim ("life's too short") to justify spending money.

This suggests that, at the very least, we should not tear out what Fiona says about positive thinking from the multifaceted structure of her comments. Let me underline this point with one more extract:

EXTRACT 1.2

Hetty:	When I first found out I had cancer, I said to myself, I said right, it's not gonna get me. And that was it. I mean (Yvonne: Yeah) obviously you're devastated because it's a dreadful thing
Yvonne:	(overlaps) Yeah, but you've got to have a positive attitude thing, I do
Betty:	(overlaps) But then, I was talking to Dr. Purcott and he said to me the most helpful thing that anybody can have with any type of cancer is a positive attitude
Yvonne:	a positive outlook, yes
Betty:	Because if you decide to fight it, then the rest of your body will st-, will start
Yvonne:	Motivate itself, yeah
Betty:	to fight it (Wilkinson & Kitzinger, 2000, p. 807)

Once again, on the surface, Extract 2 seems to support the idea that "positive thinking" is an internal, cognitive state of people with cancer. However, this overlooks the extent to which these women are discussing "thinking positive" not as a natural reaction to having cancer (the natural reaction [cited elsewhere in their data] is that, "obviously you're devastated because it's a dreadful thing"), but rather as a moral imperative: "you've got to have a positive attitude." (Wilkinson & Kitzinger, 2000, pp. 806–807)

So WK's analysis suggests two different ways in which these women formulate their situation:

Positive thinking is presented as a moral imperative, part of a moral order in which they should be thinking positive.

Other reactions (including fear and crying) are simply described as what "I did," not as "what you have got to do."

This distinction shows the value of looking at how talk is organized and not just treating it "as providing a transparent 'window' on underlying cognitive processes" (2000, p. 809). By contrast, WK's constructionist model has allowed us to get a quite different, more processual grasp of the phenomenon.

This has two useful consequences. First, we come to understand the place of "positive thinking" within a broader range of activities like troubles-telling. In so doing, we move from substantive theories to **formal theories** and, thereby, open up the possibility of broader comparisons (see Glaser & Strauss, 1967). Second, rather than simply confirm lay or medical beliefs about the phenomenon, it provides new insights of potential value to both patients and health care workers.

CONCLUDING REMARKS

Wilkinson and Kitzinger's study gives a new twist to our earlier comments about the haziness of the distinction between qualitative and quantitative research. Earlier qualitative studies of "positive thinking" have simply replicated the findings of quantitative surveys but at the cost of precision because of the smaller sample size involved. By contrast, by using a radically different research model, they have come up with new findings that would be difficult to establish through quantitative methods.

Nonetheless, we must not draw too sharp a distinction between quantitative and qualitative research. Qualitative research can mean many different things, involving a wide range of methods and informed by contrasting models.

Ultimately, everything depends on the research problem you are seeking to analyze. We conclude this chapter, therefore, with a statement that shows the absurdity of pushing too far the qualitative/quantitative distinction:

We are not faced, then, with a stark choice between words and numbers, or even between precise and imprecise data; but rather with a range from more to less precise data. Furthermore, our decisions about what level of precision is appropriate in relation to any particular claim should depend on the nature of what we are trying to describe, on the likely accuracy of our descriptions, on our purposes, and on the resources available to us; not on ideological commitment to one methodological paradigm or another. (Hammersley, 1992, p. 163)

KEY POINTS

One of the main points we have made in this chapter is that research methods should be chosen based on the specific task at hand. Amir's personal experience with a study of juvenile offenders who were charged with adult criminal offenses is a good illustration of this point (Frazier, Bishop, Lanza-Kaduce, & Marvasti, 1999). In this federally funded research, one of the goals was to isolate the factors that cause legal authorities to recommend a minor for adult judicial processing. The data came from two official sources. One was a statewide database called Client Information System (CIS). The CIS data contained numerically coded information on thousands of offenders from around the state. This information came to the researchers in the form of magnetic cartridge tapes that had to be mounted on a mainframe computer before they could be accessed and analyzed. The other source of data for the project was local court records, which contained arrest reports, indictments, sentencing reports, and a host of other documents about the cases. Summarizing and analyzing the numerical data was relatively easy. Once the data tapes were mounted on the mainframe, Amir used statistical programs like SAS or SPSS to read the data. With amazing speed, the computer programs could peruse thousands of records and extract just what was needed for analysis. For example, if Amir wanted to know the average age of offenders who had committed a violent crime like robbery, he would write a few lines of computer syntax, submit the request, and have the report, or output, back in seconds.

However, the work was much more challenging where the local court files were concerned. To transform these documents into data suitable for statistical analysis, the researchers put together a lengthy data collection instrument. After making an appointment at the appropriate courthouse, which could be hundreds of miles away, Amir and his colleagues would drive to the location and peruse the dossiers in search of information that corresponded to the hundreds of variables on the data collection instrument. For example, if the minor offender had used a firearm during an offense, that would be coded as "1," a blunt weapon, such as a baseball bat, would be coded as "2," etc. As the project proceeded, the principal investigators and Amir had to add more variables to capture the nuances of each case. For example, Amir came across a few cases that started in one jurisdiction and were transferred to another. This required the inclusion of new variables to the data collection instrument. Amir and his colleagues soon realized that no matter how many variables were added, many details of the case simply did not fit a precoded, standardized format. Additionally, they were faced with the problem of overlapping categories. For instance, Amir had difficulty recording a case in which the offender began beating his victim with a baseball bat and then pulled out a firearm and shot his victim. Should this case be coded as a "1"or "2"? To remedy these problems, Amir and his colleagues had to supplement the numerical data about a case with a qualitative narrative or a case history to capture additional nuances. These case histories were written on a blank sheet of paper that was provided on the back of the data collection form. For example, Amir would write that Offender X lost his father to cancer at the age of 12, and was placed in a foster home after his mother refused to care for him, and so on. Finally, the principal investigators for this project (Amir was a graduate student at the time and served on the project as a research assistant) added more depth to their data by conducting in-depth interviews with a small sample of offenders. They would go to prisons, halfway houses, or other venues and interview the juvenile offenders face-to-face.

As you can see from this example, methods need not guide the research but can be used as tools when they are needed. It would have been silly for Amir and his colleagues to turn away from the case study method because it seemed "too qualitative." It would have been equally unreasonable to exclude the statewide (CIS) data from the research because they were "too quantitative." As we have repeatedly noted in this chapter, you can become much more effective as a researcher if you reject arbitrary, self-imposed limitations, and instead systematically pursue knowledge about a topic wherever the data might take you.

FURTHER READING

The most useful introductory texts are Alan Bryman's *Quantity and Quality in Social Research* (1988); Nigel Gilbert (editor), *Researching Social Life* (1993); Clive Seale (editor), *Researching Society and Culture* (2004); and Keith Punch, *Introduction to Social Research* (1998). More advanced qualitative analysis is offered by Silverman's *Interpreting Qualitative Data: Methods for Analysing Talk, Text and Interaction* (2001), especially Chapter 2; Miles and Huberman's *Qualitative Data Analysis* (1984); Hammersley and Atkinson's *Ethnography: Principles in Practice* (1983); and Denzin and Lincoln (editors), *Handbook of Qualitative Research* (2000). A particularly useful source is "Inside Qualitative Research," the introduction to Seale, Gobo, Gubrium, and Silverman's edited book *Qualitative Research Practice* (2004, pp. 1–11).

In addition to these general texts, readers are urged to familiarize themselves with examples of qualitative and quantitative research. Strong (1979) and Lipset, Trow, and Coleman (1962) are good examples of each. Sue Wilkinson elaborates on her work in Wilkinson (2004). Sensible statements about the quantitative position are to be found in Marsh (1982) (on survey research) and Hindess (1973) (on official statistics).

EXERCISE 2.1

Review any research study with which you are familiar. Then answer the questions below:

1. To what extent are its methods of research (qualitative, quantitative, or a combination of both) appropriate to the nature of the research question(s) being asked?

2. Apply the criticisms of either qualitative or quantitative research discussed in this chapter to this research.

3. In your view, how could this study have been improved methodologically and conceptually?

EXERCISE 2.2

In relation to your own possible research topics,

1. Explain why you think a qualitative approach is appropriate.

2. Would quantitative methods be more appropriate? If not, why not?

3. Would it make sense to combine qualitative and quantitative methods? Explain your answer.

EXERCISE 2.3

Visit the following Web site for the journal of *Qualitative Research* at http://qrj.sagepub .com/. Browse the table of contents for the most recent issue of the journal and read the abstracts (you can do this without a subscription).

1. List the topics or questions, as listed in the abstracts, from three articles.

2. List qualitative research methods used in the three articles.

3. Describe to what extent the topics and methods are similar. In what ways are they different?

CHAPTER 3

The Research Experience

CHAPTER OBJECTIVES

By the end of this chapter, you will

1. Understand the basic issues involved in developing a research project from initial ideas to data analysis and writing

2. Understand some of the challenges student researchers face

3. Learn some effective strategies for organizing and writing a dissertation

4. Recognize the role of Institutional Review Boards in approving and monitoring university-affiliated research

"Don't touch the hot stove!" "Eat your food with a fork!" "Wash your hands before you eat." "Don't tease your brother." Most of us remember being told these things by our parents. Sometimes we boldly asked "Why?" and were told, "Because I told you so!" or "Because it's good for you, trust me." This process of learning does not change significantly as we grow older. We continue to ask questions, but we are not always told, or fully understand, why a certain approach is more fruitful or less painful than others; we sort of take it for granted and trust the expertise of others. However, this type of learning has to be balanced against direct experience and individual creativity. It is true that you should avoid being burnt by the hot stove, but you might be able devise a way to safely handle the heat—that is to say, to balance your individual interest with conventional mandates.

This is the objective of this book. In discussing the specifics of doing qualitative research, we hope to offer you strategies for both satisfying personal interests and meeting certain requirements within the field. To start with, we can assume that by picking up this book and reading through the pages, you are showing willingness to submit yourself to a learning process where you receive advice on how qualitative research is done. However, it is unlikely that you will find an exact, ideal formula for doing your research in this or any other textbook because, as you will note throughout this book, qualitative research is a growing and diverse field. This reminder about the vast and flexible terrain of qualitative research may be simultaneously exciting and daunting to novice researchers. The examples and stories presented in this chapter are intended to both reduce your anxiety and raise your enthusiasm about the field.

Learning From Others' Experiences

Switch on your television and flip through the channels. You will undoubtedly come across a talk show in which people are talking about their rise and fall from grace. Or maybe you will find a sports channel where, more often than not, instead of a game, you will see interviews with players about their hopes and feelings. We live in a world in which our yearning for people's "experiences" is more than satisfied by the popular media. Indeed, sometimes the "personal" is unduly praised as a privileged source of knowledge (see Atkinson & Silverman, 1997).

However, this is not always the case. Any book which sets out to offer information and advice about doing a piece of research without telling a few personal stories would be in danger of being received as empty and unhelpful. If we can draw out appropriate implications from these stories, moving from the personal to the practical, then we will have achieved something more substantial than merely providing some kind of experiential comfort blanket.

In this spirit, this chapter is devoted to the stories of doctoral students, who, like you, had to navigate their way through the labyrinth of qualitative research. These stories are organized in a chronological sequence that starts with selecting a research topic and ends with analysis and writing. You should note that in reality the steps presented here might overlap (e.g., you might choose a dissertation chair before you choose a research topic). Also, the sequence is not always linear. Things do not always progress as expected. For example, after selecting a topic, such as mental illness, you might realize that you cannot find any participants for your study and might have to change your topic. The steps outlined here constitute the essential components of a qualitative study. Although more can be added and some steps may be reversed or repeated, the basics do not change dramatically from one project to another.

The discussion that follows is based on the generous contributions of 12 colleagues who, in response to a list of questions, shared their experiences with us. Collectively, these stories represent an opportunity to learn about the theory and practice of qualitative research. Theses stories may be read and used in different ways. Some can be (a) *imitated*, especially if the research strategies were successful, whereas others can help you (b) *avoid* similar mistakes in cases where strategies did not work well. Still others might simply (c) *inspire* you to move in innovative directions. Finally, collectively, the stories provide a practical (d) *list* of the steps involved in the research process from start to finish based on the experiences of recent PhDs.

SELECTING A TOPIC

In this section, we discuss some common pathways to choosing topics for qualitative researchers. As you read these stories, note that in many cases researchers come across a topic by chance, or they begin studying a topic because the data or the research site were conveniently available.

Social Obligations

For some graduate students, selecting a topic derives from a sense of social obligation. For example, Karyn McKinney's research on how white college students construct their racial identity was motivated by her desire to expose the system of racial hierarchy in the United States. In a sense, she was morally driven to select this topic, or as she puts it, "I was interested in the topic out of thinking about what *I should do* to effectively change the status quo." Karyn was committed to studying race relations, and settling on a specific area within that field was a fortunate coincidence. In her words,

Eventually, my real excitement about *data* was what decided me on my topic. I was teaching a class in race and ethnicity, and had asked students, as their main project for the class, to write what I referred to as a "racial/ethnic autobiography." In my assignment for the course, students were to go chronologically through their lives, telling their stories, focusing on situations and incidents that made them more aware of their own or other people's race or ethnicity. Basically, these papers would be first-person analyses of the development of racial and/or ethnic identity. When I got the students' papers back, I was mesmerized by reading them. I literally could not put them down. All of the students told stories that showed how racial and ethnic identity is a process, not a static characteristic. They were fascinating, to me at least. Most of my students were white, and I began to think about the new area I'd been reading in, "whiteness studies."

Karyn's research agenda was not entirely planned in advance. She was simply assigning a project for a course and happened to realize the importance of the data that was pouring in—the data "mesmerized" her. Note her social obligations did not dictate her research entirely. To a large extent it was her fascination with the data that focused her interests.

Curiosity

Other researchers cite general curiosity as the main reason for selecting a particular topic. Essentially, they are intrigued by a facet of social life and want to learn more about it. Michelle Miller-Day's story is illustrative of this approach:

There is a quote from Zora Neale Hurston that, for me, captures what I hope to achieve with qualitative research. She said, Research is formalized curiosity.

It is poking and prying with purpose. It is a seeking that he who wishes may know the secrets of the world and they that dwell therein.

I have always been curious. Choosing a career as a social science researcher, I assumed I could make a living asking questions and seeking answers. (In my more noble moments) I also believed that this career would enable me to make real contributions to the understanding of social behavior and the human experience.

In Michelle's story, social obligations are not necessarily at the forefront of her work. A general sense of curiosity coupled with the "noble" desire to understand others dictated her research choices. This sense of wonder about the world guided her questions and her observations.

Being Assigned to a Research Grant

A number of the colleagues we contacted selected their research topics based on the fact that they were assigned to work on a research grant that fortuitously provided them with a topic and access to respondents. For example, Greg Boylstein writes,

I accepted a job as a research assistant (RA) at the local Veterans Administration Medical Center. Initially I did home interviews with veterans who recently had a stroke. Through time I became more intimately involved in the project, helping construct the initial theoretical framework with the principal investigator and my dissertation chair, who was a consultant on the study. Since I was a member of the research team on this large project, it became natural for me to use the first phase of data as a basis for my dissertation research. I did not have any particular interest or knowledge in stroke recovery prior to this RA position. . . . Rather than being isolated in my dissertation research, I actually became integrated into a large investigative center focused on stroke rehabilitation, with my dissertation making up one component of disseminating our initial findings.

For other researchers who received less restrictive, individual grants, the funding simply provided them with the time and resources to pursue topics of personal interest. Consider, for example, Nikitah Imani's case:

I actually did not per se select my topic for the dissertation. I received a grant from the National Science Foundation to participate in a summer qualitative methods workshop. Part of the responsibilities associated with successful completion of that workshop was the completion of a qualitative research project. . . . We were given the run of the local social theater to choose as sites and given the convenience of the university setting itself and some issues it resolved in advance (like securing primary access). I became engaged by a grant-funded psychotherapy program the university was running. It targeted presumably "dysfunctional" African American families. Initially, without a topic, I sought merely to use ethnographic tools to describe to those external to the program what was "taking place." It was not long after embarking on this quest that my pursuits turned far away from merely "test-driving" the methodology to looking at critical questions of how "dysfunctionality," which I had taken for granted in the programmatic definitions, was being articulated, defined, redefined, and reified in the implementation phase. So it would be fair to say that the "scene" and the associated circumstances gave me my topic, which, given the methodology I had chosen, seemed an appropriate line of inquiry to follow.

As we can see in Nikitah's example, selecting a research topic is often a complex process where personal interests, financial resources, and access to data converge to shape the ideal research question.

Using the Self as a Starting Point

For some, direct personal experience becomes the starting point of their research. In Amir's case, being an immigrant led him to look at homeless people.

In some ways, homelessness for him became a metaphor for the immigration experience and the struggle for belonging. Similarly, Michael Arter speaks of how being an undercover police officer became an impetus for his study of policing:

> I returned to graduate school after many years in the military and law enforcement. As I became acclimated to the academic setting and my background became known to the faculty and other students, I noticed there was a lot of emphasis placed upon and interest in my time spent as an undercover officer. Along with much misinformation that was held by many regarding such assignments, there was an unspoken mystique and subtle respect that was accorded to me for the work I had done. I realized at that time that most individuals lacked actual knowledge about such assignments and relied on media presentations and sensationalized examples for their understanding about the undercover function. At the same time, I was very aware of the impact undercover assignments had in my life and the lives of others with whom I had worked. While considering a topic for a research methods class, I conducted a literature search to assess research available relating to stress in policing and discovered there was a distinct gap in this body of literature. I decided to adopt this topic for the research class and, as I began to research the available literature, I became more entrenched in this topic as a viable venue for my dissertation.

The factors listed here, like those that will follow, often coexist and overlap in the same project. What is noteworthy here is not the distinct pattern that a particular researcher follows, but the fact that the process as a whole—that is, the practice of qualitative research—does not follow an exact uniformed model. Essentially, the lesson with selecting a topic is to always keep an eye out for a good topic, take advantage of opportunities when they present themselves, and be flexible.

SELECTING A METHODOLOGY

An obvious question for this book would be why do some students choose qualitative research? In the United States, quantitative research tends to be more prevalent. In most sociology departments, the majority of the faculty use quantitative methods in their research, and most journals publish a disproportionate number of quantitative journals. The so-called norm, at least for now, is quantitative. What then attracts some to qualitative research? Here are some answers directly from the researchers.

Because the Other Approach Is Limited

Although there is a general sense among some researchers that qualitative data is inherently more "interesting" than numbers, there are less aesthetically oriented and more analytically astute reasons for choosing qualitative methods. For example, Karyn McKinney suggests that qualitative research was a better fit for the types of questions she was asking:

> I've always found qualitative data more interesting than quantitative data. Beyond that, I believe that qualitative data is often more suited to provide me with the answers to questions I'm interested in. I find that my interests usually lie in "how" questions rather than in "how many" questions.

In her dissertation, Karyn was interested in *how* whiteness is created and sustained in everyday life. The question of how many whites live in the United States or how much money whites make compared to other groups could have easily been answered using the census data.

Similarly, Sara Crawley states that in her research on lesbian identities, quantitative measures seemed inadequate:

> My substantive interests were related to identity and sexuality. The notion that anyone could describe such intimate matters with a "6" or some quantitative measure seemed atheoretical and, frankly, ludicrous. I am not suggesting that nothing is measurable or that attempts to measure are less useful for some topics. But with a topic that is so intimate and constantly forming as sexuality and identity, it seemed extremely important to highlight individual narrators' ideas and concepts with some detail. As it turns out, I became very interested in talk and how people narrate their identities and realities. The good stuff was in their descriptions and ideas. It fascinated me every day.

A related limitation of quantitative research is highlighted in Michelle Miller-Day's story about realizing that the subjects had all but disappeared in her survey research:

> Like many students, I began my graduate training being socialized within a positivist paradigm. I was learning my statistics and how to conduct surveys and develop quasi-experimental designs. But, one day I experienced a transforming moment in graduate school. Donna, one of the participants in a survey-based study I conducted, was reading a manuscript I had written reporting the findings of this study when she exclaimed, "Where is the depth? Where is the feeling? Where am *I* in all of these words?"

"Well," I responded, "right there on Page 17!"

"I know that I'm the *subject*," Donna went on, "and I know that you are *the researcher*. But . . . uhmmm . . . I really don't get a sense of either one of us in the paper."

She was absolutely right! Donna, along with the other participants, provided a unique voice during the collection of the data, yet that voice was ultimately muted by the deadening *thud* of an aggregate statistic. In my research report she was nowhere to be found.

This experience occurred only a few months before I took my first qualitative research methods course. In that course I found my home. While my education to that point was focused on teaching me to collect information and understand social behavior, I wasn't getting at the *understanding human experience* part of my aspiration. I realized that to truly capture experience, I needed to embrace the subjective and, along with it, the humanity of social science.

Michelle's emphasis on voice and subjectivity shows how an interest in subjectivity and the authenticity of human experience is a strong feature of qualitative research. As we discussed in Chapter 2, this is one of the dominant paradigms within qualitative research.

Doing What We Already Like

For Sylvia Ansay and her dissertation on house arrest, doing qualitative research was not an epiphanic shift in her thinking, but rather a natural extension of what she "already liked doing":

As a former elementary teacher and Guardian ad Litem [a volunteer worker who functions as an advocate for abused children in the U.S. courts], I have years of experience listening to stories in context and analyzing situations and needs. For me, qualitative research merely formalized what I already did well and what I loved doing. Having chosen the dissertation topic based on a close friend's experience, I was already aware of the storied nature of his accounts, how his personality, alcoholism and his ongoing feud with a local underground were all part of the story of his house arrest as well as his criminal offense. I knew that his circumstances, such as being a small-business owner, gave him privileges that someone unemployed or on an 8-to-5 schedule wouldn't have. I had heard his descriptions of good officers and "pricks." Everyday life on house arrest was a story within stories, and I felt that perspective was necessary for understanding the *why*s and *how*s of the intensive supervision experience.

Bridging the Social Distance

Yet another colleague, John Talmage, found qualitative methodology to be an ideal way for bridging "the social distance" in his study of "the social world" of the homeless:

> While survey research is clearly an appropriate methodology for many research questions, I did not believe that it covered the depth of meaning that seemed to be so important in understanding the social world. I did a qualitative dissertation to understand the social world from the perspective of the homeless population, and to that end it seemed helpful to get closer to the data. This I eventually did by spending time with the homeless in public places, in their hobo camps and cat holes, in shelters, and in meetings with my "research team" [a group of homeless research informants]. These were ways to reduce the social distance between myself and those homeless persons with whom I worked and spoke.

Here we can see that John relies on ethnographic methods as a way of bridging the status gap between him and a marginal impoverished population.

Doing What Is Practical

Finally, sometimes qualitative research is just a good fit for the question. As Darin Weinberg states, there is nothing inherently superior about qualitative research and its practitioners. Selecting qualitative methodology could be mostly a practical matter of deciding what works best. In Darin's words,

> I would say my choice to do a qualitative dissertation was a product of both personal taste and a sense that the themes in which I was interested could be best explored through qualitative approaches. I was never committed to keeping the study strictly qualitative. As it turned out, my use of quantitative data was fairly minimal but this was more a product of contingency and how the foci of the project evolved than it was one of a priori commitments. Had I come across quantitative materials that could have helped me flesh out my analysis, I would have had no hesitation to use them.

These stories reiterate the points made in Chapter 2 about the diversity of qualitative research. Qualitative research is more than one thing. The features that attract researchers to this methodology are many, and so are the ways this methodology is practiced.

SELECTING A CHAIR

Aside from choosing the topic and the methodology, another important step in doing qualitative research as a doctoral student is selecting a committee chair. In U.S. universities, a committee is a group of faculty who supervise a dissertation. They are composed of five members, four from the PhD candidate's specific department and one outside member from another program. The most influential member of the committee is the chair. This person is expected to have more direct contact with the student than the other members. In fact, it is often the case that the other four committee members are implicitly or explicitly picked by the committee chair.

PhD students typically follow the research agenda of their chair and rely on his or her mentorship for the remainder of their academic careers. Thus selecting a chair could be one of the most important decisions a doctoral student makes. Although committee chairs can be changed, the practice is generally frowned on and could be read as lack of commitment or effort on the part of the student. So it is best to choose carefully and get it right the first time, as it were. Here are some suggestions from our colleagues about selecting a chair.

Reputation and Interest

A safe and easy way to choose a dissertation committee chair is work with someone with an extensive academic record and distinct reputation, particularly if you find their work interesting. This was the case for Karyn McKinney, who states,

I had been attending another university, where I got my master's degree. In the process of working on my thesis, I came across the work of my chair. It was unlike anything I had previously read, and I was very excited about his approach. I checked to see what university he was affiliated with, and then applied to the University of Florida for my doctoral studies. After I was accepted, I entered the program and immediately sought him out, and asked him to work with me.

Similarly, Eileen O'Brien writes,

My qualitative methods professor at my MA program referred me to an *American Sociological Review* article she had recently read and suggested I might be interested in his work. I made a point to meet the author at my first American Sociological Association meeting I attended, told him I wanted to work with him, and then went about the process of moving/ transferring to the school where he was.

Along with reputation, it is important to pick a chair whose work intrigues you. As Sylvia Ansay writes,

> I chose the professor whose own research and coursework excited me, someone whose seminar assignments included meaningful projects, someone who looked at my seminar papers and saw numerous possibilities for further research and publication. Research takes passion. I recognized in him the passion I needed to help me through the entire PhD process.

Rapport

Of course, reputation is not always the key criterion for this decision. Sometimes, picking a chair is a matter of finding someone you can have a good working relationship with, as in the case of Michelle Miller-Day, who states,

> I wish I could say that the selection of my committee members was a thoughtfully considered endeavor based on the best faculty member for the job. But I cannot. I knew who I wanted to be the chair of my committee because he and I had worked together in the past on a funded research project and I liked him, I respected him, and I knew we worked well together.

The importance of good rapport is further highlighted by Nikitah Imani in the following passage:

> I had had a negative experience as a political science major with one member of my committee, which led to me discontinuing my graduate studies in that department after completing a master's degree. That experience taught me to make sure that the members of the committee, not least of them the chairperson, would be sympathetic to me as a human being, first, and then to my research agenda.

It is obvious that selecting a reputable chair you have difficulty communicating and working with will do little to advance your career. Most of our colleagues recommend that students research the "temperament" of their candidate for a chair before finalizing their decision.

Politics

Academic institutions are not immune from politics and power games. Some faculty members, be it because of their research or personal characteristics, are more capable of supporting their students than others, particularly when the student's work is controversial and challenges mainstream views about a topic. As Nikitah Imani puts it,

> The chair's power and influence in the department was an important consideration for me. I watched a fellow student in the political science department who enrolled with an Ivy League honors masters and did not finish his dissertation. I watched a second similarly go down in flames, and the critical variable seemed to be an insufficient amount of influence on their behalf, particularly within their committees. As a graduate research professor, my chair not only was a full professor, but to a certain extent he was immune from the predilections of the department itself. He ranked sufficiently high within the department to have weight in decision making, but was not connected in many ways to the rivalries and histories of the long-term faculty.

Unfortunately, as Nikitah notes, sometimes graduate students become entangled in political struggles within their program and are directly or indirectly kept from completing their degree. Here is when a "powerful" chair can play a significant role in protecting the student from vicious, personal attacks. More important, a good chair (if you are willing to listen to him or her) can keep you from getting involved in certain issues in the first place. The thing to remember is that as a graduate student, your position in your department is temporary. Your goal is to get your degree and move on to a full-time position. In contrast, the faculty have long-term vested interests in the program. There are issues among them that preexisted before your arrival and will likely continue after you graduate. Do not inadvertently become fodder in fights that essentially have little to do with your academic success. By picking a chair who is immune from the petty in-fights, you simply increase your chances of completing your degree in a timely manner. That is why in many programs junior, untenured faculty are not permitted to serve as dissertation chairs. This is not entirely about qualifications. The fact is, disputes will come up and someone has to defend your side. A junior faculty, who is in the midst of the tenure approval process, is rarely capable of defending you.

Interviewing a Potential Chair

The most practical approach for selecting a chair is to literally interview potential candidates, just like you would interview job candidates (except with much more humility on your part). Michael Arter describes this approach most succinctly:

I developed a "short list" of potential chairs. I had developed a close relationship with those on the list from classes, social settings, and while functioning as a graduate assistant and assistant director of the undergraduate advising center. This allowed for a relaxed and comfortable discussion with each potential chair. Each professor was aware I was "interviewing" in search of a chair and all were open and honest in providing guidance and direction for the process. One of the candidates did not feel they were the best choice for a qualitative project and was dropped from consideration. The "qualitative candidate" was overcommitted and was faced with a family medical issue that prohibited serving as chair, but did allow for service on the committee. I had worked as a graduate and research assistant to the professor I finally chose as my chair. He did not consider himself a "qualitative person," but we were both very comfortable with each other from prior research projects and there was a reciprocal respect between us.

THE ROLE OF THE ADVISOR

Once you have formed a dissertation committee, it is essential that you establish and maintain rapport with the committee members, particularly the chair. The styles of chairing a dissertation range from a completely hands-off approach to micromanagement of the dissertation, with most chairs falling somewhere in the middle of this continuum.

For example, Michelle Miller-Day had a hands-off committee, or as she states,

I was pretty much blessed with a committee who said, "You are doing something that we have never done . . . so go for it!" They pretty much kept out of my way and let me do my thing, although my advisor did ask for field note updates.

In contrast, Karyn McKinney reports a different type of interaction with her advisor,

My advisor helped in many ways. Because I had already been writing with him, he had taught me how to use qualitative data to study the sociology of race. He was supportive of my topic, once I showed him how interested I was and where it would fit into the existing research. He was always available, by phone, e-mail, or face-to-face, to discuss the ideas I was having while analyzing the data. He read chapters as I completed them, and offered suggestions that made the project imminently better. Finally, he simply would not allow me to sabotage myself through unnecessary perfectionism.

It is up to doctoral students to a get a feel for their chairs' preferences. Having said that, here are some suggestions for communicating with your chair.

Sharing Ideas

Amir once heard a professor complain about a student who repeatedly bothered him with, as he put it, "brain farts" (i.e., fleeting thoughts). He has since lost respect for that professor and his unhelpful approach toward his students, but there is a lesson to be learned here. Remember that the difference between a so-called brain fart and insight is timing and packaging. First, it is generally not a good idea to pour out your thoughts at the doorstep of your advisor as she is preparing for class or trying to hurry to a meeting. Wait. Make an appointment to discuss your progress on the dissertation or invite your chair to lunch and carefully take the time to explain your ideas. Second, develop and polish your ideas before presenting them to your chair. Whereas some chairs are incredibly effective at helping you pull a string out of a mess of seemingly disconnected ideas, others lack the capacity or the inclination for this kind of brainstorming. So play it safe, and think before you speak.

"Driving the Bus"

Ultimately, the role of the advisor is to help you finish *your* project. Sara Crawley illustrated this point by using the analogy of "driving the bus":

> Throughout graduate school, I used a metaphor that guided my decisions and helped me organize my program and reason through pitfalls and politically dangerous situations. The metaphor I used was "I'm driving the bus." I began graduate school because of personal, passionate interests and I felt it important to hold on to those ideals throughout to direct my work. The metaphor extends like this: You can get on the bus and ride along. Everyone is invited and you are welcome to get off the bus if you choose. But I'm driving and I'm determining the direction. I may let someone else navigate for a while if their expertise is helpful. But I ultimately decide where we are going with my research.

The point here is although one can and should expect a good deal of assistance and support in graduate school, at the end the responsibility for completing the dissertation lies with the student. The casual atmosphere of some graduate programs may give the impression that the rules of professionalism do not apply in academia. This could be a dangerous assumption. In some ways, academia is very "corporate"—there are deadlines, expectations, and competition for limited resources. Accept these as the rules of the game without taking any of it too personally. Consider, for example, Darin Weinberg's balanced approach to his advisor:

> Though my advisor sometimes gave me feedback and advice I didn't really want to hear about my work, this was to my mind much appreciated candor and not in any way insulting or disrespectful. I didn't have any difficulties with him, and sought out his guidance as much as I could get it. We formally met perhaps every 4 to 6 weeks and once in awhile informally as well.

Note that the frequency of meetings with your chair will vary during your dissertation. The typical pattern is that you meet more frequently at first when you first conceptualize the project, maybe less so during fieldwork, and maybe more again toward the end. Regardless of how often you meet with your chair, make the most of these sessions. In particular, never give the impression that you are not willing to learn. In the haste to impress an advisor, it is easy to come across as a know-it-all. This is a deadly sin in academia, particularly at the graduate level. Once you are labeled as someone who is not educable, the doors start closing. This reaction on the part of the faculty may be justified in light of the institutional mission of academia. The academic enterprise is based on the assumption that students are there to learn, not to lecture the faculty. If you have a strong opinion about a particular issue, phrase it tentatively and, when possible, in the form of a question.

INSTITUTIONAL REVIEW BOARD (IRB) APPROVAL

The logic and necessity of protecting the dignity and safety of the research participants is widely accepted among social scientists today, but we should remember that this has not always been the case. Most of us are aware that the Nazis used concentration camp victims as guinea pigs in their diabolical medical experiments, but relatively few are familiar with equally egregious but less publicized violations of human rights under the auspices of research here in the United States. In one of the most troubling examples of unscrupulous research, a group of 399 African American men afflicted with syphilis unknowingly became participants in a medical experiment that lasted nearly forty years until it was finally exposed in the early 1970s (Jones, 1981, pp. 1–23). From the 1930s to the 1970s, the physicians assigned to these men deliberately did not treat them for their ailment, even after penicillin was developed and could have been used as a cure. Instead, the patients were secretly experimented on to examine the effects of untreated syphilis. By the time this U.S. Public Health Service study was exposed and subsequently terminated, many of the patients whose condition had gone untreated for years had either died horribly or become severely ill.

Instances of unethical research are not limited to medical experiments. Among social scientists in the United States, a well-known example of unethical research is Laud Humphreys' *Tearoom Trade* (1970). Humphreys studied anonymous homosexual encounters in semipublic places. Specifically, he was interested in the background of men who had sex with other men in public restrooms. After positioning himself in a restroom in a city park, he gained the trust of the men who frequented it by acting as a lookout for them while they engaged in sexual activities. Humphreys secretly recorded their license plate numbers, and with the help of the police, discovered who they were and where they lived. Months later, he visited the men in their homes disguised as a survey researcher. He gathered additional information about these men and their families and subsequently published his research in a book that was widely praised before questions were raised about its ethics. One of the main findings of his work was that many of the men in his study were married and of middle-class background—a discovery that was made possible through the covert invasion of the subjects' privacy.

Such flagrant abuses of research subjects in the name of science have led to the establishment of codes of research ethics. While these may vary across disciplines and national boundaries, there are a number of general principles that most researchers would agree with. Most prominent among these are (a) voluntary participation, (b) protection of research participants, (c) disclosure of potential benefits and risks to participants, and (d) obtaining informed consent. IRBs emerged in academic institutions as bureaucratic entities responsible for regulating and enforcing these important research ethics (Marvasti, 2003a).

Ideally, when you undergo and successfully complete an IRB review, you accomplish two things. First, you have benefited from the advice of several other academics trained to detect any potential flaws in your research design that could pose a threat to the participants. The advantage of this guidance cannot be overstated. A qualitative researcher's enthusiasm and his desire to become intimately familiar with a topic could blind him to the adverse consequences of his research. The IRB committee could alert you to problems before any inadvertent harm is done. Second, when you present your research participants with a university-approved informed consent, you earn their confidence that you are a trained researcher with the backing of a legitimate academic institution. This could help you establish rapport and address any concerns your respondents might have about answering your questions or sharing their private lives with you.

All studies conducted under the auspices of a federally funded university are required to receive IRB approvals. This applies to research conducted by any student or faculty member affiliated with the institutions, regardless of where the research is actually done. IRB reviews fall into three categories: full review (usually takes 2 to 4 weeks), expedited reviews (usually 2 weeks), and exemption (the researcher is exempted from all or parts of the IRB requirements). In most cases, the process of obtaining an IRB approval is relatively simple and straightforward.

However, qualitative researchers sometimes encounter unique problems in obtaining an IRB approval. Indeed, an IRB guidebook published by the U.S. Department of Health and Human Services explicitly notes the difficulties confronting qualitative researchers where informed consent is concerned. Specifically, in a section titled "Fieldwork," the guidebook states,

> Fieldwork, or ethnographic research, involves observation of and interaction with the persons or group being studied in the group's own environment, often for long periods of time. Since fieldwork is a research process that gains shape and substance as the study progresses, it is difficult, if not impossible, to specify detailed contents and objectives in a protocol.
>
> After gaining access to the fieldwork setting, the ongoing demands of scientifically and morally sound research involve gaining the approval and trust of the persons being studied. These processes, as well as the research itself, involve complex, continuing interactions between researcher and hosts that cannot be reduced to an informed consent form. Thus, while the idea of consent is not inapplicable in fieldwork, IRBs and researchers need to adapt prevailing notions of acceptable protocols and consent procedures to the realities of fieldwork. IRBs should keep in mind the possibility of granting a waiver of informed consent. (Penslar, 2007)

Evidently, even the government agency in charge of defining and enforcing guidelines for dealing with human subjects is aware that qualitative researchers face unique challenges in gaining IRB approvals (it is worth noting that this guidebook was prepared by a lawyer, Robin Levin Penslar, J.D.; the "ORRR Program Officer"; and a physician, Joan P. Porter, D.P.A.). In this section we consider the special IRB issues confronting qualitative researchers in the context of several examples.

Defining Research

As noted earlier, qualitative research as a whole is much more open-ended than quantitative research. In most cases, quantitative research officially commences with the administration of a survey to a sample of respondents, but, as shown above, qualitative researchers could begin data collection inadvertently. For example, Amir's life history as a person of Middle Eastern descent is data for his research, but he never thought about obtaining approval from anyone to write about his personal experiences. At the core of this issue is what is considered research and when it begins. U.S. federal law offers this formal definition for the word: "Research means a systematic investigation, including research development, testing and evaluation, designed to develop or contribute to generalizable knowledge" (U.S. Department of Health and Human Services, 2005).

This definition provides a seemingly clear institutional mission for IRB committees. In practice, however, numerous university workshops have been held to inform the faculty and students as to what exactly constitutes research. For example, given that qualitative research is not "generalizable," is it considered research under this regulation? The answer depends on the inclinations of the particular IRB committee and the academic institution involved.

As Cary Nelson (2003) notes, there is a good deal of confusion regarding IRB oversight on research involving in-depth interviews. For example, some universities exempt journalism students and faculty from the IRB approval process, even though they essentially do the kinds of interviews that qualitative researchers do. Nelson suggests that one explanation for this inconsistency is that IRB administrators fear that regulating journalism would border violating freedom of speech protections provided under the First Amendment of the U.S. Constitution (for a discussion on the constitutionality of IRBs, see Philip Hamburg, 2004). According to Nelson, another IRB strategy for defining research is, "If it's published in a scholarly journal, it's research" (2003, p. 33). Of course, this interpretation raises another question; namely, what is a "scholarly journal"? In light of these confusions, qualitative researchers often find themselves educating IRB members about the philosophy and methods of their approach. The rule of thumb here is that if you are not sure if you need an IRB approval, check with your committee chair and contact the university IRB for guidance.

Differing Priorities

University IRBs are governed by a set of priorities, some of which directly concern the ideal of protecting research subjects from harm whereas others are about protecting the institution as a corporate and legal entity. For example, IRB committees are very concerned about shielding the university from potential lawsuits. In fact, in some cases, the board includes an attorney whose responsibility is to ensure that a proposed research project is free from litigation risk. In the words of Michelle Miller-Day, who served on an IRB committee,

The board members are thinking, how could a participant in this study sue us? How can we protect against that (i.e., cover our asses)? And how can we protect the participant from us (i.e., cover their asses)? As long as you think of all possibilities where someone might get harmed and cover the collective potential risks, then you are halfway there.

However, for researchers, participants are not seen as potential litigators but as subjects who can provide information about a particular topic. In a sense, this results in two visions of the research participant, "the potential litigators" (the IRB view) and "the sources of information" (the researcher view). Although this distinction raises important theoretical issues (see *Qualitative Inquiry*, 2003, 10(2), for a list of articles related to this topic), the practical point for us as IRB applicants is that we must fit our priorities into the protective priorities of our academic institution. As Michelle notes, the key is to convince the IRB board that in essence there is no potential for a lawsuit. One way to provide this assurance is to ask research participants to sign what amounts to a contract detailing (a) the objectives of the study, (b) its voluntary nature, and (c) any potential harm. The participants are expected to sign this document, and it is to be archived along with the data (in case there is a lawsuit).

The challenge for doctoral students is to package the open-ended contingencies of qualitative research in a way that convinces IRB members (who often are unfamiliar with this kind of methodology) that no risk is involved. Again, survey researchers have an easier job with this because the survey questions are designed in advance and clearly demarcate the boundaries of the project. In contrast, qualitative research moves in unpredicted directions; an informant's answers to a question may result in a line of inquiry that was not planned from the start. Michelle Miller-Day offers this advice for overcoming this sort of challenge:

The biggest problem for qualitative researchers, as I see it, is that in our data collection we have to be flexible and attuned to "emergent data." While qualitative researchers can dance to our particular rendition of flexible and emergent, lawyers and some quantitative researchers find this rendition lacking in rhythm (structure) and believe it is chaotic (not systematic). We need to provide structure and a systematic *outline* of what is planned and give possible outcomes of "planned flexibility."

The phrase "planned flexibility" is one way out of the IRB dilemma. It is not enough to inform the board that you are doing qualitative research and therefore are not sure about the types of questions asked, where, and how. They just won't understand and agree with that line of reasoning. Instead, to the best of your ability give an outline of what shape or direction your research might take. In other words, give them something they can work with within the parameters of their institutional roles.

Some research projects have to be considerably modified due to IRB constraints. For example, Michael Arter states,

> In the earliest planning for my research I had considered interviewing the spouses of the officers for the familial aspect of police stress. Based upon past decisions of the IRB at my institution, the plan to attempt to interview anyone other than police officers was abandoned.

Other researchers go through such a complicated IRB approval that the experience itself becomes part of the dissertation. This was certainly the case with Sylvia Ansay, who encountered particularly stringent demands in her research on house arrestees.

> I experienced a major hurdle that seemed to come out of nowhere. I had worked closely with the IRB administrator in writing my proposal. She assured me that we had covered all our bases and there appeared to be no problems. Approval should be automatic, she said, just a matter of waiting a couple of weeks until the Board met. The process became complicated when the IRB decided that, although I was not receiving funding from the National Institutes of Health (NIH), I should have NIH approval for the project. The Board didn't give me any reasons for the decision; however, I filed the proposal with NIH as they required. An administrator at NIH telephoned me, surprised at the request because I was not seeking funding from them. I had no answers for her. She ended the conversation by saying the requirement raised "red flags," which they'd have to check out. That was the first of three or four phone calls between us. (I instigated two of these in response to letters from the administrator.) The first criticized the methodology, saying they had never heard of using life stories or narrative analysis as research. It wasn't "good science," she said. Later, I had to explain and defend every aspect of the research point by point. In the end, their argument against approval shifted to a concern with my personal safety. They requested a conference call with my professor, during which an NIH attorney urged him not to support the in-home interviews, to consider the liability. When he could not be persuaded, they approved the project with a disclaimer that approval would not have been given if I had been applying for NIH funding. My experience with NIH became a chapter of my dissertation and has been published in *Studies in Symbolic Interaction* (Vol. 25).

The IRB committee in this case seems overly protective of Sylvia and her research participants. Though she eventually secured an approval for her project, it is evident that her research would have been completely stymied without the support of her dissertation chair. This sort of overprotection is especially noticeable where sensitive topics or "deviant populations" are concerned. Consider, for example, Sara Crawley's description of the IRB mandates for her research with lesbians:

> I did have to take some pains to make the IRB comfortable with the group I was interviewing. Given that I wanted to interview "lesbians," the IRB was more worried about protecting confidentiality than most of my narrators. Although I was careful to respect narrators, I found most participants were very willing and expected that they might talk about lesbian experience in the lesbian groups they normally attended to talk about lesbian experience. Ironically, for me, getting IRB approval was more about making the IRB comfortable about issues that the naturally occurring community was already comfortable discussing.

In Sara's case, the IRB approval seems to hinge more on the board's comfort level with lesbians and talk of lesbianism than the community members' ease about discussing their lifestyles.

In a related case, Eileen O'Brien, in her study of antiracists, found that the research participants wanted to be identified by name in the research despite the IRB requirements for anonymity.

> I was dealing with an area of activists who are pretty silenced/ignored in history—white antiracists—and some people felt that this neglect was very calculated because it prevents whites from having visible alternative models of whiteness to follow, thereby subverting any major transformations of the dominant group in society. So I asked my advisor about it, and he said as long as I had it documented that they gave me permission to use their real names, he didn't think it would be a problem. But this issue never actually went back to the IRB. I think this illustrates how qualitative research needs to be adaptable, and that following "standard protocol" will not always work best depending on the topic and context of the data you need to obtain.

It is important to remember that not every researcher experiences hardships with the IRB approval process. Many projects sail through, so to speak. The extent of difficulty depends on the topic you have chosen to study and on your academic institutions' research standards. Generally, topics related to crime, deviance, and marginal populations go through a more rigorous IRB process. Again, as Michelle notes, the key phrase for getting your application through is "planned flexibility." This is echoed by Charles Bosk's (2004) recommendation that qualitative researchers should educate IRB members and work to reform the review process to suit their needs.

IRB Reviews and Controversial Topics

On a more cynical level, the IRB committees can be seen as a barrier to progressive research, or as Nikitah Imani notes, they can "stymie antioppression research." Although IRBs can play a significant role in ensuring the safety of research participants, their survey-friendly protocol may in the long run discourage more innovative research projects, especially those aimed at investing social inequality (e.g., poverty, racism, sexism). Such studies may invariably involve some degree of risk, both for the subjects and for the organization where inequality is practiced. As Nelson states,

> Of course, "respect for persons" can hardly entail respect for every human action, but IRBs are ill equipped to negotiate the difference. Instead, they often give unquestioned allegiance to a concept that might be given more nuanced application to, say, Ku Klux Klan or Nazi Party members, who might merit humanity qualified with disapproval and who might on occasion appropriately be challenged aggressively in an interview. A historian might well wish to investigate the self-understanding of a Ku Klux Klan member and might choose to present a neutral account of the organization, but academic freedom means that the decision to do so needs to be the historian's, not that of an IRB. One consequence of an unreflective commitment to "respect for persons" is that IRBs have great difficulty accepting research destined to be critical of its "human subjects." (2003, p. 32)

As seen in the passage above, an increasing number of social scientists, and academics in general, are concerned about IRBs' growing "ethics creep" (Haggerty, 2004) into their research. Initially, the social scientists responded to IRB demands with incredulity and amusement. For example, in a magazine interview, Howard Becker joked that if he was required to undergo rigorous IRB reviews, he would circumvent the bureaucracy by redefining his research as "conceptual art" (Shea, 2000). Four years later, in response to Haggerty's "Ethics Creep: Governing Social Science Research in the Name of Ethics," Howard Becker writes:

What began years ago as a sort of safeguard against doctors injecting cancer cells into research patients without first asking them if that was OK has turned into a serious, ambitious bureaucracy with interests to protect, a mission to promote, and a self-righteous and self-protective ideology to explain why it is all necessary. . . . I never had occasion to try out the idea I suggested to the reporter from *Lingua Franca*, of describing my work as conceptual art or performance art. . . . But if I did I suspect the response would be to change the rules to include art projects. (2004, pp. 415–416)

Becker goes on to point out that some of his research on medical students, for example, could not have been conducted with the same academic rigor under the new IRB rules. His final recommendation to social scientists is, "start fighting this thing full time and don't give up an inch we don't have to" (2004, p. 416).

Similarly, Nikitah speculates that IRBs may inadvertently block the aspirations of researchers who want to dig deeper, as it were. Moreover, in their capacity to monitor and approve research, IRBs can become a sort of "university research police" that controls the production of knowledge. Given that IRBs are a relatively new institutional invention, it remains to be seen how they will evolve to fulfill their mission.

For now, the IRB approval is a necessary part of doing research at most U.S. institutions of higher education. Based on our contributors' comments and our own experience with obtaining IRB approvals, we offer the following checklist to help facilitate your application process.

1. Learn about the IRB guidelines at your particular institution (typically, this can be done by visiting their Web site).

2. Describe your research in simple terms and do not assume that your application will be reviewed by someone with expertise in qualitative research.

3. Prior to submitting the final application, contact your IRB office for clarifications on the informed consent procedures. In some cases, your research may be exempt from the requirement of a written informed consent.

4. Be cordial to the IRB staff and let them know you are willing to address any concerns about privacy or potential harm to the research participants.

5. Expect some delays in the IRB process as you may be asked to revise and resubmit the original application several times before your research is deemed compliant with IRB guidelines.

6. If fellow graduate students have done projects similar to the one you are proposing, ask them how they went about obtaining their IRB approvals.

DATA COLLECTION

One of the unique features of qualitative research, and what really separates it from quantitative research, is that data collection is not limited to a particular survey instrument or a set of variables. Qualitative data collection, especially with ethnographic research, is an open-ended process that encompasses all the contextual information related to the research topic and the research site. In some cases, information that was collected for a different purpose or observations that were originally not part of your research might become data. Consider, for example, Karyn McKinney's research on white identities, which started as a class project:

I had, in a sense, already begun data collection before I decided on my dissertation topic. As an assignment for a course I was teaching, I had asked my students to write their racial autobiographies. I didn't realize this was "data" that I was collecting at that time. The students' stories showed how racial and ethnic identity is a process, not a static characteristic. They were fascinating. After deciding to use the initial student autobiographies as data, and obtaining the consent that I needed, I asked colleagues to collect more data for me in their own classes, at two other universities in the area. These colleagues offered their students extra credit for contributing to my work, and the students sent me their autobiographies via e-mail, which made it very easy later to begin analysis of them (the originals I had received were in hard copy, and I had to scan them into my computer). The extra credit was, of course, offered to students of any racial or ethnic background, although I only used those of white students for this project. In order to guide students in their writing, I gave them a list of questions, the same that I had given to my class, that would give them an idea of the kinds of stories and experiences I was interested in. They were told that they did not have to answer every question, and could add other information they felt was relevant. So the data for my dissertation came from three universities. I ended up with about 60 autobiographies.

It is not uncommon for qualitative researchers to use their existing relationships and contacts for their research. For example, Sara Crawley writes about how she used her existing rapport with the lesbian community to collect data for her research on gender roles among lesbians.

I had chosen to study lesbians, an identity that I hold myself. I was already familiar with the local community and knew where to access narrators. I found focus groups particularly easy to organize because I was looking for "naturally occurring" settings (in the sense that I did not arrange them, but participants would be there regardless of my research). So for focus groups, I approached preexisting groups and simply asked to be their topic for the evening. As a result, I intervened less as a researcher in creating the groups, as well as needed to expend little energy organizing places, time, participants, etc.

Similarly, Michael Arter, in his research on undercover police officers, used his existing contacts.

I capitalized on my prior law enforcement experience to gain access to the departments from which I collected data. Some of the agencies I contacted were personally known to me and others had individuals who worked there who knew me from my time in law enforcement.

In Amir's research on Middle Eastern Americans, he actually interviewed members of his family and incorporated a good deal of personal experiences into his research. However, using existing opportunities does imply there is no planning involved in qualitative data collection. As we will see in the coming chapters, there are still many choices to be made about the focus, scope, and duration of the study.

THE ROLE OF THEORY

Arguably, any research endeavor is theoretical. That is, certain assumptions about the social world are always present and influence our observations. Having said that, the degree to which theory is an explicit part of research varies considerably across different dissertations. Some researchers seem to have a formal theoretical model that guides their work from the start. For example, Michael Arter reports,

The theoretical schema of general strain theory seemed to comport with a substantial portion of the literature review on my topic. Basically, the academic literature on policing pointed to strain theory as a model for understanding the structural conditions of policing and police officers' behavior. I felt it was a logical decision to apply the theory directly in my study. I also allowed the data to become grounded as the collection and analytical processes evolved.

Arter's theoretical choices are guided by a review of the literature (e.g., a reading of what other academics have published on the topic). This approach is quite effective if you don't want to reinvent the wheel, so to speak. Certain ideas may be normatively accepted in the field, and your research could build on the existing knowledge. However, as Michael notes, there is also room for **grounded theory** (a la Glaser and Strauss, and Charmaz), or a sort of bottom-up, or **inductive**, approach to theorizing (we will say more on this in the later chapters).

Overall, the experience of our colleagues suggests that the role of theory in qualitative research varies on a continuum that ranges from formal theory (i.e., a line of reasoning with explicit assumptions and a particular intellectual history) to data-specific analytical orientations (a way of making sense of the data at hand that makes no attempt at universal generalizations). Some of these variations were discussed more formally in Chapter 2, in the context of Gubrium and Holstein's *New Language of Qualitative Method* (1997). Many of our colleagues fall somewhere in the middle of this continuum, as in the case of Michael Arter, whose work was simultaneously informed by formal theory and open to unique characteristics of his data.

Darin Weinberg's position on theory further highlights this kind of flexible theorizing:

My own orientation to theory is rather broader than the one we often find in theory textbooks. For me, theory simply refers to the analytic relevance of your empirical work to more general questions being debated in your academic field or fields. Hence, I was interested in issues like power, **social constructionism** versus realism, macro-/microrelationships, structure and agency, and material and ideological structure, and I thought a lot about how these issues were playing out in my own research settings and how what was going on in my settings might highlight things that my academic colleagues might find interesting or valuable with respect to these more general topics.

DATA ANALYSIS

To start with, anyone who has ever done qualitative data analysis will tell you that writing and analysis coexist. This is not necessarily the case in quantitative research, where much of the analysis is done using a computer software program, and once all the tables are generated, the writing of the results begins. In qualitative research, we write explanatory notes (i.e., analysis) as we collect and transcribe the data. Consider, for example, Karyn McKinney's approach to data analysis:

> First, I read through all of my data, and while doing so, I created a list of "themes" I found in the data, with subthemes. Of course, this was an ongoing process, where I several times added new subthemes until I had a final list. Next, I began to try to code the data using a qualitative software program, QUALPRO. I found that doing so was taking more time than it was worth. So I simply went through each autobiography in WordPerfect and placed a theme or subtheme at the beginning of various sections, in brackets. Each portion of every autobiography was coded in some way. Then, when it was time to begin writing, I simply went through files and searched for these key words for themes to select quotes for each section. I organized and wrote my dissertation according to the major categories of themes I seemed to be finding in my analysis. These were whiteness as discourse, whiteness as stories, and whiteness as identity. This organization came to me through my analysis.

As Karyn notes, analysis of data provides a method for organizing and eventually writing the dissertation. Again, the writing and analysis are not separate, sequential stages, but they are intertwined and simultaneous.

In fact, as Michelle Miller-Day notes, the trick is to not lose sight of this intricate relationship between analysis and writing. In her words, "The difficulty lies in disciplining yourself to write your field notes every night whether you feel like it or not. Writing your research memos and trying to examine connections while at the same time thinking of what questions you will pursue tomorrow." Here we can see that not only are writing and analysis linked but that the data collection is also part of the same process. Another researcher, Nikitah Imani, describes the process in this way:

> I think it is vital to synthesize and catalog a lot of the data as you are getting inputs rather than gathering the data and beginning a separate process of writing. At one level, this helps you avoid the simple human problem of trying to retroactively reconstruct events and other things through memory. At another level, writing after all the data collection could cause one to take events out of the original context in which they were derived. It is critical that a qualitative researcher maintain, as I did throughout, a three-pronged research process involving (a) the actual data collection, (b) a journal about the data collection process as it takes place, and (c) a journal about changes in the perception of both of those

processes as they unfold. Thus at the "end," one has the raw data but also the equally important analysis of how one has transformed and been transformed by the research process. Having these three projects allowed me to, say, look at conversations and interviews from a session, look at my own initial take, and finally, look at how I approached the scene for subsequent events after that initial assessment.

To do effective data analysis, you must know your data, or as one of my professors used to say, "You must court your data." Good social science writing, be it qualitative or quantitative, is embedded in the data. To ensure that the writing grows out of the data, become intimately familiar with every bit of information that your research generates. In Lara Foley's words,

> I became familiar with my interview transcripts initially during transcription. I used an extra-wide margin to make notes as I was transcribing and later when reading through transcripts and **coding**. My approach to data analysis is that I become intimately familiar with the data. Topics, themes, or specific arguments "jump out at me" or formulate in my head over time and then I pull together excerpts that work.

Believe it or not, data analysis can be fun. Sitting down and piecing together the different bits and pieces of interviews and observations into a coherent work can be an exhilarating creative process. This was the case for Sylvia Ansay, who states,

> I transcribed all my own data, along with notes about the homes and family members interviewed. It took a long time, but I viewed it as the beginning of the analysis, as a way to get close to the data. It helped me to remember families in context and to begin identifying emergent themes. I analyzed individual narratives as I went along. I enjoyed working with the data, making minute-by-minute decisions, backtracking, reviewing, rethinking, feeling satisfied, and moving to the next step. I love working with words and I was doing what I loved. Besides, I don't think I could have combined the various kinds of data and made the methodological shifts I needed to make along the way. For me, the fun of qualitative research rests in its endless possibilities.

WRITING

To the extent that qualitative writing is separate from analysis, it is mostly about knowing when to stop and deciding what should or should not be included in the text. Qualitative writing, as Sylvia Ansay notes, offers "endless possibilities." Well, in practice, tasks have to have a logical end. The challenge for most novice writers, to put it bluntly, is knowing when to shut up. Nikitah Imani, offers this advice for overcoming the problem:

> The story frame really determined the selection of data to present. At the outset, I committed to get in as much as I could of the participants' own words and ideas. Within that commitment, I wanted to make sure that I indeed told the story. Information that was not directly germane to give the reader a sense of the particular pieces of the story I wanted to render was set aside. I always say set aside, rather than excluded, since it's more a question of them not relating to what's being said than being denied arbitrarily. Much of the material I did not use in the dissertation has found its way back into the book and in other publications as good data about other questions I did not think about or choose to focus on at the time.

Nikitah's advice can be summed up this way: decide what the story is, tell the story, and save whatever is not part of the story for another project. The emphasis on the narrative is echoed in Michelle Miller-Day's account:

> For my dissertation, I felt overwhelmed, I felt unsure, and I felt like, "who am I to interpret these people's lives?" Then the chair of my committee reminded me that I was a social science narrator and I just needed to tell my story from my view trying to represent the characters in the story. This helped to get me jump-started. Then, and now, I always begin by writing a descriptive account of the story—of the people, of the setting, and of my reactions to it all. Then, once I have captured the people and their voices at least in part, I begin with my analysis of the data; trying to capture the human experience without reducing this experience to disembodied variables. I took a mountain of data and broke it into its parts and put it back together into a coherent story.

If the narrative model does not appeal to you, or just doesn't fit your data, you might want to consider Eileen O'Brien's more thematically driven approach:

> On the advice of my advisor, I looked at a couple of recent dissertations of his advisees that he suggested. This helped me with an Introduction and Methods chapter. This also probably gave me the model for the number of chapters I would have, then a conclusion. My substantive chapters

I basically organized around the three major research questions with which I originally began the project:

1. *Why* did they become antiracist?

(In other words, being white, why should they care about racism? What made them want to take it up as their life's work?)

2. *What* do they do?

(What are the specific antiracist actions they take in their everyday life? I used concrete examples here.)

3. *How* do they define racism?

(This question basically focused on the ideology that guided their work.)

QUANTITATIVE OR QUALITATIVE?

Whereas qualitative researchers might be more open to flexibility of the data and the research process as a whole than quantitative researchers, as you will see in the coming chapters, there are many similarities between the two methodologies. A quantitative dissertation in many respects involves the steps outlined previously. In fact, some graduate students combine quantitative and qualitative methods (i.e., they use "mixed methods") for their research. For example, John Linn writes,

As I was going through graduate school, there was an ongoing debate over the centrality of one form of social science research over another. Specifically, some very difficult and contentious debates revolved around the "proper place" for qualitative research in the social sciences as opposed to quantitative. My master's degree was directed by an individual who was working at the margins of both qualitative and quantitative methodologies. The underlying idea was to take qualitative data and quantify it. I was enthralled by the concept and accepted the orientation readily. As I moved to my doctoral institution, the old debates were still lingering and it was easy to identify those oriented to qualitative research as opposed to quantitative. In fact, there were no classes offered that were positioned to an in-depth study of qualitative research. Moreover, a form of implicit pressure was brought to bear on doing quantitative research—"clean and easy" was the catch phrase. Nonetheless, for my dissertation I chose to follow a mixed-methods approach. My decision was based on the realization that while quantitative methods provide very interesting data about how much or how many questions, they missed some of the "story." The analogy I used was that of people in poverty. A determination can be made as to how many, where, when, and the like, but what was missing, from my perspective, was a very simple and compelling question—what is it like to be in poverty? So, when it came to my topic, employee loyalty, it was not simply a matter of determining who might have been loyal or not, but also what underlying interpersonal dynamics were at play, how did they factor into loyalty, and what conditions had to be met for loyalty to exist.

As John's story shows, it might be wiser to think of quantitative and qualitative methodologies as complementary parts of the systematic, empirical search for knowledge.

CONCLUDING REMARKS

Admittedly, there is considerable overlap between the themes discussed in this chapter. For example, as we noted, data collection, analysis, and writing are virtually inseparable in qualitative research. Thus these categories are not intended to be treated as mutually exclusive, but their main purpose is to show you the diversity of research experiences. If, in selecting your topic, you are pushed and pulled by different forces, you are not unique. Doing qualitative research is in many respects no different than doing everyday life—it is complex and sometimes downright chaotic. The point of this book and other advice and mentorship you receive is to help you manage this chaos and direct it into a coherent research project.

Obviously, there are many different stories that research students can tell about their experience and we do not pretend that what you have read was typical or representative. Nonetheless, there are several clear messages in these stories that are worth listening to.

We set these out following this paragraph as a 16-point guide. Obviously, like any recipe, you will, of course, need to apply it to your own circumstances. Nevertheless, the following points apply to all levels of student research, from BA and MA dissertations to the PhD.

1. Begin in familiar territory: If you can, work with data that is close at hand and readily accessible. For instance, if you have data from another study that you can (re)analyze, grab the opportunity. There are no brownie points to

be obtained for gathering your data in difficult circumstances. Make it easy on yourself at this stage so that you can concentrate your energies on the infinitely more important task of data analysis.

2. Find a settled theoretical orientation: As we stress throughout this book, research is never just about techniques. Find a theoretical approach that makes sense to you and could provide a basis for inference and data analysis.

3. Narrow down your topic: Strive to find a topic that is appropriate to your theory and data and is workable (this issue is discussed at length in Chapter 6).

4. Don't try to reinvent the wheel: In Chapter 5, we discuss what original-ity might mean in research. For the moment, we recommend that you look at previous successful dissertations in your university library or departmental files and, where possible, focus on work directed by your supervisor.

5. Keep writing: Commit your ideas to paper. Don't worry how short or rough your papers are. Indeed, in some way, it makes more sense, initially at least, to submit 500-word pieces so that you can be guided in the right direc-tion before you have expended too much time and effort.

6. Begin data analysis early: Don't be deflected away from early data analysis by literature reviews and the exigencies of data gathering. If you haven't got any data yourself at an early stage, try analyzing someone else's data—published data, your supervisor's data, and so forth (see Chapter 11).

7. Think critically about data: When you start to identify a pattern in your data, don't rush to conclusions. See how robust this pattern is by working com-paratively with different parts of your data.

8. Use your dissertation chair: The chair can help you test out your ideas and give you confidence.

9. Use other resources and opportunities: Graduate students should take every opportunity to attend relevant conferences and, better still, to give con-ference papers and take appropriate training courses. Find out if there are study groups of research students working on similar topics. If not, try to establish such a group.

10. Do not expect a steady learning curve: Be prepared for the sequence of highs and lows that will inevitably happen. Treat setbacks as opportunities.

11. Keep a research diary: Keep a file of your current ideas, hopes, and worries. This file is an invaluable resource, which, as suggested in Chapter 22, can be used, in edited form, in your methodology chapter.

12.[1] Earmark blocks of working time: If you are researching part-time, it is crucial to find blocks of time in which you can focus solely on your research. Use this time for intensive data analysis and writing.

13. Do not reproach yourself: If you experience a setback, it may be best to take some time out to relax before you return to your research.

14. Treat field relations as data: How others treat you in the field is never just a technical matter. Reflect upon how your interaction with your subjects is shaping your data.

15. Understand that there is no "perfect" model of research design: Practical contingencies (e.g., access or the lack of it, the time you have available) are always going to affect any piece of research. Don't be afraid of working with what data you happen to have. Your chair and other committee members will not be comparing your research with some perfect model, but they will expect you to have thought through the limitations of your data and your analysis (see Chapter 5).

16. Realize that it is never too early to think about job prospects: As we note in Chapter 29, your job prospects will be decided by your research interests, publications, and your training (who mentored you in graduate school). As you consider your dissertation topic and choice of methods, also give some thought to how your choices will limit or expand your employability.

CASE STUDY

As with Greg and Nikitah, chance factors were crucial in David's choice of PhD topic. Whereas a research grant or access to a particular setting shaped Greg and Nikitah's research, David's committee and his own changing interests had a key influence on his topic. After having completed an MA at UCLA, David returned to the London School of Economics to do his PhD. He then discovered that one of his undergraduate teachers (Robert McKenzie, a political sociologist) expected that David would be supervised by him on a topic close to McKenzie's own interests (e.g., voting behavior).

However, by this time, David's interests had shifted away from political sociology and toward social class and status. Influenced by contemporary sociologists like C. Wright Mills and David Lockwood, he planned to conduct an interview study of white-collar workers at four different kinds of workplace, focusing on their lifestyles and aspirations. Not wishing to

(Continued)

---

1. Items 12 and 13 were suggested by Vicki Taylor after reading an earlier draft of this chapter.

(Continued)

upset his undergraduate tutor, he included him on his committee, along with an industrial relations specialist, Ben Roberts.

David began his research interviews and, after two years, published a short note on his initial findings in the *British Journal of Sociology*. This shows the value of beginning data analysis at an early stage rather than allowing the data to accumulate.

Early data analysis has a further advantage: it allows you to reconsider the direction in which your research is heading. In David's case, such reconsideration had quite a drastic result:

- He started to worry about the reliability of data gathered from his semistructured interviews. How far did his respondents' answers to his prepared questions actually reflect their own experiences? Moreover, didn't his own assumptions come into play when he interpreted their answers to some open-ended questions?

- David now had a junior faculty post where he unexpectedly found himself teaching a course on the sociology of organizations. As a result, he published a paper on organization theory in *Sociology*. Was this a better topic for his PhD?

His joint supervisor, Ben Roberts, settled the matter. Having read David's published paper, he suggested that it might make sense to develop it in the form of a library-based, theoretical PhD. Seeing how quickly such a dissertation could be written, given David's reading for his teaching work, David switched topics. This example shows what you can gain by discussing the direction of your research with your supervisor.

Two years later, David was awarded his PhD at about the same time as his dissertation was published as a book (*The Theory of Organizations*). So, as a result of chance factors and his own research experience, David's research topic was totally redefined.

KEY POINTS

1. It helps to begin your research in familiar territory.

2. Find a settled theoretical orientation that works for you.

3. Once you get a feel for your field, narrow down your topic as soon as you can.

4. Don't try to reinvent the wheel—find what has worked for others and follow it.

5. Keep writing.

6. Begin data analysis immediately.

7. Think critically about your data—don't rush to conclusions.

8. Test out your ideas with your supervisor—don't worry if, in the early stages, you are often wide of the mark.

9. Use other resources and opportunities inside and outside your own department.

10. Do not expect a steady learning curve—no research study is without some disasters.

11. Keep a research diary.

12. Earmark blocks of working time to complete different activities.

13. Do not reproach yourself about setbacks.

14. Treat your relations within the field as data.

15. Understand that there is no perfect model of research design.

FURTHER READING

The best place to look for similar research histories is in the writings of students at your own university. BA students should seek to obtain past successful undergraduate senior theses from their department. Graduate students should study MA theses and PhD dissertations in the library, focusing particularly on the work of people having your supervisor. If the methodology chapters do not include an autobiographical account, try to contact the authors and discuss what lessons they draw from their experience.

EXERCISE 3.1

Keep a research diary in which you record

- changes in your ideas about topic, data, theory, and method;

- new ideas from the literature or from lectures and talk;

- meetings with your supervisor and their consequences; and

- life events and their consequences for your work.

At regular intervals (every 3 weeks, for example), reread your research diary and assess

- what you have achieved in that period,

- what would be required for you to do better in future, and

- your achievement targets for the next equivalent period.

Exercise 3.2

Keep a diary of your changing research interests. Think through what factors are influencing the direction that your research is taking. For instance, how much have you had a free choice in your topic? Have you taken advantage of any chance factors (e.g., research access, publications) that may have arisen? How important is it for you to complete your PhD dissertation or research project speedily? If so, have you chosen an appropriate topic?

You will find that such a research diary will not only help you reflect more on the direction your research is taking but will produce material that will prove invaluable when you write your methodology section (or chapter) for your research.

Exercise 3.3

Visit the Web site for the U.S. Department of Health and Human Services at http://www.hhs.gov/ohrp/irb/irb_guidebook.htm and browse through the *IRB Guidebook*. What sections of this guidebook apply to qualitative researchers? What are their recommendations for the protection of subjects in qualitative studies? Are these guidelines different than the ones suggested for quantitative or survey researchers?

Exercise 3.4

Visit your university's IRB Web site (this is typically under something like "The Office of Research Protections") and review their IRB procedures. If your university does not have an IRB office, simply search the words *IRB guidelines* on the Internet and review other universities' guidelines. Do you note any special guidelines or exemptions for qualitative research?

CHAPTER 4

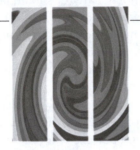

The Research Experience II

INTRODUCTION

In this part of the book, we have been attempting to set out the context in which qualitative research dissertations are written. We began with a brief overview of qualitative research. Then, in Chapter 3, we considered the lessons that could be drawn from three completed research dissertations.

Yet, for many readers of this book, their own completed graduate or undergraduate dissertation is a distant, desired object. So, in this chapter, we draw upon the accounts of research students at an early stage of their research. Through these accounts, we examine the analytical, methodological, and practical problems that confront the beginning researcher.

In some senses, the beginning researcher has far less to prove than established scholars. If you imagine a sliding scale of levels of achievement, then journal articles, as the stock in trade of established scholars, are (or should be) at the pinnacle of scholarly accomplishment. Somewhat surprisingly, books are a little further down the scale because they do not depend on the same degree of independent review. Further down the scale are completed research dissertations, which, we suggest, are properly viewed as displays of successful apprenticeship.

However, this sense of a sliding scale in research is intended simply to mark a stage of a research career—it is not a moral category. Although it is many years since we were at that stage, we do not look down upon the work of first-year research students. Indeed, frankly, we sometimes come across more exciting ideas in a first-year graduate seminar than in many journal articles!

What follows is by no means a representative survey of qualitative research at its early stages. Instead, the following material has been drawn from research students in my own department and in various social science and humanities departments of Finnish universities.[1]

Although the range of research covered in this chapter is limited, we hope you will eventually agree that it is not narrow. In other words, we hope and expect that readers will find at least some echo of their own ideas and interests represented in the following pages.

In collating these presentations for this chapter, we had to decide on an organizing principle. In particular, we had to choose whether to organize the material by topic, theory, or methodology. We reasoned that grouping by topic would be lively but might appear to exclude readers working on different topics. By contrast, a theory grouping might be too abstract and, perhaps, confusing for an audience coming from a disparate range of disciplines. By taking a methodological perspective, we hope to be more inclusive by encompassing many of the methods used (and contemplated) by qualitative researchers.

The discussion in this chapter is thus organized by method, with sections on interview studies, **ethnographies**, textual analysis, work with video- and audio-tapes, and multiple methods. However, such a focus on method is not narrowly technical. As we make clear, methods only acquire meaning and vitality by their embeddedness in particular theoretical perspectives.

As in Chapter 3, we will proceed case by case, offering some comments with each example and then summarizing the points that emerge from each methodology. The chapter concludes with some suggestions about managing the early stages of research.

After each of the following topics, we have noted the social science discipline in which the student is working as well as the student's name.

Living and Coping in a Community of Elderly People

Information Studies/Sociology: Tippi

Tippi writes about her joint research, "We wanted to ask how the inhabitants feel about living in the community where they have lived for many years." Her study is based on thematic interviews with a random sample of eight elderly people from the community. As she puts it, the aim of this study "is to [clarify] . . . the basic meaning of living [in this community]."

This is how she describes her interviews: "The elderly people were asked about their daily schedules; their attitudes to relatives, services, neighborhood and environment; their interests and their opinions about society today compared with their earlier life-experiences."

Preliminary findings suggest two things. First, members of the community told the same kinds of life stories. Second, such people described themselves as more independent than she had thought. They described "coping" by attempting to keep control of four types of issues: financial, social, health-related, and security.

An analytic issue potentially arises in such studies where interviews are used to elicit respondents' perceptions. How far is it appropriate to think that people attach a single meaning to their experiences? In this case, may not there be multiple meanings of living in the community, represented by what people say to the researcher, to each other, to carers, and so on (Gubrium, 1997)?

This raises the important methodological issue about whether interview responses are to be treated as giving direct access to "experience" or as actively constructed **narratives** (Holstein & Gubrium, 1995). Both positions are entirely legitimate but the position taken will need to be justified and explained.

Students' Views of Evaluation and Feedback

Behavioral Sciences: Laura

Laura is examining students' responses to the assessment of their Distance Education essays. Her research question is, "Does it deliver the feedback that is needed and when it is needed?" Her data is derived from thematic interviews with 11 students chosen from four different localities. Her preliminary findings suggest that students want more detailed, critical feedback on their essays so that they can know what the gaps are in their knowledge and what they can do about them.

Laura describes the theoretical basis of her research as a **hermeneutic** method based on how researcher and subjects interpret the world and attempt to merge their horizons of meaning. This is ambitious and its value will need to be demonstrated in the data analysis. Indeed, it might be simpler to settle on presenting her research as a descriptive study based on a clear social problem. Either way, the issues about the status of interview data, also raised in Tippi's project, will need to be engaged.

Football and Masculinity

Sociology: Steven

Steven's approach is based on theories of masculinity within the general area of gender studies. More specifically, his work is concerned with football supporters and masculinity. He is particularly interested in understanding the experience of football supporters as opposed to the way in which their behavior is represented (for instance, in the media).

Care needs to be taken in how such appeals to "experience" are described. This is one way of slicing the cake and other approaches (e.g., studies of media representations of sport), using other forms of data, are not directly competitive.

The data he is using derives from interviews with football supporters. As Steven acknowledges, he still needs to sort out tricky methodological issues relating to his **sampling** procedure, his involvement with his interviewees, and how he analyzes his data. A possible resource is Cornwell's study of health, gender, and poverty, *Hard Earned Lives* (1981), an interview study that shares some of his ambitions.

It is always sensible, in this situation, to familiarize yourself more deeply with the methodological literature on analyzing interview data. Even if you choose to take a position opposed to such texts, you will need to be able to justify it. Without doing this, you are in danger of trying to reinvent the wheel.

Text Processing in Foreign-Language Classrooms

English: Pia

In Finland, foreign languages are primarily taught through textbooks. Yet textbook-based learning is often defined as monotonous or boring by students. Pia's topic is whether there are different ways of talking about foreign-language teaching and is there a conflict between them? Her broader concern is with what hinders change in classroom practices.

Her data consists of 12 interviews (half with teachers and half with students). She also has five "think aloud" sessions in which students were asked to do an exercise from a text and think aloud at the same time. This is an interesting idea because it attempts to relate what people say to a particular task they are doing—although it has to cope with the likelihood that people's practical skills are far more complicated than they could tell you in so many words (Garfinkel, 1967).

Pia describes her analytical approach as **discourse analysis** (DA). This implies that she is more interested in identifying different ways of *talking* about foreign-language reading than in addressing the actual experiences of learning a foreign language through a textbook. Given that the latter can be seen as a social problem, there may be a mismatch between DA, which assumes that issues of social definition are paramount, and a direct address of social problems. This might suggest either dropping DA or reconceptualizing the problem.

If we are interested in what happens in the classroom, there is a further issue about the appropriateness of interview data. Shouldn't we observe what people do there instead of asking them what they think about it? Is how we talk about schooling directly related to what happens in schooling?

The Family Grief and Recovery Process as Narratives

Psychiatry: Katarin

Katarin is analyzing interviews with couples after the loss of their baby. She is interested in how family members construct stories about their grief and recovery processes after such a loss. She has identified three discourses at work here:

- A religious discourse ("everything is clear . . . I think my faith is strengthened")

- A medical discourse ("our baby did not have a chance to live, this is better, the lungs were undeveloped")

- A protest discourse ("who can decide who is allowed to live and who isn't?")

Katarin calls her work narrative analysis. By treating her respondents' accounts as skillfully structured stories, she gets a lively, theoretically informed grip on her data.

Only two cautions are appropriate here. First, the mere identification of different discourses in respondents' talk can lead to a simple, reductive list. At some stage, it is analytically productive to move beyond such a list in order to attempt to map the skillful way in which such discourses are laminated on one another (see Silverman, 2001, pp. 198–202).

Second, the assembly of narratives in interviews (or conversations) is always a two-way process. Therefore, we must treat the interviewer's questions not as (possibly distorted) gateways to the authentic account but as part of the process through which a narrative is collectively assembled (see Holstein & Gubrium, 1995).

Narratives by Bereaved Relatives

Sociology: Moira

We first came across Moira's research in Chapter 3. Here we describe her early thoughts on her project in a presentation at a graduate workshop. Using interview data drawn from an earlier study, Moira, like Katarin, is concerned with how bereaved relatives organize their initial stories of their bereavement. Moira's approach is drawn from **ethnomethodology**'s concern with how people demonstrate the rationality and moral accountability of their talk. In their stories, people show that they hear (and preemptively manage) possible charges against them. By doing this, the analysis can fully show how people are not "judgmental dopes" but rather display a lively concern for the maintenance and repair of the moral order.

Her method derives from Sacks's **membership categorization analysis,** using Baruch's work on the "moral tales" of mothers of handicapped children as an example. As we saw in the previous chapter, basing your work on an earlier study deriving from a clear-cut theoretical approach can be a shortcut to a successful research dissertation (see also Chapter 6).

In her presentation, Moira showed how she had started to analyze five data extracts using this method. At a later point, in line with her theoretical approach, the analysis can be deepened by working more intensively with small pieces of data to delineate precisely how particular descriptions serve to support particular activities like "doing a complaint," "excusing oneself," and so on. In this way, like Katarin, she can avoid the temptation simply to *list* different categories.

Interviews: Summary

Common themes have emerged from our six interview studies, which we summarize below. For the sake of simplicity, we present this summary in the form of a list of questions that you need to think about if you are planning to do an interview study.

It should be apparent that here, as elsewhere, we are concerned with data *analysis* rather than the mechanics of data gathering. We strongly believe that to provide recipes for data gathering is to risk either gross oversimplification or utter triteness. Moreover, in qualitative research, what happens in the **field** as you attempt to gather your data is itself a source of data rather than just a technical problem in need of a solution (see Chapter 17).

What status do you attach to your data?

Many interview studies are used to elicit respondents' perceptions. How far is it appropriate to think that people attach a single meaning to their experiences? May there not be multiple meanings of a situation (e.g., living in a community home) or of an activity (e.g., being a male football fan) represented by what people say to the researcher, to each other, to carers, and so on (Gubrium, 1997)?

This raises the important methodological issue about whether interview responses are to be treated as giving direct access to "experience" or as actively constructed narratives involving activities which themselves demand analysis (Holstein & Gubrium, 1995; Silverman, 2001). Both positions are entirely legitimate, but the position you take will need to be justified and explained.

Is your analytic position appropriate to your practical concerns?

Some ambitious analytic positions (e.g., hermeneutics, DA) may actually cloud the issue if your aim is simply to respond to a given social problem (e.g., living and coping in a community of elderly people, students' views of evaluation and feedback). If so, it might be simpler to acknowledge that there are more complex ways of addressing your data but to settle on presenting your research as a *descriptive* study based on a clear social problem.

Does interview data really help in addressing your topic?

If you are interested in, say, what happens in school classrooms, should you be using interviews as your major source of data? Think about exactly why you have settled on an interview study. Certainly, it can be relatively quick to gather interview data but not as quick as, say, perusing texts and documents. How far are you being influenced by the prominence of interviews in the media (see Atkinson & Silverman, 1997)?

In the case of the classroom, couldn't you observe what people *do* there instead of asking them what they *think* about it? Or gather documents that routinely arise in schools (e.g., pupils' reports, mission statements, etc.)?

Of course, you may still want to do an interview study. But whatever your method, you will need to justify it and show you have thought through the practical and analytical issues involved in your choice.

Are you making too large claims about your research?

It always helps to make limited claims about your own research. Grandiose claims about originality, scope, or applicability to social problems are all hostages to fortune. Be careful in how you specify the claims of your approach. Show that you understand that it constitutes one way of slicing the cake and that other approaches, using other forms of data, may not be directly competitive.

Proper Analysis Goes Beyond a List

Identifying the main elements in your data according to some theoretical scheme should only be the first stage of your data analysis. By examining how these elements are linked together, you can bring out the active work of both interviewer and interviewee and, like them, say something lively and original.

We now turn to ethnographic studies that involve some element of observation. As we shall see, these kinds of studies also raise complex methodological and analytic issues.

ETHNOGRAPHIES

Ethnographies are based on observational work in particular settings. The initial thrust in favor of ethnography was anthropological. Anthropologists argue that, if one is really to understand a group of people, one must engage in an extended period of observation. Anthropological fieldwork routinely involves immersion in a **culture** over a period of years, based on learning the language and participating in social events with them.

By contrast, nonanthropologists are more likely to study particular milieux or **subcultures** in their own society. We will see examples of this latter approach in the studies discussed next where activities in classrooms, in hospitals, and on the Internet become objects of research observation.

The Analysis of Communicative Functions
of Peer Interaction During Small-Group Learning

Education: Caroline

Working in small groups has become a common feature of modern education. The exact nature of such learning presents a clear and apparently underresearched topic tied to a recognizable social problem. As Caroline remarks, "The ways in which knowledge is constructed in children's verbal interactions during small-group-work learning without direct teacher control has not yet been fully researched."

Caroline has gathered data from children ages 10 to 12 in small classroom groups working on mathematics, science, and language. Her focus is on "the sociocognitive and interpersonal dynamics of peer interaction" using categories "based on the communicative functions identified in the interactions."

This is a theoretically defined topic, which nonetheless might have a clear practical input. It uses a clearly defined method derived from certain forms of DA. However, Caroline's study also raises a more general issue about how a researcher goes about identifying features in the data.

Caroline's use of the passive voice in her reference to "the communicative functions *identified* in the interactions" draws attention to a neglected issue in social research: that is, how does the analyst go about "identifying features" in the data? One common answer is to claim to follow proper procedural rules. For instance, coders of data are usually trained in procedures with the aim of ensuring a uniform approach.

This is a tried and trusted method designed to improve the **reliability** of a research method. However, it is sensible to be conscious that **coding** is not the preserve of research scientists. In some sense, these students, like all of us, "code" what they hear and see in the world around them. Moreover, this coding has been shown to be mutual and interactive (Sacks, 1992; Silverman, 1998).

Of course, as we said earlier, the research "cake" can be legitimately sliced in many ways. So we are *not* suggesting that the vast mass of researchers who treat coding as purely an analyst's problem abandon their work. Instead, our minimalist suggestion is that they mention and respond to this well-established critique (for an example, see Clavarino, Najman, & Silverman, 1995).

Analyzing How Radiologists Work

Information Processing Science: Julia

Radiology, like many health professions, has recently experienced a sea change of technologies, with the conventional X-ray image being complemented by computer-based, digitized images. As Julia points out, any new technology creates new constraints as well as new possibilities. Her focus is on such technologically mediated interaction in workplace settings.

Using videotapes, observation, and interviews, Julia has gathered data about radiological image interpretation conferences. By examining actual workplace interaction, she hopes to contribute to the growing body of knowledge about human-computer interaction and to inform future technological design (see Heath, 2004; Suchman, 1987).

We hope you will agree with us that this is an exciting combination of a theoretically defined approach with clear practical relevance. However, Julia writes that she is concerned about what is *missing* from both her interviews and videos. As she puts it:

Thus far in my research it has become clear that there are aspects of work which I can't "reach" through interviews (people can't readily articulate aspects that are so familiar to them as to be unremarkable) or through observation and interactional analysis of video recordings (those aspects of work that are not evident in what people can actually be seen to do).

In a sophisticated way, Julia raises a problem that often troubles research students: the necessarily "partial" character of any data source. We believe this problem is potentially huge yet, in a practical sense, easily resolved. One simply avoids trying to find the "whole picture." Instead, one analyzes different kinds of data separately, aware that all the data is partial.

So make do with what you have and understand that there are multiple phenomena available in any research setting. If you must go beyond any particular data set, save that until you have completed smaller-scale analyses. Worrying about the whole picture at the outset is, in our view, a recipe for stalling your research (see Silverman & Gubrium, 1994).

Newsgroups on the Internet

Sociology: Danny

Danny's topic is the Internet. He is concerned with how people assemble themselves as a community via the Internet, without recourse to speech inflections or body language. Broader issues relate to how the Internet is regulated, how it developed, and what is exchanged on it. He proposes to focus on newsgroups on the Internet because their messages are publicly available and offer an interesting way to look at how a "community" is assembled and develops.

Danny's approach derives from his interest in the Internet as a possible new locus of power and, to this end, he plans to draw upon the German critical theorist Jurgen Habermas's conception of distorted communication. In this way, he will compare how people actually communicate with Habermas's **normative** theory.

Danny's study shows the implications of making theoretical choices. Using Habermas's concept of "distorted communication" will give a particular thrust to his study very different from other kinds of theory.

Even if you decide to eschew such grand theories, that itself is a theoretical choice! In this sense, there is no escape (nor should there be) from theory. At the same time, however, there is nothing wrong with a descriptive study providing that the researcher is conscious about the choice that is being made.

Ethnographies: Summary

Once more, we have been concerned with how you analyze your data. We deal next with three issues that have arisen in the foregoing material.

What is involved in coding data?

As we have seen, coders of data are usually trained in procedures with the aim of ensuring a uniform approach. Later in this book, we examine how computer-aided qualitative data analysis can help in such coding (see Chapter 13).

However, as we pointed out, it is sensible to be conscious that coding is not the preserve of research scientists. All of us "code" what we hear and see in the world around us.

One response is to make this everyday coding (or interpretive practice) the object of inquiry. Alternatively, we can proceed in a more conventional manner but mention and respond to this well-established critique.

Is my data "partial"?

Of course it is. But this is not a problem—unless you make the impossible claim to give "the whole picture." So celebrate the partiality of your data and delight in the particular phenomena that it allows you to inspect (hopefully in detail).

Is my theory appropriate?

Your theory must be appropriate to the research questions in which you are interested. Indeed, rather than being a constraint, a theory should generate a series of directions for your research.

TEXTS

To introduce a separate section on texts can look a little artificial. After all, aren't people on the Internet constructing texts? Again, if we treat an interview as a narrative, this can mean looking for the same textual features as researchers working with printed material. Indeed, the mere act of transcription of an interview turns it into a written text.

In this section, we use *text* as a heuristic device to identify data consisting of words and images that have become recorded without the intervention of a researcher (e.g., through an interview). In the next section, we examine five studies of texts.

Analyzing Classroom Religious Textbooks

Teacher Education: Pertti

Since 1985, Finnish schools have had a religious instruction syllabus mainly based on three textbooks deriving from the Finnish Lutheran Church. Pertti's approach treats such textbooks as a form of literary genre (see Silverman, 2001, pp. 198–200), which filters certain values into the school. He is examining such features as tables of contents in order to ask "how is otherness constructed in these texts through particular methods of classification?" His analysis derives from Michel Foucault's (1977, 1979) discussion of the construction of subjects and disciplines.

This study benefits from a manageable body of data—three textbooks are more than enough to carry out the analysis Pertti proposes. The analysis derives from a clearly defined theoretical approach, although it may be uneconomical to work with both Foucauldian ideas and writers on literary genre. In particular, from a Foucauldian position, one would want to study education in its own right, not in terms of ideas developed to study literature.

The Form of Japanese Modernity

Sociology: Yoji

Yoji is interested in how far Japanese modernity depends on concepts and practices deriving from the West (e.g., the assumption that history involves progress) and how far it is a feature of Western colonialization. His data will be drawn from representations of urban space in Tokyo. Although a major focus will be on the family, Yoji is also interested in other institutions, including prisons, the police, the hospital, the school, and the factory.

Yoji's approach derives from Foucault's (1977) account of the micropolitics of space. From this perspective, he is concerned with how space is racialized, colonized, and gendered. It also leads to a concern with how space constructs "modern" subjects (e.g., "us" and "them") and the "inside" and "outside" (for instance, the inner city, the ghetto, etc.).

Like Pertti, Yoji is working with a clear analytic approach. However, he might learn from Pertti's limited database by focusing on one archive or body of data. He is currently working with historical data from around the Meiji Restoration, and it may be fruitful just to focus on one such period and/or to limit the material to visual images or certain texts.

The Medicalization of the Middle-Aged Female Body in the Twentieth Century

Sociology: Greta

Greta is interested in the way in which middle-aged women have become a topic for medicine and the "psy" sciences. Like Pertti and Yoji, Greta bases her analysis on a Foucauldian discourse analytic approach, concerned with the construction of subjects within various forms of power/knowledge. Using this approach, she is able to chart how the medical gaze has moved from a biomedical model to medico-psy models and, most recently, a medico-psychosocial model.

Her data derives from the *British Medical Journal*, medical textbooks, and a history of menopause clinics in the 1970s. Simple key word analysis has proved fruitful in the early stages of her research, illustrating for instance how the clinical type of "the chronic pelvic woman" emerged into discourse.

As Greta's research develops, like Katarin and Moira's interview studies (discussed previously), she will want to map how different discourses are laminated on each other. She will also have to decide whether to look for yet more sources of data (e.g., articles and letters on advice pages in women's magazines) or to narrow down the amount of data she has already collected.

The Representation of "Crime" in Local Newspapers

Sociology: Kay

Analysis of newspapers in the UK has usually focused on the mass circulation press and has used theoretical models deriving from either Marxism or literary studies. Kay's work is distinctive in that it uses data drawn from small, local newspapers and draws on the small corpus of newspaper studies using Sacks's membership categorization analysis (see Silverman, 1998, chaps. 5 and 7). The research incorporates a nice comparative perspective, as the two newspapers Kay is studying derive from different geographical locations: suburban London and a Northern Ireland city. The value of this comparison can be explored by examining the local categories that the newspapers use in their descriptions of crime (e.g., national and local boundaries).

Like Pertti, Kay has a manageable body of data. By limiting her data simply to two newspapers' headlines on crime stories, she is in a good position to say "a lot about a little." Like Greta, her clear analytic approach will pay off when used as more than a simple listing device in order to reveal the precise sets of relationships locally constructed in her data.

"Enterprise Discourse" in Higher Education

Sociology: Neil

Neil's research is concerned with strategic development documents from a higher education college arising from recent changes in the tertiary sector. He is focusing on what he calls "enterprise discourse" and how it constitutes the professional's conception of identity.

Like Kay, Neil's original approach derives from **ethnomethodology** and was based on Sacks's membership categorization analysis. However, Neil acknowledges the attraction of the Foucauldian approach and aims to recast his concerns in terms of Foucault's conception of the "architecture of the text."

Neil's problem is that Foucault provides no clear methodology (but see Kendall & Wickham, 1998). He is attempting to find a usable method from the "critical linguistics" of Norman Fairclough and from **semiotics**' concern with **syntagmatic** and **paradigmatic** relations (see Silverman, 2001, pp. 198–200). Using these approaches, the aim is to analyze whole texts rather than a few extracts. The value of these approaches will be clearer when Neil presents an extensive piece of data analysis.

However, we feel there is less to worry about in relation to Neil's concerns that working on a single case might mean that he has too little data. As Mitchell (1983) shows, the **validity** of qualitative analysis depends more on the quality of the analysis than on the size of the sample. Moreover, the comparative method can be used on a single case by isolating and comparing different elements.

Texts: Summary

Limit Your Data

Like many other qualitative approaches, textual analysis depends on very detailed data analysis. To make such analysis effective, it is imperative to have a limited body of data with which to work. So, although it may be useful initially to explore different kinds of data (e.g., newspaper reports, scientific textbooks, magazine advice pages), this should usually only be done to establish the data set with which you can most effectively work. Having chosen your data set, you should limit your material further by only taking a few texts or parts of texts (e.g., headlines).

Have a Clear Analytic Approach

All the textual studies discussed in the foregoing have recognized the value of working with a clearly defined approach. Even Neil, who was unsure which approach to use, was convinced that such a choice is crucial. Having chosen your approach (e.g., Foucauldian DA, Saussurian semiotics, Sacks's analysis of membership categorizations), treat it as a toolbox providing a set of concepts and methods to select your data and to illuminate your analysis.

Recognize That Proper Analysis Goes Beyond a List

We make no apology for repeating a point that we made previously in our discussion of interview studies. It seems to us that the distinctive contribution qualitative research can make is by utilizing its theoretical resources in the deep analysis of small bodies of publicly shareable data. This means that, unlike much quantitative research, we are not satisfied with a simple coding of data. Instead, we have to show how the (theoretically defined) elements identified are assembled or mutually laminated.

AUDIOTAPES

The three types of qualitative data discussed so far all end up in the form of some kind of text. For instance, in interviews, researchers usually work with written transcripts, and in ethnographies, one often records and analyzes written field notes.

In the same way, audiotapes of **naturally occurring** interaction are usually transcribed prior to (and as part of) the analysis. The two main social science traditions that inform the analysis of transcripts of tapes are **conversation analysis (CA)** and **discourse analysis (DA)**. For an introduction to CA, see ten Have (1998); for DA, see Potter and Wetherell (1987) and Potter (2004). Both of the following examples involve the use of CA (a further example is found in Simon's research, discussed in Chapter 2).

Team Meetings at a Hospice

Sociology: Anthony

While studying for his MA, Anthony started to do voluntary work at a hospice in a London suburb. Staff at the hospice were later happy to grant him access to tape-record some of their work. He chose team meetings for two reasons. First, focusing on such data meant that he did not need to trouble patients. Second, team meetings in which patients were discussed were scheduled events, so Anthony did not have to waste time waiting for relevant data to appear. Moreover, another researcher had already tape-recorded some team meetings at the hospice and was happy to lend him her good-quality tapes.

Anthony had used conversation analytic methods for his MA dissertation and applied the Jeffersonian CA transcription method to his new data (see the Appendix to this book). He then inspected his transcripts informed by CA's focus on the sequential organization of talk. After an initial series of discrete observations, he selected a number of sequences in which disagreements emerged and were resolved by team members. The management of agreements and disagreements has been extensively analyzed within CA through the concept of **preference organization** (Heritage, 1984, pp. 265–269). However, Anthony now realizes that his data allowed a new twist to be given to such analyses by looking at how third parties manage disagreements by others. This looks likely to be both analytically interesting and practically relevant to medical staff concerned with effective decision making.

Asymmetry in Interactions Between Native and Non-Native Speakers of English

English: Marla

Marla is working with taped, naturally occurring conversations in English between native speakers of English and Finnish (both informal conversations and professional/client encounters). As she notes, "Research in pragmatics and sociolinguistics has shown that various forms of communicative trouble may arise where the linguistic and sociocultural resources of the participants are not shared."

However, she is taking a different approach. Rather than treat asymmetries as a "trouble," her initial idea is to examine how the participants "use emerging asymmetries as a resource through which they can renegotiate the current context of discourse and their interpersonal relationship."

Like much good research, this is based on a nicely counterintuitive idea that derives from a clear theoretical perspective (CA suggests that participants can treat apparent troubles as local resources). As in Anthony's case, Marla's data, method, and analytical approach are elegantly intertwined.

Audiotapes: Summary

Choose a Single Concept or Problem

Choosing a clear analytic approach is a help but is not everything. The danger is that you seek to apply too many findings or concepts deriving from that approach. This can make your analysis both confused and thin or a naive listing of observations consonant with each of these concepts. By narrowing down to a single issue (e.g., preference organization or troubles as a local resource), you may begin to make novel observations.

Give a Problem a New Twist

As the data analysis proceeds, you should aim to give your chosen concept or issue a new twist. In the foregoing studies, we have seen this done by pursuing a counterintuitive idea and by noting an additional feature little addressed in the literature.

Make Data Collection as Easy as Possible

There are no "brownie points" given by most disciplines for having gathered your own data—perhaps with the exception of anthropology's expectation that most researchers will have spent their statutory year with their "tribe." Indeed, by choosing difficult situations to gather data (difficult either because nothing relevant may happen or even because background noise may mean you have a poor-quality tape), you may condemn yourself to having less time to engage in the much more important activity of data analysis.

Marla and Anthony found practical ways of efficiently gathering data. Both chose to study scheduled encounters, and Anthony was able to supplement his own data with tapes collected by somebody else. As we pointed out in the previous chapter, secondary analysis of other people's data is to be commended rather than condemned.

VIDEOTAPES

When people interact face to face, they do not use merely verbal cues. Researchers who work with videos have access to many of these cues. However, as we shall see, complicated data can often mean complicated analysis!

Talk, Text, and Visual Communication in Desktop Videoconferencing Environments

English: Erkki

Erkki is studying a 1-month teaching experiment in which a university course was given on the Internet in two places in Finland and Sweden. Ideas and papers were regularly exchanged and weekly presentations and feedback sessions were held through videoconferencing (Internet seminars). Recordings of the video-mediated sessions between the two centers were obtained and transcribed (see Heath, 2004).

Erkki is combining CA with ideas from Goffman (1974) about "participation frameworks" adopted in particular settings. This setting is, of course, pretty unusual in that participants' sharing of time and space is technologically mediated. In some sessions, the camera positions were fixed. In others, the camera zoomed in and out on the participants. This is allowing Erkki to get a hold on how different use of videoconferencing technology affects interaction.

Erkki's work combines a manageable body of data and a clear theoretical approach (participation frameworks) with a likely practical input for systems design. As she recognizes, however, it is very complex to work with video data because both transcription and analysis are more complex than is the case with audio data. Fortunately, there is a growing body of CA-inspired work on technologically mediated interaction, which Erkki can use as a model (see Heath, 2004).

The Early Interaction Between a
Mother and a Baby Aged Less Than 1

Finnish: Suzanne

This is a study of interaction between Suzanne and her baby, Sara, as well Sara's interaction with other family members while Suzanne was present based on 9.5 hours of videos of 22 episodes up till Sara's first birthday. Suzanne's initial interest was at what age a baby begins to imitate other people. Consequently, she is attempting to describe what (and how) she says to her baby at different ages and what linguistic elements begin to emerge in the baby's vocalizations.

Like Erkki, she is using transcription methods and analytic ideas from CA. Based on this approach, she is treating mother-baby talk as interactional (e.g., how does the mother interpret the baby's utterances and behavior in concrete situations and how does she act in response to them)?

At the time of her presentation, Suzanne submitted a set of written questions, which are set out below with David's answers:

- *Is one baby (my own) enough data?* For qualitative work, one case study is sufficient. Obviously, there are issues to be thought through where you are yourself a principal actor. However, from a CA point of view, the complexity of what all of us do is so great that we are unable to grasp it or indeed to change it significantly at the time.

- *Is one video camera enough, particularly as you don't always see mother and baby together?* This is not a major objection. Once you recognize that there can be no "perfect" recording of interaction, it is always a case of making do with what you have.

- *How far can you reconstruct all aspects of the interaction between a baby and her family from 10 hours of videotape?* Never attempt to reconstruct *everything* about an interaction! Not only is this an impossible task but it is likely to deflect you from establishing a clear focus on one manageable topic.

- *Does an analysis of interactional situations give any hints as to how the baby reciprocally interprets her mother's actions?* Who knows what baby (and mother) are thinking? CA instructs us to look at what each party does without speculating about what they are thinking.

- *Should imitations associated with gestures and expressions be analyzed separately from vocal imitations?* No! Use your rich video data to examine the interweaving of talk, gesture, and expression.

- *Should more approaches be used (e.g., hermeneutics)?* Don't even think about it! Once you have found an approach that suits you, stick with it. Using multiple approaches is uneconomical and likely to delay completion of your research.

- *How do we distinguish "imitation" from other activities such as "repetition"?* Look at how baby's utterances are treated by mother (e.g., praise). But be prepared to change topic. "Imitation" may give you an early hold on the topic but detailed description may lead in different directions.

The Construction of Ethnic Identity Among Spanish Immigrants in London

Sociology: Viviana

Viviana's work focuses on styles of cultural consumption in relation to intergenerational differences within families of first- and second-generation immigrants. She has moved from an interview-based study to one based largely on observation and videotaping of Spanish families watching television together.

Viviana's research involves two overlapping areas—media studies and nationality. It is important for her to think through whether her main focus is on media reception or on national identity, using the media as a case study. Again, although video data is potentially exciting material, it is notoriously difficult to analyze. Even though the analysis of interview data has all kinds of difficulties attached to it (see previous paragraphs), it may be more suited to her focus on ethnic identity. With a video, you have to infer identities. Through interviews, you can ask people to speak about their identity.

How the Female Experience Is Presented and Problematized on Television

Sociology: Nora

Nora's research is concerned with confessional television as represented by Oprah Winfrey and other chat shows. She has a particular interest in how "psychological health" is invoked in such programs.

She argues that most existing research focuses on audience participation in terms of issues relating to democracy and resistance. As she points out, the problem with such studies is that they simply posit general structures of power, class, and gender. Instead, Nora, following Foucault, wants to problematize subjectivity. In particular, she is interested in the productivity of power in relation to what it means to be a woman, the kind of ethical agent who might adopt this subject position, and the forms of knowledge that have helped to construct it.

By its focus on media products from a Foucauldian perspective, her research promises to break new ground. Her major difficulty is the lack of any detailed direction for empirical work on media products within Foucault's work. Given this absence, David suggested that she speedily review methodologies deriving from other traditions to see if there are any useful points to be derived. In particular, CA offers a detailed way of transcribing video material and is beginning to address issues of **validity** and **reliability** in relation to single case studies (see Peräkylä, 2004).

Videotapes: Summary

All the points made in the preceding paragraphs about audio data apply here, so we limit ourselves to a few additional observations arising from our four video studies.

Beware of Complexity

Although video data is very attractive, it is very complex to work with because both transcription and analysis are more difficult than is the case with audio data. So think very carefully about whether you need video data for your research. For instance, unlike CA, neither Foucault nor theories of identity provide a clear template for video analysis.

Keep It Simple

You are not making a feature film! One video camera is fine for most purposes. When you have your data, maintain a clear focus. Never attempt to reconstruct all aspects of the interaction from the videotape.

Stick With One Approach

By all means test out different ways of analyzing your data, but always settle on one clear analytic approach. Draw on other approaches only for particular technical skills (e.g., in transcribing video data).

MULTIPLE METHODS

Researchers are often tempted to use multiple methods. For instance, ethnographers often seek to combine observation with the interviewing of "key informants." In the next section, we consider four examples of ethnographic work involving methods additional to observation.

How Texts Are Reconstructed

Sociology: Anne

Anne's research is concerned with how a text changes as it moves from a book to television or radio. She is also concerned with the effects of mediation on performance.

Her approach derives from an extensive literature on theories of mediation dealing with literary products, film, sound/music, and art. This seems to form a good basis for her research, although perhaps more work needs to be done on distinguishing these theories from our everyday assumption that something is "lost" when books are turned into mass media products.

Anne intends to study media practices during the process of production as well as to interview translators, script writers, and actors to try to understand the principles that inform mediators. This looks like an interesting project working with accessible data, but her data analysis might be simplified by focusing on media practice and products and leaving out any reference to the intentions of those involved in the process and/or by just following through the transformation of one text.

Botswana Women in Public Life (From 1800)

Sociology: Mercy

This study is a development of Mercy's earlier research. It centers on questions of women, power, and politics in the context of Botswana society and culture. Her research derives from a feminist focus on the factors limiting women's political influence in Botswana. This means concentrating on forms of patriarchy as expressed in the *kgotla* system and in women's fragile citizenship rights. The research questions that flow from this concern women's changing experiences, the limits to women's participation in political life, and the role of outside influences.

To answer these questions, Mercy proposes to use three methods: interviews, **focus groups**, and the analysis of archive material perhaps using ideas from Foucault. However, she may be limited by the need to obtain government approval for her research.

This is an ambitious project, which may be made more manageable by considering using only one data set and not pursuing her reading of Foucault unless she decides to make the textual data her primary focus. However, as in all field research, it makes sense to treat her dealings with official authorities as data rather than as a technical difficulty prior to data gathering (see Chapter 17).

American "Concert Dance" in the Postwar Era

Sociology: Rita

Rita's background is in dance studies and, more recently, sociology. After the Second World War, Rita found that the U.S. government was building a new relationship with the dance community through sending out cultural "ambassadors." The period also coincided with the development of an American dance style eschewing expressionism in favor of formalism.

Rita wants to explain both the politics of U.S. support for dance and the emergence of a style that avoided seeking to express the self or inner emotions. She will focus on two groups of dance companies, as well as examining performances and texts by dance theorists.

Rita describes her approach as deriving from the work of Pierre Bourdieu, drawing on his account of the body as a site in which agents struggle for domination. Bourdieu's work should help her achieve her ambitious aim to bring together history and social theory.

It remains to be seen whether it will be possible to effectively combine data deriving from different methods. Not only does this increase the scope of the research, but also it raises complicated issues about how to "map" one set of data upon another (see our critique of **triangulation** in Chapter 14).

How Women Experience Depression

Sociology: Philippa

Philippa's research is concerned with how women, as user communities of psychiatry, experience depression, self, and identity. Her interest in this topic arose partly from family and work experience and partly because of her curiosity about the statistics that seem to show that women are twice as likely as men to be diagnosed as depressives.

Her approach derives from Foucauldian **genealogical** analysis and hence leads to a focus on how "depression" is discursively constituted. This approach differs from feminist concerns with patriarchy and misogyny and from an interactionist focus on labeling by psychiatrists. The research questions that arise for her from this approach are the following: How do women speak of themselves as subjects who are "depressed"? How do women position/speak about themselves compared to "normal" gendered subjects? And how far do we find traces of a "pharmacological culture" in how depression is constituted and treated?

Her data is drawn from women whom she meets through her work as a counselor. Unusually, given her approach, Philippa has opted, initially at least, for a questionnaire (partly this reflects her lack of confidence in interviewing women she also counsels). A pilot of this questionnaire showed a high rate of nonresponse. She is currently revising her questionnaire as well as planning to do some archive analysis.

Philippa is aware that there might be more fruitful research designs. In particular, the use of focus groups or of open-ended interviews based on a single question (such as, "tell me your story") might overcome the problem of using leading or incomprehensible questions. Nonetheless, her project is ambitious and she might consider working entirely with available archives in the usual Foucauldian manner.

Multiple Methods: Summary

Keep It Simple I

Like videotapes, multiple methods are tempting because they seem to give you a fuller picture. However, you need to be aware that multiple sources of data mean that you will have to learn many more data-analysis skills. You will need to avoid the temptation to move to another data set when you are having difficulties in analyzing one set of material.

Keep It Simple II

Often the desire to use multiple methods arises because you want to get at many different aspects of a phenomenon. However, this may mean that you have not yet sufficiently narrowed down your topic. Sometimes a better approach is to treat the analysis of different kinds of data as a dry run for your main study. As such, it is a useful test of the kind of data that you can most easily gather and analyze.

Keep It Simple III

"Mapping" one set of data upon another is a more or less complicated task depending on your analytic framework. In particular, if you treat social reality as constructed in different ways in different contexts, then you cannot appeal to a single phenomenon that all your data apparently represents.

Research design should involve careful thought rather than seeking the most immediately attractive option. However, none of the previous points exclude the possibility of using multiple means of gathering data. Ultimately, everything will depend on the quality of your data analysis rather than on the quality of your data.

CONCLUDING REMARKS

In this chapter, we have examined the early stage of student research projects. The following suggestions have been made:

- Define your research problem analytically.

- Limit your data.

- Demonstrate that your data analysis goes beyond a list.

- Limit the claims you make about your study.

- Think about the relevance of your research for other scholars and for "society."

These points are explained in the following paragraphs.

Define Your Problem

1. Research "problems" do not arise out of a clear blue sky! Sometimes their source is a scholarly debate; sometimes a pressing social problem. In any event, you will need to think through the analytic basis of your way of defining your research problem. Having chosen an approach, treat it as a toolbox providing a set of concepts and methods to select your data and to illuminate your analysis.

2. Your approach must be appropriate to the research questions in which you are interested. Indeed, rather than being a constraint, a theory should generate a series of directions for your research (see Chapter 6). It will influence

what status you attach to your data—for instance, as a true or false representation of reality—and how you code it.

Limit Your Data

1. Decide which data to use by asking yourself which data is most appropriate to your research problem—for instance, are you more interested in what people are thinking or feeling or in what they are doing?

2. To make your analysis effective, it is imperative to have a limited body of data with which to work. So, although it may be useful initially to explore different kinds of data, this should usually only be done to establish the data set with which you can most effectively work (see Chapter 8).

3. Make data collection as easy as possible. There are no brownie points given by most disciplines for having gathered your own data. Indeed, by choosing difficult situations to gather data (difficult either because nothing relevant may happen or even because background noise may mean you have a poor-quality tape), you may condemn yourself to have less time to engage in the much more important activity of data analysis.

4. Beware of complexity. For instance, as we have seen, although video data is very attractive, it is very complex to work with. So keep data gathering simple. Go for material that is easy to collect. Do not worry if it only gives you one angle on your problem. That is a gain as well as a loss!

Data Analysis Goes Beyond a List

1. Choosing a clear analytic approach is a help but is not everything. The danger is that you seek to apply too many findings or concepts deriving from that approach. This can make your analysis both confused and thin or a naive listing of observations consonant with each of these concepts. By narrowing down to a single issue, you may begin to make novel observations.

2. Identifying the main elements in your data according to some theoretical scheme should only be the first stage of your data analysis. Go on to examine how these elements are linked together (see Chapters 11 and 12).

3. As your data analysis proceeds, you should aim to give your chosen concept or issue a new twist, perhaps by pursuing a counterintuitive idea or by noting an additional feature little addressed in the literature.

Limit the Claims You Make About Your Research

It always helps to make limited claims about your own research. Grandiose claims about originality, scope, or applicability to social problems are all hostages to fortune. Be careful in how you specify the claims of your approach. Show that you understand that it constitutes one way of slicing the cake and that other approaches, using other forms of data, may not be directly competitive.

Issues of Relevance

1. When you have finished, reflect on the contribution your research makes to contemporary scholarly debates. How does it add to knowledge or change our sense of the role of particular methods or concepts? (See Chapter 24.)

2. Is your analytic position appropriate to any practical concerns you have? For instance, many contemporary social theories look at the world quite differently from respondents, policymakers, or practitioners. If you use such an approach, you will need to think carefully about what you can offer such groups—although it may well turn out that you can offer them more interesting findings than rather more conventional research (see Chapters 24 and 28).

KEY POINTS

In this chapter, we have examined the early stage of student research projects. The following suggestions have been made:

1. Define your research problem analytically.

2. Limit your data.

3. Demonstrate that your data analysis goes beyond a list.

4. Limit the claims you make about your study.

5. Think about the relevance of your research for other scholars and for "society."

FURTHER READING

An excellent practical guide to the business of writing a dissertation is Pat Cryer's *The Research Student's Guide to Success* (1996). Judith Bell's *Doing*

Your Research Project (1993) is a much more basic treatment, mainly aimed at undergraduate dissertations. If you plan to do qualitative interviews, a useful Web site is http://www.andrle.org.uk.

NOTE

1. These research ideas derive from presentations during graduate workshops David coordinated at Goldsmiths College and at Oulu University, Finland. In the Finnish material, he has been able to draw upon research abstracts written by the students prior to the workshop. He was dependent on his contemporary notes for the Goldsmiths material and apologizes for any inaccuracies present. In any event, it should be borne in mind that this is an account of the early stages of research studies, which, no doubt, have developed and changed. For this reason, students' names have been anonymized.

EXERCISE 4.1

The following exercise is meant to help you think through the issues raised in this chapter about the value and implications of different ways of gathering and analyzing qualitative data. Please go through the following steps, ideally with another student:

1. Define your research topic in no more than two sentences.

2. Explain which method you propose to use to gather data. Why that method?

3. Why would other methods not be possible or appropriate?

4. How big a data sample do you intend to collect? Could you manage with less data? Might you need more?

5. What theoretical approach do you favor? How will it help or hinder you in the analysis of your data?

6. What other approaches might be appropriate or inappropriate? Why?

7. Is there anything about your theory/method/data that could be simplified to make a more effective study?

CHAPTER 5

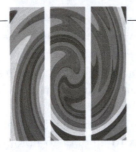

What Counts as Originality?

INTRODUCTION

All students speculate about the standards by which they will be assessed. Many students beginning a research study crave to be "original." Whether the research is for a PhD, MA, or a humble BA dissertation, originality is, for many, both a goal and a perceived critical standard that will be used by your examiners to beat you with!

Such fears are associated with a lack of knowledge about what is expected at a new, "higher" level of your education. In this respect, we are talking about a common experience when we reach the next step on any ladder.

Many social transitions are associated with rites of passage, and educational careers are no exception. In English secondary schools, after the age of 16, one enters the sixth form where one is expected to specialize narrowly and to become more self-reliant and less spoon-fed. At David's own school, boys just out of short trousers suddenly found themselves addressed by their sixth-form teacher as "gentlemen." They looked around the room but, weirdly, the appellation was directed at them.

The process is repeated in some form all over the world when you begin a BA at a university. Now, it seems, you are truly on your own, having to meet strange new criteria of achievement without any obvious means of support. Your time tends to be much more your own and you have to decide how much time to allocate to the library or computer center—or, at British universities, the Students' Union bar.

How much worse, then, when you register to do an MA or PhD. Suddenly, everything you could count on in the past now seems to amount to nothing. You are no longer the outstanding undergraduate but just one of many students, all of whom, presumably, achieved good first degrees. In the past, university examinations were mysteries that you had cracked. Now, although some further written examinations may await, you know that this is not how you are going to be mainly judged.

To some extent, this transition from BA to PhD is eased by the provision of taught courses for first-year research students, many of whom will have already taken an MA. However, a nagging doubt is still likely to torment many beginning PhD students. Are you up to it? Above all, do you have the capacity to be original? Or is originality, like so many things these days, something you can learn?

ORIGINALITY

> Original: not derived, copied, imitated or translated from anything else; novel; creative; independent in invention. (Chambers English Dictionary, 1990)

Consulting a dictionary about *originality* brings mixed blessings. You are not planning to plagiarize anybody else and so should have no problem in meeting the "negative" definition of *originality*: your dissertation is unlikely to be "derived, copied, imitated or translated from anything else."

But how about the "positive" components of *originality*? Can you be "novel; creative; independent in invention"? Moreover, since *imaginativeness* is linked to *originality* by Roget's *Thesaurus*, have you the talent to be imaginative?

However you answer these questions, you are going to be in trouble! Obviously, if you don't feel that your intellect is especially novel, creative, inventive, and imaginative, then you are going to worry yourself sick about whether you are up to doing a worthwhile piece of research. Conversely, if you are full of confidence about these matters, it is very likely that you are underestimating what is required to be granted these epithets.

If you doubt me, scan the book review pages in a journal in your field. Our guess is that you will not find such words thrown around freely. And, remember, many of the books reviewed will be authored by established scholars, well past their own PhDs.

If the work of established scholars is not regularly judged to be novel, creative, inventive, or imaginative, what chance do you have? The answer is surprising—you have no problem.

Such epithets are rarely used by the examiners of successful PhD dissertations. Most dissertations are no more than solid and competent. Indeed, it would cheapen the currency of academic description to use the vocabulary of *originality* too frequently. Even Nobel Prize laureates never fail to cast doubt on their own supposed genius. Instead, they regularly refer to the support of their research teams and to the old metaphor: "one percent inspiration, ninety-nine percent perspiration" (see Mulkay, 1984).

As Phillips and Pugh point out, in the context of a PhD, "an original contribution to knowledge" is a very shaded term: "it does not mean an enormous breakthrough which has the subject rocking on its foundations" (1994, p. 34). Following Kuhn (1970), PhD research is unlikely to involve a **paradigm** shift in your discipline. Instead, Phillips and Pugh suggest, it demonstrates that you have a good grasp of how research is normally done in your field (i.e., that you can do what Kuhn calls "normal science"). What does this mean in practice?

Among other things, it can mean

making a synthesis that hasn't been made before; using already known material but with a new interpretation, bringing new evidence to bear on an old issue (and) adding to knowledge in a way that hasn't been done before. (Phillips & Pugh, 1994, pp. 61–62)

So Phillips and Pugh suggest that a PhD is less to do with originality and is more about displaying that you are "a fully professional researcher" (p. 19). In turn, this means showing

- That you have something to say to which your peers will want to listen

- That you are "aware of what is being discovered, argued about, written and published by your academic community across the world" (Phillips & Pugh, 1994, p. 19).

The upshot of this is that a PhD is best viewed as an apprenticeship prior to the admission to a community of scholars. This implies that "you are not doing research in order to do research; you are doing research in order to demonstrate that you have learned how to do research to fully professional standards" (Phillips & Pugh, 1994, p. 20).

BEING A PROFESSIONAL

Originality is only one of four criteria upon which examiners of the University of London PhD must report. To get a London PhD, the examiners must report

- That the thesis is genuinely the work of the candidate

- That the thesis forms a distinct contribution to the knowledge of the subject, and affords evidence of originality by the discovery of new facts and/or the exercise of independent critical power

- That the thesis is satisfactory as regards literary presentation

- That the thesis is suitable for publication as submitted or in abridged or modified form

Despite the passing reference to originality in the second item, all these criteria are really about professionalism. We only need to concern ourselves about the second criterion: the discovery of new facts and the exercise of independent critical thought.

Considered on its own, "the discovery of new facts" is rarely an important or even challenging criterion in most of the social sciences. In the natural sciences, perhaps, a PhD researcher may discover a new substance or process and be applauded. But, in our experience, it is much more rare for qualitative social science PhDs to argue that they have found new "facts." Indeed, if they did so, they would most likely be greeted with the riposte, "So what?"

For example, say such a dissertation claims it has discovered that a particular group has beliefs or displays behaviors that were previously unknown. Any examiner worth his or her salt would then want to ask, "Why, on earth, should it matter that this is the case?" In other words, what analytical or practical significance are we being asked to attach to this "finding"?

Such a line of questioning is *not* a case of the examiner being difficult. As we argue in Chapter 7, any scientific finding is always to be assessed in relation to the theoretical perspective from which it derives and to which it may contribute.

This means that, although facts are never unimportant, they derive their relevance from the theoretical perspectives from which they stem and to which they contribute. The clear implication is that "the exercise of independent critical thought" is the major criterion through which your dissertation will be assessed.

How can you satisfy this criterion? If professionalism consists in the display of independent critical thought, what is the secret of being independent, critical, and professional?

INDEPENDENT CRITICAL THOUGHT

In fact, as is the usual case in research, there is no secret or magic process to be revealed. In Chapter 3, we saw how Moira, Sally, and Simon went about their research as solid craftspersons. Although occasionally they may have jumped out of their bath shouting "Eureka," most of the time they just plodded along, building a competent analysis in the face of setbacks and opportunities.

Using their experience and the work of other students David has supervised, in the following we outline four procedures that contribute to the successful display of "independent critical thought":

- Developing a concept or a methodology

- Thinking critically about your approach

- Building on an existing study

- Being prepared to change direction

Develop a Concept and/or a Methodology

In 1997, Acourt completed a theoretical dissertation on the emergence and apparent disappearance of discussion of "progress" in the social science literature. Armed with a well-supported argument about the analytical and practical relevance of such a concept, he was able to convince his examiners of his "independent critical thought."

Many social science dissertations have a more empirical content. Sally used Goffman's (1974) concept of **frames** to understand how a mental health team made decisions about what services to offer to homeless people. Moira and Simon employed the concepts and methodology that the sociologist Harvey Sacks used to study the descriptive process.

Moira applied **membership categorization device** analysis (MCDA) and **conversation analysis (CA)** to interviews with the partners of people who had recently died in the hospital. Simon used CA to study the sequential organization of talk at parent–teacher meetings.

Twenty years earlier, Baruch (1981) had used one of these approaches (MCDA) to analyze transcripts of interviews with parents of handicapped children. Like Moira and Simon, he showed the ability to work with and to advance Sacks's specialist approach. Indeed, Moira used Baruch's thesis as a baseline for her own research and showed how his analysis of interviews as "moral tales" could be developed.

In the normal way, Moira, Simon, and Baruch were influenced by the interests and skills of their supervisor. In David's case, he had a long-standing interest in making Sacks's work more widely known (see Silverman, 1998), and four of David's other successful PhD students have used the concepts and methodology of the subdiscipline Sacks founded.

Of course, social science has a broad and rich stream of concepts and methodologies, and David's students' work has expressed this breadth while reflecting his interests in processes of language and representation. So Kobena Mercer used some ideas from the French tradition of semiotics in his research on the speeches of an English politician, Enoch Powell (Mercer, 1990). The related concepts of Foucauldian discourse analysis were used by Mary Fraser in her study of representations of children in a British nursing journal (Fraser, 1995).

In all these cases, because the approach was theoretically informed, the dissertation could justifiably argue that it had contributed to conceptual development.

Think Critically About Your Approach

As we saw in Chapter 3, your prior experience usually has an important bearing on how you approach your data. For instance, Sally was constantly aware of how her own nursing experience might be influencing how her health professionals related to her and how she might be taking for granted certain aspects of their behavior.

Sometimes, doubts about an overall approach can have far-reaching consequences for how you think about your data. So Moira became dissatisfied with the conventional version of open-ended interviews as a potential window into people's experiences. Instead of using brief extracts from her interviews to illustrate particular categories, she started to analyze the devices through which her interviewees told recognizable "stories." Similarly, Simon was determined not to treat his parents' evenings as mere "products" of familiar social structural **variables** (e.g., class and ethnicity of the parents, measured ability of the child).

Fifteen years earlier, another of David's students, Gill Chapman, had devised an unusual way of demonstrating her independent critical thought. Having discussed a range of possible ways of analyzing her audiotapes of nurses' meetings, she decided to experiment with a wide range of concepts and methodologies. Each of the empirical chapters of her dissertation is thus both an analysis of her data and a critical evaluation of the approach used (Chapman, 1987).

Build on an Existing Study

Don't try to reinvent the wheel! Try to find a previous study that, in some respect, mirrors your own interests and topic. Then model your own research on that study and develop some aspect of it.

Of course, with limited resources, you are unlikely to be able to offer a complete test of the findings of that study. But by careful analysis of your limited data, you can reflect on its approach and conclusions in an informed way.

Sometimes a more realistic model is a previous PhD thesis. It is worth recalling that Moira used an earlier PhD thesis that David had supervised as a model for her research. So, at the outset, look at earlier dissertations in your university library and, where possible, focus on work directed by your supervisor.

Be Prepared to Change Direction

Sometimes students believe that what matters most is showing that their research has followed a logical sequence. Based on how research is sometimes reported, this structure seems to display the following sequence:

Research problem

Hypothesis

Data analysis

Conclusion

However, anyone who has ever done any research knows that such a rigid sequence is rarely followed. Moreover, it sometimes makes sense to divert from an expected path if you come across new data or a new concept or if your data suggests a different focus (see Chapter 12 for a discussion of how David changed paths in his research on a pediatric cardiology clinic).

So, as we argue in Chapter 25, although your examiners will look for evidence of a logical structure to your research, they will also want to see that you have been prepared to be flexible and to change direction when appropriate. After all, originality is not consonant with always following a predetermined plan.

CONCLUDING REMARKS

The message of this chapter is that a successful dissertation does not require genius. Once you define the task of the research student in terms of the display of professional competence, then you can abandon those sessions in front of the mirror wondering whether you really look like Einstein, Keynes, or Marie Curie!

In any event, you are likely to discover these things after a while through the response of your supervisor to your work. As Phillips and Pugh point out, worrying about the originality of your thought tends to be a concern only during the first few months. After that, this problem tends to disappear.

The case of a PhD examination many years ago makes this point very nicely. The thesis of the philosopher Ludwig Wittgenstein was being examined by two famous professors: Bertrand Russell and G.E. Moore. Although these two had no doubt about its merits, there is some evidence that both examiners found Wittgenstein's thesis somewhat beyond them. In their report, Russell and Moore make clear that getting a PhD is different from being a genius. As they put it, "This is a work of genius. It is also up to the standard required for a Cambridge PhD." (Monk, 1991)

KEY POINTS

Students at all levels desire to be original. However, BA and MA students can comfort themselves that even PhDs are rarely awarded for originality. In the context of a research degree, originality is largely about your ability to display independent critical thought. In turn, such thought can be shown by:

1. Developing a concept or a methodology

2. Thinking critically about your approach

3. Building on an existing study

4. Being prepared to change direction

FURTHER READING

Estelle Phillips and Derek Pugh's *How To Get a PhD* (1994, Chapters 3–6) gives a realistic, supportive account of what is required to achieve a PhD. Another helpful account of what counts as originality in student research is Pat Cryer's *The Research Student's Guide to Success* (1996, Chapters 15–17).

EXERCISE 5.1

Cryer has suggested that we can understand originality in research through an analogy with a travel expedition: "the research student is the explorer and the expedition is the research programme" (1996, p. 145). Cryer uses the expedition analogy to suggest different senses of "original research."

Review each of the following kinds of originality in terms of what you think your research might contribute and decide which kind is most likely to be applicable to your work:

- Originality in tools, techniques and procedures

- Originality in exploring the unknown

- Originality in exploring the unanticipated

- Originality in use of data

- Originality in outcomes

- Originality in by-products (Cryer, 1996, pp. 146–148)

You might return to this exercise at regular intervals to review any changes in how you view your research.

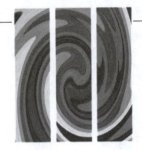

PART II

Starting Out

Part I of this book was aimed at the beginning research student. Part II assumes that you have overcome your initial doubts and now need to deal with the nitty-gritty issues that arise when you start to design a research study. Chapter 6 discusses how to select a topic. Chapters 7 and 8 deal with using theories and choosing a methodology. The tricky question of selecting which case(s) to study is discussed in Chapter 9. The final chapter in Part II considers how to write a research proposal.

CHAPTER 6

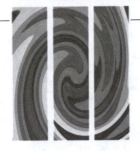

Selecting a Topic

CHAPTER OBJECTIVES

By the end of this chapter, you will be able to

1. Understand why you need a clear research topic

2. Recognize the main problems that stop you narrowing down your topic

3. Find solutions to these problems

INTRODUCTION

In this chapter, we discuss the problems you may encounter in defining your research topic. We then suggest some strategies you can use to overcome these problems.

People are often impressed when they find out that you are "doing research." They may even want to know more. If you have ever been in this situation, you will know how embarrassing it can be if you are unable to explain clearly exactly what you intend to study. Such embarrassment can be multiplied a thousandfold if your interrogator is, say, a smart professor you have never met before. How are you to respond? The answer to this question becomes easier if you recognize that there are practical as well as social reasons for having a clear research topic. Above all, such clarity can give your research focus, as shown in Table 6.1.

Table 6.1   The Role of Research Questions

---

1. They organize the project and give it direction and coherence.

2. They delimit the project, showing its boundaries.

3. They keep the researcher focused.

4. They provide a framework when you write up your research.

5. They point to the methods and data that will be needed.

SOURCE: Adapted from Punch (1998), p. 38.

Unfortunately, many undergraduate social science courses reward passive knowledge rather than the ability to use ideas for yourself, an essential requirement for developing original research questions. This way of learning often emphasizes formal assessment and test-taking skills. However, formulating a workable research project calls for the ability to apply knowledge beyond the boundaries of mechanical classroom learning.

As you take your qualitative methodology courses, do not be overly concerned with their critique of quantitative research, but learn how you can practice alternative methods. In this regard, we can learn from quantitative methods courses that are less preoccupied with critiquing their competition. Instead, through their rote recipe knowledge, they offer practical guidelines for drafting research proposals (e.g., formulating research **hypotheses** and defining variables).

Selecting a research topic for a qualitative research project can be a considerable challenge and to some degree a risk. This is because it involves committing oneself to a particular course of action and set of practices and not just the idle criticism of what quantitative researchers cannot understand and capture in their data. Selecting a topic sets you on the path of practice. Your proposed alternative will invariably mean that you will expose your weaknesses as a researcher and open yourself to criticism from others.

Faced with this risk, students often try to play it safe by opting for one of three apparently low-risk strategies:

- Simplistic inductivism

- The "'kitchen sink" gambit

- **Grand theory**

We briefly discuss each in the following sections before offering some more satisfactory solutions.

SIMPLISTIC INDUCTIVISM

In many social sciences, the qualitative tradition was initially characterized by its opposition to the strict research designs demanded in most quantitative work. So anthropologists would select their tribe, take up residence, learn the language, and do no more than keep a field diary. Similarly, sociological ethnographers would identify an activity, institution, or subculture and just "hang out." In both cases, the idea was to grasp reality in its daily accomplishment.

The hope was that somehow meaning would emerge by itself from such "in-depth" exposure to the field. It was believed that any prior definitions of topics or concepts would only stand in the way of a sensitive understanding of the slice of the cultural world to which one was being exposed.

In the 1960s, this belief was apparently supported by Glaser and Strauss's (1967) famous idea of theory grounded in data rather than presumed at the outset of a research study. Ironically, but understandably, the idea of qualitative research as unstructured exposure to the world was also supported by quantitative researchers. So we learn, in one quantitative text, that "field research is essentially a matter of immersing oneself in a naturally occurring . . . set of events in order to gain firsthand knowledge of the situation" (Singleton, Straits, Straits, & McAllister, 1988, p. 11).

In common with crude inductivists, Singleton et al. refer to "the situation" as if "reality" were a single, static object awaiting observation. Like such qualitative researchers, they emphasize "immersion," which they implicitly contrast with later, more focused, research. This is underlined in their subsequent identification of qualitative or field research with "exploration" and "description" (p. 296) and their approval of the use of field research "when one knows relatively little about the subject under investigation" (pp. 298–299).

This apparent unanimity at both ends of the research spectrum is noted by the authors of one qualitative methodology text: "The conventional image of field research is one that keeps prestructuring and tight designs to a minimum" (Miles & Huberman, 1984, p. 27). Miles and Huberman note two objections to this position and the cozy consensus that supports it: the omnipresence of theory and the need for a research design. We will briefly consider each in turn.

First, "any researcher, no matter how unstructured or inductive, comes to fieldwork with some orienting ideas, foci and tools" (Miles & Huberman, 1984, p. 27). As Gubrium and Holstein (1997) note, the apparently atheoretical position of some ethnographers itself derives from a theory: "The directive to 'minimize presuppositions' in order to witness subjects' worlds on their own terms is a key to *naturalistic* inquiry" (1997, p. 34, our emphasis).

So the idea of just hanging out with the aim of faithfully representing subjects' worlds is a convenient myth derived from a theory that Gubrium and Holstein term naturalism. Of course, without some conceptual orientation, one would not recognize the field one was studying. So the problem is that many closet naturalists seem oblivious to the theory-dependent nature of their research.

A second objection to simply going out into the field and inducing observations is that it can be an excuse for sloppy, unfocused research. Mason (1996, p. 6) rejects the suggestion that qualitative research can just "describe" or "explore" the social world. As Miles and Huberman point out, such unfocused research can be a recipe for disaster: "The looser the initial design, the less selective the collection of data; everything looks important at the outset to someone waiting for the key constructs or regularities to emerge from the site, and that wait can be a long one" (Miles & Huberman, 1984, p. 28).

Moreover, such a purely inductive approach can be blind to the need to build cumulative bodies of knowledge, which is an important goal of any scientific research endeavor. In the 1920s and 1930s, research students in Chicago, following Robert Park's injunction to get out of their armchairs into the virgin territory of urban street life (see Bulmer, 1984), could justify their inductivist aims. By the 1960s, however, even Glaser and Strauss (1967) were requiring that field researchers think about the formal theories that might be developed out of apparently isolated substantive, inductive studies.

In the new century, qualitative research is becoming more respected and established in large part because it has helped develop theories and related cumulative bodies of knowledge. As David has commented recently, "We no longer need to regard qualitative research as provisional or never based on initial hypotheses. This is because qualitative studies have already assembled a usable, cumulative body of knowledge" (Silverman, 1997, p. 1).

As qualitative researchers, we need not be dogmatically opposed to formal knowledge and learning from the past. Sometimes, the previous literature or (for experienced researchers) one's own work will suggest a hypothesis crying out to be tested or a finding ripe for retesting. When this happens, particularly where the earlier study derived from a theoretical approach to which you are sympathetic, an attempt to strike out afresh would be in danger of reinventing the wheel.

Of course, as the stories in Chapter 3 show, this does not mean that you should necessarily be stuck with your initial ideas. The beauty of qualitative research is that its rich data can offer the opportunity to change focus as the ongoing analysis suggests. But such changes of direction, like the initial research proposal, do not come out of the blue but reflect the subtle interplay between theory, concepts, and data.

THE KITCHEN SINK GAMBIT

Like any piece of advice, you can take too far the suggestion that you should avoid simplistic inductivism. In drafting your first research proposal, it is tempting to select a very broad topic. By including every aspect of a problem that you can think of, you hope to show the breadth of your knowledge and to impress potential supervisors. Unfortunately, this "kitchen sink" approach is a recipe for disaster. Unless you have the resources for a big team of researchers, depth rather than breadth is what characterizes a good research proposal. If you define your topic very widely, you will usually be unable to say anything at great depth about it. As David tells his students, your aim should be to say "a lot about a little (problem)." This means avoiding the temptation to say "a little about a lot." Indeed, the latter path can be something of a cop-out. Precisely because the topic is so wide ranging, one can switch from one aspect to another without being forced to refine and test each piece of analysis.

The following case study illustrates how one research student worked to refine and narrow down her problem. Over time, Seta Waller moved from quite a broad psychological interest in the "alcoholic" to a quite narrow but workable concern with the narrative structure of patients' accounts.

A CASE STUDY: SETA'S PROCESS OF NARROWING DOWN HER TOPIC

My interest in developing a research study in the field of alcoholism came about naturally as I had been working in this field for many years. My research experience and training, however, had been exclusively in quantitative sociomedical studies on alcoholism. Following training in social policy and administration, I joined the Alcohol Treatment Unit (ATU) of a Psychiatric hospital. At the ATU, I was involved in a set of quantitative studies designed to measure treatment outcome in alcoholic patients.

When I decided to develop a PhD study, my initial interest was to find out what patients thought of their drink problem—how they conceptualized it. This would have been a quantitative study but quite different from the usual measurement of outcome studies. I therefore began designing a quantitative study inquiring into alcoholic patients' concepts of alcoholism. The sample was to be drawn from groups of alcoholics admitted to a 4-week inpatient treatment program in the alcohol treatment unit where I was employed.

Having developed some rating scales on concepts of alcoholism, following interviews with patients, I carried out a pilot study on a small sample. Patients were asked to complete

(Continued)

(Continued)

5-point rating scales consisting of statements, by indicating whether they agreed or not with each statement, with responses ranging from "agree strongly" to "disagree strongly."

This whole process took about 8 months. However, I was feeling uncomfortable with the results of my pilot study as I tried to make sense of the data. I felt very uncertain about the attitudes and beliefs expressed in the scales; I began to question how one could consider that all patients who, for instance, stated "agree strongly" on the rating scales, meant the same thing.

I started thinking of a new study with a qualitative methodology, which I was introduced to on my MA course in sociology at Goldsmiths' College. In this course, I became aware of the relevance of the status of interview data, how naturally occurring data or unstructured interview data can be treated as analyzable texts which do not need to be considered as being true or false.

As my main interest in my work had been alcoholism for many years, I decided to look at alcoholic patients' accounts of their experiences by means of open-ended interviews rather than the traditional structured methods. I therefore asked the patients to tell me about their drinking, allowing them to talk with a nondirective approach. I tape-recorded some interviews in the beginning, and, when I looked at my transcripts, I knew this was what I ought to do. The qualitative data resulting from this kind of approach was so rich and rewarding that I decided to proceed in this way and carried out 40 interviews.

At first my approach to the analysis of the data was to look at "social meanings," concerned mainly with "why" certain causes of alcoholism were given as explanations, partly inspired by Mary Douglas's work (1975). I then tried a frame analysis following Goffman's methodology (Goffman, 1974). After having applied frame analysis to some patients' interview data, I still was not satisfied with the results as I had no means of knowing if the staff used similar frames. Patients' hospital notes did not reveal sufficient data to study this. I realized that my interest lay in how patients were formulating and presenting their drinking problem and then to attempt to look at "why" they were presenting in these particular ways.

Adopting a qualitative approach, I was able to look at the narrative structure of patients' accounts to see how the texts were accomplished and organized. The structure of the accounts seemed to have a common chronologically organized pattern. Examination of the narratives made me realize that patients were showing their skills in presenting themselves as morally adequate individuals, as Baruch (1981) had found in his sample of parents of children with congenital illness. I also found that patients were displaying considerable insights into their problems and were emerging as well-informed individuals.

My current approach is therefore not simply an analytical shift, but another way of looking at interview data to see how it can help our understanding of alcoholic patients' versions and presentations of their problems.

This case study illustrates how ideas derived from methodology and theory can help in specifying a research topic. However, some people are more comfortable working solely at a theoretical level and seek to substitute theoretical syntheses or critiques for data analysis. Following Mills (1959), we call this approach grand theory.

THE GRAND THEORIST

Whereas the kitchen-sinker moves about trying this and that, the grand theorist is kept busy building theoretical empires. Stuck firmly in their armchairs, such theorists need never trifle with mere facts. Instead, they may sometimes spin out cobwebs of verbiage, which, as C. Wright Mills (1959) shows, can be reduced to a few sentences.

Nonetheless, a situation in which you can obtain a research degree without ever leaving your familiar university library is not to be despised. Indeed, David should be the last to criticize grand theory as his own PhD was obtained by this very method!

However, it is usually wise to assume that every "solution" contains seeds of further problems. In the case of grand theory, these problems include the following:

• Can you ever get out of the library in order to write your thesis or dissertation? One book will surely have a list of further "crucial" references and so on, ad infinitum. Anybody who thinks a library PhD is a quick fix would be well advised to ponder whether he or she has the willpower to stop reading. He or she would also be wise to consult a short story called "The Library of Babel" by the Argentinean writer Borges. This tells a chastening tale of scholars who believe that, if they only keep on looking, all knowledge will finally be revealed by yet another book.

• Theoretical fashions change—nowhere more so than in the social sciences. If you commit yourself to a theoretical topic, you must always be looking over your shoulder at the prospect of some change in direction in the theoretical wind from, say, New York, to an obscure location with a school of thought of which you are totally unfamiliar.

If you do grand theory, you may spend so much time constructing elegant accounts of the world that you never touch base with the ground upon which the world rests. Kafka's (1961) wonderful short story "Investigations of a Dog" (the story of an old dog's life journey to find the source of his food) creates a marvelous image of "airdogs" or "soaring dogs" (*Lufthunde*) who float on cushions above the ground, surveying the world of other dogs from on high, yet cut off from any contact with it (so cut off that Kafka's hound investigator wonders how they manage to reproduce). In Kafka's words, "They have no relation to the general life of a community; they hover in the air, and that is all" (1961, p. 294). The practical lesson here is, beware of the temptation of theorizing. It can become a self-indulgent process so detached from the real world as to be worthy of the label "pointless jargon."

However, readers of this book will be more interested in solutions than in critiques. In response to this, we set out in the following paragraphs some practical strategies that may be of use to potential simplistic inductivists, kitchen-sinkers, and grand theorists.

STRATEGIES FOR SIMPLISTIC INDUCTIVISTS

If your previous education has equipped you with few research ideas of your own, comfort yourself that your predicament is not unusual and can be resolved. We outline three strategies that you can use if you find yourself in this boat. Each seeks to encourage you to use the knowledge you have already gained as a resource in generating a researchable problem. The three strategies are

- Using concepts as sensitizing resources

- Following up findings from other studies

- Introducing a third variable

Using Concepts

Treating the knowledge you have learned as a resource involves thinking about how it can sensitize you to various researchable issues. In an earlier book (Silverman, 2001, pp. 9–11), David distinguished three types of sensitivity: historical, political, and contextual.

Historical sensitivity means that, wherever possible, one should examine the relevant historical evidence when setting up a topic to research. Political sensitivity shows the vested interests behind current media "scares" and reveals that this way of determining our research topics is just as fallible as designing research in accordance with administrative or managerial interests.

Contextual sensitivity is the least self-explanatory and most contentious category in the present list. A longer explanation is, therefore, set out below:

By contextual sensitivity, David means two things:

1. The recognition that apparently uniform institutions like "the family," "a tribe," or "science" take on a variety of meanings in different contexts

2. The understanding that participants in social life actively produce a context for what they do and that social researchers should not simply import their own assumptions about what context is relevant in any situation (Silverman, 2001, pp. 10–11)

Such contextual sensitivity would suggest that matters like "recovery from depression," "quality care," and "urban healing" are not uniform phenomena but take on particular meanings in different local contexts and local cultures (Gubrium, 1988), depending, among other things, on who is the audience for the description.[1]

There is one final point. The three kinds of sensitivity we have been considering offer different, sometimes contradictory, ways of generating research topics. We are not suggesting that all should be used at the beginning of any research study. However, if we are not sensitive to any of these issues, then we run the danger of lapsing into a commonsensical way of defining our research topics. This is a topic to which we shall return, particularly in Chapter 7.

Following Up Other Findings

Phillips and Pugh (1994, pp. 49–52) suggest that one aid for the sluggish research imagination is to begin with previously proposed generalizations and then try to find their limits by postulating new conditions.

Because most undergraduate social science teaching places a great deal of emphasis on the classic literature, you can sometimes mobilize your knowledge of classical work in order to generate a research problem. In an earlier book (Silverman, 1985, pp. 10–11), David gives two sociological examples of postulating a new condition for a classical generalization:

Alvin Gouldner (1954) observed that Max Weber's "ideal type" of bureaucracy was largely based on studies of government bureaucracies. This meant that Weber stressed the role of democratically defined formal rules in obtaining consent. By studying rule following in the private sector, Gouldner was able to identify varying levels and bases of consent by staff to rules. Lipset, Trow, and Coleman (1962) noted that Robert Michels' "Iron Law of Oligarchy" had encouraged a focus on the factors that make organizations undemocratic. By studying a highly democratic organization, Lipset et al.

identified both antidemocratic and democratic pressures in how organizations operate. Thus they were able to question the inevitability of this iron law.

More recently, David became interested in the conditions under which clients were likely to demonstrate uptake of the advice that they were given in interviews with health professionals. In a study of interviews between British health visitors and first-time mothers, Heritage and Sefi (1992) had found that mothers were more likely to acknowledge the relevance of advice that was related to their expressed concerns.

In David's study of HIV-test counseling (Silverman, 1997), he began with Heritage and Sefi's findings as his initial research focus. However, he observed that time constraints in many counseling centers meant that it was very difficult for counselors to adopt such an apparently client-centered approach. David's research question then changed to considering how both parties acted to prevent open disagreements while giving or receiving potentially irrelevant advice (Silverman, 1997, pp. 154–181).

Similarly, Amir began his research on homelessness (Marvasti, 2003b) with the commonsense and widely accepted notion that homeless clients who are neediest receive the most help from their service providers. In this model, human service organizations are passive agents, objectively and methodically documenting client needs and responding to them. As it turned out in Amir's ethnography of a homeless shelter, "service-worthiness" and "neediness" were actively constructed in interactions between clients and the shelter staff. The presumed potential for recovering from homelessness as reflected in client attitude and demeanor was a better predictor of who received help than their immediate and apparent need for food and shelter. It was not uncommon for hungry clients to be turned away on the grounds that they were treatment resistant.

Introducing a Third Variable

As described by Rudestam and Newton (1992, pp. 12–16), introducing a third variable involves adding a focusing factor to your area of research interest. These authors give the example of a student interested in how young people view the elderly. You can make this topic less general, more researchable and interesting, by introducing a third variable. For instance, you can ask, does living with a grandparent influence this? Alternatively, you can focus on the effect on young people of media representations of the elderly. Further, using contextual sensitivity, as described previously, you can limit your focus even more by asking how, when, and where young people generate descriptions of elderly people.

If you find yourself routinely resorting to simplistic inductivism in your research, try Exercise 6.1 at the end of this chapter. It is a useful tool for helping you narrow your research interests.

STRATEGIES FOR KITCHEN-SINKERS

"Do less, more thoroughly." (Wolcott, 1990, p. 62)

Wolcott's advice is sound. Narrowing down is often the most crucial task when drafting a research proposal. Kitchen-sinkers have so many ideas buzzing around in their heads that getting down to a focused piece of research is entirely beyond them.

Every issue seems so fascinating. Each aspect seems interconnected and each piece of reading that you do only adds further ideas (and suggests further readings). So, although you can grasp the value of making a lot out of a little, it is easier said than done. The question remains: how do you go about narrowing your ideas down?

Following are three practical techniques that help answer this question:

- Draw a flow chart

- Find a puzzle

- Look through a zoom lens

The Flow Chart

Dealing with data means moving from passive reading to active analysis. If you do not narrow down your topic in the early stages of your research, data analysis is going to be very difficult: "Having a large number of research questions makes it harder to see emergent links across different parts of the data base and to achieve successful integration of findings" (Miles & Huberman, 1984, p. 36).

To help you narrow down, it can make sense to do an early flow chart setting out your key concepts and how they might relate. Following Miles and Huberman, "Conceptual frameworks are best done graphically, rather than in text. Having to get the entire framework on a single page is salutary" (1984, p. 33). The single-page flow chart is a useful technique in writing books as well as in doing research. For instance, as we write these words, we regularly move to a second document that houses the outline of this book. This outline was continually revised as we did our preliminary reading. It is still being revised as we write each chapter.

Several attempts will usually be needed to get your flow chart into a state that will be useful to you. Miles and Huberman recommend experimenting with different ways of specifying your research focus. But their basic advice is to "begin with a foggy research question and then try to defog it" (1984, p. 35).

A good dissertation chair could be tremendously helpful with this process of outlining your research. He or she can help you develop this flow chart into a polished table of contents for your dissertation. Do not be afraid to share your ideas with your chair in these preliminary stages. You can think of your outline as representing the different scenes in a movie; you decide what is relevant in telling the story and what is not.

Find a Puzzle

One way to break out of the vicious circle of unending facts and theories is to put your books to the side and ask yourself, What am I really trying to find out? More specifically, what puzzle am I trying to solve?

Think of research as one of many kinds of puzzle solving among a set of activities like doing jigsaws, completing crosswords, or solving crimes. Each activity will be associated with its own set of more or less unique activities (but see Alasuutari, 1995, on the parallel between the qualitative researcher and Sherlock Holmes). Jennifer Mason has argued that "all qualitative research should be formulated around an intellectual puzzle" (Mason, 1996, p. 6). She distinguishes three kinds of questions that may generate the type of intellectual puzzle qualitative researchers would recognize, namely:

How or why did X develop? (a developmental puzzle)

How does X work? (a mechanical puzzle)

What causes X or what influence does X have on Y? (a causal puzzle) (Mason, 1996, p. 14)

Let us consider how, following Mason, you might find a puzzle. Say you have a general interest in child abuse. You might narrow down your topic by choosing among the following questions:

- How or why was child abuse first recognized? (a developmental puzzle)

- How (and by whom) is child abuse identified? (a mechanical puzzle)

- What are the characteristics of child abusers and abused children? What effect does child abuse have on each group? (a causal puzzle)

Once you make a list of this kind, you should see that it is impossible to solve satisfactorily all these puzzles. So which puzzle do you choose? The following are some further questions that are worth asking:

- Which puzzle most interests me?

- Which puzzle might most interest my advisor or funding body?

- Which puzzle most relates to issues on which I already have some theoretical, substantive, or practical background?

- Which puzzle would generate questions that could be answered using my own resources and with readily available data?

The Zoom Lens

Wolcott (1990) gives the example of one PhD student who never finished his study of classroom behavior. The true kitchen-sinker, this student was always reading more or gathering yet more data.

Wolcott uses the analogy of a zoom lens to suggest a practical solution. Say you want to take some photographs of a holiday resort. You could find some suitably high place, say a nearby hill, and try to take a picture of the whole resort. Then, as Wolcott points out, "if you want to take in more of the picture, you must sacrifice closeness of detail" (1990, p. 63). Alternatively, you can zoom in on one small image. What you lose in breadth, you may well gain in telling detail—say a particular dish that you enjoyed or the interaction between two local people.

Now apply the zoom lens analogy to defining your own research task. Wolcott suggests "taking some manageable 'unit of one' as a focus" (1990, p. 69). So if, like his student, you are interested in classroom behavior, focus on one student, one day, one lesson, or one critical event. The beauty of this narrowing of focus is that it will produce a manageable and achievable research task. Moreover, you are not locked forever in this close-up picture. Just like the photographer you can "zoom in progressively closer and closer until your descriptive task is manageable, then zoom back out again to regain perspective" (Wolcott, 1990, p. 69).

Following Wolcott, later on you can always attempt to broaden your generalizations through more data at different levels of reality. But your initial zooming in will have you going out of the library and into dealing with data.

For example, in his doctoral dissertation on homelessness, Amir could have studied a number of topics such as "how the homeless tell their stories, what kind of stories they tell, how the organizational context affects the storytelling, how charity work is performed in an institutional setting, the effect of interorganizational communication on the storytelling, the survival strategies of the homeless, and friendship and family networks" (Marvasti, 2004, p. 122). As you can see, each topic could have provided more than enough material for a dissertation. Amir opted to save some of his ideas for later projects and mainly focus on how stories of homelessness are mediated by institutional priorities of human service organizations (i.e., how poverty is articulated and dealt with in a modern charity organization).

If you have a tendency to be a kitchen-sinker, you should now attempt Exercise 6.2 at the end of this chapter.

A Caution: Avoid Reductionism

One of the advantages of introducing a third variable is that it guards against the tendency to try to explain complex social processes in terms of a single cause. Such reductionism is regularly demanded in both legal cross-examinations ("answer yes or no!") and in media interviews (where the demand for simple answers sometimes makes research scientists seem like incoherent babblers).

So the diagnosis of kitchen-sinking and recommendations for specifying a research problem should not be confused with a mandate to reduce the complexities of the social world to a single variable. It is very disheartening when a detailed seminar on one's research is greeted by some bright spark with a version of "that's all very interesting, but surely what you've described is all to do with power and postmodernity, etc.," or its quantitative equivalent of "that's all very nice, but how do we know if the variation in your dependent variable is statistically significant?" What a nice, simple world it would be if everything could be reduced to one factor! For the moment, however, we should leave the pursuit of this kind of simplicity to bigots and to those theoretical physicists who valiantly are seeking a single theory of matter.

So narrowing down a research problem should not be confused with this kind of reductionism. We can only echo the arguments of the authors of a recent qualitative methodology textbook:

> Such reductive arguments are always distressing, given the variety and complex organization of social worlds. They reflect mentalities that cannot cope with the uncertainties and ambiguities of social research. (Coffey & Atkinson, 1996, p. 15)

STRATEGIES FOR GRAND THEORISTS

Reducing reality to ungrounded sets of categories is an obvious potential failing of grand theorizing. However, those who feel they have the flair and temperament for theorizing will not, we suspect, be easily dissuaded. Indeed, sometimes, as stated earlier, library-based work can be a quick way to write an acceptable paper. In this situation, we offer two suggestions. First, try to ignore fashions. Second, think about how some data may actually help you theorize better. We set out these suggestions in the following paragraphs.

Ignore Fashions

Having found the corner of the intellectual garden that suits you, stick with it. Do not worry about those smart alecks who have always read a crucial book by some new author—nine times out of ten, it will just distract you. Guided by your advisor, work out the set of readings that will be your central material and stay with them. When you have written most of your thesis or dissertation, you may then have the luxury of reading more widely and using that reading to reflect on the implications and limitations of your position—perhaps for your final chapter. Till then, don't be distracted.

Find Some Data

Even the most active minds can become a little stilted when confined to their armchairs. So think about examining empirical materials of some kind. Even though these may not be central to your dissertation, they may work as an aid to the sluggish imagination.

Take the case of two students in David's department who wrote theoretical PhDs. Nick was interested in what he calls "the refusal of work," which he linked to theoretical ideas about "the ontology of desire." Despite this highly complex theory, Nick still felt it worthwhile to gather material on the history of Autonomia—an Italian movement to refuse work—and the organization of unemployment benefits in the U.K.

Jake was interested in a critique of existing theories of the community. In this context, he attempted what he described as largely a philosophical exercise. Nonetheless, to aid his thinking, he observed and interviewed homeless people, beggars, and the mainstream community. Attempting what he called "a situated phenomenology of the moral encounter," his data was intended to be only illustrative.

STRATEGIES FOR ALL RESEARCHERS

Whether you tend to be this kind of a grand theorist or you are a kitchen-sinker or simplistic inductivist, there are certain general issues that apply to everybody who wants to select a research topic. These issues are

- Finding a workable (not just narrow) research topic

- Recognizing feedback loops between topic(s) and data analysis

- Understanding that your categories (or variables) are always theoretically saturated

We deal with each issue in the next paragraphs.

Find a Workable Research Topic

Narrowing down is necessary but not sufficient for a good research project. It is possible to have a narrowly defined, clear, and unambiguous research topic (using concepts which clearly connect to data indicators) that is simply not workable. For instance, there may be no way you could obtain appropriate data, or the topic may simply not be very interesting or important. Table 6.2 lists three features of workable research questions.

Recognize Feedback Loops

Good research rarely moves smoothly from A (research topic) to B (findings). As Seta's case (discussed previously) shows, alert researchers are always

Table 6.2   Workable Research Questions

1. *Answerability*: We can see what data are required to answer them and how the data will be obtained.

2. *Interconnectedness*: The questions are related to each other in some meaningful way, rather than being unconnected.

3. *Substantively relevant*: The questions are interesting and worthwhile, so justifying the investment of research effort.

SOURCE: Adapted from Punch (1998), p. 49.

prepared to change their focus as they learn new things from others and from their own data.

David Wield has called this to and fro between data and topic a "feedback loop" (2002, p. 42). This is how he addresses the issue of research focus in the context of such feedback:

> Each stage of the research work will result in challenging a project's focus and lead to some re-evaluation. At all times, you will find that you have to maintain a careful balancing act between the desirable and the practical. Too strong a focus early on may lead to you ignoring what actually are more important issues than the ones you have chosen. Too weak a focus results in following up each side issue as it emerges and not getting anywhere! So focus needs to remain an issue as the research progresses in order to avoid the pitfall of these extremes (Wield, 2002, p. 42).

Recognize the Theoretical Saturation of Categories

Seta's case, discussed previously, nicely illustrates that the categories we use to formulate our research problem are not neutral but, inevitably, theoretically saturated. In her case, the issue revolved around the status she should attach to her interviewees' accounts. To take two extreme formulations: were these the raw experiences of alcoholics or provoked narratives in which a drinking story was constructed?

These kinds of issues have already been discussed in Chapter 4 when we examined several interview studies. They are considered at greater length in Silverman (2001, pp. 83–118). The interdependence between research design and such analytical issues is examined in the next chapter of this book.

IRB Considerations in Selecting a Topic

As noted in Chapter 3, IRB stands for institutional review board or a university committee responsible for ensuring that research, especially when dealing with human subjects, follows the basic guidelines of (a) informed consent or voluntary participation, (b) anonymity and/or confidentiality when possible, and (c) minimal risk to subjects. IRBs originally focused on medical research, given its greater potential to endanger research participants. However, a growing number of academic institutions in the United States are also requiring social scientists to obtain IRB approvals before proceeding with their research. In fact, a new journal, titled *Journal of Empirical Research on Research*

Ethics, is entirely devoted to the study of ethical guidelines and violations in scientific research.

A number of factors have motivated universities to form and enforce IRB policies. First, there is the obvious ethical obligation of researchers not to abuse their status in dealing with human subjects. Second, there is the problem of legal liability. Universities are corporate entities that can be held legally responsible for ethical violations. In simpler terms, universities can be sued and ordered to pay monetary damages for the misconduct of their employees (i.e., professors) or those under their supervision (i.e., students) when they are acting as agents of the university. IRB oversight committees limit the legal liability of your school by setting and enforcing ethical guidelines. If you fail to follow their recommendations, your school cannot be held liable for a course of action you chose to take against their advice. In essence, your institution can wash its hands of you and distance itself from any research they did not approve. Finally, federal guidelines require the establishment of IRB policies for all institutions that receive research funds from the U.S. government. Overall, it is reasonable to assume that IRBs are here to stay and will only grow in their supervisory role in the coming years.

What does this mean for a qualitative researcher who is contemplating a new research project? Beware that with some topics it is very difficult to obtain the necessary IRB approval. For example, Amir was interested in studying the institutionalized mentally ill. He specifically wanted to do fieldwork on how mental illness is constituted in an asylum with a particular emphasis on how those officially labeled as "mentally ill" communicate with each other. The question was inspired by his casual observations from his part-time work in a crisis stabilization unit (CSU) for the mentally ill who were apprehended by the police and temporarily detained for observation and further processing. Amir had noticed that some patients used the term *crazy* in very sane ways. For example, at the CSU, Amir met Carlo, who had been officially diagnosed as a schizophrenic. Carlo was allowed a few personal possessions, including a small radio that was coveted by other patients. Inevitably, one of the other patients took Carlo's radio from his room without permission. After noticing this offense, Carlo grabbed his radio back, clutched it to his chest, and yelled to the other patients, "Don't mess with me. I'm CRAZY!" This defensive and very practical use of mental illness came from someone who was officially designated as out of touch with reality and imprisoned because he posed a danger to himself and others. There were other cases where it seemed that the mentally ill in the CSU were quite capable of rationally communicating with one another. So Amir thought he could learn a great deal about both sanity and insanity from these interactions among the involuntarily committed mentally ill.

Alas, the topic was not workable. Among other things, gaining access to a mental institution for research purposes and with the approval of Amir's university

IRB turned out to be practically impossible. The issue of informed consent was particularly insurmountable in this case. In order to conduct his research, Amir had to obtain the approval of the director of the CSU. She could not give the approval without consulting her supervisors, who in turn had to contact their supervisor ad infinitum. A related problem was that the patients themselves had to give consent, and of course, because they were mentally incapable, the consent had to come from their parents or guardians. The CSU staff could not give Amir the parents' contact information without violating confidentiality policies regarding the disclosure of patients' personal records (e.g., their family background information). After realizing the absurdity of this situation, Amir abandoned the project. It is possible that a more ambitious and persistent researcher could have found a way around all these obstacles, but for a PhD student like Amir, burdened with coursework, financial obligations, and the pressure to complete his degree in a timely fashion, the problems seemed insurmountable.

Therefore, before settling on a topic, familiarize yourself with your university's IRB policies and procedures. Most have Web sites you can consult, and if you do not find the answers there, send them an e-mail or make a phone call. The composition of IRB committees varies greatly across universities. Some, for example, have separate IRB committees, one for medical research and another for social science or behavioral research. This dual committee oversight is advantageous to social scientists, who find it difficult to convey the purpose and methodology of their research in the concrete language of the so-called hard sciences. Regardless, be prepared to fill out lengthy standardized applications that contain questions that seem to have no relevance to your proposed project. Once you submit your IRB application, you should not be surprised if you are asked to make revisions and submit additional information. This is routine, especially for qualitative researchers whose work rarely fits into the predetermined IRB expectations of researcher–respondent encounters. Specifically, survey researchers, because of their formulaic approach (i.e., formulating a hypothesis, sampling, administering questionnaires, doing data analysis, and writing), typically cruise through the IRB process. By contrast, qualitative research is not always so predictable from the start and uncertainty is something that administrative bodies, such as an IRB committee, are not comfortable with. So the more specific you are about your research plan, the more quickly you obtain their approval (see Michelle Miller-Day's discussion of planned flexibility in Chapter 3).

Recognize the Chance Limitations and Opportunities

Scientific publications lead one to believe that every phase of the research was carefully planned from the start and proceeded as expected. However, as stated in Chapter 3, sometimes chance factors or unexpected opportunities play a significant role in how research is done. In fact, serendipity and chance are widely recognized in the world of natural science. Everyone knows Archimedes' bathtub story and his chance discovery of measuring volume through the amount of displaced water. Reportedly, Archimedes was so elated with his discovery that he jumped out of his tub and ran into the streets undressed, screaming "Eureka!" (i.e., "I have found it!"). The point is that many scientific breakthroughs happen by chance. As W. I. B. Beveridge put it, "Most discoveries that break new ground . . . are by their very nature unforeseeable" (cited in Deming, 1998, p. 19).

As a qualitative researcher, you should be especially open to chance learning. Indeed, qualitative methods incorporate chance into the research process. For example, snowball sampling (e.g., asking a contact to introduce you to another and letting the sample exponentially grow from there) is a method of data gathering based on chance meetings. Similarly, grounded theory, inductivism, and open-ended or unstructured questions are all founded on the belief that researchers cannot know from the start where their observations may lead.

Let us consider some actual research experiences that involve chance learning. In the following excerpt, Lara Foley speaks of how she came across her research site:

> I sort of picked my topic by convenience. I wanted to do an ethnography. I had been volunteering at an organization that would have been perfect for my general interests in gender, health, and sexuality. When I approached the local people in charge about doing research, they were excited, but the national organization required quite a bit of red tape to approve research proposals. While I loved graduate school, I was ready to finish and get a real paycheck. I didn't want to wait the time it would take to jump through that organization's hurdles. I waffled around for a bit and then one day I was driving on the outskirts of town and a large sculpture of hands caught my eye. Next to the sculpture was a small building that housed a midwifery school. I called them up, told them I wanted to do research, and they were thrilled. I started volunteering right away.

As seen in the next excerpt, chance also comes into play in the literature review phase of a dissertation. For example, when you are perusing books and other publications, you may learn a good deal of new material unexpectedly. As Darin Weinberg explains,

> I am convinced that, at least in my case, it would have been a pipe dream to think I might be able to get comprehensively acquainted with some

particular literature that was decisively relevant to my research. What I found was quite the opposite. The more I read the more I realized that there were any number of directions in which the dissertation might have been fruitfully pursued. The topics about which I read evolved in part due to the purely chance discovery of materials in the literature that bore unanticipated influences on the direction of my own thinking. This chance development of my thinking, rather than some set of artificially imposed a priori boundaries on what might conceivably be relevant to my research, dictated the shape the dissertation ultimately took.

Finally, chance factors also influence data collection. In John Talmage's case, his research subjects would disappear and reappear from his site (i.e., the street of a large city in the Southeast) as a function of police practices, or as he puts it, "the city's efforts to control the homeless population through police crackdowns."

Given the importance of chance learning, as indicated in these stories, you should choose your research topic with a good deal of flexibility. This is not an excuse for wandering through the universe waiting for that moment of enlightenment when everything becomes clear. That kind of Zen, epiphanic, or "eureka" experience is rare. Instead, what we have in mind is similar to what Michelle Miller-Day referred to earlier in this chapter as planned flexibility. Instead of choosing a topic first and then forcing the analysis to fit your selection, let your empirical observations inform what your research topic is. Of course, as you get further along with your work, with the help of your advisor, you will have to disengage from the world of chance and slowly commit yourself to patterns, recurrent themes, and analytical categories.

CONCLUDING REMARKS

Like most dispositions, whether you tend to be a simplistic inductivist, kitchen-sinker, or grand theorist is likely to arise from a combination of temperament and experience. As such, you are unlikely to be deflected by simply reading a chapter in a book. So it is likely that reading this chapter will not convert you, but we hope it at least helps you to become more skilled in your chosen path.

On the other hand, it may be overly reductionist to view these three tendencies as personal dispositions. Jay Gubrium (personal correspondence) has suggested to me that simplistic inductivism, kitchen-sinkism, and grand theory are occupational hazards of all social science inquiry. In this sense, they are tendencies present in all of us and we need to be constantly wary of them if our enterprise is going to be theoretically informed and empirically grounded.

CASE STUDY

The following narrative is based on Michelle Miller-Day's chance discovery of her dissertation topic. As you read this story, note how, although she was more or less directed by a set of interests, the direction those interests took and how she found related data for her dissertation presented themselves purely by chance.

While in graduate school, I was directing a play about mothers and daughters that was based on the actual stories of mothers and daughters who lived in my community. The post-performance discussions after this play were really very interesting and at times very heated! The mother–daughter relationship touches a nerve among many women.

At the same time I was directing this play and was taking my first qualitative methods course, I received a phone call from a friend saying that her cousin had made a very serious suicide attempt and had been hospitalized. While sitting and chatting in the hospital, family members of this young woman began to realize that not only had she attempted suicide, but so had two of her aunts, her mother, her grandmother, and her great-grandmother at one point or another in their lives. Over a 50-year period, six women across four generations had tried to take their own lives and all had been hospitalized after their attempts. Surprisingly, most family members were unaware that most of the attempts had ever happened. This family kept their secrets, they kept what was private *private*, and even immediate family members were unaware of other women's earlier suicide attempts. This young woman's attempt provided a catalyst for everyone to begin talking, sharing their experiences, and expressing concern and fear that somehow the women in the family were "cursed."

My friend knew that I was interested in exploring the mother–daughter relationship (mother–daughter communication in particular) and so she thought this family would be an interesting "case study" for me. The family was interested in getting an outsider's perspective on the family "curse" and I was interested in how the communication processes in this family might have contributed to the suicidal tradition in the family. So, my dissertation began to be conceptualized as a study of the intergenerational transmission of messages (mother–daughter communication) that were perceived as contributing to the suicidal behavior of women in this family. As a final project for my qualitative course, I conducted a "pilot study" for the dissertation idea. I traveled to the town where all the women in this family lived and spent three weeks with this family conducting semistructured and unstructured interviews, observing their interactions. I tried to collect the experiences of these women and make some sense of them. I wrote up this research and began to develop my dissertation proposal.

NOTE

1. See Chapter 15 for further discussion of studies of these topics in relation to evaluating the "quality" of qualitative research.

KEY POINTS

Selecting a research topic can be made easier if you resist three temptations:

Simplistic inductivism assumes that we need make no assumptions in studying the world. Instead, hypotheses will somehow just emerge if we just "hang out" with the aim of faithfully representing subjects' worlds. Simplistic inductivism is at best a convenient myth that ignores the theory-saturated nature of any observation and can be an excuse for sloppy, unfocused research.

It is best countered by

- Using concepts as sensitizing resources

- Using other people's generalizations

- Introducing a third variable

The kitchen-sink gambit seeks to include every aspect of a problem that you can think of in order to show the breadth of your knowledge and to impress potential supervisors. However, if you define your topic very widely, you will usually be unable to say anything at great depth about it. Depth rather than breadth is what characterizes a good research proposal.

It can be countered by

- Drawing a flow chart

- Finding a puzzle

- Looking through a zoom lens

Grand theorists build theoretical empires. Stuck firmly in their armchairs, such theorists need never trifle with mere facts. The consequence may not be enlightenment but merely cobwebs of verbiage.

This tendency can be countered by

- Ignoring the latest fashions

- Finding some data

FURTHER READING

To help you think some more in defining your research, we recommend three basic texts: Amanda Coffey and Paul Atkinson's *Making Sense of Qualitative*

Data (1996), Chapter 1; Jennifer Mason's *Qualitative Researching* (1996), Chapters 1–2; and David Silverman's *Interpreting Qualitative Data: Methods for Analysing Talk, Text and Interaction* (2001), Chapter 1. Useful but more specialized texts are Pertti Alasuutari's *Researching Culture* (1995), Chapter 13; Martyn Hammersley and Paul Atkinson's *Ethnography: Principles in Practice* (1983), Chapter 2; and Anselm Strauss and Juliet Corbin's *Basics of Qualitative Research* (1990), Chapters 1–4.

EXERCISE 6.1: STRATEGIES FOR SIMPLISTIC INDUCTIVISTS

1. Attempt to relate your research ideas to ONE or ALL of the types of "sensitivity" discussed previously:

   - Historical

   - Political

   - Contextual

How might this lead you to reformulate your research interest?

2. Review any theoretical or research study with which you are familiar. Try to postulate new conditions that might allow you to develop a new but related research topic.

3. Try adding a few extra variables into your area of research interest. Now work out which of these variables would add the most depth to your project and/or be most simply researched (e.g., is the data available and can it be relatively easily gathered?).

EXERCISE 6.2: STRATEGIES FOR KITCHEN-SINKERS

1. Draw a flow chart of no more than one page setting out your key concepts and how they relate.

2. Review your area of research interest in terms of the following questions and formulate your research problem in terms of ONE kind of puzzle:

   - How or why did X develop? (a developmental puzzle)

   - How does X work? (a mechanical puzzle)

   - What causes X or what influence does X have on Y? (a causal puzzle) (Mason, 1996, p. 14)

3. Use the zoom lens technique to focus in on some manageable "unit of one" which might serve as an initial data set to resolve your puzzle.

EXERCISE 6.3: A TRICK FROM HOWARD BECKER

Howard Becker is the author of a very useful book for research students called *Tricks of the Trade* (1998). One trick he suggests is the following exercise:

1. Ask your supervisor (or a fellow student who knows your work reasonably well) to offer a snap characterization of what you are trying to find out.

2. Now respond to this characterization of your work (e.g., by denying it or modifying it).

This exercise, says Becker, should help you get a better understanding of what you are trying to do.

EXERCISE 6.4: WHAT DID GREAT MASTERS WRITE THEIR DISSERTATIONS ABOUT?

1. Use Internet resources or online library search engines to find out what your favorite theorists or sociologists wrote their dissertations about. Do you see any similarity or continuity between the dissertation topic and the later work for which these scholars are known?

2. Do the same research on your advisor and/or committee members. If they don't mind, ask them how or why their research stayed or did not stay on the same track as their dissertation.

3. Do you discern a pattern? That is, is it true that successful social scientists are typically those whose dissertation topic is closely related to their later work? If so, what is the implication of this observation for your own dissertation research?

CHAPTER 7

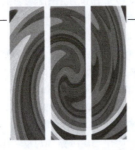

Using Theories

CHAPTER OBJECTIVES

By the end of this chapter, you will be able to

1. Know what a **theory** is

2. Distinguish between a theory, a **model**, and a **concept**

3. Think about ways of building theories from your data

INTRODUCTION

Some people become qualitative researchers for rather negative reasons. Perhaps they are not very good at statistics (or think they are not) and so are not tempted by quantitative research. Or perhaps they have not shone at library work and so are not tempted to write a purely theoretical dissertation.

However, the latter disposition begs the question of the relevance of **theory** to research. In part, this varies among social science disciplines. For, at least until recently, the different social sciences seemed to vary in the importance they attached to theory. To take just two examples, psychologists and anthropologists, for all their differences, both seemed to downplay theory.

For psychologists, the benchmark was the laboratory study. Their motto seemed to be, "demonstrate the facts through a controlled experiment and the theories will take care of themselves." Anthropologists were just as interested in "the facts," although their most important facts were revealed in observational case studies of groups or tribes usually found in faraway lands. Until recently, however, most English-speaking anthropologists followed psychologists in elevating facts above theories.

By contrast, generations of British sociology students have been made very aware of the primary importance attached to theory in their discipline. For instance, although undergraduate sociology courses tend to be split into three main areas (the "holy trinity" of social theory, **social structure**, and research methods), it is the course in social theory that is usually given the most prestige. Moreover, theory has recently become much more important in psychology and anthropology, as battles have commenced between traditionalists and qualitative **discourse analysts** (in psychology), and postmodern and gender theorists (in anthropology).

The social sciences' concern with theory is reflected in how PhD dissertations are assessed. As we saw in Chapter 5, the discovery of new facts is rarely an important or even challenging criterion in the assessment of most qualitative research. Any scientific finding is usually to be assessed in relation to the theoretical perspective from which it derives and to which it may contribute. This means that, although facts are never unimportant, they are always subsidiary to theories. Successful dissertations display "independent critical thought" (in the words of the University of London PhD regulations) by engaging with theory.

However, this begs an important question. What is theory? In the next section, we show why, for qualitative researchers, theory is altogether more interesting than the dry pages of theory textbooks. Later sections deal with the differences between theories, models, and **hypotheses** and the role of generalizations in building theories. The chapter concludes with some tips about how to theorize with your data.

WHAT IS THEORY?

O'Brien has used the example of a kaleidoscope to answer this question. As he explains,

> A kaleidoscope . . . [is a] child's toy consisting of a tube, a number of lenses and fragments of translucent, coloured glass or plastic. When you turn the tube and look down the lens of the kaleidoscope the shapes and colours, visible at the bottom, change. As the tube is turned, different lenses come into play and the combinations of colour and shape shift from

one pattern to another. In a similar way, we can see social theory as a sort of kaleidoscope—by shifting theoretical perspective the world under investigation also changes shape. (1993, pp. 10–11)

How theory works as a kaleidoscope can be vividly seen in a concrete example taken from Livingston (1987). He asks us to imagine that we have been told to carry out some social research on city streets. Where should we begin? Some alternatives are set out in Table 7.1.

Table 7.1   Viewing a Street: Data Possibilities

1. Official statistics (traffic flow, accidents)

2. Interviews (how people cope with rush hours)

3. Observation from a tower (viewing geometric shapes)

4. Observation/video at street level (how people queue/organize their movements)

SOURCE: Adapted from Livingston (1987), pp. 21–27.

As Livingston points out, each of these different ways of looking involves basic theoretical as well as methodological decisions. Very crudely, if we are attached to social theories that see the world in terms of correlations between social facts (think of demography or macroeconomics), we are most likely to consider gathering official statistics (option 1 in Table 7.1). By contrast, if we think that social meanings or perceptions are important (as in certain varieties of sociology and psychology), we may be tempted by the interview study (option 2). Or if we are anthropologists or those kinds of sociologists who want to observe and/or record what people actually do *in situ*, we might elect options 3 or 4. But note the very different views of people's behavior we get from looking from on high (3), where people look like ants forming geometrical shapes like wedges, versus from street level (4), where behavior seems much more complex.

The point is that none of this data is more real or more true than the others. For instance, people are not really more like ants or complex actors. It all depends on our research question. And research questions are inevitably theoretically informed. Even earth policy–oriented research designed to evaluate some social service will, as Livingston implies, embed itself in theoretical issues as soon as it selects a particular evaluation method (see our discussion on HIV counseling research in Chapter 8).

So we *do* need social theories to help us to address even quite basic issues in social research. Howard Becker quotes a famous American social psychologist of the past to make just this point:

One can see the empirical world only through some scheme or image of it. The entire act of scientific study is oriented and shaped by the underlying picture of the empirical world that is used. This picture sets the selection and formulation of problems, the determination of what are data, the kinds of relations sought between data, and the forms in which propositions are cast. (Blumer, 1969, pp. 24–25)

However, O'Brien's analogy of a kaleidoscope and Livingston's example of viewing a city street only take us so far. But what precisely is a theory? And how does it differ from a hypothesis?

Questions like this mean that we can no longer postpone the potentially tiresome business of defining our terms. Once we have completed these definitions, we will, once again, provide a set of concrete examples to clarify what we mean.

THEORIES, MODELS, AND HYPOTHESES

In this section, we shall be discussing models, concepts, theories, hypotheses, methods, and methodologies. In Table 7.2, we set out how each term will be used.

Table 7.2   Basic Research Terms

Term	Meaning	Relevance
Model	An overall framework for looking at reality (e.g., behavioralism, feminism)	Usefulness
Concept	An idea deriving from a given model (e.g., "stimulus-response," "oppression")	Usefulness
Theory	A set of concepts used to define and/or explain some phenomenon	Usefulness
Hypothesis	A testable proposition	Validity
Methodology	A general approach to studying research topics	Usefulness
Method	A specific research technique and methodology	Good fit with model, theory, hypothesis

SOURCE: Silverman (2001), p. 3.

As we see from Table 7.2, *models* provide an overall framework for how we look at reality. In short, they tell us what reality is like and the basic elements it contains (ontology) and what is the nature and status of knowledge (epistemology). In this sense, models roughly correspond to what are more grandly referred to as **paradigms**.

In social research, examples of such models are functionalism (which looks at the functions of social institutions), behavioralism (which defines all behavior in terms of stimulus and response), **interactionism** (which focuses on how we attach symbolic meanings to interpersonal relations), and **ethnomethodology** (which encourages us to look at people's everyday ways of producing orderly social interaction).

Within the narrower sphere of qualitative research, Gubrium and Holstein (1997) use the term *idiom* to encompass both the analytical preferences indicated by model and tastes for particular vocabularies, investigatory styles, and ways of writing. They distinguish (and criticize) four different **idioms**:

- *Naturalism*: a reluctance to impose meaning and a preference to "get out and observe the field"

- *Ethnomethodology*: shares naturalism's attention to detail but looks in detail at people's taken-for-granted ways of creating orderly social interaction

- *Emotionalism*: desires "intimate" contact with research subjects and favors the personal biography

- *Postmodernism*: seeks to deconstruct the concepts of the subject and the field

Concepts are clearly specified ideas deriving from a particular model. Examples of concepts are *social function* (deriving from functionalism), *stimulus/response* (behavioralism), *definition of the situation* (interactionism), and *the documentary method of interpretation* (ethnomethodology). Concepts offer ways of looking at the world that are essential in defining a research problem.

Theories arrange sets of concepts to define and explain some phenomenon. As Strauss and Corbin put it, "Theory consists of plausible relationships produced among concepts and sets of concepts" (1994, p. 264).

Without a theory, such phenomena as death, tribes, and families cannot be understood. In this sense, without a theory there is nothing to research. So theory provides a footing for considering the world, separate from, yet about, that world. In this way, theory provides both

1. a framework for critically understanding phenomena and

2. a basis for considering how what is unknown might be organized (Jay Gubrium, personal correspondence).

By provoking ideas about the presently unknown, theories provide the impetus for research. As living entities, they are also developed and modified by good research. However, as used here, models, concepts, and theories are self-confirming in the sense that they instruct us to look at phenomena in particular ways. This means that they can never be disproved but only found to be more or less useful.

This last feature distinguishes theories from hypotheses. Unlike theories, *hypotheses* are tested in research. Examples of hypotheses, discussed in Silverman (2001), are

- How we receive advice is linked to how advice is given

- Responses to an illegal drug depend upon what one learns from others

- Voting in union elections is related to nonwork links between union members

In many qualitative research studies, there is no specific hypothesis at the outset. Instead, hypotheses are produced (or induced) during the early stages of research. In any event, unlike theories, hypotheses can, and should, be tested. Therefore, we assess a hypothesis by its validity or truth.

A *methodology* refers to the choices we make about cases to study, methods of data gathering, forms of data analysis, and so on, in planning and executing a research study. So our methodology defines how one will go about studying any phenomenon. In social research, methodologies may be defined very broadly (e.g., qualitative or quantitative) or more narrowly (e.g., **grounded theory** or **conversation analysis**). Like theories, methodologies cannot be true or false, only more or less useful.

Finally, *methods* are specific research techniques. These include quantitative techniques, like statistical correlations, as well as techniques like observation, interviewing, and audio recording. Once again, in themselves, techniques are not true or false. They are more or less useful, depending on their fit with the theories and methodologies being used and the hypothesis being tested and/or the research topic that is selected. So, for instance, behavioralists may favor quantitative methods and interactionists often prefer to gather their data by observation. But, depending on the hypothesis being tested, behavioralists may sometimes use qualitative methods—for instance, in the exploratory stage of research. Equally, interactionists may sometimes use simple quantitative methods, particularly when they want to find an overall pattern in their data.

The relation among models, concepts, theories, hypotheses, methodology, and methods can be set out schematically as in Figure 7.1.

Reading Figure 7.1 downward, each concept reflects a lower level of generality and abstraction. The arrows from "findings" to "hypotheses" indicate a feedback mechanism through which hypotheses are modified in the light of findings.

SOME EXAMPLES

Let me now try to put flesh on the skeleton set out in Figure 7.1 through the use of some concrete examples. Imagine that we have a general interest in the gloomy topic of death in society. How are we to research this topic?

Before we can even define a research problem, let alone develop a hypothesis, we need to think through some very basic issues. Assume that we are the kind of social scientist that prefers to see the world in terms of how social structures determine behavior, following sociologist Emile Durkheim's (1951) injunction to treat social facts as real "things." Such a model of social life will suggest concepts that we can use in our research on death. Using such a model, we will tend to see death in terms of statistics relating to rates of death (or mortality). And we will want to explain such statistics in terms of other social facts such as age or social class.

Armed with our concepts, we might then construct a theory about one or another aspect of our topic. For instance, working with our assumption that death is a social fact, determined by other social facts, we might develop a theory that the rate of early death among children, or infant mortality, is related to some social

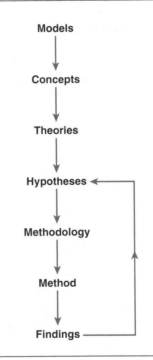

Figure 7.1   Levels of Analysis

fact about their parents, say their social class. From this theory, it is a quick step to the hypothesis that the higher the social class of its parents, the lower the likelihood of a child dying within the first year of its life. This hypothesis is sometimes expressed as saying that there is an inverse relationship between social class and infant mortality.

As already implied, a model concerned with social facts will tend to favor a quantitative methodology, using methods such as the analysis of official statistics or the use of large-scale **social surveys** based on apparently reliable fixed-choice questionnaires. In interpreting the findings of such research, one will

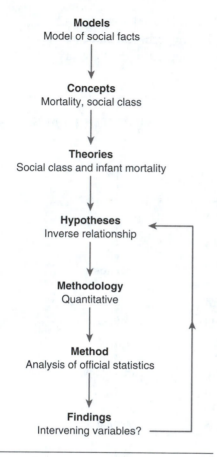

Models
Model of social facts

Concepts
Mortality, social class

Theories
Social class and infant mortality

Hypotheses
Inverse relationship

Methodology
Quantitative

Method
Analysis of official statistics

Findings
Intervening variables?

Figure 7.2   Death as a Social Fact

need to ensure that due account is taken of factors that may be concealed in simple correlations. For instance, social class may be associated with quality of housing and the latter factor (here called an **intervening variable**) may be the real cause of variations in the rates of infant mortality.

This overall approach to death is set out schematically in Figure 7.2.

Figure 7.3 sets out a very different way of conceiving death. For certain sociologists, social institutions are created and/or stabilized by the actions of participants. A central idea of this model is that how we label phenomena defines their character. This, in turn, is associated with the concept of *definitions of the situation*, which tells us to look for social phenomena in how meaning gets defined by people in different contexts. The overall message of this approach is that death should be put in inverted commas and hence leads to a theory in which death is treated as a social construct.

Of course, this is very different from the social fact model and, therefore, nicely illustrates the importance of theories in defining research problems. Its immediate drawback, however, may be that it appears to be counterintuitive. After all, you may feel, death is surely an obvious fact. Either we are dead or not dead and, if so, where does this leave **constructionism**?

Let us cite two cases that highlight the counterargument. First, in 1963, after President Kennedy was shot, he was taken to a Dallas hospital with, according to contemporary accounts, half of his head shot away. Our hunch is that if one of us were to arrive in a casualty department in this state, we would be given a cursory examination and then recorded as "dead on arrival" (DOA). Precisely because they were dealing with a president, the staff had to do more than this. So they worked on Kennedy for almost an hour, demonstrating thereby that they had done their best for such an important patient (cf. Sudnow, 1968a).

Now think of contemporary debates about whether or when severely injured people should have life-support systems turned off. Once again, acts of definition constitute whether somebody is alive or dead. And note that such definitions have real effects.

Of course, such a way of looking at how death is socially constructed (sometimes called social constructionism) is just one way of theorizing this phenomenon, not intrinsically better or worse than the social fact approach. But, once we adopt one or another model, it starts to have a big influence on how our research proceeds. For instance, as we have seen, if "DOA" can be a label applied in different ways to different people, we might develop a hypothesis about how the label "dead on arrival" is applied to different hospital patients.

Because of our model, we would then probably try to collect research data that arose in such **naturally occurring** (or non-research-generated) contexts as actual hospitals, using methods like observation and/or audio or video recording. Note, however, that this would not rule out the collection of quantitative data (say from hospital records). Rather, it would mean that our main body of data would probably be qualitative. Following earlier research (e.g., Dingwall & Murray, 1983; Jeffery, 1979), our findings might show how age and presumed moral status are relevant to such medical decision making as well as social class. In turn, as shown in Figure 7.3, these findings would help us refine our initial hypothesis.

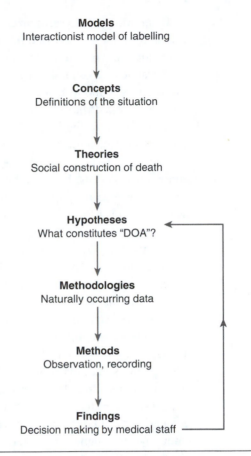

Figure 7.3   Death as a Social Construction

GENERALIZATIONS AND THEORY BUILDING

Theorizing about data does not stop with the refinement of hypotheses. In this section, we will show how we can develop generalizations out of successfully tested hypotheses and, thereby, contribute to *building* theories. Further discussion of theory building, in the context of grounded theory (Strauss & Corbin, 1990), is found in Chapters 12 and 13.

First, we need to recognize that case studies, limited to a particular set of interactions, still allow one to examine how particular sayings and doings are embedded in particular patterns of social organization.

A classic case of an anthropologist using a case study to make broader generalizations is found in Douglas's (1975) work on a Central African tribe, the Lele. Douglas noticed that an anteater, what Western zoologists call a pangolin, was very important to the Lele's ritual life. For the Lele, the pangolin was both a cult animal and an anomaly. It was perceived to have both animal and human characteristics—for instance, it tended only to have one offspring at a time, unlike most other animals. It also did not readily fit into the Lele's classification of land and water creatures, spending some of its time on land and some time in the water. Curiously, among animals that were hunted, the pangolin seemed to the Lele to be unique in not trying to escape but almost offering itself up to its hunter.

Fortunately, Douglas resisted what might be called a tourist response, moving beyond curiosity to systematic analysis. She noted that many groups who perceive anomalous entities in their environment reject them out of hand. To take an anomalous entity seriously might cast doubt on the "natural" status of your group's system of classification.

The classic example of the rejection of anomaly is found in the Old Testament. Douglas points out that the reason why the pig is unclean, according to the Old Testament, is that it is anomalous. It has a cloven hoof, which, following the Old Testament, makes it clean, but it does not chew the cud—which makes it dirty. So it turns out that the pig is particularly unclean precisely because it is anomalous. Similarly, the Old Testament teachings on intermarriage work in relation to anomaly. Although you are not expected to marry somebody of another tribe, to marry the offspring of a marriage between a member of your tribe and an outsider is even more frowned upon. In both examples, anomaly is shunned.

However, the Lele are an exception: they celebrate the anomalous pangolin. What this suggests to Douglas is that there may be no *universal* propensity to frown upon anomaly. If there is variability from community to community, then this must say something about their social organization.

Sure enough, there is something special about the Lele's social life. Their experience of relations with other tribes has been very successful. They exchange goods with them and have little experience of war.

What is involved in relating well with other tribes? It means successfully crossing a frontier or boundary. But what do anomalous entities do? They cut across boundaries. Here is the answer to the puzzle about why the Lele are different.

Douglas is suggesting that the Lele's response to anomaly derives from experiences grounded in their social organization. They perceive the pangolin favorably because it crosses boundaries just as they themselves do. Conversely, the Ancient Israelites regarded anomalies unfavorably because their own experience of crossing boundaries was profoundly unfavorable. Indeed, the Old Testament reads as a series of disastrous exchanges between the Israelites and other tribes.

By means of this historical comparison, Douglas has moved from a single-case explanation to a far more general theory of the relation between social exchange and response to anomaly. Glaser and Strauss (1968) have described this movement toward greater generality as a move from **substantive** to **formal theory**. In their own research on hospital wards caring for terminally ill patients, they show how, by using the comparative method, we can develop accounts of people's own awareness of their impending death (i.e., a substantive theory) to accounts of a whole range of *awareness contexts* (formal theory).

Douglas's account of the relation between responses to anomaly and experiences of boundary crossing can also be applied elsewhere. Perhaps bad experiences of exchanges with other groups explains why some Israeli Jews and Palestinian Muslims are so concerned to mark their own identity on the "holy places" in Jerusalem and reject (as a hateful anomaly) multiple use of the same holy sites?

In any event, Douglas's study of the Lele exemplifies the need to locate how individual elements are embedded in forms of social organization. In her case, this is done in an explicitly Durkheimian manner which sees behavior as the expression of a "society" which works as a "hidden hand" constraining and forming human action. Alternatively, Moerman (1974) indicates how, by using a constructionist framework, one can look at the fine detail of people's activities without treating social organization as a purely external force. In the latter case, people cease to be "cultural dopes" (Garfinkel, 1967) and skillfully reproduce the moral order.

HOW TO THEORIZE ABOUT DATA

Unlike Moerman or Douglas, most readers will not bring to their research any very well-defined set of theoretical ideas. If you are in this position, your problem will be how you can use data to think in theoretical terms. The following list is intended merely as a set of suggestions. Although it cannot be exhaustive, it should serve as an initial guide to theorizing about data. It can also be read in conjunction with our discussion of the three kinds of research sensitivity in Chapter 6.

In carrying out your research, it is suggested that you think about the following six issues:

1. *What* and *how* questions: Avoid the temptation to rush to explanations of your data. Don't begin with *why* questions. Instead, ask yourself *what* verbal and behavioral and contextual resources are being used

here and look for the detail of *how* they are being used (and with what consequences).

2. *Chronology*: Look at the timing of people's behavior or their use of time in their accounts. Alternatively, gather data over time in order to look at processes of change. If appropriate, try searching out historical evidence that may at least suggest how your research problem came into being.

3. *Context*: How is your data contextualized in particular organizational settings, social processes, or sets of experiences? For instance, as Moerman shows, answering an interviewer's question may be different from engaging in the activity that is the topic of the interview. Therefore, think about how there may be many versions of your phenomenon.

4. *Comparison*: Like Douglas, who generated her theory by comparing how different groups treated anomalies, always try to compare your data with other relevant data. Even if you cannot find a comparative case, try to find ways of dividing your data into different sets and compare each one. Remember that the comparative method is the basic scientific method.

5. *Implications*: When you are reporting your research, think about how what you have discovered may relate to broader issues than your original research topic. In this way, a very narrow topic (e.g., how the Lele perceive the pangolin) may be related to much broader social processes (e.g., how societies respond to anomalous entities).

6. *Lateral thinking*: Be like the Lele. Don't erect strong boundaries between concepts but explore the relations between apparently diverse models, theories, and methodologies. Celebrate anomaly!

CONCLUDING REMARKS

The philosopher of science Thomas Kuhn (1970) has described some social sciences as lacking a single, agreed set of concepts. In Kuhn's terms, this makes social research "pre-paradigmatic" or at least in a state of competing paradigms. As we have already implied, the problem is that this has generated a whole series of social science courses, which pose different social science approaches in terms of either/or questions.

Such courses are much appreciated by some students. They learn about the paradigmatic oppositions in question, choose A rather than B and report back, parrot fashion, all the advantages of A and the drawbacks of B. It is hardly surprising that such courses produce very little evidence that such students have ever thought about anything—even their choice of A is likely to be based on their teacher's implicit or explicit preferences. This may, in part, explain why so many undergraduate social science courses actually provide a learned incapacity to go out and do research.

Learning about rival "armed camps" in no way allows you to confront research data. In the field, material is much more messy than the different camps would suggest. Perhaps there is something to be learned from both sides, or, more constructively, perhaps we start to ask interesting questions when we reject the polarities that such a course markets?

Even when we decide to use qualitative and/or quantitative methods, we involve ourselves in theoretical as well as methodological decisions. These decisions relate not only to how we conceptualize the world but also to our theory of how our research subjects think about things.

But theory only becomes worthwhile when it is used to explain something. Becker (1998, p. 1) reports that the great founder of the Chicago School, Everett Hughes, responded grumpily when students asked what he thought about theory. "Theory of what?" he would reply. For Hughes, as for us, theory without some observation to work upon is like a tractor without a field.

Theory, then, should be neither a status symbol nor an optional extra in a research study. Without theory, research is impossibly narrow. Without research, theory is mere armchair contemplation.

KEY POINTS

Research questions are inevitably theoretically informed. So we do need social theories to help us address even quite basic issues in social research. But theories need to be distinguished from models and concepts:

Models provide an overall framework for how we look at reality.

Concepts are clearly specified ideas deriving from a particular model.

Theories arrange sets of concepts to define and explain some phenomenon.

Methodologies define how one will go about studying any phenomenon.

Methods are specific research techniques.

You can improve your ability to theorize about data by thinking about

- *What* and *how* questions
- *Chronology*: gathering data over time in order to look at processes of change

- *Context*: considering how your data is contextualized in particular organizational settings, social processes, or sets of experiences

- *Comparison*: trying to find ways of dividing your data into different sets and comparing each one

- *Implications*: thinking about how what you have discovered may relate to broader issues than your original research topic

- *Lateral thinking*: exploring the relations between apparently diverse models, theories, and methodologies

FURTHER READING

Seale, Gobo, Gubrium, and Silverman's edited book *Qualitative Research Practice* (2004) contains seven chapters that show the relevance of seven contemporary theories to qualitative research (Part II, "Analytic Frameworks", pp. 107–213). Becker's (1998) book *Tricks of the Trade* contains two chapters that are highly relevant to learning how to theorize about your data (Chapter 2 on "Imagery" and Chapter 4 on "Concepts"). Jaber Gubrium and James Holstein's (1997) text *The New Language of Qualitative Method* is an invaluable, thought-provoking guide to the vocabularies, investigatory styles, and ways of writing of different theoretical idioms.

EXERCISE 7.1

Howard Becker reports that his colleague Bernard Beck responded to students seeking to theorize about their data by instructing them, "Tell me what you've found out, but without using any of the identifying characteristics of the actual case" (Becker, 1998, p. 126).

Becker gives the example of his own research on Chicago teachers, which seemed to show that these teachers sought to improve their situation by moving to different schools rather than trying to get promoted in their present school. Using his data but forbidden to talk about teachers or schools, how might Becker have generated an account of his research that would have satisfied Beck?

CHAPTER 8

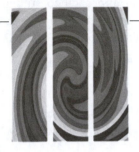

Choosing a Methodology

INTRODUCTION

As we saw in Chapter 7, decisions about **methodology** are always theoretically loaded. In this chapter, we provide more specific advice about the role of methodological issues in the way you design your research study. First, we introduce the concept of *research strategy*. This is then illustrated by a case study. Next we discuss the contentious topic of whether naturally occurring data has a special place in qualitative research design. Finally, we examine whether it makes sense to use multiple research methods.

YOUR RESEARCH STRATEGY

In Chapter 7, we defined *methodology* as "a general approach to studying research topics." In this sense, your choice of method should reflect an "overall research strategy" (Mason, 1996, p. 19), as your methodology shapes which methods are used and how each method is used.

Four issues arise when you decide that strategy:

- Making an early decision about which methods to use

- Understanding the link between methods, methodologies, and society

- Appreciating how models shape the meaning and use of different methods

- Choosing method(s) appropriate to your research topic

An Early Decision

Knowing what you want to find out leads inexorably to the question of how you will get that information. (Miles & Huberman, 1984, p. 42)

In quantitative research, it is expected that you begin by establishing a set of variables and methods (often using already-existing, proven measures). However, when you are at the start of a piece of qualitative research, how far are you forced to choose between different methods?

This question is raised by Miles and Huberman (1984), who suggest that qualitative researchers have a range of options in how far they use what the authors call "prior instrumentation" (i.e., predefined methods and measures):

- *No prior instrumentation*: Fieldwork must be open to unsuspected phenomena, which may be concealed by "prior instrumentation"; all you really need are "some orienting questions, some headings for observations (and) a rough and ready document analysis form" (Miles & Huberman, 1984, p. 42).

- *Considerable prior instrumentation*: If the research is not focused, you will gather superfluous data; using measures from earlier studies allows for comparability.

- *An open question*: Exploratory studies need to be far less structured than confirmatory studies; if your sample size is very small, then cross-case comparison will be more limited and, therefore, the need for standardized research instruments will be less.

Miles and Huberman show that, although prior structuring of a research design is more common in quantitative studies, such structuring is worth considering in more qualitative work. Thus, there have to be good reasons for any decision to begin a study with no prior instrumentation. Qualitative research can be highly structured, and what Miles and Huberman call "no prior instrumentation" should not be regarded as the default option for nonquantitative research. An early decision about your preferred methods is therefore preferable.

Methods Are Linked to Methodologies and to Society

Most research methods can be used in research based on either qualitative or quantitative methodologies. This is shown in Table 8.1. The table underlines our earlier point that methods are techniques that take on a specific meaning according to the methodology in which they are used. All this means is that we need to resist treating research methods as mere *techniques*.

To take just one example, although there are quantifiable, standardized observation schedules, observation is not generally seen as a very important method of data collection in quantitative research. This is because it is difficult to conduct observational studies on large samples. Quantitative researchers also argue that observation is not a very reliable data-collection method because different observers may record different observations. If used at all, observation is held to be only appropriate at a preliminary, or exploratory, stage of research.

Table 8.1   Different Uses for Four Methods

| | Methodology | |
Method	Quantitative Research	Qualitative Research
Observation	Preliminary work, e.g., prior to framing questionnaire	Fundamental to understanding another culture
Textual analysis	Content analysis, i.e., counting in terms of researchers' categories	Understanding participants' categories
Interviews	Survey research: mainly fixed-choice questions to random samples	Open-ended questions to small samples
Transcripts	Used infrequently to check the accuracy of interview records	Used to understand how participants organize their talk and body movements

SOURCE: Silverman (2001), p. 12.

Conversely, observational studies have been fundamental to much qualitative research. Beginning with the pioneering case studies of non-Western societies by early anthropologists (Malinowski, 1922; Radcliffe-Brown, 1948) and continuing with the work by sociologists in Chicago prior to the Second World War (Hughes, 1984), the observational method has often been the chosen method to understand another **culture** or **subculture**.

But there is a broader, societal context in which methods are located and deployed. As a crude example, texts depended on the invention of the printing press or, in the case of television or audio recordings, on modern communication technologies.

Moreover, such activities as observation and interviewing are not unique to social researchers. For instance, as Foucault (1977) has noted, the observation of the prisoner has been at the heart of modern prison reform, whereas the method of questioning used in the interview reproduces many of the features of the Catholic confessional or the psychoanalytic consultation. Its pervasiveness is reflected by the centrality of the interview study in so much contemporary social research. Think, for instance, of how much interviews are a central (and popular) feature of mass media products, from "talk shows" to celebrity interviews. Perhaps we all live in what might be called an **interview society** in which interviews seem central to making sense of our lives (see Atkinson & Silverman, 1997).

This broader societal context may explain qualitative researchers' temptation to use methods such as the interview. Of course, such a link between culture and method should be an opportunity to question ourselves about our methodological preferences. However, such self-questioning (sometimes, mistakenly, we think, referred to as **reflexivity**) does not itself provide a warrant for the choices we make. As we argue in Chapters 14 and 15, such a warrant depends on the robustness and **credibility** of our research design.

Models Shape the Meaning of Methods

Many qualitative researchers believe that they can provide a deeper understanding of social phenomena than would be obtained from purely quantitative data. However, such purportedly "deep" understanding arises in qualitative researchers' claims to have entered and mapped very different territories such as inner experiences, language, narratives, sign systems, or forms of social interaction. Some of these claims, associated with different qualitative models, are set out in Table 8.2.

Each activity shown in Table 8.2 is not neutral but depends on an implied model of how social reality works. In this table, we have simplified different

Table 8.2   Methods and Models of Qualitative Research

Method	Model I	Model II
Observation	"Background" material	Understanding of subcultures
Texts and documents	"Background" material	Understanding of language and other sign systems
Interviews	Understanding "experience"	Narrative construction
Audio- and videorecording	Little used	Understanding how interaction is organized

approaches into just two models. However, in terms of Gubrium and Holstein's (1997) four **idioms** discussed in Chapter 7, **naturalists** give priority to understanding subcultures, **emotionalists** favor understanding "experience" and focus on the open-ended interview, **ethnomethodologists** prefer to understand interaction, and postmodern theorists prioritize sign systems.

Such idioms or models are a necessary but not sufficient warrant for a claim that any given research method has been properly used. So a purely theoretical warrant does not guarantee that a method will be appropriately used in a particular data analysis.

Choosing an Appropriate Method

There are no right or wrong methods. There are only methods that are appropriate to your research topic and the model with which you are working.

Let us take two contrasting examples from Chapter 4. Tippi was interested in the experience of living in a community of elderly people. Her concept of *experience* clearly derives from an emotionalist model. This makes her choice of open-ended interviews entirely appropriate. By contrast, if she were interested instead in how people *behave* in such a community, this naturalist topic might have suggested that she should use observational methods.

Anne's research was concerned with how a narrative changes as it is moved from book to television or radio. Her intention to observe what happens during the process of production seems to be a highly appropriate method for this topic. However, she also wanted to interview the participants to understand their motivation.

The problem here is the potential conflict within her research design between emotionalist and naturalist models. If she primarily wants to understand behaviors, then the naturalist stress on observation makes most sense. By contrast, if experience and motivation are really her thing, then she should stick with the interview method. This argument is developed in our discussion of multiple methods later in this chapter.

Of course, sometimes it does make sense to think laterally and to combine methods and models. But the safest option for most apprentice researchers is to keep it simple and to have a straightforward fit among the topic, method, and model.

What follows next is an extended discussion of one case. It shows how David encountered these issues in designing a study of HIV-test counseling (Silverman, 1997).

CHOOSING A METHODOLOGY: A CASE STUDY

Studying Counseling

The counseling study discussed here emerged out of David's work as a medical sociologist. Between 1979 and 1985, he worked on data from British outpatient consultations that involved parents and children. At the same time, he also conducted a small study of adult oncology clinics, comparing National Health Service and private consultations conducted by the same doctor. This research was reported in a number of papers (Silverman, 1981, 1983, 1984; Silverman & Bloor, 1989) and brought together in a book (Silverman, 1987). In that book, David focused on how apparently "patient-centered" medicine can work in many different directions.

In 1987, he was given permission to sit in at a weekly clinic held at the Genito-Urinary Department of an English inner-city hospital (Silverman, 1989). The clinic's purpose was to monitor the progress of HIV-positive patients who were taking the drug AZT (Retrovir). AZT, which seems able to slow down the rate at which the virus reproduces itself, was then at an experimental stage of its development.

Like any observational study, the aim was to gather firsthand information about social processes in a naturally occurring context. No attempt was made to interview the individuals concerned because the focus was on what they actually did in the clinic rather than on what they thought about what they did. The researcher was present in the consulting room at a side angle to both doctors and patient.

Patients' consent for the researcher's presence was obtained by the senior doctor. Given the presumed sensitivity of the occasion, tape recording was not attempted. Instead, detailed handwritten notes were kept, using a separate sheet for each consultation. The sample was small (15 male patients seen in 37 consultations over seven clinic sessions), and no claims were made about its representativeness. Because observational methods were rare in this area, the study was essentially exploratory. However, as we shall see, an attempt was made to link the findings to other social research about doctor-patient relations.

As Sontag (1979) has noted, illness is often taken as a moral or psychological metaphor. The major finding of this early study was the moral baggage attached to being HIV-positive. For instance, many patients used a buzzer to remind themselves to take their medication during the night. As one commented, "It's a dead giveaway. Everybody knows what you've got."

However, despite the social climate in which HIV infection is viewed, there was considerable variation in how people presented themselves to the medical team. Four styles of "self-presentation" (Goffman, 1959) were identified, which David called "cool," "anxious," "objective," and "theatrical" (Silverman, 1989). But there was no simple correspondence between each patient and a particular style of self-presentation. Rather, each way of presenting oneself was available to each patient within any one consultation, where it might have a particular social function. So the focus was on social processes rather than on psychological states.

Along the way, he also discovered how an ethos of "positive thinking" was central to many patients' accounts and how doctors systematically concentrated on the bodies rather than the minds of their patients. This led to some practical questions about the division of labor between doctors and counselors.

About the time David was writing up this research, Kaye Wellings, who then was working for the publicly funded Health Education Authority (HEA), approached him about the possibility of extending his research to HIV counseling. Until that time, the HEA had been funding research on the effectiveness of "safer sex" messages carried in the mass media. In the light of the explosion in the number of HIV tests in the UK in the late 1980s, Kaye thought it might be useful to take a longer look at the effectiveness of the health promotion messages being delivered in counseling people before and after the HIV antibody test.

David was interested in such a study for two reasons. First, it was the logical development of his study of medical interviews with AIDS patients. Second, it offered the opportunity to pursue his interest in looking at how communication between professionals and their clients worked out in practice—as opposed to the injunctions of textbooks and training manuals. Consequently, he submitted a research proposal and received funding from the HEA for 30 months beginning in late 1988.

The Quantitative Bias

McLeod has reminded us that "almost all counseling and psychotherapy research has been carried out from the discipline of psychology" (1994, p. 190).

One consequence has been a focus on quantitative studies concerned with the attributes of individuals. This has meant that linguistic and sociological issues, such as language use and social context, have been downplayed (see Heaton, 1979).

Such a psychological focus has also had an impact on research design, leading to the dominance of experimental and/or statistical methods, which are favored in psychology. Of course, no research method is intrinsically better than any other; everything will depend on one's research objectives. So it is only a question of restoring a balance between different ways of conceiving counseling research.

In designing his research proposal, David therefore needed to balance two competing objectives:

1. His desire to examine how HIV counseling worked in actual counselor–client interviews

2. Having to adjust to a context in which most counseling research had been informed by either a quantitative methodology or **normative** assumptions about what constitutes "good" counseling

Designing a Methodology: Three Familiar Options

Quantitative or normative approaches suggest three obvious ways of researching counseling, all of which appear to take seriously the demands of **validity** and **reliability**. These three methodologies are set out in Table 8.3.

In order to underline the methodological options that arise in the early stages of research design, we review each strategy in the next paragraphs. In doing so,

Table 8.3   Three Methodologies for Counseling Research

1. Measuring clients' response to counseling by means of research interviews that elicit their knowledge and reported behavior. This would involve a longitudinal study, following a cohort of patients. The study could have either an experimental or nonexperimental design.

2. Measuring clients' response to counseling by means of objective behavioral indicators. This also would involve a longitudinal study, following a cohort of patients.

3. Measuring the degree of fit between actual counseling practice and certain agreed normative standards of "good counseling."

SOURCE: Silverman (1997), p. 16.

we will see that each raises both methodological and analytic questions. We shall suggest that, in terms of either or both of these questions, none of these three strategies is entirely satisfactory.

The Research Interview

As noted in Table 8.3, this might have either an experimental or nonexperimental design.

In the experimental design, we might randomly assign clients to two groups. In Group 1, clients are counseled, whereas in Group 2, the **control group**, no counseling is provided. Both groups are then interviewed about their knowledge of AIDS and how they intend to protect themselves against the disease. This interview is followed up, some months later, with a further interview examining their present behavior compared with their reported behavior prior to the experiment.

In the nonexperimental design, existing counseling procedures are evaluated by a cohort of patients. Again, we might follow up with a cohort some time later.

The advantage of such research designs is that they permit large-scale studies that generate apparently hard data, seemingly based on unequivocal measures. However, a number of difficulties present themselves. Of course, we recognize that these problems are recognized by researchers who use such research instruments. In turn, they have ingenious methods for dealing with them. Here are a few:

1. How seriously are we to take patients' accounts of their behavior? Isn't it likely that clients will tend to provide answers that they think the counselors and researchers will want to hear (see McLeod, 1994, pp. 124–126)?

2. Doesn't the experimental study ignore the *organizational* context in which health care is delivered (e.g., relations between physicians and other staff, tacit theories of "good counseling," resources available, staff turnover, etc.)? Such contexts may shape the nature and effectiveness of counseling in nonlaboratory situations.

3. Even if we can overcome the practical and ethical problems of not providing, say, pretest counseling to a control group, may not the experience of being allocated to a control group affect the reliability of our measures and the validity of our findings (see McLeod, 1994, p. 124)?

4. Don't both studies treat subjects as "an aggregation of disparate individuals" who have no social interaction with one another (Bryman,

1988, p. 39)? As such, they give us little hold on how counseling is organized as a local, step-by-step social process and, consequently, we may suspect that we are little wiser about how counseling works in practice.

The nonexperimental study may have either a quantitative or qualitative design. In the latter case, we might expect to carry out a relatively small number of open-ended interviews in order "to enter, in an empathic way, the lived experience of the person or group being studied" (McLeod, 1994, p. 89).

This pursuit of "lived experience" means that many qualitative researchers favor the open-ended interview (see Chapter 15). Unfortunately, both the in-depth accounts apparently provided by the open-ended interview and the apparently unequivocal measures of information retention, attitude, and behavior that we obtain via laboratory or questionnaire methods have a tenuous basis in what people may be saying and doing in their everyday lives. Moreover, if our interest is in the relation of counseling to health-related behavior, do such studies tell us how people actually talk with professionals and with each other as opposed to via responses to researchers' questions?

An example makes the point very well. At a recent meeting of social scientists working on AIDS, much concern was expressed about the difficulty of recruiting a **sample** of the population prepared to answer researchers' questions about their sexual behavior. As a result, it was suggested that a subsequent meeting should be convened at which we could swap tips about how to recruit such a sample.

Now, of course, this issue of recruiting a sample is basic to survey research. And, for potentially delicate matters, like the elicitation of accounts of sexual behavior, survey researchers are quite properly concerned about finding willing respondents.

At the same time, it is generally acknowledged that the best chance of limiting the spread of HIV may be by encouraging people to discuss their sexual practices with their partners. This implies something about the limits of interview-based research in this area. Such research necessarily focuses on finding people prepared to talk about their sexuality in an interview. However, it can say nothing about how talk about sexuality is organized in naturally occurring environments such as talk between partners or, indeed, talk about sexuality in the context of real-time counseling interviews.

Behavioral Indicators

This method seeks to elicit behavioral measures that reliably report the effectiveness of counseling. Its advantage is that, unlike the research interview, it does not depend on potentially unreliable client perceptions and self-reports of behavior and behavioral change. Moreover, by eliminating a concern with the information that clients may acquire from counseling, it takes on board the research that shows that acquired knowledge does not have any direct link with behavioral change.

In relation to HIV-test counseling, it was suggested to me by a senior physician at an AIDS unit in Sweden that an appropriate behavioral indicator is seroconversion (developing antibodies to the HIV virus). Presumably, then, we would need to study a cohort of patients who test seronegative and are counseled. We could then retest them after a further period, say 12 months, to establish what proportions from different counseling centers and with different counselors have seroconverted. In this way, it would be claimed, we could measure the effectiveness of counseling in relation to promoting safer behavior.

As already noted, the advantage of this approach is that it generates quantitative measures of behavior that are apparently objective. However, like the research interview, its reliability also has serious shortcomings:

1. How do we know that the counseling alone is the variable that has produced the reported behavior? Although we may be able to control for some gross intervening variables (like gender, age, sexual preference, drug use, etc.), it is likely that some nonmeasured variables may be associated with the reported behavior (e.g., access to other sources of information, availability of condoms or clean injecting equipment, etc.).

2. Ad hoc decisions are often made about which part of a counseling interview should be assessed. The scope extends from one whole interview (or even several interviews with the same client) down to a microsegment of one interview. The latter approach gains precision but with a loss of context. Such context is provided by studying whole interviews but at a likely loss of precision.

3. Even if such measures are reliable and precise, the result "assesses only the presence or absence of a mode, and not the skilfulness with which it is delivered" (McLeod, 1994, p. 151).

Such problems in attempts to use internal, normative standards of evaluation look even worse when viewed in the context of studies that seek to relate such measures to particular outcomes. As McLeod (1994) notes, one such study (Hill et al., 1988) found that only 1 percent of variance in client responses was related to observed measures of counselor behavior!

The Methodology Chosen

It is now time to lay David's cards on the table and to offer the alternative approach on which his research was based—**conversation analysis** (henceforth CA). CA, as we saw in the studies discussed in Chapters 3 and 4, is centrally concerned with the organization of talk, although its concern with social organization leads it to describe its subject matter as "talk-in-interaction."

Equally, counselors, by definition, treat talk as a nontrivial matter. However, even if we concede the centrality of talk to social life, why should counseling researchers give priority to recording and transcribing talk? Given the usefulness of other kinds of data derived, say, from observations of behavioral change or interviews with clients, what is the special value of transcripts of tape recordings of conversation?

One way to start to discuss this question is to think about how research based upon data that arises in subjects' day-to-day activities can seek to preserve the "phenomenon" of interactions like counseling interviews. Although such **naturally occurring data** is never uncontaminated (for instance, it may need to be recorded and transcribed), it usually gives us a very good clue about what participants usually do outside a research setting.

Conversely, in research interviews, as Heritage puts it, "the verbal formulations of subjects are treated as an appropriate substitute for the observation of actual behaviour" (Heritage, 1984, p. 236).The temptation here is to treat respondents' formulations as reflections of some preexisting social or psychological world.

However, even when counseling researchers contemplate tape recording actual interactions, they sometimes become easily deflected away from the counseling session itself. For instance, although McLeod (1994) calls for a study of "the interior of therapy," he also cites favorably attempts at "interpersonal process recall" where participants are played back the tape "to restimulate the actual experience the person had during the session" (1994, p. 147). Thus, in common with many qualitative researchers, what matters for McLeod is what people think and feel rather than what they do.

However, if we follow this temptation in designing a study of counseling, then we deny something that all counselors recognize: that talk is itself an activity. Although this is recognized in many normative versions of counseling, to base our research on such versions would be to narrow our focus to those activities we already know about.

An alternative is to investigate how counseling interviews actually proceed without being shackled by normative standards of "good" communication. In this way, we might discover previously unnoticed skills of both counselors and clients as well as the communicational functions of apparently dysfunctional counselor behavior.

Summary and Implications

In this section, we have used the case of a study of HIV counseling to illustrate several options that are available in designing a qualitative study. We do not want to imply that a CA study of counseling interviews is the "one right method." Instead, we want to demonstrate that choosing a particular method always has more implications than you might think. We have shown here how those implications encompass preferred analytical models, questions of reliability and validity and, in this particular case, relevance for professional practice. To follow up this point, you should attempt Exercise 8.1 now.

In developing his research design in this study, David took a position on two issues that need further discussion: He chose to study behaviour *in situ* (i.e., naturally occurring data) and he rejected combining multiple methods. This reflected his own preferences. Since other choices can (rightfully) be made by others, it is worth reviewing both issues.

NATURALLY OCCURRING DATA?

Some qualitative researchers prefer to avoid creating data through setting up particular "artificial" research environments like interviews, experiments, **focus groups**, or survey questionnaires. They argue that, since so much data occurs naturally (i.e., without the intervention of a researcher), why not study that and, thereby, access what people are routinely up to without, say, being asked by a researcher? To those who argue that such access can be difficult, the answer is that lateral thinking can move you into areas that *are* accessible.

For instance, to use an example raised by someone at a recent talk David gave, we might think that how couples negotiate the consequences of their different sleeping patterns can only be elicited by interviewing those involved. However, if indeed this is a real problem to members of society, it should crop up, say, in the advice or letters pages of certain magazines. Why not try looking for actual instances first, before resorting to interviews?

Moreover, the problem with methods like interviews and (to some extent) focus groups is that the researcher has to set things up by asking questions of respondents. By contrast, the beauty of naturally occurring data is that it may show us things we could never imagine. As Sacks once put it, "Thus we can start with things that are not currently imaginable, by showing that they happened" (Sacks, 1992, Vol. 2, p. 420).

Although David is highly sympathetic to this argument, it also has limitations (see Speer, 2002). For instance,

- Data cannot be intrinsically unsatisfactory; it all depends on what you want to do with the data

- No data can be "untouched by human hands" (e.g., recording equipment is sometimes present, and this has to be positioned by a researcher)

- The difference between what is natural and nonnatural should be investigated rather than used as a tacit research resource

These are powerful arguments. However, rather than abandon his preference, David preferred to take a nondogmatic position. This involves the following two elements:

- Everything depends on your research topic. So, as Speer (2002) notes, if you want to study how counseling gets done, it may not make sense to seek retrospective accounts from clients and practitioners or to use a laboratory study.

- We need to consider how far any research setting is *consequential* for our research topic. For instance, in one laboratory study, limitations were placed on who could speak. This made the experimental setting consequential for its topic (of "self-repair") and undercut its conclusions (Schegloff, 1991, p. 54). Without such limitations, the study would have been sound.

To conclude: choosing any method, based on any kind of data, can never be intrinsically right or wrong. However, as a nonemotionalist, David is sympathetic to Potter's argument that, given the (unthought?) dominance of open-ended interviews in qualitative research, "the justificatory boot might be better placed on the other foot. The question is not why should we study natural materials, but why should we not?" (J. Potter, 2002, p. 540).

MULTIPLE METHODS?

So far, we have been assuming that you will always want to choose just one method. However, the methods presented in Table 8.2 are often combined. For instance, many qualitative case studies combine observation with interviewing. This may be because you have several research questions or "because you want to use different methods or sources to corroborate each other so that you are using some form of methodological **triangulation**" (Mason, 1996, p. 25).

For instance, Miles and Huberman (1984, p. 42) give the example of research on how police suspects are arrested and booked. You might think here of combining several methods, for instance,

- Interviews (with suspects, police, and lawyers)

- Observation (of arrests and bookings)

- Collecting documents (produced by this process)

- Recording (of arrests and bookings)

If you are a pure **empiricist**, uninterested in the theoretical bases of research design, multiple methods may look like a good idea. By having a cumulative view of data drawn from different contexts, we may, as in trigonometry, be able to triangulate the "true" state of affairs by examining where the different data intersect. In this way, some qualitative researchers believe that triangulation may improve the reliability of a single method. But do multiple methods always make analytical sense?

As we remarked in Chapter 4, mapping one set of data upon another is a more or less complicated task depending on your analytic framework. In particular, if you treat social reality as constructed in different ways in different contexts, then you cannot appeal to a single phenomenon that all your data apparently represents (see Chapter 14).

Mason (1996, p. 27) gives the example of the mistaken attempt to combine (say) interview data on individuals' perceptions with **discourse analysis** (DA) of particular texts. The mistake arises because DA treats all accounts as socially constructed and, therefore, cannot treat interview accounts as providing a definitive version of reality.

Such triangulation of data seeks to overcome the context-boundedness of our materials at the cost of analyzing their sense in context. For purposes of social research, it may simply not be useful to conceive of an overarching reality to which data, gathered in different contexts, approximates.

At the very least, we need to note Fielding and Fielding's (1986) suggestion that the use of triangulation should operate according to ground rules, set out in the following:

- Always begin from a theoretical perspective or model

- Choose methods and data that will give you an account of structure and meaning from within that perspective (e.g., by showing the structural contexts of the interactions studied)

Many theoretical perspectives in sociology and elsewhere suggest we cannot simply aggregate data in order to arrive at an overall "truth." This implies that we should receive with caution the clarion calls for multiple methods in areas like nursing, family medicine, and elsewhere. As Hammersley and Atkinson point out, "One should not adopt a naively 'optimistic' view that the aggregation of data from different sources will unproblematically add up to produce a more complete picture" (1983, p. 199).

As already noted in Chapter 4, multiple methods are often adopted in the mistaken hope that they will reveal "the whole picture." But this whole picture is an illusion, which speedily leads to scrappy research based on underanalyzed data and an imprecise or theoretically indigestible research problem. For instance, multiple methods may tempt novice researchers to move to another data set when they are having difficulties in analyzing one set of material. It is usually far better to celebrate the partiality of your data and delight in the particular phenomena that it allows you to inspect (hopefully in detail).

CONCLUDING REMARKS

The debate about multiple methods and naturally occurring data illustrates the theoretically laden environment in which we make methodological choices. It underlines the fact that many apparently technical choices are saturated with theoretical import.

Of course, to some extent this complicates the picture when you are attempting to design a research study. However, a concern at this stage with theoretical issues also helps in at least two ways. First, it may allow you to simplify your research design as you realize that it is often misleading to attempt to research the whole picture. Second, thereby, it may add theoretical consistency and even some elegance to the research design. As we remarked in Part I, often the best research says "a lot about a little."

KEY POINTS

- Your choice of method should reflect both your research topic and your overall research strategy, as your methodology shapes which methods are used and how each method is used.

- Although most research methods can be used in either qualitative or quantitative studies, research methods are more than mere techniques. Different theoretical idioms or models provide different justifications for using particular research methods.

- Methods do not just belong to social researchers. Before choosing a method, you should reflect upon the broader, societal context in which this method is located and deployed.

- Think carefully before you generate data through research instruments like interviews and focus groups. Sometimes such methods may indeed be appropriate to your topic and model. Sometimes, however, you may be neglecting to study illuminating, naturally occurring data.

- Think carefully before adopting multiple methods. Many models suggest that we cannot simply aggregate data in order to arrive at an overall "truth." Choose simplicity and rigor rather than the often-illusory search for the full picture.

FURTHER READING

David Silverman's (ed.) *Qualitative Research: Theory, Method and Practice* (2004b) provides state-of-the-art accounts by leading scholars of the uses of interviews, observations, texts, Internet data, and audio and visual data. Other useful books on methodology are Amanda Coffey and Paul Atkinson's *Making Sense of Qualitative Data* (1996), Jennifer Mason's *Qualitative Researching* (2002), Pertti Alasuutari's *Researching Culture* (1995) and David Silverman's *Interpreting Qualitative Data: Methods for Analysing Talk, Text and Interaction* (2001).

EXERCISE 8.1

Mason (1996, p. 19) notes that your choice of a methodology is likely to reflect your own biography and the knowledge and training your education has given you. As she comments, "Whilst practical issues to do with training and skill are . . . relevant in your choice of method . . . they should not govern your choice" (p. 19). She suggests instead making a list of possible research methods and data source options and to think through why you are accepting or rejecting each one.

1. Follow Mason's suggestion about making a list of possible research methods and data source options. Explain why you are accepting or rejecting each one.

2. Answer the following questions (adapted from Mason, 1996, pp. 20–21):

- What data sources and methods of data generation are potentially available or appropriate?

- What can these methods and sources feasibly tell me?

- Which phenomena and components or properties of social "reality" might these data sources and methods potentially help me to address?

- Which of my research questions could they help me to address?

CHAPTER 9

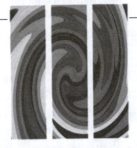

Selecting a Case

INTRODUCTION

We concluded the previous chapter with David's favorite research maxim: "make a lot out of a little." If you take us seriously, you will have every chance of producing a thorough, analytically interesting research study. However, at least three nagging doubts may well remain. We list them next, together with some soothing words about each:

- *"My case may not be important."* Here you are worried that the case you are studying may be seen by others as trivial or not a real problem. The famous ethnographer Howard Becker remarks that such criticisms have been made of his own work on several occasions. As he puts it, "Just as some people think tragedy is more important than comedy . . . some problems are seen as inherently serious and worthy of grownup attention, others as trivial, flyspecks on the wallpaper of life . . . mere exotica" (Becker, 1998, p. 92). There is a very good response to this kind of complaint: what seems to be important is usually governed by little more than current fashions; who knows what might become important? Apparently trivial cases may, through good analysis, turn out to have far-reaching implications.

- *"I can only study the (part of the) case to which I have access."* This is a more serious issue. When we are studying an organization, we are dependent on the whims of **gatekeepers**. Such people will usually seek to limit what we can study, assuring us that, if we need to know more, they can tell us about it (Becker, 1998, p. 90). How do we get around this problem? Becker suggests two answers. First, "doubt everything anyone in power tells you." Second, look for other opinions (1998, p. 91). Like Dalton (1959), in his classic study of middle managers, case study researchers should systematically attempt to assess the likely linkages between opinions, activities, and interests.

- *"I have so little data—just one case."* This is a serious problem. As we shall see, even in qualitative research it is important to consider what kinds of generalizations can be made from a single case.

The rest of this chapter will be devoted to the issue of **generalizability** in case study research. First, however, we need to define both terms.

WHAT IS A CASE STUDY?

This question has a relatively simple answer. As Punch puts it,

> The basic idea is that one case (or perhaps a small number of cases) will be studied in detail, using whatever methods seem appropriate. While there may be a variety of specific purposes and research questions, the general objective is to develop as full an understanding of that case as possible. (1998, p. 150)

There are, of course, an endless variety of possible "cases." If, like Becker, we are interested in occupations, cases to study may range from dance-hall musicians to student physicians. By contrast, if you are interested in childhood, a case may be a single child, a classroom or clinic, or a charity or other organization concerned with the welfare of children. So, as Stake suggests, "A case may be simple or complex . . . (but) it is one among others. In any given study, we will concentrate on the one" (2000, p. 436).

All this is purely descriptive. Table 9.1 identifies three analytic features of case study research.

Table 9.1   Case Study Research

1. Each case has boundaries that must be identified at an early stage of the research (e.g., if you are studying a school, does this include classroom behavior, staff meetings, parent–teacher meetings, etc.?).

2. Each case will be a case of something in which the researcher is interested. So the unit of analysis must be defined at the outset in order to clarify the research strategy.

3. Case studies seek to preserve the wholeness and integrity of the case. However, in order to achieve some focus, a limited research problem must be established geared to specific features of the case.

SOURCE: Adapted from Punch (1998), p. 153.

GENERALIZING FROM CASES

Generalizability is a standard aim in quantitative research and is normally achieved by statistical sampling procedures. Such sampling has two functions. First, it allows you to feel confident about the representativeness of your sample: "If the population characteristics are known, the degree of representativeness of a sample can be checked" (Arber, 1993, p. 70). Second, such representativeness allows you to make broader inferences: "The purpose of sampling is usually to study a representative subsection of a precisely defined population in order to make inferences about the whole population" (1993).

Such sampling procedures are, however, usually unavailable in qualitative research. In such studies, our data is often derived from one or more cases and it is unlikely that these cases will have been selected on a random basis. Very often, a case will be chosen simply because it allows access. Moreover, even if you were able to construct a representative sample of cases, the sample size would probably be so large as to preclude the kind of intensive analysis usually preferred in qualitative research (Mason, 1996, p. 91).

This gives rise to a problem, familiar to users of quantitative methods: "How do we know . . . how representative case study findings are of all members of the population from which the case was selected?" (Bryman, 1988, p. 88).

TYPES OF CASE STUDIES

Stake (2000, pp. 437–438) has identified three different types of case study:

1. The *intrinsic case study*, where "this case is of interest . . . in all its particularity and ordinariness." In the intrinsic case study, according to Stake, no attempt is made to generalize beyond the single case or even to build theories.

2. The *instrumental case study*, in which a case is examined mainly to provide insight into an issue or to revise a generalization. Although the case selected is studied in depth, the main focus is on something else.

3. The *collective case study*, where a number of cases are studied in order to investigate some general phenomenon.

The idea of a purely *intrinsic case study* is resisted by many qualitative researchers. If all you aim to do is simply to describe a case, you may rightly get the response, "so what?" Description itself is a tricky activity which is inevitably theoretically laden. If you doubt this, you might look back at Table 7.1 in Chapter 7.

In this context, most supervisors of student qualitative research would expect your study of a case to be based on some **concept**(s) that is developed as a result of your study. For examples of concept development through case study research, see Chapter 3.

Furthermore, empirical issues arise in case studies just as much as theoretical concerns. It is reasonable to ask what knowledge your case study has produced. If you are to answer this question, you must consider the degree of generalizability of your research. As Mason puts it,

> I do not think qualitative researchers should be satisfied with producing explanations which are idiosyncratic or particular to the limited empirical parameters of their study. . . . Qualitative research should (therefore) produce explanations which are generalizable in some way, or which have a wider resonance. (1996, p. 6)

So description of a case for description's sake (the intrinsic case study) is a weak position. Quite rightly, the problem of representativeness is a perennial worry of many qualitative or case study researchers. How do they attempt to address it? Can we generalize from cases to populations without following a purely statistical logic?

In the rest of this chapter, we will discuss four different but positive answers to this question of how we can obtain generalizability:

- Combining qualitative research with quantitative measures of populations

- Purposive sampling guided by time and resources

- Theoretical sampling

- Using an analytic model that assumes that generalizability is present in the existence of *any* case

COMBINING QUALITATIVE RESEARCH WITH QUANTITATIVE MEASURES OF POPULATIONS

Quantitative measures may sometimes be used to infer from one case to a larger population. Hammersley (1992) suggests three methods through which we can attempt to generalize from the analysis of a single case:

- Obtaining information about relevant aspects of the population of cases and comparing our case to them

- Using survey research on a random sample of cases

- Coordinating several ethnographic studies

Hammersley argues that such comparisons with a larger sample may allow us to establish some sense of the representativeness of our single case.

However, two of Hammersley's methods are very ambitious for the student researcher. For instance, you are unlikely to have the funds for even a small piece of survey research, while the coordination of several ethnographic studies requires substantial resources of time and personnel as well as good contacts with other researchers. Such contacts allowed Miller and Silverman (1995) to apply the comparative approach in describing talk about troubles in two counseling settings: a British hemophilia center counseling patients who are HIV-positive and a family therapy center in the United States. In this study, they focused on similarities in three types of discursive practices in these settings: those concerned with trouble definitions, trouble remedies, and the social contexts of the clients' troubles (see also Gubrium, 1992).

Without such contacts and resources, the student researcher is left with Hammersley's first method: obtaining information about relevant aspects of the population of cases and comparing our case to them. This is more useful because, at its simplest, this method only involves reading about other cognate studies and comparing our case to them. For instance, in David's study of HIV counseling (Silverman, 1997), he compared his counselor–client interviews with Heritage and Sefi's (1992) data on interviews between health visitors and first-time mothers. Although this had little to do with establishing the representativeness of his sample, it gave a firmer basis to his generalizations about advice-sequences in his data (Silverman, 1997, pp. 124–128). The comparative method used here allows you to make larger claims about your analysis without leaving your library. As Peräkylä puts it, "The comparative approach directly tackles the question of generalizability by demonstrating the similarities and differences across a number of settings" (2004, p. 296).

In this sense, your literature review (see Chapter 17) has as much to do with the issue of generalizability as with displaying your academic credentials.

PURPOSIVE SAMPLING

Before we can contemplate comparing our case to others, we need to have selected our case. Are there any grounds other than convenience or accessibility to guide us in this selection?

Purposive sampling allows you to choose a case because it illustrates some feature or process in which you are interested. However, this does not provide a simple approval to any case you happen to choose. Rather, purposive sampling demands that you think critically about the parameters of the population you are studying and choose your sample case carefully on this basis.

As Denzin and Lincoln put it,

Many qualitative researchers employ . . . purposive, and not random, sampling methods. They seek out groups, settings and individuals where . . . the processes being studied are most likely to occur. (2000, p. 370)

Stake (2000, pp. 446–447) gives the example of a study of interactive displays in children's museums. He assumes that you only have resources to study four such museums. How should you proceed?

He suggests setting up a *typology*, which would establish a matrix of museum types as in Table 9.2.

The typology set out in Table 9.2 yields 6 cases which could be increased further by, say, distinguishing between museums located in small and big cities—bringing the number of cases to 12. Which cases should you select?

Table 9.2   A Typology of Children's Museums

| | Type of Museum | | |
Program Type	Art	Science	History
Exhibitory	1	2	3
Participative	4	5	6

SOURCE: Adapted from Stake (2000), pp. 446–447.

You will be constrained by two main factors. First, there may not be examples to fit every cell. Second, your resources will not allow you to research every existing unit. So you have to make a practical decision. For instance, if you can cover only two cases, do you choose two participatory museums in different locations or in different subjects? Or do you compare such a museum with a more conventional exhibit-based museum?

Provided you have thought through the options, it is unlikely that your selection will be criticized. Moreover, as we see in the next section, how you set up your typology and make your choice should be grounded in the theoretical apparatus you are using. Sampling in qualitative research is neither statistical nor purely personal: it is, or should be, theoretically grounded. To improve your understanding of this point, you could now attempt Exercise 9.1.

THEORETICAL SAMPLING

Theoretical and purposive sampling are often treated as synonyms. Indeed, the only difference between the two procedures applies when the *purpose* behind *purposive* sampling is not theoretically defined.

Bryman argues that qualitative research follows a theoretical, rather than a statistical, logic: "The issue should be couched in terms of the generalizability of cases to *theoretical* propositions rather than to *populations* or universes" (1988, p. 90, our emphasis).[1]

The nature of this link between sampling and theory is set out by Mason:

Theoretical sampling means selecting groups or categories to study on the basis of their relevance to your research questions, your theoretical position . . . and most importantly the explanation or account which you are developing. Theoretical sampling is concerned with constructing a sample . . . which is meaningful theoretically, because it builds in certain characteristics or criteria which help to develop and test your theory and explanation. (1996, pp. 93–94)

Theoretical sampling has three features, which we discuss in the following paragraphs:

- Choosing cases in terms of your theory
- Choosing "deviant" cases
- Changing the size of your sample during the research

Choosing Cases in Terms of Your Theory

Mason writes about "the wider universe of social explanations in relation to which you have constructed your research questions" (1996, p. 85). This theoretically defined universe "will make some sampling choices more sensible and meaningful than others." Mason describes choosing a kind of sample that can represent a wider population. Here we select a sample of particular "processes, types, categories or examples which are relevant to or appear within the wider universe" (Mason, 1996, p. 92). Mason suggests that examples of these would include single units such as "an organization, a location, a document . . . (or) a conversation."

Mason gives the example of a **discourse analysis** of gender relation as discourses that construct subjects of gender relations. In this approach, as she puts it: "you are . . . unlikely to perceive the social world in terms of a large set of gender relations from which you can simply draw a representative sample of people by gender" (Mason, 1996, p. 85).

So in qualitative research, the relevant or "sampleable" units are often seen as theoretically defined. This means that it is inappropriate to sample populations by such attributes as gender, ethnicity, or even age because how such attributes are routinely defined is itself the *topic* of your research.

As an example of theoretically defined sampling, Bryman uses Glaser and Strauss's discussion of "awareness contexts" in relation to dying in the hospital:

> The issue of whether the particular hospital studied is "typical" is not the critical issue; what is important is whether the experiences of dying patients are typical of the broad class of phenomena . . . to which the theory refers. Subsequent research would then focus on the validity of the proposition in other milieux (e.g., doctors' surgeries). (Bryman, 1988, p. 91)

We can understand better the theoretical logic behind choice of a sample in a further example of a study of police work. Say you are interested in the arrest and booking of suspects (see Miles & Huberman, 1984, pp. 37–38). You are now confronted with a series of choices which relate to

- The particular setting to be studied

- The elements or processes on which you will focus

- How you might generalize further

Let us look at each of these in turn.

Settings

In independent, unfunded research, you are likely to choose any setting that, while demonstrating the phenomenon in which you are interested, is accessible and will provide appropriate data reasonably readily and quickly. In the police study, this might well lead you to study the police station rather than a squad car, the scene of the crime, or the suspect's residence or hangout. In the police station, at the very least, you will keep warm and dry, you will be safe, and you can expect several arrests and bookings on any visit. However, so far you are being guided by quite practical influences.

The Research Focus

In focusing your research, you necessarily are making a theoretically guided choice. By opting to focus on particular individuals, events, or processes, you are electing particular theoretical frameworks. For instance, a focus on differential behavior between police officers and suspects with different characteristics may draw on some version of the structural determinants of action. Conversely, a focus on how laws are interpreted in practice (cf. Sudnow, 1968b) may derive from a concern with the creative power of commonsense interpretive procedures.

Generalizing Further

When wedded to other studies that share your theoretical orientation, a single police station may provide enough data to develop all the generalizations you want about, say, how commonsense reasoning works. However, if you have a more "structural" bent, it may now be necessary to widen your sample in two ways: first, to add more observations of arrests in this police station and, second, to compare it with other stations, perhaps in a range of areas.

In all these cases, the sample is not random but theoretical. It is "designed to provide a close-up, detailed or meticulous view of particular units which may constitute . . . cases which are relevant to or appear within the wider universe" (Mason, 1996, p. 92).

Choosing "Deviant" Cases

Mason notes that you must overcome any tendency to select a case which is likely to support your argument. Instead, it makes sense to seek out negative instances as defined by the theory with which you are working.

One of Becker's "tricks of the trade" is:

> Just to insist that nothing that can be imagined is impossible, so we should look for the most unlikely things that we can think of and incorporate their existence, or the possibility of their existence, into our thinking. (1998, pp. 85–86)

For instance, in a study of the forces that may make trade unions undemocratic, Lipset, Trow, and Coleman (1962) deliberately chose to study a U.S. printing union. Because this union had unusually strong democratic institutions, it constituted a vital deviant case compared with most American unions of the period. Lipset et al.'s union was also deviant in terms of a highly respected theory that postulated an irresistible tendency toward oligarchy in all formal organizations.

So Lipset, Trow, and Coleman chose a deviant case because it offered a crucial test of a theory. As our understanding of social processes improves, we are increasingly able to choose cases on such theoretical grounds.

Changing the Size of Your Sample During the Research

So far, we have been discussing theoretical sampling as an issue at the *start* of a research study. However, we can also apply such sampling during the course of a piece of research. Indeed, one of the strengths of qualitative research design is that it often allows for far greater (theoretically informed) flexibility than in most quantitative research designs. As Mason puts it,

> Theoretical or purposive sampling is a set of procedures where the researcher manipulates their analysis, theory, and sampling activities interactively during the research process, to a much greater extent than in statistical sampling. (1996, p. 100)

Such flexibility may be appropriate in the following cases:

- As new factors emerge, you may want to increase your sample in order to say more about them (for instance, a gatekeeper has given you an explanation that you doubt on principle).

- You may want to focus on a small part of your sample in the early stages, using the wider sample for later tests of emerging generalizations.

- Unexpected generalizations in the course of data analysis lead you to seek out new deviant cases.

Alasuutari has described this process using the analogy of an hourglass:

A narrow case-analysis is broadened . . . through the search for contrary and parallel cases, into an example of a broader entity. Thus the research process advances, in its final stages, towards a discussion of broader entities. We end up on the bottom of the hourglass. (1995, p. 156)

Alasuutari (1995, p. 155) illustrates this hourglass metaphor through his own study of the social consequences of Finnish urbanization in the 1970s. He chose local pubs as a site to observe these effects and eventually focused on male "regulars." This led to a second study even more narrowly focused on a group in which drinking was heavier and many of the men were divorced. As he puts it, "Ethnographic research of this kind is not so much generalization as extrapolation . . . the results are related to broader entities" (Alasuutari, 1995, p. 155).

GENERALIZABILITY IS PRESENT IN A SINGLE CASE

The fourth and final way of thinking about how we generalize in qualitative research is far more radical than our earlier alternatives. According to this approach, since the basic structures of social order are to be found anywhere, it does not matter where we begin our research. Look at *any* case and you will find the same order.

 For this linguistically inspired approach, the possibility that something exists is enough. As Peräkylä suggests,

Social practices that are possible, i.e., possibilities of language use, are the central objects of all conversation analytical case studies on interaction in particular institutional settings. The possibility of various practices can be considered generalizable even if the practices are not actualized in similar ways across different settings. (2004, p. 297)

Peräkylä illustrates his argument by the example of his own study of AIDS counseling in a London teaching hospital (Peräkylä, 1995). This study focused on specific questioning practices used by counselors and their clients. As he puts it,

> As possibilities, the practices that I analysed are very likely to be generalizable. There is no reason to think that they could not be made possible by any competent member of (at least any Western) society. In this sense, this study produced generalizable results. The results were not generalizable as descriptions of what other counsellors or other professionals do with their clients; but they were generalizable as descriptions of what any counsellor or other professional, with his or her clients, can do, given that he or she has the same array of interactional competencies as the participants of the AIDS counselling sessions have. (Peräkylä, 2004, p. 297)

As the most cogent proponent of this view once put it, "Tap into whomsoever, wheresoever and we get much the same things" (Sacks, 1984b, p. 22).

Sacks had a strategy of working with any data that crossed his path. This clearly conflicts both with the standard approach of quantitative social scientists, who usually work with random samples from particular populations, and with the common defensiveness of their qualitative brethren about the representativeness of the cases that they study.

Sacks's lack of defensiveness on this issue stems from his argument about the obvious pervasiveness of the social forms (or what he calls the "machinery") with which he is concerned. For example, Sacks notes the ability of a child to learn a culture from very limited contacts and of the sociolinguist Whorf to build a Navajo grammar from talking to just one person (Sacks, 1992, Vol. 1, p. 485).

The pervasiveness of structures that these examples suggest imply to Sacks that it does not matter what data you select. As he argues,

> Now if one figures that that's the way things are . . . then it really wouldn't matter very much what it is you look at—if you look at it carefully enough. And you may well find that you [have] got an enormous generalizability because things are so arranged that you could get them; given that for a member encountering a very limited environment, he has to be able to do that, and things are so arranged as to permit him to. (Sacks, 1992, Vol. 1, p. 485)

However, apprentice researchers have to be very cautious about simply parroting Sacks's "solution" to the problem of the generalizability of research findings. This solution is really only appropriate to the most basic research on social order guided by theoretically sophisticated positions like Sacks's own **conversation analytic** (CA) approach (or, perhaps, French **structuralism**). If you are interested in this sort of research, you should now attempt Exercise 9.2.

Within CA, following Sacks,

> the baseline assumption is that the results are or should be generalizable to the whole domain of ordinary conversations, and to a certain extent even across linguistic and cultural boundaries. (Peräkylä, 1995, p. 214)

However, even Peräkylä notes that this depends on the type of CA research:

> Even though the most primordial conversational practices and structures—such as turn-taking or adjacency pairs—are almost universal, there are others, such as openings of telephone calls (see Schegloff, 1986; Houtkoop-Steenstra, 1991; Lindström, 1994), which show considerable variation in different cultures. This variation can only be tackled through gradual accumulation of studies on ordinary conversation in different cultures and social milieux. (1995, pp. 156–157)

Peräkylä's observation about the need for comparative work shows that even the most potentially radical approach, like CA, has to take seriously the issue of the empirical generalizability of its findings. Sometimes, an appeal to "possibilities" will be sufficient. Often, however, other examples will be required.

CONCLUDING REMARKS

In this chapter, we have set out various strategies you can use to defend your research against the charge that it "merely" depends upon a single case. My overall message is that there is usually no need to be defensive about the claims of qualitative research. As Becker argues,

> Sampling is a major problem for any kind of research. We can't study every case of whatever we're interested in, nor should we want to. Every scientific enterprise tries to find out something that will apply to everything of a certain kind by studying a few examples, the results of the study being, as we say "generalizable" to all members of that class of stuff. We need the sample to persuade people that we know something about the whole class. (1998, p. 67)

Following Becker, **sampling** is not a simple matter even for quantitative researchers. Indeed, as we have seen, the relative flexibility of qualitative research can improve the generalizability of our findings by allowing us to include new cases after initial findings are established.

The crucial issue here seems to be thinking through one's theoretical priorities. Providing that you have done that and can demonstrate a research design driven by those priorities, nobody should have cause for complaint.

So the secret seems to be to substitute theoretical cogency for the statistical language of quantitative research. In this sense, as Alasuutari has suggested, perhaps *generalizability* is the wrong word to describe what we attempt to achieve in qualitative research. As he puts it,

> Generalization is . . . [a] word . . . that should be reserved for surveys only. What can be analyzed instead is how the researcher demonstrates that the analysis relates to things beyond the material at hand . . . extrapolation better captures the typical procedure in qualitative research. (Alasuutari, 1995, pp. 156–157)

KEY POINTS

There are four positive answers to the question of how we can generalize from qualitative data:

- Combining qualitative research with quantitative measures of populations
- Using purposive sampling guided by time and resources
- Using theoretical sampling
- Using an analytic model that assumes that generalizability is present in the existence of *any* case

NOTE

1. As Clive Seale (personal correspondence) has pointed out, theoretical sampling may have more to do with generating theories than with empirical generalization. We take up Seale's point at the end of this chapter in relation to Alasuutari's argument that the idea of empirical generalization "should be reserved for surveys only" (Alasuutari, 1995, p. 156).

FURTHER READING

Clive Seale et al.'s edited book *Qualitative Research Practice* (2004, pp. 420–472) contains three very useful chapters on case studies by Flyvberg, Gobo, and Emerson. The most thorough book on this topic is Clive Seale's *The Quality of Qualitative Research* (1999). Other useful discussions are Jennifer Mason's *Qualitative Researching* (2002); Pertti Alasuutari's *Researching Culture* (1995), Chapter 12 ("Generalization"); and Howard Becker's *Tricks of the Trade* (1998), Chapter 3 ("Sampling"). Robert Stake's chapter "Case Studies" is a good account of the conventional qualitative methods position on generalizability (in N. Denzin and Y. Lincoln's edited *Handbook of Qualitative Research*, 2000), and Anssi Peräkylä's chapter "Reliability and Validity in Research Based Upon Transcripts" is an excellent, more specialist treatment (in David Silverman's edited *Qualitative Research*, 2004).

EXERCISE 9.1

Assume that you are studying a single case. On what basis do you think you might generalize from your findings? Distinguish your possible empirical contribution from any potential development of concepts.

EXERCISE 9.2

Imagine that you have the resources to study four cases of the phenomenon in which you are interested. Following our discussion of Stake (Table 9.2), draw up a typology to indicate the universe of cases potentially available. This typology should include between 6 and 12 possible cases.

Now explain why you propose to select your four cases in terms of the logic of purposive sampling.

EXERCISE 9.3

Using conversation analysis, Harvey Sacks has argued, "Tap into whomsoever, wheresoever and we get much the same things" (Sacks, 1984b, p. 22).

Consider how far your own theoretical model might allow you to use Sacks's argument to justify working with a very small data set.

CHAPTER 10

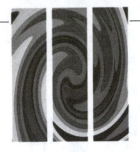

Writing a
Research Proposal

INTRODUCTION

Before you can set out on your research, you will usually need to submit a research proposal for approval. Although this is, in one sense, a bureaucratic hurdle, it is also an opportunity for you to make sure that you are perfectly clear about the direction you want your research to take.

Writing a research proposal allows you to clarify in your own mind that you have fully grasped the issues we have been discussing in Part II of this book. Moreover, it adds a useful discipline. Now it is not just a matter of convincing yourself but of convincing a potentially skeptical audience who will expect you to answer briefly and clearly a set of difficult questions. These questions are set out in Table 10.1.

177

The best way to answer these questions with brevity and clarity is to follow a standard format. Table 10.2 indicates a basic structure for a qualitative research proposal.

In preparing your proposal, it is worth bearing in mind the special difficulties qualitative researchers can face in achieving credibility. Particularly if you are within a university department where quantitative research is the

Table 10.1   Questions Answered by a Research Proposal

1. What? What is the purpose of my research? What am I trying to find out?

2. How? How will the proposed research answer these questions?

3. Why? Why is the research worth doing (and/or funding)? What will we learn and why is it worth knowing?

SOURCE: Adapted from Punch (1998), p. 268.

Table 10.2   A Structure for a Qualitative Research Proposal

1. Title

2. Abstract (further advice on titles and abstracts is found in Chapter 20)

3. Background or introduction (e.g., contemporary debates in social policy/social science)

4. Statement of purpose or aims: the research question ("The intellectual problem[s] I may help solve through this research is[are]. . . .")

5. Review of the relevant literature (showing the importance of the project in the context of the classic or definitive pieces of research in this area)

6. Methods (description of cases[s] chosen, procedures for data collection and data analysis in terms of [a] their appropriateness to your theoretical orientation and [b] how they satisfy criteria of validity and reliability [see Chapters 8 and 14])

7. Ethical issues (see Chapter 17)

8. Dissemination and policy relevance: explain how you will communicate your findings (see Chapters 17, 27, and 28)

9. A timetable indicating the length of time to be devoted to each stage of the research

10. References—use a standard system such as those available in the American Sociological Association guidelines, *The Publication Manual of the American Psychological Association*, or *The Chicago Manual of Style*

SOURCE: Adapted from Morse (1994), p. 228; Kelly (1998), pp. 115–121; and Rudestam and Newton (1992), p. 18.

mainstream, bear in mind that your proposal is likely to receive highly skeptical reviews.

Such skeptics may make the following assumptions:

- Qualitative research is unstructured

- The results of qualitative research are unpredictable

- The outcome is uncertain (Morse, 1994, p. 227)

Moreover, most experienced qualitative researchers will expect their potential students to be aware of such concerns and to have thought about how to respond to them. How, then, can you convince a potential university supervisor to support your research proposal?

Of course, following the format set out in Table 10.2 should help. But how should you frame your proposal in a way likely to maximize acceptance?

The following suggestions form the rest of this chapter:

- Aim for crystal clarity.

- Plan before you write.

- Be persuasive.

- Be practical.

- Make broader links.

AIM FOR CRYSTAL CLARITY

The proposal should use language and terminology that is understandable to an intelligent lay person as well as to a subject expert. (Cryer, 1996, p. 15)

Although it is tempting to seek to display your newly acquired technical jargon, bear in mind that your proposal is likely to be read, in the first instance, by a faculty member who is unlikely to be a specialist in your area of the discipline. So never be content with a proposal that can look like a stream of (perhaps undigested) theories or concepts. Always aim for clear language that describes your research in a way that nonspecialists can comprehend.

As Morse suggests, this means that you should resist the temptation to lapse into pure jargon: "because some of the reviewers will be from other disciplines, the proposal writer should assume nothing and explain everything" (Morse, 1994, p. 227).

By explaining everything, you will have demonstrated the ability to think (and write) clearly. Not only is this the way to write a research proposal, but also it is the best indicator that your research itself will be organized in a clear and logical way: "A sloppily prepared proposal will, at best, send a message to the agency that if it funds the proposal, the research may also be sloppy" (Morse, 1994, pp. 226–227).

For instance, your objectives "should be clear and it should be easy to decide whether they have been achieved or not" (Kelly, 1998, p. 117). The ways to achieve this are

- Be concise (there is no reason why a proposal for a piece of student research should be more than 500 words)

- Use short, simple sentences

- Use headings as in Table 10.2

PLAN BEFORE YOU WRITE

The writer must show that the design is the result of a series of decisions that she made because of knowledge gained from the . . . literature. (Marshall & Rossman, 1989, p. 13)

The proposal must demonstrate that it is based on an intelligent understanding of the existing literature, and also it must show that you have thought about the time you will need to conduct each stage of the research, from obtaining access to writing up your data analysis. So, as Arber notes, your research proposal will partly be judged by how you state you are going to use your time: "You need to adopt a systematic and logical approach to research, the key to which is the planning and management of your time" (1993).

Kelly (1998, pp. 120–121, adapted here) offers an example from an interview study planned to last 32 weeks:

Week 2: Submit proposal to University Ethical Committee

Week 6: Draw up sample

Week 8: Begin interviews

Week 15: End interviews

Week 23: Complete data analysis

Week 26: Send out first draft for comments

Week 32: Submit final report

We are not born with a natural ability to prepare research timetables! To help you plan such a timetable, seek the assistance of a trusted teacher in your department. Failing that, seek out an existing research student. With their help, make a list of all the options available in relation to your research problem, method, and case(s) to be studied. Now you are in a better position to write a reasoned research proposal that explains the actual choices you have made.

BE PERSUASIVE

It is easy to get very wrapped up in the subject and think that, because we are convinced of the particular value of our research, others will be too. The way in which the proposal is presented can enable the reader to appreciate what you are planning to do. (Kelly, 1998, p. 121)

Kelly is reminding us that, in framing a research proposal, one must think first of the audience who is going to read it (and judge it). This means that it should set out to convince such readers that this is something worth supporting:

The first principle of grantsmanship is to recognize that a good proposal is an argument . . . for the researcher's project. The proposal must make a case to the granting agency that the research question is interesting (and) that the study is important. . . . Thus the proposal must be written persuasively. (Morse, 1994, p. 226)

Morse is suggesting that you try to "sell" your proposal. This means that you must recognize that the craft of selling (e.g., your proposal, yourself) is not incongruent with working in a university. "Ivory towers" were never so isolated as the term suggests!

However, this persuasiveness must be balanced with a realistic understanding about what you can achieve within a few years as a single researcher. Like any good salesperson, do not oversell your goods!

BE PRACTICAL

One way to persuade nonspecialists, Morse suggests, is to show the specific ways that your research can address a social problem or solve an organizational trouble (e.g., staff turnover).

Such a concern with practical problems cannot be shrugged off even if you are proposing to do a purely academic piece of research with no expectation that it will be read outside the university. Academic funding bodies are increasingly demanding practical payoffs as well as analytic insights. For instance, Kelly (1998, p. 112) quotes a policy statement by the body that funds social science PhDs in the UK:

> Any lingering public perception of social science as a source of irrelevant, introverted and incoherent output is set for radical alteration. . . . In future, research which makes a difference to the health and wealth of the population, rather than merely supports "ivory tower" academic excellence will be the ESRC's priority. (Economic and Social Research Council newsletter, 1996)

The issue of *audiences* for your research is discussed further in Chapter 28. However, if what you are proposing is "basic research," i.e., a study deriving from debates and concepts internal to social science, then all is not lost. You can strengthen the persuasiveness of your case by showing nonspecialists why they ought to take your ideas seriously. One way to do this is to try to make broader links between your (very narrow) research proposal and wider issues.

MAKE BROADER LINKS

Realism need not mean that you must present your research as a narrow, anemic exercise. Even if you cannot cover every aspect of the field yourself, you should demonstrate your understanding of the broader implications of your proposed research.

One way to do that is to hint at a wider context: "Place the problem in context to show, for instance, that 'when we understand this, we will be able to work on that'" (Morse, 1994, p. 227).

Of course, you will be studying very few cases or maybe only a single case. Be positive about the gains as well as the losses of this! Show how a relatively small database will enable you to conduct an in-depth analysis (see Chapters 8 and 13). And argue that your case can indicate far larger phenomena: "The writer must show how, in examining a specific setting or group of individuals, she is studying a case of a larger phenomenon" (Marshall & Rossman, 1989, p. 12).

CONCLUDING REMARKS

If you eventually submit a research proposal with the kind of logical structure we have been suggesting, you may be plagued by a horrible thought. Will you actually have to follow, word for word, every idea you have suggested? If things turn out differently than the way you now expect, will your supervisor insist that you follow your self-prescribed route?

Fortunately, the answer to these kinds of questions is "generally no." Your research proposal should not be regarded as some kind of contract, which, if approved, is legally enforceable. Every practitioner recognizes that all researchers may, at some stage, find it worthwhile to divert from an initial path. This is particularly true of qualitative research, where analysis of **field** data often leads in unexpected but fruitful directions (see Chapter 12).

Of course, this does not mean that you may not be asked to justify any diversion. But any research proposal should not be set in stone for all time.

What, then, is the point of having to write an initial proposal? Let us suggest two answers to this reasonable question.

First, having had to work out a clear, persuasive research proposal is a wonderful discipline which will help you work out exactly what it is you want to do. As such, it can guide you in the initial stages of your research. Second, such a proposal helps others. In particular, it allows your potential supervisors to see if you are the kind of student who is able to think critically and, just as important, to move outside your own inner world in order to work out what others may be looking for.

This means that ultimately a research proposal should not be regarded as a legal contract but as a way of responding to the potential questions experienced researchers may ask about your plans. These questions are summarized in Table 10.3.

Table 10.3   Questions a Research Proposal Must Answer

1. Why should anyone be interested in the research?

2. Is the research design credible, achievable, and carefully explained?

3. Is the researcher capable of doing the research?

SOURCE: Adapted from Marshall and Rossman (1989), p. 2.

KEY POINTS

When preparing a research proposal, try to find answers to three questions suggested by Punch (1998, p. 268):

1. *What?* What is the purpose of my research? What am I trying to find out?

2. *How?* How will the proposed research answer these questions?

3. *Why?* Why is the research worth doing (and/or funding)? What will we learn and why is it worth knowing?

You can answer these questions better by following *five* principles:

1. Aim for crystal clarity.

2. Plan before you write.

3. Be persuasive.

4. Be practical.

5. Aim for broader links.

FURTHER READING

A research proposal is crafted according to the level of your research. Beginning researchers should turn to Moira Kelly's "Writing a Research Proposal" (in C. Seale [Ed.], *Researching Society and Culture*, 2004, pp. 111–122). At PhD level, useful references are Pat Cryer's *The Research Student's Guide to Success* (1996), Chapter 2; and Keith Punch's *Developing Effective Research Proposals* (2000) (a much shorter version is contained in Punch's book *Introduction to Social Research*, 1998, pp. 268–279). Beyond the PhD, you should consult Janice Morse's "Designing Funded Qualitative Research" (in N. Denzin and Y. Lincoln [Eds.], *Handbook of Qualitative Research*, 1994, pp. 220–235).

EXERCISE 10.1

Prepare a draft proposal about your research (no more than 1500 words) covering the following elements:

1. Title

2. Abstract

3. Background or introduction

4. Statement of purpose or aims

5. Review of the relevant literature

6. Methods (description of case[s] chosen, procedures for data collection, and data analysis)

7. Ethical issues

8. Practical relevance

9. A timetable

10. A set of preliminary references

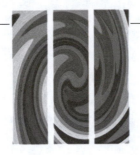

PART III

Analyzing Your Data

CHAPTER 11

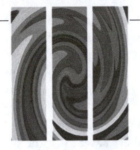

Beginning Data Analysis

CHAPTER OBJECTIVES

By the end of this chapter, you will be able to

1. Recognize the problem of "drowning in data"

2. Understand the uses of secondary data

3. Employ methods to kick-start your data analysis

4. Recognize the major issues involved in early analysis of different kinds of qualitative data

INTRODUCTION

After their first year of research, people have varying degrees of certainty about the future. As Coffey and Atkinson (1996) put it, the end of year 1 sees two kinds of researcher. The uncertain one feels he or she is drowning in data and asks: "I've collected all this data, now what should I do?" The other, more confident, researcher states, "I've collected all my data; now I'm going to analyze it and write it up."

The temptation might be to find merit in both positions. After all, self-questioning and self-confidence both seem to be worthy qualities in a researcher.

In fact, *neither* position is satisfactory and both reflect a more or less wasted first year of research:

> Both positions imply a woeful lack of appreciation of what is and can be meant by analysis. . . . [Such analysis] is a *pervasive* activity throughout the life of a research project. Analysis is not simply one of the later stages of research, to be followed by an equally separate phase of "writing up results." (Coffey & Atkinson, 1996, pp. 10–11, our emphasis)

Research designs that devote the first year solely to a literature review and/or data gathering may look excellent on paper. Indeed, they may be just the thing in quantitative studies more concerned with implementing predesigned measures rather than employing a theoretical imagination. But in most qualitative research, unless you are *analyzing* data more or less from day 1, you will always have to play catch-up.

That's all very well, you might respond, but where on earth am I going to get my data from on day 1? Surely, most of my first year is going to be spent on getting access to some research site or set of respondents and then, if successful, gathering my data. How is it going to be possible to start data analysis so quickly?

In the rest of this chapter, we show you how to kick-start your data analysis very early on. We then discuss ways to begin data analysis on many different kinds of qualitative data: interviews, field notes, texts, visual data, and transcripts of conversation.

KICK-STARTING DATA ANALYSIS

As already noted, you might well ask, where am I going to get my data on day 1? There are five very practical, complementary solutions to this puzzle:

- Analyze data already in the public sphere.
- Beg or borrow other people's data.
- Seek advice from your supervisor.
- Analyze your own data as you gather it.
- Ask key questions about your data.

We briefly discuss each strategy in the following paragraphs.

Analyze Data Already in the Public Sphere

Some types of naturally occurring materials are already waiting for you. For instance, when undergraduate students doing a dissertation at David's London college used to approach him with their concerns about gathering and analyzing data in, say, a 3-month time slot, he usually gave the following advice: Hop on a train to Colindale in North London. Turn right out of the station and you will come to a big building marked British Museum Newspaper Library. Now select a few newspapers that covered a particular story (e.g., Princess Diana's death, the O.J. Simpson trial, or the McCann baby missing in Portugal). Of course, you still lack a research problem and a method of analysis, and you will need to think long and hard about both. But you have your data, so go to it!

Needless to say, the public sphere contains much more than newspapers. There are all the other kinds of written texts, from novels to the contents of different Web sites on the Internet. There are the products of the broadcast media, radio, and TV programs, from phone-ins to soap operas and news broadcasts. Then there are those rare qualitative studies that reproduce large portions of data, making them available for your own reanalysis, perhaps following up different questions from those originally asked.

Even if you intend, in due course, to gather your own data, these materials are immediately available. As such, they provide a marvelous opportunity to refine your methods and to get a feel for the joys (and torments) of hands-on data analysis.

Beg or Borrow Other People's Data

Perhaps your research interests cannot be accommodated by data in the public sphere. If so, it is always worth making inquiries in your department about relevant data that other people may be willing to share with you.

Your supervisor is an obvious person to turn to. Having agreed to supervise you and thereby acknowledging a common research interest, it is probable that your supervisor will have already gathered data that may be relevant to your project. Don't be shy to ask if you might have access to it. This was exactly the strategy that David's student Vicki Taylor followed. He was delighted to pass on his data to her so she could explore a research problem that was different from his.

Of course, there may be ethical or other reasons why such access is not always possible. But most supervisors will be delighted, perhaps even flattered, if you are interested in their own data. After all, your research may lead to new ideas that will help them in their own work.

If your supervisor cannot deliver the goods, explore your various peer groups. Fellow research students in your department, perhaps two or three years into their research, may, like your supervisor, welcome passing on some of their own data. Or perhaps you can turn to members of study groups in your area or even to visiting speakers talking on a relevant topic.

Above all, you must remember that, in most disciplines, no brownie points are usually given for having your own data. It is the quality of your data *analysis* that will matter, not whether you can show how clever you were in accessing your data. Perhaps only in anthropology may the display of how, in pursuit of your "tribe," you have traveled thousands of miles, learned a foreign language, and endured endless hardships count for something—but not much, we suspect.

Even if you feel happier to have your own data, remember that this does not exclude the first two strategies. In the early stages, analysis of other people's data or public data may still give you the impetus you need for research "liftoff" when you are ready to analyze your own materials.

You should now attempt Exercise 11.1.

Seek Advice From Your Supervisor

As an undergraduate, your main face-to-face contact with a faculty member may have been when you submitted a term paper or, occasionally, when you got some feedback after such a submission. However, this model of a student–staff relationship is totally inappropriate when you are doing your own research.

Supervisors are there to offer support when you most need it (see Chapter 18). If you feel that you are drowning in data, that is a prime time to ask for help.

One way they can help you gain focus is to suggest a small and hence achievable task. Two examples of such tasks from Becker and Wolcott follow:

- Offering a snap characterization of what seems to be happening in your data and asking you to respond to it. It really doesn't matter how wide of the mark this idea is if it can get you to start working with your data (Becker, 1998)

- Asking you to take "some manageable *unit of one* as a focus" (Wolcott, 1990, p. 69, discussed at greater length in Chapter 5). In this way, instead of confronting your data as one large, threatening mass, you can narrow down and achieve a focus on one topic, one activity, or one day (or one minute).

These kinds of tasks should help you overcome the kinds of mental blocks we all too readily erect for ourselves when first confronting data. If we are set a small task, we are more likely to succeed and to gain confidence. Moreover, through such small tasks, we can start to see subtleties in our data that may be hidden if we ask big questions at the outset. As Becker (1998) reminds us, don't overtheorize early on in data analysis. Instead, begin from a situation or a piece of data and then build theories out of this limited material.

Analyze Your Own Data as You Gather It

Data analysis should happen not only after all your data has been safely gathered. Even if you only have one interview or recording or set of field notes, go to it! Where appropriate, start transcribing. In all cases, start reviewing your data in the light of your research questions.

Now is the time to test out methods, findings, and concepts. Here are some good questions to ask yourself:

- Do I feel comfortable with my preferred method of data analysis (e.g., grounded theory, narrative, conversation, or discourse analysis)?

- Is my data-analysis method suggesting interesting questions?

- Is it giving me a strong grip on my data that looks as though it might generate interesting generalizations?

- Do previous research findings seem to apply to my data? If not, why not? If so, how can I use my data to develop these findings?

- How do particular concepts from my preferred model of social research apply to my data? Which concepts work best and hence look likely to be most productive?

None of these questions can be properly answered from the armchair or drawing board. No matter how elegant your original research proposal, its application to your first batch of data is always salutary. In most qualitative research, sticking with your original research design can be a sign of inadequate data analysis rather than demonstrating a welcome consistency.

None of this will you know until you begin analyzing your data. Of course, this will mean committing yourself to writing up your analysis at a very early stage. As Wolcott (1990, p. 20) argues, "You cannot begin writing early enough." Even a 200-word shot at data analysis will give your supervisor something to go on. And even if your understandable initial hesitancy means that you are not "off and running," at least you will have started.

You should now attempt Exercise 11.2.

Ask Key Questions About Your Data

Of course, what is a "key" question will depend on your research topic and your preferred model of qualitative research. Although this means that there are few if any "free-floating" key questions, the following list has worked with David's own students and is worth posing about your own research:

- What are the main units in your data and how do they relate to one another? Remember that no meaning resides in a single unit and so everything depends on how your units fit together. This is an issue of articulation.

- Which categories are actually used by the people you are studying? Remember that, unlike quantitative researchers, we do not want to begin with our own categories at the outset. This is an issue of *definition*.

- What are the contexts and consequences of your subjects' use of categories? Remember that it is rarely right to ask *why?* questions before you have identified the local phenomena involved. This is an issue of *hows?* and *whats?*

- How do your difficulties in the field over, say, access and how you are defined by your research subjects provide you with further research topics? Remember that the beauty of qualitative research is that it offers the potential for us to topicalize such difficulties rather than just treat them as methodological constraints. This is an issue of the creative use of *troubles*.

So far we have been discussing ways to kick-start your data analysis. However, our attempt to offer useful tips for any kind of study has meant that we have had to talk about qualitative research in general. We now want to move to a lower level of generality and to examine how you may begin to analyze different kinds of qualitative data. We will consider five different kinds of data:

- Interviews

- Field notes

- Texts

- Visual data

- Transcripts

For each data source, we will offer an example of how, in a particular study, data analysis took off.

INTERVIEWS

In Chapter 4, we examined the various ways that researchers can read sense into answers that respondents give to open-ended interview questions. The most popular approach is to treat respondents' answers as describing some external reality (e.g., facts, events) or internal experience (e.g., feelings, meanings). Following this approach, it is appropriate to build into the research design various devices to ensure the accuracy of your interpretation, so you can check the accuracy of what your respondents tell you by other observations (see Chapter 14 on the method of **triangulation**). And you can treat such measures as intercoder agreement (see Chapter 14) and computer-assisted qualitative data programs (see Chapter 13) as a means of securing a fit between your interpretations and some external reality. Let us call this a realist approach to interview data.

As Clive Seale has pointed out (personal correspondence), realism is here used in the sense of the literary genre whose aim is to describe the gritty reality of people's lives. In this approach, typical of tabloid journalism, confessional stories are gathered and presented to the reader as new "facts" about personalities. This form of realism has had much influence on qualitative research (see Atkinson & Silverman, 1997).

An alternative approach treats interview data as accessing various stories or narratives through which people describe their world (see Holstein & Gubrium, 1995). This approach claims that, by abandoning the attempt to treat respondents' accounts as potentially true pictures of reality, we open up for analysis the culturally rich methods through which interviewers and interviewees, in concert, generate plausible accounts of the world. Although this second approach may use similar measures to achieve *quality control* (e.g., group data sessions to ensure agreement about the researchers' reading of a transcript), these measures are used in pursuit of a different, narrated reality in which the *situated*, or locally produced, nature of accounts is to the fore.

We are aware that many readers of this volume will favor the former approach. At the same time, we do not want to neglect the latter, **narrative** approach—particularly as it is closer to David's own theoretical orientation. Fortunately, there are examples available that show how you can kick-start a piece of interview research using both these approaches.

Miller and Glassner (2004) describe a study involving in-depth, open-ended interviews with young women (aged 13 to 18) who claim affiliation with youth gangs in their communities (Miller, 1996). These interviews follow the completion of a survey interview administered by the same researcher.

Here is how the authors describe the purposes of each form of data:

> While the survey interview gathers information about a wide range of topics, including the individual, her school, friends, family, neighborhood, delinquent involvement, arrest history, sexual history, and victimization, in addition to information about the gang, the in-depth interview is concerned exclusively with the roles and activities of young women in youth gangs, and the meanings they describe as emerging from their gang affiliation. (Miller & Glassner, 2004, p. 131)

Let us focus on the data that Miller obtained from her in-depth interviews. This is one example:

Describing why she joined her gang, one young woman told Miller, "Well, I didn't get any respect at home. I wanted to get some love and respect from somebody somewhere else." (Miller & Glassner, 1997, p. 107)

Here is another respondent's explanation of why she joined a gang: "I didn't have no family. . . . I had nothin' else" (1997, p. 107).

Another young woman, when asked to speculate on why young people join gangs, suggested,

> Some of 'em are like me, don't have, don't really have a basic home or steady home to go to, you know, and they don't have as much love and respect in the home so they want to get it elsewhere. And, and, like we get, have family members in gangs or that were in gangs, stuff like that. (1997, p. 107)

Let us assume that you have gathered this data and now want to begin analysis. Put at its starkest, what are you to do with it?

In line with the realist approach, using software programs such as ETHNOGRAPH or NUD•IST (see Chapter 13), you may start by coding respondents' answers into the different sets of reasons that they give for participation in gangs. From this data, two reasons seem to predominate: *push* factors (unsupportive families) and *pull* factors (supportive gangs).

Moreover, given the availability of survey data on the same respondents, you are now in a position to correlate each factor with various background characteristics that they have. This seems to set up your research in good shape. Not only can you search for the subjective meanings of adolescent gangs, but also you can relate these meanings to objective **social structures**.

The realist approach thus has a high degree of plausibility to social scientists who theorize about the world in terms of the impact of (objective) social structures upon (subjective) dispositions. Moreover, the kind of research outputs that it seeks to deliver are precisely those demanded by "users" in the community, seeking immediate practical payoffs from social science research.

However, say we are not entirely satisfied by the apparent plausibility of realism. How can the narrative approach kick-start data analysis?

Miller and Glassner (2004, pp. 134–135) suggest that one way to begin is to think about how respondents are using culturally available resources in order to construct their stories. They refer to Richardson's suggestion that "participation in a culture includes participation in the narratives of that culture, a general understanding of the stock of meanings and their relationships to each other" (Richardson, 1990, p. 24).

How, then, can the previous data be read in these terms? The idea is to see respondents' answers as *cultural stories*. This means examining the rhetorical force of what interviewees say, as "interviewees deploy these narratives to make their actions explainable and understandable to those who otherwise may not understand" (Miller & Glassner, 1997, p. 107).

In the data already presented, Miller and Glassner note that respondents make their actions understandable in two ways. First, they do not attempt to challenge public views of gangs as bad. But, second, they do challenge the notion that the interviewee herself is bad.

However, Miller and Glassner note that not all their respondents glibly recycle conventional cultural stories. As they put it,

Some of the young women go farther and describe their gang involvement in ways that directly challenge prevailing stereotypes about gangs as groups that are inherently bad or antisocial and about females' roles within gangs. (1997, p. 108)

This is some of the respondents' accounts that they have in mind:

It was really, it was just normal life, the only difference was, is, that we had meetings.

[We] play cards, smoke bud, play dominoes, play video games. That's basically all we do is play. You would be surprised. This is a bunch of big kids. It's a bunch of big old kids in my set. (1997, p. 109)

In accounts like these, Miller and Glassner argue that there is an explicit challenge to what the interviewees know to be popular beliefs about youth gangs. Instead of accepting the conventional definition of their behavior as "deviant," the girls attempt to convey the normalcy of their activities.

These narratives directly challenge stereotypical cultural stories of the gang. Following Richardson, Miller and Glassner refer to such accounts as "collective stories," which "resist the cultural narratives about groups of people and tell alternative stories" (Richardson, 1990, p. 25).

Miller's research on adolescent gang culture follows an earlier study of American adolescents' perception and use of illegal drugs. In this study, Glassner and Loughlin (1987) treat interview responses as *both* culturally defined narratives and as possibly factually correct statements. So, for instance, when someone says she uses marijuana because her friends do, Glassner and Loughlin (1987, p. 35) take this to suggest *two* findings:

> She has made use of a culturally prevalent way of understanding and talking about these topics [identifying a narrative].
> We now have evidence that marijuana smoking is part of peer gatherings [the realist version].

Glassner and Loughlin argue that narrative analysis works through examining the nature and sources of the "frame of explanation" used by the interviewee. However, the character of what the interviewee is saying can also be treated, through a realist approach, as a factual statement and validated by observation (e.g., of the series of interactions through which her friends' use comes to affect her own).

If we treat interviewees' responses as factual statements, then it becomes crucial to ask, "Can we believe the kids?" Clearly, the authors take this to be a serious question, arguing that, indeed, we should trust (their report of) what the kids are saying. They base this assertion on a set of claims about how rapport was established with subjects: interviewers were accepted as peer-group members, showed "genuine interest" in understanding the interviewee's experiences and guaranteed confidentiality (1987, p. 35).

Calling their approach a "methodology for listening," Glassner and Loughlin are thus centrally concerned with "seeing the world from the perspective of our subjects" (1987, p. 37). In this respect, they share the same assumptions about the authenticity of experience as do other realists and **emotionalists**. However, their sensitive address of the narrative forms from which perspectives arise suggests an alternative path for interview analysis (for a more developed version of the narrative approach, see Gubrium & Holstein, 1997).

FIELD NOTES

Tape-recorded interviews, like texts and tapes of **naturally occurring** interaction, allow you to return to your data in its original form as often as you wish. The problem with field notes is that you are stuck with the form in which you made them at the time and that your readers will only have access to how you recorded events.

There are two partial solutions to this problem: following strict conventions in writing field notes and adhering to a consistent theoretical orientation. The issue of field note conventions will be discussed in Chapter 12. In this chapter, we discuss an observational research study that began from a well-defined theory.

In the early 1980s, David obtained access to a number of clinics treating cancer patients in a British National Health Service (NHS) hospital. Following Strong's (1979) account of the "ceremonial order of the clinic," David was interested in how doctors and patients presented themselves to each other. For instance, Strong had noted that NHS doctors would adhere to the rule "politeness is all" and rarely criticize patients to their faces.

While at the hospital, David noticed that one of the doctors regularly seemed to "go missing" after his morning clinics. His curiosity aroused, he made inquiries. He discovered that most afternoons the doctor was conducting his "private" practice at consulting rooms in a salubrious area of London's West End. Nothing ventured, nothing gained, so David tried asking this doctor if he could "sit in" on the doctor's private practice. To David's great surprise, the doctor consented on condition that David did not tape-record. David happily agreed, even though this meant that his data was reduced to (what he saw as) relatively unreliable field notes.

Obviously, in making field notes, one is not simply recording data but also analyzing it. The categories you use will inevitably be theoretically saturated— whether or not you realize it! Given David's interest in Strong's use of Goffman's (1974) concept of frames, he tried to note down the activities through which the participants managed their identities. For instance, he noted how long the doctor and patient spent on social "small talk" and how subsequent appointments were arranged.

However, if the researcher is physically present, two different kinds of issues should never be neglected:

- What you can see (as well as hear)

- How you are behaving/being treated

What You Can See

Both NHS clinics were held in functional rooms, with unadorned white walls, no carpets, simple furniture (a small desk, one substantial chair for the doctor and a number of stacking chairs for patients, families, and students). Like most NHS hospitals, heating pipes and radiators were very obtrusive.

To enter the consulting rooms of the private clinic was to enter a different world. The main room had the air of an elegant study, perhaps not unlike the kind of room in a private house where a wealthy patient might have been visited by an 18th-century doctor. The walls were tastefully painted and adorned with prints and paintings. The floor had a fine carpet. The furniture was reproduction antique and included a large, leather-topped desk, several comfortable armchairs, a sofa, a low table covered with coffee table books and magazines, and a bookcase that held ivory figures as well as medical texts. Plants were placed on several surfaces, and the room was lit by an elegant central light and a table lamp. To add an executive touch, there were three phones on the desk, as well as a pen in a holder.

This room established an air of privacy as well as luxury. At the NHS clinics, patients were nearly always examined in curtained-off areas. Here, however, the examination couch was in a separate room, which could only be entered through the consulting room. Although more functional than the latter, it was nonetheless carpeted and kept at a high temperature to keep patients warm. Even the doctor himself might knock before entering this examination room while the patient was dressing or undressing.

How You Are Being Treated

The emphasis on privacy in British "private" medicine creates a special problem for the researcher. While at the NHS clinics, David sheltered happily behind a nametag, but at the private clinic his presence was always explained, if ambiguously ("Dr. Silverman is sitting in with me today, if that's all right?"). Although identified and accepted by the patient, David remained uncomfortable in his role in this setting. Its air of quiet seclusion made him feel like an intruder.

Like the doctor, David found himself dressing formally and would always stand up and shake hands with the patient. He could no longer merge into the background as at the NHS clinics. He regularly experienced a sense of intruding on some private ceremony.

His impression was that the private clinic encouraged a more personalized service and allowed patients to orchestrate their care, control the agenda, and obtain some "territorial" control of the setting. In David's discussion of the data, like Strong, he cites extracts from consultations to support these points, while referring to deviant cases and to the continuum of forms found in the NHS clinics.

David's interest in how observers are treated in medical settings is nicely demonstrated in Peräkylä's (1989) study of a hospital ward for terminally ill people. Peräkylä shows how staff use a psychological frame to define themselves as objective surveyors of the emotional reactions of such patients. The psychological frame is a powerful means of resolving the identity disturbances found in other frames—when a patient resists practical or medical framing, staff can explain this in terms of the patient's psychological state.

However, the psychological frame also turns out to be highly relevant to understand staff's response to Peräkylä himself. By seeing him as a researcher principally interested in patients' feelings, the staff had a ready-made explanation of his presence to give to patients and also were able to guess which of their own activities might need explaining to him.

Like Peräkylä, by examining his own involvement in the framing of the interaction, and using his eyes as well as his ears, David had kick-started his analysis. However, were there other ways in which he could systematically compare the two NHS clinics with the private clinic? In Chapter 12, we discuss some simple quantitative measures he used in order to respond to this problem.

TEXTS

Quantitative researchers try to analyze written material in a way that will produce reliable evidence about a large sample. Their favored method is **content analysis**, in which the researchers establish a set of categories and then count the number of instances that fall into each category. The crucial requirement is that the categories are sufficiently precise to enable different coders to arrive at the same results when the same body of material (e.g., newspaper headlines) is examined (see Berelson, 1952).

In qualitative research, small numbers of texts and documents may be analyzed for a very different purpose. The aim is to understand the participants' categories and to see how these are used in concrete activities like telling stories (Propp, 1968; Sacks, 1974), assembling files (Cicourel, 1968; Gubrium & Buckholdt, 1982), or describing "family life" (Gubrium, 1992).

The constructionist orientation of many qualitative researchers thus means that they are more concerned with the processes through which texts depict reality rather than with whether such texts contain true or false statements. As Atkinson and Coffey put it,

> In paying due attention to such materials, however, one must be quite clear about what they can and cannot be used for. They are "social facts," in that they are produced, shared and used in socially organized ways. They are not, however, transparent representations of organizational routines, decision-making processes, or professional diagnoses. They construct particular kinds of representations with their own conventions. (2004, p. 58)

The implications of this are clear:

Documentary sources are not surrogates for other kinds of data. We cannot, for instance, learn through written records how an organization actually operates day-by-day. Equally, we cannot treat records—however "official"—as firm evidence of what they report. . . . This recognition on reservation does not mean that we should ignore or downgrade documentary data. On the contrary, our recognition of their existence as social facts (on constructions) alerts us to the necessity to treat them very seriously indeed. We have to approach documents for what they are and what they are used to accomplish. (2004, p. 58)

What does it mean to approach texts "for what they are"? Let us take a concrete example. In two of Sacks's lectures, he refers to a *New York Times* story about an interview with a navy pilot about his missions in the Vietnam War (Sacks, 1992, Vol. 1, pp. 205–222, 306–311). Sacks is especially interested in the story's report of the navy pilot's reported answer to a question in the following extract.

The Navy Pilot Story

How did he feel about knowing that even with all the care he took in aiming only at military targets, someone was probably being killed by his bombs?

I certainly don't like the idea that I might be killing anybody," he replied. "But I don't lose any sleep over it. You have to be impersonal in this business. Over North Vietnam I condition myself to think that I'm a military man being shot at by another military man like myself. (Sacks, 1992, Vol. 1, p. 205)

Sacks invites us to see how the pilot's immediate reply ("I certainly don't like the idea") shows his commitment to the evaluational scheme offered by the journalist's question. For instance, if the pilot had instead said, "Why do you ask?" he would have shown that he did not necessarily subscribe to the same moral universe as the reporter (and, by implication, the readers of the article).

Having accepted this moral schema, Sacks shows how the pilot now builds an answer that helps us see him in a favorable light. The category "military man" works to defend his bombing as a category-bound activity, which reminds us that this is, after all, what military pilots do. The effect of this is magnified by the pilot's identification of his coparticipant as "another military man like myself." In this way, the pilot creates a pair (military man/military man) with recognizable mutual obligations (bombing/shooting at the other). In terms of this pair, the other party cannot properly complain or, as Sacks puts it, "There are no complaints to be offered on their part about the error of his ways, except if he happens to violate the norms that, given the device used, are operative" (1992, Vol. 1, p. 206).

Notice also that the pilot suggests that "you have to be impersonal in this business." Note how the category "this business" sets up the terrain on which the specific pair of military men will shortly be used. So this account could be offered by either pair-part.

However, as Sacks argues, the implication is that "this business" is one of many where impersonality is required. For,

> if it were the case that, that you had to be impersonal in this business held only for this business, then it might be that doing this business would be wrong in the first instance. (1992, Vol. 1, p. 206)

Moreover, the impersonality involved is of a special sort. Sacks points out that we hear the pilot as saying not that it is unfortunate that he cannot kill "personally" but rather that being involved in this "business" means that one must not consider that one is killing persons (1992, Vol. 1, 209).

However, the pilot is only *proposing* a pair of military man–military man. In that sense, he is inviting the North Vietnamese to "play the game" in the same way a child might say to another, "I'll be third base." However, as Sacks notes, in children's baseball, such proposals can be rejected:

> If you say "I'll be third base," unless someone else says "and I'll be . . . " another position, and the others say they'll be the other positions, then you're not that thing. You can't play. (1992, Vol. 1, p. 307)

Of course, the North Vietnamese indeed did reject the pilot's proposal. Instead, they proposed the identification of the pilot as a "criminal" and defined themselves as "doing police action."

As Sacks notes, these competing definitions had implications that went beyond mere propaganda. For instance, if the navy pilot were shot down, then the Geneva Conventions about his subsequent treatment would only properly be applied if he indeed were a "man" rather than a "criminal" (1992, Vol. 1, p. 307).

Sacks's analysis derives from his particular way of treating texts (like Atkinson and Coffey) as representations. Like Garfinkel (1967), Sacks wanted to avoid treating people as "cultural dopes," representing the world in ways that some culture demanded. Instead, Sacks approached **culture** as an "inference-making machine": a descriptive apparatus, administered and used in specific contexts. The issue for Sacks was not to second-guess societal members but to try to work out "how it is that people can produce sets of actions that provide that others can see such things . . . [as] persons doing intimacy . . . persons lying, etc." (1992, Vol. 1, p. 119).

Given that many categories can be used to describe the same person or act, Sacks's task was "to find out how they [members] go about choosing among the available sets of categories for grasping some event" (1992, Vol. 1, p. 41).

So Sacks does not mean to imply that "society" determines which category one chooses. Instead, he wants to show the active interpretive work involved in rendering any description and the local implications of choosing any particular category. Whether or not we choose to use Sacks's precise method, he offers an inspiring way to begin to analyze the productivities of any text.

VISUAL DATA

Visual data is a very broad category which can encompass anything from videos to photographs to naturally occurring observational data like that discussed in the section on British private medicine and to such aspects of our environment like street signs and advertisements (see Emmison & Smith, 2000).

The analysis of visual data can be very complicated and, in some hands, can be so overtheorized that one feels that the theoretical tail is wagging the empirical dog! To simplify matters for the beginning researcher, we will use as an example a relatively straightforward study and illustrate how data analysis took off.

Sharples, Davison, Thomas, and Rudman (2003) had the interesting idea of studying the kinds of photographs made by children. A total of 180 children of three different ages (7, 11, and 15) were given single-use cameras and asked to use them in any way they pleased over a weekend. Over 4300 photographs were generated by this means.

Data analysis took off through using a form of content analysis that produced a kind of "radar screen . . . a two-dimensional scatterplot showing the principal axes of variability" (Sharples et al., p. 311). This data was set up in this way in order to answer some early, key research questions:

- What is the content of each photograph?

- Are the people or objects shown posed?

- Who are the people shown?

- How do each of these features vary by the age of the photographer?

The analysis showed significant variation by the age of the child. For instance, 7-year-old children were more likely to take photographs of toys and other possessions. They also took more photographs of their home and family. By contrast, the 11-year-olds concentrated on outdoor and/or animal photographs (usually their pets), whereas the 15-year-olds mainly took photographs of their friends, usually of the same sex and often in "informal and striking poses" (pp. 316–317).

This study shows that an apparently simple count of such apparently basic features can raise a number of interesting issues. In this case, the researchers sought to pursue these issues by qualitative interviews with their child photographers.

Following the suggestion in the section titled "Ask Key Questions About Your Data," this study took off by beginning with descriptive questions of *what?* and *how?* This generated *why?* questions, which they later sought to answer through interviews with subjects. The interviews also allowed the comparison of the categories that the researchers used with those used by the children themselves.

TRANSCRIPTS

Like any kind of data, the analysis of tapes and transcripts depends on the generation of some research problem out of a particular theoretical orientation. As with the writing of field notes, the preparation of a transcript from an audio- or videotape is a theoretically saturated activity. Where there is more than one researcher, debate about what you are seeing and hearing is never just about collating data—it is data *analysis*. But how do you push the analysis beyond an agreed transcript?

The temptation is to start at line 1 of your transcript and to work your way down the page making observations as you go. However, the danger of proceeding in this way is that your observations are likely to be ad hoc and commonsensical. Moreover, if you are committed to an approach (like CA or DA), which looks at how the participants coproduce some meaning, then beginning with a single utterance gets you off on the wrong foot. How else can you proceed?

In Chapter 6, we came across Mason's (1996) idea of formulating a research topic in terms of different kinds of puzzles. Identifying a puzzle can also be the way to kick-start the analysis of a transcript. Once you have found your puzzle, the best method is often to *work back and forth* through your transcript to see how the puzzle arises and is resolved.

As in the other sections, let us take a concrete example. David was working on some transcripts of parent-teacher interviews gathered in Australian schools by Carolyn Baker and Jayne Keogh (1995). The following examples involve a student, Donna (S); her parents (F and M); and her teacher (T). In Extracts 11.1 and 11.2, there are no audible responses from Donna or Donna's parents to a piece of advice from the teacher (• indicates turn-slots where receipts are absent):

Extract 11.1

T: that's the only way I can really (1.0) really help at the moment and (.) for Donna herself to um do a little bit more in class and not chat so much down the back with Nicky and (.) Joanne?

      (1.0)

T: um(2.0)

Extract 11.2

T: Or we maybe, if- our next unit of work, Donna? if it's (.) another group do you think you- you'd perform better not working with the same girls?

      (1.0)

T: work with a different, with someone different in the class?

      (2.0)

T: you'd prefer to work with the same girls

In Extract 11.3, Donna's father eventually responds after a pause in a turn-slot in which Donna might have spoken:

Extract 11.3

T: I- don't- know it's really the three of you got to pull up your socks sort of thing or (.) or you sit somewhere different but

      (2.0)

T: [( )

F: [I think you should sit somewhere different

Finally, in Extract 11.4, Donna does not respond to her father's advice:

EXTRACT 11.4

F: I think you should sit somewhere different

M: Mm?

F: well think of your marks it's just (4.0) it's pretty rubbishy

The absence of (spoken) responses by a student to her teacher's or parents' advice in Extracts 11.1–11.4 gave them the puzzle that kick-started their analysis (Silverman, Baker, & Keogh, 1997). Such silence is a puzzle because it does not appear to fit with what we know about conversation, where the absence of a response by someone selected for next turn is remarkable and accountable (Sacks, Schegloff, & Jefferson, 1974).

To try to solve this puzzle, they searched other data for comparable findings. In over sixty advice sequences in pre-HIV-test counseling, David had only one example of such a silent response to advice (Silverman, 1997). This is shown in Extract 11.5 [C = counselor, P = patient]:

EXTRACT 11.5

[A01] C: this is why we say hh if you don't know the person that

[A02]   you're with (0.6) and you're going to have sex with them hh

[A03]   it's important that you tell them to (0.3) use a condom

[A04]   (0.8)

[A05] C: or to practice safe sex that's what using a condom means.

[A06]   (1.5)

[A07] C: okay?

[A08]   (0.3)

[A09] P: uhum

[10]   (0.4)

[11] C: has your partner ever used a condom with you? (Silverman, 1997, p. 118)

Notice the 1.5-second pause at the second •. Because this follows a possible turn-completion point as C concludes her advice, the pause can be heard as P's pause. Moreover, C demonstrates that she monitors it this way by using "okay?" to go in pursuit of some utterance to indicate that at least P is listening. When, after a further pause, she obtains "uhum," C can now continue.

However, it is also worth noting C's explanation (or gloss), which follows "use a condom." As that phrase could also have been heard as terminating C's advice, she seems to have interpreted the 0.8-second pause that follows as representing an absent **continuer** and, therefore, a possible lack of understanding. So she provides her gloss in order, unsuccessfully as it turns out, to create a stronger environment in which to get a continuer.

Extract 11.5 shares one further similarity with the teacher–pupil advice sequences. The patient in Extract 11.5 is a 16-year-old person, by far the youngest of all the clients in the HIV counseling extracts.

On a nonanalytic level, what we seem to be dealing with here is the social problem well known to both professionals and parents: that is, the common nonresponse of adolescents when told what to do by adults (or even when asked questions). This social problem is seen massively in hospital clinics run for adolescents and evokes continual, unsuccessful attempts to get the child to speak (see Silverman, 1987). In Extracts 11.6–11.8 below, taken from such clinics, we also find nonresponse to advice (D = doctor, P = patient, and M = mother):

EXTRACT 11.6

D: What should we do about your diabetes? Because you've not been doing your testing (untimed pause)

D: I know at the moment your feeling sod all this altogether

P: Don't know

D: Would it help if we got off your back?

(untimed pause) (Diabetic clinic 1 [NH:17.7])

EXTRACT 11.7

D: The blood sugar is really too high

(untimed pause) (P is looking miserable)

M: We have to fight this all the way

D: One or two units, does this really upset you?

(untimed pause) (P is looking down and fiddling with her coat) (Diabetic clinic 2 [S:12.2])

EXTRACT 11.8

D: Um (2.0) but you're satisfied with your lip, are you, we don't want any-
       thing done to that?

M: She doesn't (1.0) it doesn't seem to worry her

D: Heh heh don't want anything done about any[thing?

M: [heh heh

D: Not your nose?

       (3.0) (Cleft-palate clinic [14.32-3])

Throughout Extracts 11.5–11.8, adolescents fail to respond in the second-turn position to advice and questions. In Extracts 11.5 and 11.6, they eventually offer a minimal response after a second prompt. By contrast, in Extracts 11.7 and 11.8, when these young patients fail to take a turn when nominated as next speaker, their mothers speak for them, offering a commentary on their child's behavior or feelings. Finally, in Extract 11.8, when D once more renominates the patient as next speaker, nothing is heard.

However, if David and his colleagues had stopped at the observation of a congruence between professional-client encounters involving young people in both medical and educational settings, they would only be restating a social problem well known to parents and professionals dealing with young people. We work on the assumption that the skills of social scientists arise precisely in their ability to look at the world afresh and hence hold out the possibility of offering insights to practitioners. The question was, then, how could they move from their commonplace observation to a social science analysis?

Earlier in this book, we suggested that qualitative research is at its strongest in answering questions like *how?* and *what?* rather than *why?* So their initial response was to shift the focus away from *explaining* their observation and moving toward locating its interactional *achievement*. Thus they asked, how is questioning and advice giving interactionally managed, turn by turn, where the ostensible answerer or advice recipient is apparently nonresponsive?

In multiparty professional–client settings, the recipient of a particular turn is not given by some institutional rule but is actively "worked at" by the participants. Extract 11.8 is a very nice example of this and is given here again:

EXTRACT 11.8

D: Um (2.0) but you're satisfied with your lip, are you, we don't want any-
       thing done to that?

M: She doesn't (1.0) it doesn't seem to worry her

D: Heh heh don't want anything done about any[thing?

M: [heh heh

D: Not your nose?

(3.0) (Cleft-palate clinic [14.32-3])

As we have already remarked, in line 1, D appears to nominate as next speaker someone who might appropriately make an assessment about her "lip." However, although the next speaker orients to this nomination (talking about "she" and "her" rather than "I" and "me" in line 3), she is not the next speaker so nominated. Moreover, when D appears to renominate M's daughter as next speaker (lines 4 and 6), although she is silent, M claims recipiency via her laughter at line 5.

Extract 11.8 shows that recipiency is constructed on a turn-by-turn basis. Moreover, even within a single turn, the recipient may be redefined. Notice, for instance, how D switches from the voice of "you" to "we" within line 1.

Such a switch is interactionally ambiguous. First, "we" may be heard as no more than the patronizing way of referring to organizational clients quite common in England (and, sometimes, the object of a sarcastic response, e.g., "me and who else?"). Second, in this local context, it creates the possibility that D's question about "lip satisfaction" is addressed to both or either mother and daughter. Indeed, it may be this very possibility that allows a parent to respond without a pause (in line 3) in a slot in which the child might have been expected to answer a question.

Extract 11.8, from a cleft-palate clinic, shows how the parties play with the ambiguity about who is the recipient of a particular question. Rather than treating ambiguity as a communication *problem*, the analysis has begun to show how the interactants can use ambiguity as a *resource*.

The same interpretation may be attached to the child's silence. Instead of treating this silence as indicating some *deficiency* on the part of the child, they argued that, faced with the ambivalence built into such questions and comments by teachers (and parents), silence can be treated as a display of interactional *competence*. Finally, moving on to the *why?* question, they speculated that this is because silence (or at least lack of verbal response) allows children to avoid implication in the collaboratively accomplished adult moral universe and, thus, enables them to resist the way in which an institutional discourse serves to frame and constrain their social competencies.

CONCLUDING REMARKS

In this chapter, we have shown how, using the four main kinds of qualitative data, you can begin data analysis. By generating a puzzle by early inspection of some data, whether your own or borrowed, you can kick-start any research project. In Chapter 12, we examine how data analysis can be developed after these first stages.

KEY POINTS

Avoid spending the first period of your research without analyzing any data. There are several ways to kick-start data analysis:

- Analyze data already in the public sphere

- Beg or borrow other people's data

- Seek advice from your supervisor

- Analyze your own data as you gather it

- Ask key questions about your data

When analyzing different kinds of qualitative data, the following issues arise:

Interviews: Is your aim to describe the gritty reality of people's lives (realism) or to access the stories or narratives through which people describe their worlds (constructionism)?

Field notes: You need to note what you can see (as well as hear) as well as how you are behaving and being treated.

Texts and visual material: Is your goal precise content analysis in which you establish a set of categories and then count the number of instances that fall into each category? Or is your aim to understand the participants' categories and to see how these are used in concrete activities like telling stories, assembling files, or taking photographs?

Transcripts: The preparation of a transcript from an audio- or videotape is a theoretically saturated activity. Where there is more than one researcher, sorting out what you are seeing and hearing is never just about collating data—it is data *analysis*.

FURTHER READING

Harry Wolcott's little book *Writing Up Qualitative Research* (Sage Qualitative Research Methods Series, Number 20, 1990), especially Chapter 2, is a helpful, informal guide to beginning data analysis. Other relevant sources are Amanda Coffey and Paul Atkinson's *Making Sense of Qualitative Data* (1996), Chapter 2, and Jennifer Mason's *Qualitative Researching* (2002). For further details of the case studies discussed in this chapter, see Jody Miller and Barry Glassner's "The Inside and the Outside: Finding Realities in Interviews," in David's edited collection *Qualitative Research* (2004); David's two monographs *Communication in the Clinic* (Silverman, 1987) and *Discourses of Counselling* (Silverman, 1997); and Harvey Sacks's *Lectures on Conversation* (Vol. 1, 1992), pages 205–222 and 306–311. If you are interested in using Internet data, consult Annette Markham's chapter "Internet Communication as a Tool for Qualitative Research" in David's book *Qualitative Research* (Silverman, 2004).

EXERCISE 11.1

This gives you the opportunity to think about relevant data sets to which you may have early access.

1. Review relevant data already in the public sphere, for instance on the media (from newspapers to television and radio to the Internet). Select a data set and begin to analyze it.

2. Ask your supervisor and/or fellow students about any relevant data that they might have that you could borrow either as a preliminary exercise or possibly to develop long-term collaboration. Do a brief analysis of some of it.

EXERCISE 11.2

This gives you an opportunity to analyze your own data as soon as you obtain it.

1. Which questions does your preferred method of data analysis suggest? What interesting generalizations can you start to pull out of your data?

2. Do previous research findings seem to apply to your data? If not, why not? If so, how can you use your data to develop these findings?

3. How do particular concepts from your preferred model of social research apply to your data? Which concepts work best and hence look likely to be most productive?

CHAPTER 12

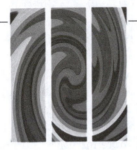

Developing Data Analysis

CHAPTER OBJECTIVES

By the end of this chapter, you will be able to

- Systematize and analyze field notes

- Know what to look for in audiotapes

- Feel confident about developing good data analysis

INTRODUCTION

Chapter 11 stressed the importance of early data analysis and showed how to kick-start such analysis. In this chapter, we will examine how you can develop your research after these beginnings. Although we will focus here just on observational and tape-recorded data, many of the suggestions equally apply to other kinds of qualitative data.

However, a checklist of suggestions can appear somewhat anemic and without substance. This chapter begins, therefore, with an account of how data analysis developed in one qualitative study. The beauty of qualitative research is that it gives you access to the nitty-gritty reality of everyday life viewed through a new analytic lens. Through the example that follows, you will learn how to take advantage of that access in order to focus and then refocus your data analysis.

A CASE STUDY

In the early 1980s (see Silverman, 1987, chaps. 1–6), David was directing a group of researchers studying a pediatric cardiology (child heart) unit. Much of their data derived from tape recordings of an outpatient clinic that was held every Wednesday.

It was not a coincidence that they decided to focus on this clinic rather than upon, say, interaction on the wards. Pragmatically, they knew that the clinic, as a scheduled and focused event lasting between 2 and 4 hours and tied to particular outcomes, would be likely to give them a body of good-quality data. By contrast, on the ward, tape recording would be much more intrusive and produce tapes of poorer quality because of multiple conversations and background noise. Even if these technical problems could be overcome, the (apparently) unfocused character of ward life meant that it would be far harder to see order than in the outpatient clinic. For instance, unlike the latter, there would be no obvious repetitive structures like scheduled meetings by appointment, physical examinations, and announcements of diagnosis and prognosis.

Of course, this does not mean that a researcher should never study apparently unfocused encounters—from the hospital ward to the street corner. But it does mean that, if you do, you must be prepared for long vigils and apparently unpromising data before researchable ideas start to gel.

At their hospital clinic, they became interested in how decisions (or "disposals") were organized and announced. It seemed likely that the doctor's way of announcing decisions was systematically related not only to clinical factors (like the child's heart condition) but also to social factors (such as what parents would be told at various stages of treatment). For instance, at a first outpatients' consultation, doctors would not normally announce to parents the discovery of a major heart abnormality and the necessity for life-threatening surgery. Instead, they would suggest the need for more tests and only hint that major surgery might be needed. They would also collaborate with parents who produced examples of their child's apparent wellness. This step-by-step method of information giving was avoided in only two cases. If a child was diagnosed as healthy by the cardiologist, the doctor would give all the information in one go and would engage in what the researchers called a "search and destroy" operation, based on eliciting any remaining worries of the parent(s) and proving that they were mistaken.

In the case of a group of children with the additional handicap of Down syndrome, as well as suspected cardiac disease, the doctor would present all the clinical information at one sitting, avoiding a step-by-step method. Moreover, atypically, the doctor would allow parents to make the choice about further treatment, while encouraging them to dwell on nonclinical matters like their child's "enjoyment of life" or friendly personality.

The researchers then narrowed their focus to examine how doctors talked to parents about the decision to have a small diagnostic test on their children. In most cases, the doctor would say something like this: "What we propose to do, if you agree, is a small test."

No parent disagreed with an offer that appeared to be purely formal—like the formal right (never exercised) of the Queen not to sign legislation passed by the British Parliament. For Down syndrome children, however, the parents' right to choose was far from formal. The doctor would say things to them like the following:

I think what we would do now depends a little bit on parents' feelings.

Now it depends a little bit on what you think.

It depends very much on your own personal views as to whether we should proceed.

Moreover, these consultations were longer and apparently more democratic than elsewhere. A view of the patient in a family context was encouraged and parents were given every opportunity to voice their concerns and to participate in decision making.

In this subsample, unlike the larger sample, when given a real choice, parents refused the test—with only one exception. Yet this served to reinforce rather than to challenge the medical policy in the unit concerned. This policy was to discourage surgery, all things being equal, on such children. So the democratic form coexisted with (and was indeed sustained by) the maintenance of an autocratic policy.

The research thus discovered the mechanics whereby a particular medical policy was enacted. The availability of tape recordings of large numbers of consultations, together with a research method that sought to develop hypotheses inductively, meant that David and his colleagues were able to develop their data analysis by discovering a phenomenon for which they had not originally been looking.

The lessons to be drawn from this study are summarized in Table 12.1.

Table 12.1   Four Ways to Develop Data Analysis

- Focus on data that is of high quality and is easiest to collect (tape recordings of clinics)
- Look at one process within that data (how medical "disposals" are organized)
- Narrow down to one part of that process (announcing a small diagnostic test)
- Compare different subsamples of the population (Down syndrome children and the rest)

In the second half of this chapter, we discuss the more general research strategies available to you when your data, as in the case study, is in the form of tape recordings of **naturally occurring data**. But perhaps you do not possess your data on tape. Does this mean that everything is lost?

In the next section, we attempt to show how you can shore up the quality of your field notes. Even if, in the final analysis, field notes can never rival the **reliability** of a good-quality tape and transcript, thoughtfully constructed field notes can provide the impetus for advanced data analysis.

FIELD NOTES AND DATA ANALYSIS

Why Detail Matters

> Field researchers seek to get close to others in order to understand their way of life. To preserve and convey that closeness, they must describe situations and events of interest in detail. (Emerson, Fretz, & Shaw, 1995, p. 14)

By preserving the details of interaction, you are in a better position to analyze the issues set out in Table 12.2.

Like any set of animating questions, the kind of issues set out in Table 12.2 reflect a particular **model** of the social world. As in David's study of heart clinics, Emerson et al. assume a **constructionist** or **ethnomethodological** model in which the meaning of events is not transparent but is actively constructed by the participants (**members**).

Two methodological imperatives flow from this model. First, a concern with what participants take to be *routine* or obvious. Second, a recognition that what is routine is best established through watching and listening to what people do

Table 12.2   Functions of Detailed Field Notes

- To identify and follow processes in witnessed events
- To understand how members themselves characterize and describe particular activities, events, and groups
- To convey members' explanations for when, why, or how particular things happen and, thereby, to elicit members' theories of the causes of particular happenings
- To identify the practical concerns, conditions, and constraints that people confront and deal with in their everyday lives and actions

SOURCE: Adapted from Emerson et al. (1995).

rather than asking them directly. So, unlike much **ethnographic** fieldwork, the interview is not regarded as a major research tool. Instead,

> the distinctive procedure is to observe and record naturally occurring talk and interaction . . . [while] it may be useful or essential to interview members about the use and meaning of specific local terms and phrases . . . the researcher's deeper concern lies in the actual, situated use of those terms in ordinary interaction. (Emerson et al., 1995, p. 140)

Such a concern with what participants take to be ordinary and unexceptional gives a clear focus to making and analyzing field notes. Data analysis can then develop through asking the sorts of questions set out in Table 12.3.

Two Ways of Developing Field Note Analysis

Two practical rules have been suggested for developing ethnographic work beyond the initial questions shown in Table 12.3:

- Thinking about what we can see as well as what we hear

- Expanding field notes beyond immediate observations

Using Your Eyes

In a study of the social organization of a restaurant, Whyte (1949) reaped rich rewards by using his eyes to observe the spatial organization of activities. More recently, in a study of interaction in hospital wards, Anssi Peräkylä (personal correspondence) notes how spatial arrangements differentiate groups

Table 12.3   Six Groups of Questions for Field Note Analysis

1. What are people doing? What are they trying to accomplish?

2. How exactly do they do this? What specific means and/or strategies do they use?

3. How do members talk about, characterize, and understand what is going on?

4. What assumptions are they making?

5. What do I see going on here? What did I learn from these notes?

6. Why did I include them?

SOURCE: Emerson et al. (1995), p. 146.

of people. There are the wards and patient rooms, which staff may enter any-time they need to. Then there are patient lounges and the like, which are a kind of public space. Both areas are quite different from areas like the nurses' room and doctors' offices, where patients enter only by invitation. Finally, if there is a staff coffee room, you never see a patient there.

As Peräkylä points out, one way to produce different categories of human beings in a hospital is the allocation of space according to categories. At the same time, this allocation is reproduced in the activities of the participants. For instance, the perceptive observer might note the demeanor of patients as they approach the nurses' room. Even if the door is open, they may stand outside and just put their heads around the door. In doing so, they mark out that they are encroaching on foreign territory.

Unfortunately, we have all become a little reluctant to use our eyes as well as our ears when doing observational work. However, these are exceptions. Stimson (1986) has noted how "photographs and diagrams are virtually absent from sociological journals, and rare in sociological books" (p. 641). He then discusses a room set out for hearings of a disciplinary organization responsible for British doctors. The Professional Conduct Committee of the General Medical Council sits in a high-ceilinged, oak-paneled room reached by an imposing staircase. There are stained-glass windows, picturing 16 crests and a woman in a classical Greek pose. As Stimson comments,

This is a room in which serious matters are discussed: the room has a pres-ence that is forced on our consciousness . . . speech is formal, carefully spoken and a matter for the public record. Visitors in the gallery speak only, if at all, in hushed whispers, for their speech is not part of the pro-ceedings. (1986, pp. 643–644)

In such a room, as Stimson suggests, even without anything needing to be said, we know that what goes on must be taken seriously. Stimson aptly contrasts this room with a McDonald's hamburger restaurant:

Consider the decorations and materials—plastic, paper, vinyl and poly-styrene, and the bright primary colours. [Everything] signifies transience. This temporary character is further articulated in the casual dress of cus-tomers, the institutionally casualized dress of staff and the seating that is constructed to make lengthy stays uncomfortable. (1986, pp. 649–650)

Stimson and Peräkylä show that ethnographers who fail to use their eyes as well as their ears are neglecting a crucial source of data. This lesson is most readily learned if you imagine a sighted person being forced to make sense of the world while blindfolded!

Expanded Field Notes

Fieldwork is so fascinating and coding usually so energy-absorbing, that you can get preoccupied and overwhelmed with the flood of particulars—the poignant quote, the appealing personality of a key informant. You forget to think, to make deeper and more general sense of what is happening, to begin to explain it in a conceptually coherent way. (Miles & Huberman, 1984, p. 69)

In order to make "deeper and more general sense of what is happening," Spradley (1979) suggests that observers keep four separate sets of notes:

1. Short notes made at the time

2. Expanded notes made as soon as possible after each field session

3. A fieldwork journal to record problems and ideas that arise during each stage of field work

4. A provisional running record of analysis and interpretation (discussed by Kirk & Miller, 1986, p. 53)

Spradley's suggestions help systematize field notes and thus improve their reliability (see Chapter 14). Like Spradley, Miles and Huberman offer systematic ways of expanding what gets recorded in field notes. They suggest writing "contact summary sheets" or extended memos after each observation (Miles & Huberman, 1984, pp. 50–51, 69–71).

An example of how to use a contact summary sheet to encourage analytic thinking is set out in Table 12.4.

Table 12.4   Questions for Contact Summary Sheets

- What people, events, or situations were involved?
- What were the main themes or issues in the contact?
- Which research questions did the contact bear most centrally on?
- What new hypotheses, speculations, or guesses about the field situations were suggested by the contact?
- Where should the fieldworker place most energy during the next contact, and what sorts of information should be sought?

SOURCE: Miles and Huberman (1984), p. 50.

Miles and Huberman suggest five reasons why such contact sheets are valuable:

1. To guide planning for the next contact

2. To suggest new or revised codes

3. To coordinate several fieldworkers' work

4. To serve as a reminder of the contact at a later stage

5. To serve as the basis for data analysis (adapted from Miles & Huberman, 1984, p. 51).

How we record data is important because it is directly linked to the quality of data analysis. In this sense, field notes and contact sheets are, of course, only a means to an end—developing the analysis.

Developing Analysis of Field Data

The move from coding to interpretation is a crucial one. . . . Interpretation involves the transcendance of "factual" data and cautious analysis of what is to be made of them. (Coffey & Atkinson, 1996, p. 46)

As Miles and Huberman (1984) point out, qualitative data comes in the form of words rather than numbers. The issue, then, is how we move from these words to data analysis.

They suggest that data analysis consists of three concurrent flows of activity: data reduction, data display, and conclusion drawing/verification (Miles & Huberman, 1984, p. 21):

- *Data reduction* "refers to the process of selecting, focusing, simplifying, abstracting, and transforming . . . 'raw' data" (p. 21). Data reduction involves making decisions about which data chunks will provide your initial focus.

- *Data display* is "an organized assembly of information that permits conclusion drawing and action taking" (p. 21). It involves assembling your data into displays such as matrices, graphs, networks, and charts, which clarify the main direction (and missing links) of your analysis.

- *Conclusion drawing* means "beginning to decide what things mean, noting regularities, patterns, explanations, possible configurations, causal flows and propositions" (1984, p. 22).

- *Verification* means testing the provisional conclusions for "their plausibility, their sturdiness, their 'confirmability'—that is, their validity" (p. 22).

Miles and Huberman demonstrate that in **field** studies, unlike much quantitative research, we are not satisfied with a simple coding of data. As we argued in Chapter 4, this means that qualitative researchers have to show how the (theoretically defined) elements that they have identified are assembled or mutually laminated. The distinctive contribution qualitative research can make is by utilizing its theoretical resources in the deep analysis of usually small bodies of publicly shareable data.

This means that coding your data according to some theoretical scheme should only be the first stage of your data analysis. You will then need to go on to examine how these elements are linked together. At this second stage, lateral thinking can help. For instance, you can attempt to give your chosen concept or issue a new twist, perhaps by pursuing a counterintuitive idea or by noting an additional feature little addressed in the literature. In any event, as we show in the next section, one way of achieving better data analysis is by a steadily more narrow focus.

Progressive Focusing in Fieldwork

We only come to look at things in certain ways because we have adopted, either tacitly or explicitly, certain ways of seeing. This means that, in observational research, data collection, hypothesis construction, and theory building are not three separate things but are interwoven with one another.

This process is well described by using an analogy with a funnel:

Ethnographic research has a characteristic "funnel" structure, being progressively focused over its course. Progressive focusing has two analytically distinct components. First, over time the research problem is developed or transformed, and eventually its scope is clarified and delimited and its internal structure explored. In this sense, it is frequently only over the course of the research that one discovers what the research is really "about," and it is not uncommon for it to turn out to be about something quite remote from the initially foreshadowed problems. (Hammersley & Atkinson, 1983, p. 175)

Atkinson (1992) gives an example of such a redefinition of a research problem. Many years after completing his PhD, Atkinson returned to his original field notes on medical education. He shows how the original data can be reread in a quite different way. Atkinson's earlier method had been to fragment his field notes into relatively small segments, each with its own category. For instance, a surgeon's description of postoperative complications to a surgical team was originally categorized under such headings as "unpredictability," "uncertainty," "patient career" and "trajectory." When Atkinson returns to it, it becomes an overall narrative, which sets up an enigma ("unexpected complications"), which is resolved in the form of a "moral tale" ("beware, unexpected things can always happen"). Viewed in this way, the surgeon's story becomes a text with many resemblances to a fairy tale!

Two studies of British medical clinics that David carried out in the 1980s also nicely illustrate Hammersley and Atkinson's funnel. As we showed, David's observation of a pediatric cardiology unit moved unpredictably in the direction of an analysis of disposal decisions with a small group of Down syndrome children. Similarly, David's research on cancer clinics, discussed in Chapter 9, unexpectedly led into a comparison of fee-for-service and state-provided medicine (Silverman, 1981, 1987).

These two cases had three features in common:

1. The switch of focus—through the "funnel"—as a more defined topic arose.

2. The use of the comparative method as an invaluable tool of theory building and testing.

3. The generation of topics with a scope outside the substantive area of the research. Thus, the "ceremonial orders" found in the cancer clinics are not confined to medicine, whereas the "democratic" decision making found with the Down children had unexpected effects of power with a significance far beyond medical encounters.

As we have noted elsewhere (Silverman, 2001), working this way parallels Glaser and Strauss's (1967) famous account of **grounded theory**. A simplified model of this involves these stages:

- An initial attempt to develop categories that illuminate the data

- An attempt to "saturate" these categories with many appropriate cases in order to demonstrate their relevance

- The development of these categories into more general analytic frameworks with relevance outside the setting

Glaser and Strauss use their research on death and dying as an example. They show how they developed the category of "awareness contexts" to refer to the kinds of situations in which people were informed of their likely fate. The category was then saturated and finally related to nonmedical settings where people learn about how others define them (e.g., schools).

Grounded theory has been criticized for its failure to acknowledge implicit theories that guide work at an early stage. It also is clearer about the generation of theories than about their test. Used unintelligently, it can also degenerate into a fairly empty building of categories or into a mere smoke screen used to legitimize purely empiricist research (see our critique of four qualitative studies in Chapter 15 and Bryman, 1988, pp. 83–87). At best, grounded theory offers an approximation of the creative activity of theory building found in good observational work, compared to the dire abstracted **empiricism** present in the most wooden statistical studies.

However, quantification should not be seen as the enemy of good field research. In the next section, we discuss one example of how simple tabulations were used to test an emergent hypothesis in the study of cancer clinics.

Using Tabulations in Testing Fieldwork Hypotheses

In the cancer study, David used a coding form that enabled him to collate a number of crude measures of doctor and patient interactions (Silverman, 1984). The aim was to demonstrate that the qualitative analysis was reasonably representative of the data as a whole. Occasionally, the figures revealed that the reality was not in line with David's overall impressions. Consequently, the analysis was tightened and the characterizations of clinic behavior were specified more carefully.

The crude quantitative data David had recorded did not allow any real test of the major thrust of this argument. Nonetheless, it did offer a summary measure of the characteristics of the total sample, which allowed closer specification of features of private and NHS clinics. In order to illustrate this, let us briefly show you the kind of quantitative data he gathered on topics like consultation length, patient participation, and the scope of the consultation.

David's overall impression was that private consultations lasted considerably longer than those held in the NHS clinics. When examined, the data indeed did show that the former were almost twice as long as the latter (20 minutes versus 11 minutes) and that the difference was statistically highly significant. However, David recalled that for special reasons, one of the NHS clinics had abnormally short consultations. He felt a fairer comparison of consultations in the two sectors should exclude this clinic and should only compare consultations taken by a single doctor in both sectors. This subsample of cases revealed that the difference in length between NHS and private consultations was now reduced to an average of less than 3 minutes. This was still statistically significant, although the significance was reduced. Finally, however, if he compared only *new* patients seen by the same doctor, NHS patients got 4 minutes more on average—34 minutes compared to 30 minutes in the private clinic. This last finding was not suspected and had interesting implications for the overall assessment of the individual's costs and benefits from "going private." It is possible, for instance, that the tighter scheduling of appointments at the private clinic may limit the amount of time that can be given to new patients.

As a further aid to comparative analysis, David measured patient participation in the form of questions and unelicited statements. Once again, a highly significant difference was found: on this measure, private patients participated much more in the consultation. However, once more taking only patients seen by the same doctor, the difference between the clinics became very small and was *not* significant. Finally, no significant difference was found in the degree to which nonmedical matters (e.g., patient's work or home circumstances) were discussed in the clinics.

This quantitative data was a useful check on overenthusiastic claims about the degree of difference between the NHS and private clinics. However, as we argued in Chapter 10, David's major concern was with the "ceremonial order" of the three clinics. He had amassed a considerable number of exchanges in which doctors and patients appeared to behave in the private clinic in a manner deviant from what they knew about NHS hospital consultations. The question was, would the quantitative data offer any support to his observations?

The answer was, to some extent, positive. Two quantitative measures were helpful in relation to the ceremonial order. One dealt with the extent to which the doctor fixed treatment or attendance at the patient's convenience. The second measured whether patients or doctor engaged in polite small talk with one another about their personal or professional lives. (David called this "social elicitation.") As Table 12.5 shows, both these measures revealed significant differences, in the expected direction, according to the mode of payment.

Table 12.5   Private and NHS Clinics: Ceremonial Orders

	Private Clinics (n = 42)	NHS Clinics (n = 104)
Treatment or attendance fixed at patients' convenience	15 (36%)	10 (10%)
Social elicitation	25 (60%)	31 (30%)

SOURCE: Adapted from Silverman (2001), p. 243.

NOTE: Percentage in parentheses indicates percentage in all such clinics.

Now, of course, such data could not offer proof of David's claims about the different interactional forms. However, coupled with the qualitative data, the data provided strong evidence of the direction of difference, as well as giving him a simple measure of the sample as a whole, which contexted the few extracts of talk he was able to use. Counting can be as arbitrary as qualitative interpretation of a few fragments of data. However, providing researchers resist the temptation to try to count everything, and base their analysis on a sound conceptual basis linked to actors' own methods of ordering the world, then both types of data can inform the analysis of the other.

In Chapter 14, we return to the role of counting as an aid to **validity** in qualitative research. In the case of observational studies, such counting will often be based on the prior coding of field notes. We now, therefore, turn to the issues that arise in such coding.

Limits in Coding Field Notes

The tabulations used in the cancer study derived from

that well-established style of work whereby the data are inspected for categories and instances. It is an approach that disaggregates the text (notes or transcripts) into a series of fragments, which are then regrouped under a series of thematic headings. (Atkinson, 1992, p. 455)

Such coding by thematic headings has recently been helped by computer-aided qualitative data analysis systems, as discussed in Chapter 13. In larger projects, the reliability of coding is also buttressed by training coders of data in procedures that aim to ensure a uniform approach.

However, there remain two problems with coding field notes. The first, and more obvious, problem is that every way of seeing is also a way of not seeing. As Atkinson points out, one of the disadvantages of coding schemes is that, because they are based on a given set of categories, they furnish "a powerful conceptual grid" (Atkinson, 1992, p. 459) from which it is difficult to escape. Although this "grid" is very helpful in organizing the data analysis, it also deflects attention away from uncategorized activities. Therefore, as Clive Seale (personal correspondence) has noted, "A good coding scheme would reflect a search for 'un-categorized activities' so that they could be accounted for, in a manner similar to searching for deviant cases."

The second, less obvious, problem is that, as we pointed out in Chapter 4, coding is not the preserve of research scientists. All of us "code" what we hear and see in the world around us. This is what Garfinkel (1967) and Sacks (1992) mean when they say that societal members, like social scientists, make the world observable and reportable.

Put at its simplest, this suggests that researchers must be very careful how they use categories. For instance, Sacks quotes from two linguists who appear to have no problem in characterizing particular (invented) utterances as "simple," "complex," "casual," or "ceremonial." For Sacks, such rapid characterizations of data assume "that we can know that [such categories are accurate] without an analysis of what it is [members] are doing" (1992, Vol. 1, p. 429).

How should we respond to Sacks's radical critique of ethnography? The first point is not to panic! Sacks offers a challenge to conventional observational work of which everybody should be aware. In particular, Sacks's lecture "Doing 'Being Ordinary'" (Sacks, 1992, Vol. 2, pp. 215–221) is essential reading for every fieldworker.

However, awareness does not mean that everybody has to follow Sacks's radical path. So one response is to state something like "thanks but no thanks." For instance, grounded theory is an equally respectable (and much more popular) way of theorizing (about) fieldwork.

To this effective but essentially defensive maneuver, we can add two more ambitious responses. First, we can seek to integrate Sacks's questions about *how* the social world is constituted with more conventional ethnographic questions about the *whats* and *whys* of social life (Gubrium & Holstein, 1997). Or, second, as we describe in the next section, we can make this everyday "coding" (or "interpretive practice") the object of inquiry by asking *how* questions about talk-in-interaction.

TRANSCRIPTS AND DATA ANALYSIS

The two main social science traditions that inform the analysis of transcripts of tapes are **conversation analysis** (CA) and **discourse analysis** (DA). For an introduction to CA, see ten Have (1998); for DA, see Potter and Wetherell (1987) and Potter (2004).

In this book, however, we are, of course, more concerned with the practicalities of doing qualitative research. In the rest of this chapter, we will, therefore, deal with two practical issues:

- The advantages of working with tapes and transcripts

- The elements of how to do analysis of such tapes

Why Work With Tapes?

The kinds of phenomena I deal with are always transcriptions of actual occurrences in their actual sequence. (Sacks, 1984b, p. 25)

The earlier ethnographers had generally relied on recording their observations through field notes. Why did Sacks prefer to use an audio recorder?

Sacks's answer is that we cannot rely on our recollections of conversations. Certainly, depending on our memory, we can usually summarize what different people said. But it is simply impossible to remember (or even to note at the time) such matters as pauses, overlaps, inbreaths, and the like.

Now whether you think these kinds of things are important will depend on what you can show with or without them. Indeed, you may not even be convinced that conversation itself is a particularly interesting topic. But, at least by studying tapes of conversations, you are able to focus on the "actual details" of one aspect of social life. As Sacks put it,

My research is about conversation only in this incidental way, that we can get the actual happenings of on tape and transcribe them more or less, and therefore have something to begin with. If you can't deal with the actual detail of actual events then you can't have a science of social life. (1992, Vol. 2, p. 26)

Tapes and transcripts also offer more than just "something to begin with." In the first place, they are a public record, available to the scientific community in a way that field notes are not. Second, they can be replayed and transcriptions can be improved and analyses take off on a different tack unlimited by the original transcript. As Sacks told his students,

I started to play around with tape recorded conversations, for the single virtue that I could replay them; that I could type them out somewhat, and study them extendedly, who knew how long it might take. . . . It wasn't from any large interest in language, or from some theoretical formulation of what should be studied, but simply by virtue of that; I could get my hands on it, and I could study it again and again. And also, consequentially, others could look at what I had studied, and make of it what they could, if they wanted to disagree with me. (1992, Vol. 1, p. 622)

A third advantage of detailed transcripts is that, if you want to, you can inspect sequences of utterances without being limited to the extracts chosen by the first researcher. For it is within these sequences, rather than in single turns of talk, that we make sense of conversation. As Sacks points out,

> Having available for any given utterance other utterances around it, is extremely important for determining what was said. If you have available only the snatch of talk that you're now transcribing, you're in tough shape for determining what it is. (1992, Vol. 1, p. 729)

It should not be assumed that the preparation of transcripts is simply a technical detail prior to the main business of the analysis. The convenience of transcripts for presentational purposes is no more than an added bonus.

As Atkinson and Heritage (1984) point out, the production and use of transcripts are essentially "research activities." They involve close, repeated listenings to recordings, which often reveal previously unnoted recurring features of the organization of talk.

Such listenings can most fruitfully be done in group data sessions. As described by ten Have, work in such groups usually begins by listening to an extract from a tape with a draft transcript and agreeing upon improvements to the transcript. Then,

> the participants are invited to proffer some observations on the data, to select an episode which they find "interesting" for whatever reason, and formulate their understanding or puzzlement, regarding that episode. Then anyone can come in to react to these remarks, offering alternatives, raising doubts, or whatever. (ten Have, 1998, p. 124)

However, as ten Have makes clear, such group data sessions should be rather more than an anarchic free-for-all:

> Participants are, on the one hand, free to bring in anything they like, but, on the other hand, required to ground their observations in the data at hand, although they may also support them with reference to their own data-based findings or those published in the literature. (ten Have, 1998, p. 124)

Analyzing Tapes

There is a strongly inductive bent to the kind of research that ten Have and Sacks describe. As we have seen, this means that any research claims need to be identified in precise analyses of detailed transcripts. It is therefore necessary to avoid premature theory construction and the idealization of research materials, which uses only general, nondetailed characterizations.

Heritage sums up these assumptions as follows:

> Specifically, analysis is strongly "data-driven"—developed from phenomena which are in various ways evidenced in the data of interaction. Correspondingly, there is a strong bias against a priori speculation about the orientations and motives of speakers and in favour of detailed examination of conversationalists' actual actions. Thus the empirical conduct of speakers is treated as the central resource out of which analysis may develop. (1984, p. 243)

In practice, Heritage adds, this means that it must be demonstrated that the regularities described can be shown to be produced by the participants and attended to by them as grounds for their own inferences and actions. Further, **deviant cases**, in which such regularities are absent, must be identified and analyzed.

However, the way in which CA obtains its results is rather different from how we might intuitively try to analyze talk. It may be helpful, therefore, if we conclude this section by offering a crude set of prescriptions about how to do CA. These are set out in Tables 12.6 and 12.7.

Table 12.6 How to Do CA

1. Always try to identify sequences of related talk.
2. Try to examine how speakers take on certain roles or identities through their talk (e.g., questioner–answerer or client–professional).
3. Look for particular outcomes in the talk (e.g., a request for clarification, a repair, laughter) and work backward to trace the trajectory through which a particular outcome was produced.

SOURCE: Silverman (2001), p. 177.

Table 12.7 Common Errors in CA

1. Explaining a turn at talk by reference to the speaker's intentions
2. Explaining a turn at talk by reference to a speaker's role or status (e.g., as a doctor or as a man or woman)
3. Trying to make sense of a single line of transcript or utterance in isolation from the surrounding talk

SOURCE: Silverman (2001), p. 177.

If we follow these rules, the analysis of conversations does not require exceptional skills. As Schegloff puts it, in his introduction to Sacks's collected lectures, all we need to do is "begin with some observations, then find the problem for which these observations could serve as . . . the solution" (Schegloff in Sacks, 1992, Vol. 1, p. xlviii).

This means that doing the kind of systematic data analysis that CA demands is not an impossibly difficult activity. As Sacks once pointed out, in doing CA we are only reminding ourselves about things we already know:

> I take it that lots of the results I offer, people can see for themselves. And they needn't be afraid to. And they needn't figure that the results are wrong because they can see them. . . . [It is] as if we found a new plant. It may have been a plant in your garden, but now you see it's different than something else. And you can look at it to see how it's different, and whether it's different in the way that somebody has said. (1992, Vol. 1, p. 488)

CONCLUDING REMARKS

Using the examples of tapes and field notes, we have seen how data analysis can be developed after the first stages. However, as we have implied throughout, good data analysis is never just a matter of using the right methods or techniques but always is based on theorizing about data using a consistent model of social reality. This commitment to theorizing about data makes the best qualitative research far superior to the stilted empiricism of the worst kind of quantitative research.

However, theorization without methodological rigor is a dangerous brew. In Chapter 13, we consider how computer software can aid qualitative research. Then, in Chapter 14, the issues of validity and reliability are discussed.

KEY POINTS

Develop data analysis by

- Working with data that is easy to collect and reliable

- Focusing on one process within those data

- Narrowing down to one part of that process

- Comparing different subsamples of the population concerned

FURTHER READING

Miles and Huberman's book *Qualitative Data Analysis* (1984) provides a useful treatment of coding observational data. For a more recent discussion, see Robert Emerson et al.'s *Writing Ethnographic Fieldnotes* (1995). Martyn Hammersley and Paul Atkinson's *Ethnography: Principles and Practice* (1983), Chapters 7–8, is a classic discussion of how to analyze ethnographic data. A development of some of these ideas can be found in Martyn Hammersley's *What's Wrong with Ethnography? Methodological Explorations* (1992). A relatively recent treatment of grounded theory is to be found in Anselm Strauss and Juliet Corbin's *Basics of Qualitative Research* (1990). Sacks's work on conversation analysis is discussed in David's book *Harvey Sacks: Social Science and Conversation Analysis* (1998). The case studies of the cancer and heart clinics discussed here are found in David's book *Communication and Medical Practice* (1987), Chapters 6–7.

EXERCISE 12.1

This exercise is based on the various ways to develop data analysis discussed in this chapter. With reference to your own data,

1. Focus on one process within that data. Now narrow down your focus to one *part* of that process. Survey your data in terms of this narrow focus. What can you now find?

2. Compare different subsamples of your data in terms of a single category or process. What does this show?

3. Decide what features of your data may properly be counted, and tabulate instances of a particular category. What does this tabulation indicate? Identify deviant cases and explain what you will do with them.

4. Attempt to develop your categories into more general analytic frameworks with relevance outside the setting you are studying.

CHAPTER 13

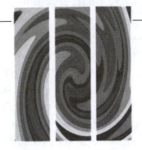

Using Computers to Analyze Qualitative Data

Clive Seale

CHAPTER OBJECTIVES

By the end of this chapter you will be able to:

- Understand the strengths and limitations of computer software for qualitative data analysis

- Recognize the key features of some of the main **CAQDAS** software packages

- Find the details of CAQDAS software packages on the Internet and evaluate their usefulness for your research project

INTRODUCTION

The use of computers for basic **content analysis** of text became popular in the humanities from the 1960s onward. Scholars of literature, for example, found that they could use the large mainframe computers of the time for counting the number of times particular words occurred in a text. A computer might have been used to count the frequency of Shakespeare's use of a particular word or phrase and to compare this with some other dramatist, or to make the comparison between Shakespeare's late plays and his early ones, or his comedies and tragedies, plays versus poetry, and so on. The co-occurrence of particular words, or the incidence of particular phrases characteristic of particular writing

233

genres, could be reported objectively, meaning that literary analysis could be based on apparently more rigorously reported evidence. Computers could do these things because of their capacity for rapidly processing large volumes of text (Miall, 1990).

Social researchers also exploited the advantages of computers for data analysis, but this was largely confined to statistical work until the early 1980s, when qualitative researchers began to catch up. There are several reasons for the delay. Before the widespread availability of personal computers, use of mainframes was expensive and slow, requiring a degree of certainty about the analysis required so that it could be prespecified accurately. Statistical procedures could be programmed into computers because they were well described. They were planned on one day and often run on data during the night, with results being examined the following morning. By contrast, qualitative analysis was (and still is) far less formulaic, often requiring an approach to computing that gives quick feedback on the results of emergent questions, involving an interactive cycle of thinking and innovation only really made possible with the personal computer.

Additionally, qualitative research, as a social movement like many others, emerged as an initially radical response to a dominant orthodoxy: that of quantitative research work. This involved a heartfelt rejection of the technological appearance of statistical work, which smacked of dehumanization, overcontrol, and obsession with technical puzzles rather than engagement with pressing social and political issues of the time. The computer symbolized these things, and many qualitative researchers remain distanced from this technology because of feelings that it may impose an alien logic on their analytic procedures. This, though, can impede a more balanced assessment of the advantages and disadvantages of the computer-assisted analysis of qualitative data (CAQDAS), which is, of course, not suitable for all the things qualitative researchers wish to do with data, but does offer significant benefits.

In this chapter, I propose to show you how CAQDAS can be helpful in doing the kind of qualitative data analysis discussed in the last two chapters—while also pointing out its limitations. I will describe features of programs that have been widely used by qualitative researchers since specialized packages were introduced from the early 1980s on. I will also discuss some of the less often used but more advanced features of packages, such as those involved in theory building.

Although particular packages will be mentioned, I do not aim to review all of them, or seek to describe the finer details of how particular packages work. Such information would probably become out of date quickly, because software developers continue to release new versions with extra features. At the end of this chapter is a section to help you gain access to the many free demonstration versions of the latest software that exist, so that this type of learning can occur. As in statistical analysis, you will learn best when you have a specific project in mind and have time to explore how various available techniques might benefit what you want to do.

ADVANTAGES OF CAQDAS

The advantages of CAQDAS fall into four main categories:

1. Speed at handling large volumes of data, freeing the researcher to explore numerous analytic questions

2. Improvement of rigor, including producing counts of phenomena and searching for deviant cases

3. Facilitation of team research, including the development of consistent coding schemes

4. Help with **sampling** decisions, be these in the service of representativeness or theory development

Speed

This advantage is most obvious to the researcher faced with a large amount of word-processed qualitative data and wanting to sort it into categories or coded segments, which may then be filed and retrieved easily. For someone in this position, the speed at which programs can carry out sorting procedures on large volumes of data is remarkable. This saves time and effort that might otherwise be expended on boring clerical work, perhaps involving mounds of photocopied paper, color coded, sorted into piles on the floor, cut up, pasted, and so on. In turn, this gives the data analyst more time to think about the meaning of data, enabling rapid feedback on the results of particular analytic ideas so that new ones can be formulated. Qualitative data analysis then becomes more devoted to creative and intellectual tasks, less immersed in routine.

In the initial stages of analysis, the rapidity with which CAQDAS can identify patterns in large volumes of text can be useful. Fisher (1997) gives an example using a feature similar to those used in the Shakespeare example earlier. This was from a project involving 244 interviews with children, parents, and social workers about local authority child care procedures. The data had been analyzed previously using manual methods. Fisher's analysis was done in order to assess the contribution that different CAQDAS software packages could make. He used a program (SONAR) to search for the word *discipline* in the interviews and found that different family members appeared to have different meanings for the word, a feature that had been missed in the original manual analysis. This led to some creative thinking about what could have led to this and what it might mean for child care issues. In turn, this thinking led to the development of ideas for **coding** segments of text. Fisher likens this sort of pattern searching to an aerial view of a landscape. Patterns can sometimes be seen from the air that, to the person on the ground, are merely random features.

A further example is a project at the University of Ulm, Germany, by Mergenthaler (1996) in which some 2 million words of transcription from 300 hours of transcribed psychotherapy sessions were searched for the incidence of particular words. It was found that a high incidence of certain words used in sessions, selected because they related to the researcher-generated concepts of *emotion* and *abstraction*, were associated with particular sessions evaluated by participants as "good." Of course, the issue of why there is this connection requires more meaningful analysis of the interactions, perhaps using a coding approach or conversational analysis, but as an initial finding generated by the simple word counting facilities of a CAQDAS program, it helped focus the minds of the researchers on particular lines of inquiry rather than others.

Rigor

An additional advantage of CAQDAS is that it can help researchers demonstrate that their conclusions are based on rigorous analysis. This adds to the trust placed in research texts by readers, a matter with which most authors are still concerned in spite of some radical postmodern analyses of research texts (e.g., Denzin, 1997; Tyler, 1986). This can involve counting the number of times things occur as well as demonstrating that you have searched for negative instances by examining the whole corpus of data rather than selecting only anecdotes supporting your interpretation. This is made relatively easy by CAQDAS.

Mention of counting is a reminder that the days of a great divide between qualitative and quantitative research work have now largely passed. The argument that each of these methodologies is inextricably linked to separate philosophical or theoretical positions (e.g., Smith & Heshusius, 1986) is less and less convincing to most practicing social researchers. The alternative position (e.g., Bryman, 1988; Hammersley, 1992) is that for many purposes the two forms of analysis can be helpfully combined (see also Chapter 14).

CAQDAS helps you to make this combination. First, as already mentioned, events can be counted. These may be word strings in the text, as in the use made by literary scholars described previously, or coded segments of text. I can give an example of this from my own work, where I had coded interviews with 163 people who had known elderly people living alone in private households in the year before their deaths. For this project, I was using the Ethnograph program. I wanted to show what the speakers had said about the elderly people's attitudes to receiving help from others, and I wrote in the final report,

It was very common for the people living on their own to be described either as not seeking help for problems that they had (65 instances covering 48 people), or refusing help when offered (144 instances in 83 people). Accounts of this often stressed that this reflected on the character of the person involved, although other associations were also made. In particular, 33 speakers gave 44 instances where they stressed the independence that this indicated:

"[She] never really talked about her problems, was very independent. . . ."

"[She] was just one of those independent people who would struggle on. She wouldn't ask on her own."

"She used to shout at me because I was doing things for her. She didn't like to be helped. She was very independent."

Being "self sufficient," "would not be beaten," and being said to "hate to give in" were associated with resisting help. (Seale, 1996)

As you can imagine, the 163 interviews generated a large amount of text. Because I had read through each interview, marking segments of text with code called *Help* to indicate when speakers had discussed the topic of the elderly person's attitude to help, which I had then entered on the computer, I was able to generate a listing of all these coded segments. Reading through this, I was able to code these into subcategories, distinguishing segments describing elderly people not seeking help in spite of problems, instances where a refusal of help was described, and, within this, those segments that involved explicit reflections on the character of the person. A code called *Indep* marked segments where independence was mentioned. For all these things, the CAQDAS program I was using allowed me to generate counts, some of which can be seen in the excerpt. I could then select illustrative quotations that gave good, typical examples of the things I was talking about.

If I had wanted to take this analysis further, I could have asked the computer to show me quotations about women separately from men, or to compare what neighbors as opposed to adult children said about the elderly person's attitude to help. Such an analysis might have been done as part of a more general investigation of the effect of gender on the experience of living alone toward the end of life, or as a part of an investigation into kinship obligations in contemporary society. The computer would have generated lists of quotations separately, which might then have been subjected to more detailed scrutiny (e.g., how do women discuss *independence* compared with men?) but would also have enabled these to be counted. Such counts help the reader to see how widespread phenomena are, and guard against excessive emphasis on rare things that happen to suit the researcher's preferred arguments.

Durkin (1997) reports these benefits of CAQDAS, too, in his study of people's experience of asbestosis litigation. For example, a comparison of interviews done in the United States with those done in the UK showed doctors and lawyers mentioning different issues. In the UK, there was an emphasis on the medical aspects of asbestosis claims; in the United States, people were more likely to discuss the role of the media in encouraging claims, and the state of crisis that the volume of claims had produced. Lawyers had rather different views from doctors. These types of systematic comparisons (between countries, or between professional perspectives) are greatly facilitated by the rapid retrieval of coded segments enabled by CAQDAS.

Team Research

In addition, Durkin notes its impact in the context of an international, collaborative research project where researchers needed to agree on the meaning of codes and so had to assess interrater **reliability**. Some qualitative researchers who claim a separate philosophical position from the majority have suggested that a concern with interrater reliability smacks of naive realism (see the review in Armstrong, Gosling, Weinman, & Marteau, 1997, for more details on this debate), preferring the view that all researchers will see a different reality in a given text. Most, however, feel that for collaborative work to proceed, it is necessary to create some sort of shared agreement about the meaning of particular segments of data. Durkin found that CAQDAS helped the team check whether it was interpreting segments in the same way. This was particularly useful as coding moved from the more descriptive and mundane codes to ones that reflected broader theoretical concerns. Researchers could pass coded interviews between them, and compare the results of blind second coding rapidly, using the counting facilities made available by the computer. Lee and Fielding (1995), who have interviewed many researchers about their use of CAQDAS, note that in collaborative projects, one of the major impacts has been the encouragement that this gives to researchers to agree to shared meanings for codes, a matter that is easier to ignore without the discipline imposed by the use of computers.

Sampling

As well as in counting, avoidance of **anecdotalism,** and the encouragement of consistent coding of data, CAQDAS has been found helpful in relation to sampling issues. Durkin's project, like most qualitative work, did not involve representative random sampling of the type used to ensure external **generalizability** in statistical work. Instead, the project used snowball and volunteer sampling, as the people involved in the legal and medical networks of asbestosis litigation were mostly known to each other:

> [CAQDAS] made it . . . easier to keep track of which actors we had spoken to. It was simple enough to compare a list of mentioned names with the interview directory [made available by the CAQDAS program]. . . . We knew we had reached near closure on the influential actors when the snowball sample question ("who else do we need to interview?") yielded only names of people we had already interviewed. (Durkin, 1997, p. 97)

I am now going to show you how CAQDAS can help a writer take an idea forward. I am writing about sampling and CAQDAS at the moment. Whenever I read an article or a book, I make notes of what I read in handwriting. Recently, I have been preparing a book on the quality of qualitative research, for which I have read a large number of books and articles over the past few months. First, I studied all my notes about this reading, typing the main ideas I had noted into my word processor, along with relevant code words to indicate the topics concerned. Two of the topics were CAQDAS and sampling issues, for which I have coded, although CAQDAS will not be a major preoccupation of the book and thus the level of detail I have given on this topic in my typed notes is fairly thin. However, I am now at the point in writing this chapter where I would like to say more about these two subjects. I can half-remember that there are issues about representativeness that someone has written about in relation to CAQDAS, but I cannot remember who it was or what they said. I am going to switch from my word processor into NUD•IST, the CAQDAS program I have been using for this project. I am going to search for overlaps between the code words *caqdas* and *sample* and see what happens. Then I will show you the result.

Okay, I have done this. I have used the "copy" command of NUD•IST to paste the results into my word-processing program. The whole thing took 2–3 minutes, as I had to load the NUD•IST software. It looks as though there are several references, so I will edit the output from NUD•IST to reduce this, showing just one "hit."

Figure 13.1 shows that NUD•IST has given me a lot of extraneous information about the number of segments ("text units") I have found with this search.

This sort of thing might have been useful were I using NUD•IST for analysis of data, but this usage is different—I just want a reference and I don't want to

Q. S. R. NUD•IST Power version, revision 3.0 GUI.
Licenses: Clive Seale.

PROJECT: VALREL. PRJ, User Clive, 11:13 am, Jan 19, 1998.

****

(1 1)   /auton/IndSysSrch
***   Definition:
Search for (intersect (30) (57))
◆◆◆◆◆◆◆◆◆◆◆◆◆◆◆◆◆◆◆◆◆◆◆◆◆◆◆◆◆◆◆
◆◆◆   ON-LINE DOCUMENT: DATA
◆◆◆   Retrieval for this document: 11 units out of 1034 = 1.1%

Kelle (1995) 3 – Smith style relat*ivism a waste of time.
                482
Most research reports contain an implied realism (q). R/I*
Kerlinger a
positiv* ist at other extreme from Smith. Hammersley is in the
middle –
Reals* – though Denzin and Lincoln (postmod*) call him a
post-positivist.
You need to take a fallibilistic approach and try to reduce error,
without going for perfect correspondence between text and reality.
Neginst* Caqdas* can help with sample* issues and rel* of
coding.   483

◆◆◆◆◆◆◆◆◆◆◆◆◆◆◆◆◆◆◆◆◆◆◆◆◆◆◆◆◆◆
◆◆◆   Total number of text units retrieved = 11
◆◆◆   Retrievals in 1 out of 1 documents = 100%.
◆◆◆   The documents with retrievals have a total of 1034 text units,
        so text units retrieved in these documents = 1.1%.
◆◆◆   All documents have a total of 1034 text units,
        so text units found in these documents = 1.1%.

◆◆◆◆◆◆◆◆◆◆◆◆◆◆◆◆◆◆◆◆◆◆◆◆◆◆◆◆◆◆◆

Figure 13.1   An Example of Data Analysis Using NUD•IST

spend hours leafing through my notes to find it. The item of interest is Kelle (1995), an edited book on CAQDAS. The output tells me that on the third page of my notes about this book, Kelle discusses the work of Smith (as in Smith & Heshusius, 1986, mentioned earlier), rejecting the **relativistic** philosophical position of this writer.

As you can see, my summary of the arguments here is pretty brief! If I wanted to see more on this topic, I would go back to the handwritten notes, or look again at the book. Then, there is a summary of the arguments of a number of writers concerning philosophical issues in social research, the topics indicated by the code words with asterisks next to them. Right at the end is "Caqdas* can help with sample* issues," which indicates that this text contains material on these topics, though without specifying the detail of the argument.

Looking now at my handwritten notes, I see that this is a reference to a chapter by Kelle and Laurie on "computer use in qualitative research and issues of validity" in a book edited by Kelle (1995). Here, they make the point that the rapid retrieval that CAQDAS makes possible can help in dealing with larger samples, thus enhancing the confidence with which empirical generalizations are made. However, their main point is that theoretical sampling in qualitative research has a different purpose from random sampling. The aim is not so much to create empirical generalizations through large representative samples, but to develop theory. For example, this can be done by comparing cases where a phenomenon exists with those where it does not, thus seeing which other conditions appear to be associated with the phenomenon. This is the strategy of constant comparison described in the **grounded theory** approach of Glaser and Strauss (1967)—see Chapter 12. CAQDAS can help with this, say these authors, by ensuring that comparison of cases is systematic rather than impressionistic. If thorough coding has occurred across a number of cases, a CAQDAS program can rapidly indicate which cases show a phenomenon, as well as showing what other conditions are present in each case.

You can see from this example of my use of NUD•IST that, as well as using CAQDAS for data analysis, programs can be adapted for other purposes, too, often not envisaged by the original software developers. I use NUD•IST as a reference manager, too. On the market at present are a number of such managers that promise to produce lists of references in a variety of conventional forms, suitable for the different demands of particular academic journals. These can create searchable databases, very similar to those available at computer terminals in libraries. My problem, though, was that I did not wish to key in afresh several hundred references that I had already in electronic form, from a variety of books and articles I had done over the years. NUD•IST has been helpful here, allowing me to import these files in the rough and ready formats in which they are typed, to which I have added code words for particular topics. When I was asked to write this chapter, my first step was to go to this database and search for a list of articles I had read on the topic of CAQDAS, which I could then retrieve from my paper files and use for a more thorough investigation of the academic literature that is now emerging on this topic.

LIMITATIONS AND DISADVANTAGES

My computer search tells me, in the objective and balanced way that computers generally do, that I must now restrain my personal enthusiasm for CAQDAS and attend to the documented disadvantages and limitations that have been reported in the literature and that I have found in my personal experience and duly jotted down in the CAQDAS database that now reports them to me. My computer-assisted survey tells me that there are three major subtopics here:

1. Do specialist CAQDAS packages do anything that cannot be done by a good word processor?

2. Do computers impose a narrowly exclusive approach to the analysis of qualitative data?

3. Although clearly of use in analyzing large volumes of data, CAQDAS packages are of little help in examining small data extracts, of the sort often examined by **conversation analysts** and some **discourse analysts**.

Using Word Processors for CAQDAS

Reid (1992) makes the first point, going on to describe ways in which word processors can help the qualitative data analyst. Most CAQDAS programs expect data to have been entered into a word-processing package, and this task, along with reading and coding large volumes of data, remains one of the major time-consuming elements of qualitative data analysis, which computers do not remove. The time-saving elements of CAQDAS occur at a later stage of data searching and retrieval. Having said this, data in the typed or printed form used in some qualitative projects (e.g., newspaper articles, reports of political speeches) can be scanned into a computer using optical character recognition software (see Fisher, 1997, for an example of this).

Reid is helpful in pointing out a number of analytic tasks feasible with a word processor. For example, it is possible to search for strings of text. This feature can be exploited if the researcher enters code words near particular topics, which can subsequently be retrieved using the string search facility. Reid outlines a *macro* (a sequence of keystrokes contained in a command file) that will search for paragraphs in which a particular code word (say, *discipline*) is embedded, saving each paragraph it finds to a separate "results" file. One can then repeat a similar macro on this results file to search and save only those paragraphs containing a second code word (say, *children*), in which case one will have retrieved data where the two codes (*discipline* and *children*) overlap. The file management capacities of most word processors mean that this can be done for separate files, if need be, so that perhaps one could compare files for male with files for female interviewees. Not described by Reid, but also valuable for the qualitative data analyst, is a feature known as a *spike* (available in Microsoft Word, for example). This feature enables one to visually inspect a text, extract a segment of the text, temporarily store it in a clipboard, and then add to it with the contents of the next spiking operation. All the spiked material thus collected can then be copied to a separate document.

Clearly, then, word processors can do some of the things done by specialized packages. However, to an experienced user of CAQDAS programs, the procedures described by Reid appear unnecessarily time-consuming. In CAQDAS programs, the complex macro-style instructions are already programmed in and available with just a few simple clicks or keystrokes. Additionally, they offer facilities not available on word processors, such as the export of counts to statistical packages, or visualization of conceptual maps. The cost of moving from a word processor is not a strong argument since CAQDAS programs are less expensive than, for example, most statistical software (e.g., SPSS) and, indeed, most commercial word-processing software.

A Narrow Approach to Analysis

The second issue, concerning the possible imposition of a narrowly exclusive approach to analysis, has been raised most intelligently by Coffey and Atkinson (1996). I say "most intelligently" because I think concerns about the computer imposing a particular analytic logic, alien to the spirit of qualitative research, can be fueled by the slight paranoia about technology felt by some qualitative researchers, which was discussed at the start of this chapter. In contrast, Coffey and Atkinson begin with a description of a variety of analytic strategies used by researchers working within different qualitative genres. As well as the conventional and popular code-and-retrieve approach, typical of researchers working within the grounded theory approach, they also describe analysis of the formal structures of **narratives** (see also Riessman, 1993) and what they call "domain analysis," which involves close examination of actors' use of language, seen through their choice of particular words, phrases, and metaphors. Domain analysis involves a fine-grained attention to the way in which language constructs meaning, along the lines of a semiotic or discourse analytic approach (see, e.g., Potter & Wetherell, 1994). This contrasts with the code-and-retrieve approach of grounded theory that relies on commonsense interpretations of the meaning of particular segments of text. Coffey and Atkinson's comment, therefore, reflects a balanced analysis of the extent to which CAQDAS packages support particular forms of analysis, though they do not discuss conversation analysis in any depth.

By now, you should be convinced that CAQDAS supports the code-and-retrieve operations of grounded theorizing adequately. Indeed, two of the leading packages (Ethnograph and ATLAS) were designed with this methodology in mind. For discourse analysts, concerned to discover how particular speakers use particular words and phrases, the capacity for rapid retrieval of word strings in large bodies of data will be attractive in a preliminary identification of areas of text likely to repay closer analysis. For such researchers, it is useful, too, to make comparisons of different settings or speakers, to identify systematic differences in the language chosen. However, for the discourse analyst or semiotician, CAQDAS would be pointless for detailed analysis of short data extracts and would not substitute for in-depth consideration of the meaning of particular, telling instances. Barthes (1973) would not have found CAQDAS particularly useful for *Mythologies*.

Coffey and Atkinson (1996) make the point that most CAQDAS software does not support analysis of the formal structure of narratives, but note that one program, ETHNO (Heise, 1988), is devoted to this. Heise shows this by using the software to analyze the formal structure of the Little Red Riding Hood story. The analyst identifies events in narratives and enters them into the computer. For example, there may be a point in most stories where the hero's task is outlined, another point where the first difficulty is overcome, another where good defeats evil, and so on. The computer generates diagrams of such events and allows the user to explore and test logical relationships between events across different narratives, as well as to compare different narrative structures. The formal structure of fairy stories, biographical accounts, observed rituals, and so on can all be analyzed and compared in this way.

Coffey and Atkinson observe that CAQDAS software "generally is more valuable for the organization and retrieval of content than the discovery of form or structure" (1996, p. 176), and Heise's program clearly offers features unavailable in other packages, but it is worth considering how more conventional code-and-retrieve software could support the analysis of narrative form. Clearly, code words can refer to form as well as content. One might code what the wolf said to Red Riding Hood as being about big eyes, or big teeth, or hunger, or sexual terrorism, in which case we would be coding for content (though the last example relies on an underlying theory that might not be obvious or agreed by some readers). On the other hand, we could use code words like *springing the trap* or *villain tricks victim* to indicate that a recurrent formal feature of fairy stories occurs at that moment in the text. Retrieval of all *springing the trap* moments in the Brothers Grimm or the Arabian Nights collections could be a part of an analysis of narrative form. Once coded, one could search for co-occurring forms (e.g., the presence of a savior figure in a fairy story) in order to test logical propositions about formal structures.

Small Data Extracts

The point I have been discussing merges with the third limitation of CAQDAS listed at the head of this section: the issue of small data extracts. This is not controversial. It has long been conventional advice to users of statistical packages that there is no point in spending time entering data from a ten-question interview schedule, done with ten people, in order to find out how many people answered "yes" or "no" to each question. You can work this out by hand more quickly. This advice also applies to CAQDAS. For the conversation analyst interested in reading and rereading a particular 10-second extract of talk, or the discourse analyst paying close attention to a single paragraph of text, there is no point in using CAQDAS.

Having said this, it is increasingly recognized that these more advanced and theory-driven modes of qualitative analysis have established a body of basic findings that can be extended by the comparative analysis of different data extracts. This can involve quite large bodies of data. For example, Silverman (1997) presents a conversation analytic study of a large number of HIV counseling sessions, drawn from several different clinics. He finds that counseling sessions in this highly focused setting vary, for the most part, between a directive *information delivery* (ID) format that has the virtue of being brief, but is not designed to elicit or address the particular concerns of clients, and an *interview* (IV) format that takes longer, is more recognizable as being "counseling" in the conventional sense implying elicitation of clients' concerns, and has the virtue of resulting in "recipient-designed" advice. The IV format is effective, in that it is accompanied by overt acknowledgement of the relevance of advice by clients, whereas the ID format sometimes shows clients resisting advice. These findings are based on an unusually large body of data, by comparison with most other CA studies. Clearly, it would be possible to build on these findings by examining data from a variety of other counseling settings, searching and marking transcribed extracts for the formal characteristics of ID or IV formats, perhaps as a part of some broader enterprise searching for the co-occurrence of particular formats and particular outcomes. For a study like this, CAQDAS would have some relevance in storing, retrieving, and counting coded segments.

Like narrative analysis, though, the more popular CAQDAS packages are unable to support many of the things conversation analysts wish to do. This is particularly evident when it comes to transcription of talk from sound recordings. Here, it is useful to have software that can store and replay sound records, and time events within talk, such as the length of pauses. A program called Code-A-Text (http://www.code-a-text.co.uk/index.htm) allows the computer storage and replay of sound recordings. (ATLAS, reviewed in the next section, also allows the storage of audio recordings). In Code-A-Text, hypertext links allow the user to work concurrently with transcript and sound or video. One can also add codes to audio segments without transcription. The transcription system of Code-A-Text has a number of features useful for CA, including the automatic recording of the length of silences and the insertion of this into the transcript, as well as supporting the use of CA transcription symbols (see the Appendix to this book). The program can export counts of words or other letter strings, and counts of code words, to spreadsheets for numerical analysis.

Using CAQDAS is no substitute for thinking hard about the meaning of data. This is often said in response to fears that computer technology will be used uncritically for data analysis. No doubt this fear is partly generated by the perception that just such a process has occurred too often in statistical research. However, experienced quantitative researchers have long been aware of the need to treat computers as instruments for pursuing arguments about data, rather than limiting thought to what the computer can do. Additionally, different packages offer different things, and if you think you want to do something that your package cannot do, search for one that can and you will often find it. I hope the examples of ETHNO and Code-A-Text in this section, neither of which are mainstream CAQDAS packages, will show you that this can result in some welcome finds. I will now give you a brief description of three "mainstream" packages, before discussing some more advanced analytic strategies supported by CAQDAS.

MAINSTREAM PACKAGES: ETHNOGRAPH, NUD•IST, NVIVO, N7, AND ATLAS

A full account of the range of CAQDAS packages is available in Miles and Weitzman (1995). As I've said, new versions continually emerge, and for the latest versions it is best to explore relevant Internet sites (see p. 255) rather than read books, which quickly lose their currency. These sites have the advantage of containing demonstration versions of the commercial packages, and free versions of shareware. There are also e-mail discussion groups where software developers will engage with issues users raise, as well as allowing users to communicate with each other from around the world. However, a brief review of the features of three mainstream packages is appropriate here in order to show you more about what such packages can support and illustrate the view that different programs suit different needs.

Ethnograph

Ethnograph (http://www.QualisResearch.com) was one of the first CAQDAS programs and, in the 1980s, was the one most often used by qualitative researchers. Developed initially as a DOS program, it is easy to learn. Because of this, I use it to teach CAQDAS to beginners, rather than any other package. The documentation is very explicit, and the continual prompts it offers the user to double-check a chosen action are, although very helpful to beginners, a little irritating after a while. The core is a straightforward code-and-retrieve system. As I write, version 5.0 for Windows is due to be released. This promises a number of welcome new features, which will overcome limitations of earlier versions. The number of data files will no longer be limited to 80, for example, and it will be possible to do on-screen coding with a mouse. For the first time it will be possible to export counts of code words to files that can be read by statistical software.

The program, like all CAQDAS software, requires the user to enter text with another program (either a word processor or optical character recognition). Once imported, lines are numbered. Codes can be attached to the numbers associated with particular segments of text. Memoranda about the meaning of codes can be recorded so that their development is logged, and these and other memos can themselves be incorporated as elements of data during searches (a feature the developers of NUD•IST would call an instance of "system closure"). Searching for segments of text has become more sophisticated in successive versions of the program. One can restrict searches to particular files, or to particular features of files recorded on attached *facesheets* (e.g., male/female interviewee, institutional or community setting, and so on). If data takes the form of a conversation between several people, the capacity to restrict searches to particular speakers, or categories of speaker, is useful. *Boolean* searches are feasible, so that overlaps of codes, and retrieval of segments coded with one word but not with another, are supported. A new feature is the capacity automatically to scan data files for code words that were entered along with the data. This can be very useful if the researcher has a robust coding scheme developed before all data has been entered.

NUD•IST, NVivo, and N7

NUD•IST (http://www.qsr.com.au) entered the scene somewhat later than Ethnograph, initially as a Macintosh program, but with a PC Windows version soon developed. In recent years, the developers of NUD•IST have also created NVivo and finally N7, which merges the features of NUD•IST and NVivo. Our comments here relate to NUD•IST. Readers should explore the latest software from this manufacturer themselves to assess how relevant these comments are to N7. NUD•IST offers more features than Ethnograph but is a little harder to learn. The documentation is less explicit for the novice, and things that are quite simple in Ethnograph, such as printing out the results of a search, are made more complex in NUD•IST. As well as enabling just about everything that Ethnograph can do, NUD•IST offers more complex Boolean searches.

NVivo is a very flexible tool, allowing pictures and sound files to be associated with a project as well as raw text. Coding text involves operations that are very similar to those involved in highlighting text in a word processor. The program allows the user to alter original data files (e.g., the transcript of an interview) after they have been coded. Cutting and pasting between NVivo and word processor Windows is straightforward, and complex searches are feasible. Additionally, like ATLAS (see p. 255), NVivo has a built-in *modeler*, which allows the user to map out ideas in visual displays whose nodes are linked to the underlying data associated with them (see Figure 13.2 for an example).

ATLAS

ATLAS (http://www.atlasti.de) was explicitly developed to enable a grounded theory approach, resulting in a program of considerable sophistication. Unlike

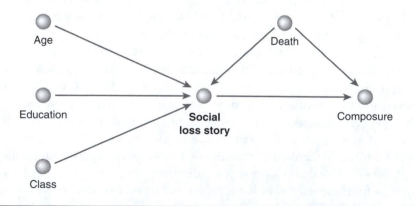

Figure 13.2   Conceptual Network Drawn With the NVivo Modeler

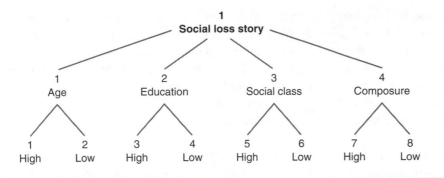

Figure 13.3   Conceptual Network of the Type Supported by NUD•IST

the other two programs reviewed here, ATLAS allows graphics (pictures and so on) to be used as data. This means that, for example, handwritten documents can be electronically scanned as pictures, sections of which can be marked and coded for later retrieval. ATLAS also offers more extended features for theory development, including the capacity to create conceptual diagrams showing links between emerging ideas. These diagrams are themselves linked to instances of data, meaning that quotations illustrating theoretical statements can be gathered very quickly. This is an advance on the hierarchical structure imposed by NUD•IST's graphical display, although it is possible to export codes from NUD•IST to other conceptual mapping software. The appearance of ATLAS is initially rather complex, as the default toolbar contains many buttons whose purpose is not easily apparent. Some users will feel that the ease with which Ethnograph is learned outweighs the sophisticated advantages offered by ATLAS. Coding and retrieving text segments will be all that many researchers wish to do. Others will find the new analytic possibilities opened up by ATLAS a considerable attraction. At this point, it is appropriate to consider some more advanced analytic strategies, involving theory building and testing, which packages like ATLAS are designed to support.

THEORY BUILDING WITH CAQDAS

Most researchers who use CAQDAS confine their use to coding and retrieval of text segments, using the computer as an electronic filing cabinet (Lee & Fielding, 1995). Theory building is generally done in the mind, or with the aid of paper, if at all. Although in one sense all research studies, indeed all observations, are theory driven, not all research studies need to be explicitly theorized. Much qualitative research is, in commonsense parlance, descriptive and does not require the explicit elaboration of conceptual thought generally referred to as theory. However, CAQDAS does support theorizing, and examples of this are available in the literature. Additionally, I use the term *theory building* to incorporate both the generation of theory and its testing. It is, in fact, hard to discuss one without the other, and an important perception of later researchers responding to the original outline of grounded theory (Glaser & Strauss, 1967) has been that the testing of emerging ideas is important in contributing new theoretical ideas. Indeed, the constant comparative method for generating theory (see Chapter 14) can be understood as involving continual tests of ideas against data. The concept of *abduction* (see Blaikie, 1993) is a helpful halfway house between the poles of induction and deduction, indicating this understanding of data analysis.

The capacity to map out ideas in diagrams or conceptual networks, supported particularly well by ATLAS and NVivo, has already been mentioned. Software that is exclusively devoted to conceptual mapping is also available (such as Decision Explorer; http://www.banxia.com/demain.html). Links between concepts can be visually represented in a variety of forms, so that one type of link can mean "X causes Y," and another "X is associated with Y," "X loves Y," "X depends on Y," or "X is a property of Y," and so on. Because the network is linked to coded segments of data, instances of X and instances of Y, or instances of X where Y also occurs, or instances of Y where X is not present (and so on) can be generated by the application of Boolean search statements.

Let us imagine, for a moment, that CAQDAS had been available when Glaser and Strauss (1964) generated their grounded theory of social loss, an example of the use of the constant comparative method. These researchers recorded, among other things, instances of nurses talking about the care of patients who had died. Let us imagine that they searched through all of these stories, perhaps coded as *Nursetalk*, and discovered what, in the 1960s, they found through manual methods, that some of these were instances of "social loss stories." These were comments made that indicated the extent to which nurses felt a particular death constituted a serious loss or not. A code (let us imagine that it is called *Socialoss*) might have been attached to these stories, enabling their later retrieval and further analysis.

Glaser and Strauss report that the category "social loss story" contained some variable examples, whose properties Glaser and Strauss were able to explore by comparing different incidents where nurses spoke about the deaths of patients. Thus, a nurse might regretfully say of a 20-year-old man, "he was to be a doctor," or of a 30-year-old mother, "who will look after the children?" or of an 80-year-old widow, "oh well, she had a good life." This might have been established by close examination of these stories, retrieved by computer. Such an examination could have involved searches for word strings like *age* or *years*. Glaser and Strauss concluded that the age of a patient was a key factor in determining the properties of social loss stories, as well as the educational and occupational class of the person who died. Additionally, they found that nurses' "composure" (itself a category with variable properties) was often disrupted at moments of high social loss. Thus, relationships between two categories were mapped out. Eventually Glaser and Strauss were to incorporate this into a general theory of relationships between professionals and their clients, suggesting that clients of high social value were more likely to receive rapid attention from professionals.

The conceptual network that might then have helped this developing theory to emerge would have looked like that shown in Figure 13.2 (created with the NVivo modeler). The arrows indicate the features of patients considered in social loss stories, which can have two different outcomes, depending on the content of the story. At each stage, retrievals of data would have supported or refuted the emerging theory. Note, too, that further refinement is then possible. Glaser and Strauss (1964) suggest, for example, that the properties of social loss stories interact. If an elderly person of high education and social class status died, this would be less likely to result in loss of composure than a situation involving a younger person of high education and social class. Such relationships might be indicated by further arrows indicating the conditions influencing particular outcomes. Other types of diagrams are possible for representing these ideas. For example, the hierarchical tree supported by NUD•IST could look as in Figure 13.3. If the researcher wishes to retrieve instances where the great age of a person was mentioned in a social loss story, the "address" of this "node" for such a retrieval (to use the terms used in NUD•IST) would be 1, 1, 1. Note, though, that unlike Figure 13.2, the tree structure of 13.3 does not allow lines of supposed influence to be shown, making it hard to distinguish the properties of social loss stories (patients' characteristics) from their consequences (composure outcomes).

This example can also help in understanding the theory-testing capabilities of CAQDAS. Before going into this, though, it is important to distinguish between two broad types of code. It is possible to code material *factually* rather than *heuristically*. Thus, for example, a segment of text might be described as being about "composure" or about "religion" or about "alienation." These are examples of heuristic codes, often reflecting the researcher's theoretical **concepts**, useful for retrieving segments of data so that examples of such talk can be thought about more deeply, subcategorized, and so on. However, one might also want to code that composure, in a particular segment, has been retained or lost, that a person is a Catholic or a Protestant, or that someone is alienated or not. These are examples of factual codes. It is necessary to code "factually" in this way in order to pursue the rigorous hypothesis testing supported by CAQDAS.

Hesse-Biber and Dupuis (1995) give an example of hypothesis testing from a study of the causes of anorexia. Using factual coding with CAQDAS, these researchers could test the proposition that weight loss related to certain antecedent conditions. A logical relationship between factual coding categories was written along the following lines: "*If* mother was critical of daughter's body image *and* mother-daughter relationship was strained *and* daughter experiences weight loss *then* count as an example of mother's negative influence on daughter's self-image." Once particular interviews were identified as containing the codes involved, the text could be retrieved for further examination in order to see whether support for this causal interpretation could be justified for each case.

Clearly, the example from Glaser and Strauss could have been treated in a similar fashion. Selecting all examples of the loss of composure, the researchers could have examined to see whether these were accompanied by co-occurrences of codes for high education, high social class, and low age, or particular combinations of these. This strategy would have searched out and retrieved negative instances, thus supporting an approach to data analysis that, in Chapter 14, we describe as analytic induction. Kelle (1995) contains a number of examples of these uses of CAQDAS, as well as references to programs that have been developed to support particular approaches to theory testing, such as AQUAD (Huber & Garcia, 1991).

HYPERLINKS TO POSTMODERN READINGS OF TEXT

The previous section may have made you feel that some of the fears that computers might take over analytic thought are justified. A technical fantasy seems to have emerged, uncomfortably close to quantitative work, with a language of counting, **hypothesis** testing, and causal analysis that is alien to the interpretive freedom supported by qualitative approaches. Perhaps in response to these tendencies, Coffey, Holbrook, and Atkinson (1996) have outlined an approach to CAQDAS that is more in line with postmodern sensibilities, where deconstruction of a single authorial voice to enable multiple readings of text and data is enabled (the approach is also described in Coffey & Atkinson, 1996).

This approach makes use of a feature that I have not discussed so far, that of the hypertext link, whereby the analyst of data, or reader of a report, can click on a highlighted word or icon and go instantly to some link that has been previously made. Thus, a click on a code word might lead to an associated segment of text, or to a picture or sound file illustrating the concept. This feature will be familiar to users of the Internet. It has been promoted in certain CAQDAS packages (e.g., Hypersoft; Dey, 1993) as avoiding the "decontextualization" of data that can occur in simple code-and-retrieve approaches, such as those supported by Ethnograph. This is because the hypertext link does not retrieve the relevant segment, but shows it in its original location, surrounded, for example, by the rest of the interview in which the segment of speech occurs. Additionally, the analyst can attach explanations, interpretations, and memos to particular links.

Coffey and Atkinson argue that, as an example, "we might also attach additional details, such as career details of particular respondents, their family trees, or details about their domestic lives." (1996, p. 183). This means that the "reader" of a research report will in fact interact with a computer rather than a book, with a research "report" being written to a CD-ROM rather than on paper. The reader will be able to explore original data in as much depth as is needed, thereby being free of the need to attend to an overarching and exclusive presentation by a single author.

The presentation of these ideas, like many new and interesting developments in qualitative research, has been couched initially in the form of a critique, to which the use of hypertext in these ways is offered as a solution. It seems that innovators often form their ideas as a response to perceived limitations of the dominant orthodoxy (or perhaps this is a rhetorical ploy to add to the persuasive appeal of the new idea). The ideas of Coffey et al. (1996) are presented as emerging in response to the limitations of the dominant grounded theory approach, which they perceive to be supported by most CAQDAS software.

This critique has duly received a sophisticated reply from a representative of that approach, namely Kelle (1997), who rejects the simple dichotomizing of hypertext versus coding, postmodernism versus grounded theory. Kelle draws on a learned and interesting discussion of the German **hermeneutic** tradition of Biblical scholarship to show that both approaches can be fruitfully combined.

Here, we are in the realms of advanced methodological debate, a fascinating and somewhat self-sustaining arena of discourse which, however, is a little distanced from the practicalities faced by researchers grappling with particular research tasks. In the spirit of grounding the methodological debate, I would note that the ideas outlined by Coffey et al. seem like good and creative ones that could benefit some researchers in what they want to do. In particular, the authors extend the topic of data analysis by pointing to the intimate links between data, analysis, interpretation, and presentation to readers. In one sense, too, they have the potential to address more traditional concerns with reliability and validity, as a CD-ROM can contain a great deal more text and other data than a conventional book. This will enable one of the long-standing problems of qualitative researchers to be addressed, that of anecdotalism, as "readers" will be able to examine the full corpus of data on which conclusions are based. This would, of course, still be an exhaustive task, and it is likely that the single-paragraph abstract of findings will retain a greater appeal for readers wanting to survey a range of studies in order to extract the major research findings of a particular field.

CONCLUDING REMARKS

In this chapter, I have introduced you to some of the basic features of CAQ-DAS, emphasizing the utility of many such programs for the electronic storage, filing, and retrieval of large bodies of textual data.

The time-saving element of this has been stressed, as well as the advantages that are gained in addressing issues of validity and reliability by the simple counting enabled by most such programs. The limitations of CAQ-DAS have also been discussed, including the issue of whether computer programs are likely to impose a narrowly exclusive approach to qualitative data analysis.

As a result, I hope that you will feel able to use CAQDAS for your own ends, rather than have it dictate an analytic strategy to you. There are many such programs available, and if you find that a particular one does not support what you want to do, the odds are that another package will contain something more useful if you look hard enough.

More elaborate uses of CAQDAS, for theory building and testing, were also described, as well as the more speculative use of hypertext and computer presentations in general, to create research reports that allow readers to engage in interpretive work relatively free from a dominant authorial interpretation.

KEY POINTS

- Specialized computer software (CAQDAS) can speed up the routine tasks of sorting and searching through large quantities of qualitative data. This frees up time for analytic thought.

- Such software also tends to promote certain aspects of rigor. It does not tie the researcher to a particular form of qualitative analysis.

- CAQDAS does not do the thinking for you. It may not be needed where small segments of data are being considered.

- "Code, search, and retrieve" are basic and much-used features of the major CAQDAS packages. However, you should not neglect other features designed to facilitate theory building and innovative approaches to presenting and reading research reports (including visual modeling and hyperlink facilities).

FURTHER READING

Kelle (1995) is a good collection of articles showing a variety of uses of CAQ-DAS, and this author has written thoughtfully on coding for computerized analysis elsewhere (Kelle, 2004). Fielding and Lee (1991) is an edited collection of similar pieces. Richards and Richards (1994), who are the producers of NUD•IST and NVivo, have written an excellent review of the field. Seale (2002) provides a guide to the use of CAQDAS software with interview material. The following list of CAQDAS and NUD•IST Web sites contain plentiful advice, and training and self-help tutorials on the subject, as well as links to books and articles:

Ethnograph (http://www.QualisResearch.com)

NUD•IST, NVivo, and N7 (http://www.qsr.com.au)

ATLAS (http://www.atlasti.de)

CAQDAS networking project at Surrey University, UK (http://caqdas.soc .surrey.ac.uk/)

Details of how to join user discussion groups are available at the above sites. The Sage Scolari site is included because Sage distributes NUD•IST and ATLAS and contains links to the producers' Web sites.

EXERCISE 13.1

If you have an Internet connection, visit the Web sites listed in the "Further Reading" section of this chapter. Download a demonstration version of one of the mainstream programs described in this chapter (i.e., Ethnograph, NVivo, NUD • IST, or ATLAS). When you have spent some time getting to know the package and what it can do, jot down answers to the following questions:

1. How could I use this program to save time on my research project?

2. How could I use this program to improve the rigor of my study?

3. How could I use this program to develop the theoretical aspects of my study?

4. What are the limitations and disadvantages of using this for my study? Would another program overcome these, or should I opt for a manual approach?

Exercise 13.2

Select a published qualitative research project that you already know quite well, which was done without the use of CAQDAS. It could, for example, be an early, classic study of Chicago School ethnography, or a well-known study relevant to your research topic. Examine the way in which the researcher appears to have collected and analyzed the data and answer the following questions:

1. How might a CAQDAS program have been used to aid data collection on this study?

2. How might a CAQDAS program have been used to develop a coding scheme on this study?

3. How might the use of CAQDAS have improved the quality and rigor of data reporting on this study?

4. What other questions might have been asked of the data in the study, and could a CAQDAS program have helped in answering these?

CHAPTER 14

Quality in Qualitative Research

CHAPTER OBJECTIVES

By the end of this chapter, you will be able to

- Understand the concepts of validity and reliability

- Incorporate into your research design methods for improving both of the above

- Design and generate research sensitive to quality issues

INTRODUCTION

Quality has been a continuing theme of this book. Deciding to do qualitative research is not a soft option. Such research demands theoretical sophistication and methodological rigor.

Just because we do not use complicated statistical tests or do much counting does not mean that we can wallow in comforting hot baths of "empathic" or "authentic" discussions with respondents. After all, if this is the limit of our ambitions, can we do better than a talk show presenter?

In his excellent book *The Quality of Qualitative Research*, Seale (1999) identifies quality issues with what he calls "methodological awareness." As he puts it,

Methodological awareness involves a commitment to showing as much as possible to the audience of research studies . . . the procedures and evidence that have led to particular conclusions, always open to the possibility that conclusions may need to be revised in the light of new evidence. (Seale, 1999, p. x)

It follows that unless you can show your audience the procedures you used to ensure that your methods were reliable and your conclusions valid, there is little point in aiming to conclude a research dissertation. Having good intentions or the correct political attitude is, unfortunately, never the point. Short of reliable methods and valid conclusions, research descends into a bedlam where the only battles that are won are by those who shout the loudest.

In Chapter 9, we were able to be reassuring about the scientific status of case studies based on small amounts of data. However, we are less tempted to assure qualitative researchers that they need not be concerned about the reliability of their data or the quality of their interpretations. The reader has only to refer to Chapter 15 to see that our concerns about these matters extend to some published research.

This chapter is the first of two chapters that deal with quality considerations. In this chapter, we will attempt a diagnosis of the problem and suggest some practical solutions for you to use in your own research. In Chapter 15, we suggest how you can apply quality rules to evaluate research publications.

But first it is important to be clear about the relevant terms—*validity* and *reliability*. For simplicity, we will work with two straightforward definitions set out in Table 14.1.

Using examples of actual research studies, we review in the next section the pitfalls and opportunities that the demands of validity and reliability create for the novice researcher. Let us begin with validity.

Table 14.1   Validity and Reliability

Validity

"By validity, I mean truth: interpreted as the extent to which an account accurately represents the social phenomena to which it refers." (Hammersley, 1990, p. 57)

Reliability

"Reliability refers to the degree of consistency with which instances are assigned to the same category by different observers or by the same observer on different occasions." (Hammersley, 1992, p. 67)

VALIDITY

Validity is another word for truth. Sometimes one doubts the validity of an explanation because the researcher has clearly made no attempt to deal with contrary cases. Or sometimes, the demands of journal editors for shorter and shorter articles and the word limits attached to university courses mean that the researcher is reluctantly led to use only "telling" examples.

Of course, such challenges to validity are not confined to qualitative research. The same sorts of problems can happen in the natural sciences. The demands of journal editors and university courses are little different in most fields. Nor is the temptation to exclude contrary cases unique to qualitative research. Moreover, the large research teams that sometimes collaborate in the natural sciences can unexpectedly threaten the credibility of findings. For instance, laboratory assistants have been shown to select "perfect" slides for their professor's important lecture, while putting to the side slides about which awkward questions might be asked (see Lynch, 1984).

It also should not be assumed that quantitative researchers have a simple solution to the question of validity. As Fielding and Fielding point out, some interpretation takes place even when using apparently "hard" quantitative measures:

> Ultimately all methods of data collection are analyzed "qualitatively," in so far as the act of analysis is an interpretation, and therefore of necessity a selective rendering. Whether the data collected are quantifiable or qualitative, the issue of the *warrant* for their inferences must be confronted. (1986, p. 12, our emphasis)

So, as you prepare your qualitative study, you should not be overly defensive. Quantitative researchers have no "golden key" to validity.

Nonetheless, qualitative researchers, with their in-depth access to single cases, have to overcome a special temptation. How are they to convince themselves (and their audience) that their "findings" are genuinely based on critical investigation of all their data and do not depend on a few well-chosen examples? This is sometimes known as the problem of **anecdotalism**.

As Mehan (1979) notes, the very strength of ethnographic field studies—its ability to give rich descriptions of social settings—can also be its weakness. Mehan identifies three such weaknesses:

1. Conventional field studies tend to have an anecdotal quality. Research reports include a few exemplary instances of the behaviour that the researcher has culled from field notes.

2. Researchers seldom provide the criteria or grounds for including certain instances and not others. As a result, it is difficult to determine the typicality or *representativeness* of instances and findings generated from them.

3. Research reports presented in tabular form do not preserve the materials upon which the analysis was conducted. As the researcher abstracts data from raw materials to produce summarized findings, the original form of the materials is *lost*. Therefore, it is impossible to entertain alternative interpretations of the same materials. (1979, p. 15, our emphasis)

Some years later, this problem was succinctly expressed by Bryman:

There is a tendency towards an anecdotal approach to the use of data in relation to conclusions or explanations in qualitative research. Brief conversations, snippets from unstructured interviews . . . are used to provide evidence of a particular contention. There are grounds for disquiet in that the representativeness or generality of these fragments are rarely addressed. (1988, p. 77)

The complaint of anecdotalism questions the validity of much qualitative research. Two common responses to it are to suggest method and data triangulation and/or respondent validation.

Triangulation refers to the attempt to get a "true" fix on a situation by combining different ways of looking at it or different findings. In Chapter 4, we showed some of the difficulties that novice researchers can get into by attempting such triangulation. In Chapter 9, we discussed in more detail the analytical limitations of this approach.

Broadly, many of the models that underlie qualitative research are simply not compatible with the assumption that "true" fixes on "reality" can be obtained separately from particular ways of looking at it. Of course, this does not mean that you should not use different data sets or deploy different methods. The problem only arises when you use such multiplicity as a way of settling validity questions.

Respondent validation suggests that we should go back to the subjects with our tentative results and refine them in the light of our subjects' reactions (Reason & Rowan, 1981). Like triangulation, however, we fear it is a flawed method.

Of course, the subjects we study can, if we ask them, give us an account of the context of their actions. The problem only arises if we attribute a privileged status to that account (see Bloor, 1983; Bryman, 1988, pp. 78–79). As Fielding and Fielding put it,

There is no reason to assume that members have privileged status as commentators on their actions . . . such feedback cannot be taken as direct validation or refutation of the observer's inferences. Rather such processes of so-called "validation" should be treated as yet another source of data and insight. (1986, p. 43)

Of course, this leaves to one side the ethics, politics, and practicalities of the researcher's relation with subjects in the field (see Chapters 17 and 18). Nonetheless, these latter issues should not be *confused* with the validation of research findings.

If triangulation and respondent validation are fallible paths to validity, what more satisfactory methods remain? We discuss next five interrelated ways of thinking critically about qualitative data analysis in order to aim at more valid findings. These are

- The refutability principle

- The constant comparative method

- Comprehensive data treatment

- **Deviant-case analysis**

- Using appropriate tabulations

The Refutability Principle

One solution to the problem of anecdotalism is simply for qualitative researchers to seek to refute their initial assumptions about their data in order to achieve objectivity. As Kirk and Miller argue,

The assumptions underlying the search for objectivity are simple. There is a world of empirical reality out there. The way we perceive and understand that world is largely up to us, but the world does not tolerate all understandings of it equally. (1986, p. 11)

Following Kirk and Miller, we need to recognize that "the world does not tolerate all understandings of it equally." This means that we must overcome the temptation to jump to easy conclusions just because there is some evidence that seems to lead in an interesting direction. Instead, we must subject this evidence to every possible test.

The critical method implied here is close to what Popper (1959) calls "critical rationalism." This demands that we must seek to refute assumed relations between phenomena. Then, only if we cannot refute the existence of a certain relationship, are we in a position to speak about "objective" knowledge. Even then, however, our knowledge is always provisional, subject to a subsequent study that may come up with disconfirming evidence.

Popper puts it this way:

> What characterizes the empirical method is its manner of exposing to falsification, in every conceivable way, the system to be tested. Its aim is not to save the lives of untenable systems but, on the contrary, to select the one which is by comparison the fittest, by exposing them all to the fiercest struggle for survival. (1959, p. 42)

Of course, qualitative researchers are not alone in taking Popper's critical method seriously. One way in which *quantitative* researchers attempt to satisfy Popper's demand for attempts at "falsification" is by carefully excluding spurious correlations (see Table 2.3 and associated text in Chapter 2).

To do this, the survey researcher may seek to introduce new variables to produce a form of multivariate analysis that can offer significant, nonspurious correlations (see Mehan, 1979, p. 21). Through such an attempt to avoid spurious correlations, quantitative social scientists can provide a practical demonstration of their orientation to the spirit of critical inquiry that Popper advocates.

How can qualitative researchers satisfy Popper's criterion? The remaining four methods suggest an interrelated way of thinking critically during data analysis.

The Constant Comparative Method

The comparative method means that the qualitative researcher should always attempt to find another case through which to test out a provisional hypothesis. In an early study of the changing perspectives of medical students during their training, Becker and Geer (1960) found that they could test their emerging hypothesis about the influence of career stages on perceptions by comparing different groups at one time and also by comparing one cohort of students with another over the course of training. For instance, it could only be claimed with confidence that beginning medical students tended to be idealists if several cohorts of first-year students all shared this perspective.

Similarly, when David was studying what happened to Down syndrome children in a heart hospital, he tested out his findings with tape recordings of consultations from the same clinic involving children without the congenital abnormality (Silverman, 1981). And, of course, his attempt to analyze the ceremonial order of private medical practice (Silverman, 1984) was highly dependent on comparative data on public clinics.

However, beginning researchers are unlikely to have the resources to study different cases. Yet this does not mean that comparison is impossible. The constant comparative method involves simply inspecting and comparing all the data fragments that arise in a single case (Glaser & Strauss, 1967).

While such a method may seem attractive, beginning researchers may worry about two practical difficulties involved in implementing it. First, they may lack the resources to assemble all their data in an analyzable form. For instance, transcribing a whole data set may be impossibly time consuming—as well as diverting you from data analysis! Second, how are you to compare data when you may have not yet generated a provisional hypothesis or even an initial set of categories?

Fortunately, these objections can be readily overcome. In practice, it usually makes sense to begin analysis on a relatively small part of your data. Then, having generated a set of categories, you can test out emerging hypotheses by steadily expanding your data corpus.

This point has been clearly made by Peräkylä using the example of studies based on tape-recorded data:

> There is a limit to how much data a single researcher or a research team can transcribe and analyse. But on the other hand, a large database has definite advantages . . . a large portion of the data can be kept as a resource that is used only when the analysis has progressed so far that the phenomena under study have been specified. At that later stage, short sections from the data in reserve can be transcribed, and thereby, the full variation of the phenomenon can be observed. (2004, p. 288)

David employed this constant comparative method, moving from small to larger data sets, in his study of AIDS counseling (Silverman, 1997). For instance, having isolated an instance of how a client resisted a counselor's advice, David trawled through his data to obtain a larger sample of cases where advice resistance was present. This example is discussed in greater detail in Silverman (2001, pp. 244–246).

However, the constant comparative method, because it involves a repeated to and fro between different parts of your data, implies something much bigger. All parts of your data must, at some point, be inspected and analyzed. This is part of what is meant by "comprehensive data treatment."

Comprehensive Data Treatment

Ten Have notes the complaint that in CA, like other kinds of qualitative research, "findings . . . are based on a subjectively selected, and probably biased, 'sample' of cases that happen to fit the analytic argument" (ten Have, 1998, p. 135).

This complaint, which amounts to a charge of anecdotalism, can be addressed by what ten Have, following Mehan (1979), calls "comprehensive data treatment." This comprehensiveness arises because, in qualitative research, "all cases of data . . . [are] incorporated in the analysis" (Mehan, 1979, p. 21).

Such comprehensiveness goes beyond what is normally demanded in many quantitative methods. For instance, in survey research one is usually satisfied by achieving significant, nonspurious, correlations. So, if nearly all your data supports your hypothesis, your job is largely done.

By contrast, in qualitative research, working with smaller data sets open to repeated inspection, you should not be satisfied until your generalization is able to apply to every single gobbet of relevant data you have collected.

The outcome is a generalization that can be every bit as valid as a statistical correlation. As Mehan puts it, "The result is an integrated, precise model that comprehensively describes a specific [phenomenon], instead of a simple correlational statement about antecedent and consequent conditions" (1979, p. 21).

Deviant-Case Analysis

What is important in depicting anomalies precisely? If you cannot do it, that shows you do not know your way around the concepts. (Wittgenstein, 1980, p. 72e)

Comprehensive data treatment implies actively seeking out and addressing anomalies or deviant cases. Again, Mehan makes the point:

The method begins with a small batch of data. A provisional analytic scheme is generated. The scheme is then compared to other data, and modifications made in the scheme as necessary. The provisional analytic scheme is constantly confronted by "negative" or "discrepant" cases until the researcher has derived a small set of recursive rules that incorporate all the data in the analysis. (1979, p. 21; see also Becker, 1998, pp. 211–212)

Mehan notes that this is very different from the sense of deviant-case analysis in quantitative survey research. Here you turn to deviant cases in two circumstances:

- When the existing variables will not produce sufficiently high statistical correlations

- When good correlations are found but you suspect these might be spurious

By contrast, the qualitative researcher should not be satisfied by explanations that appear to explain nearly all the variance in their data. Instead, as we have already argued, in qualitative research, every piece of data has to be used until it can be accounted for.

Let us show you two examples that use deviant-case analysis with the aim of a comprehensive data treatment. The first is drawn from an interview study of reports by relatives about family members who had died alone (Seale, 1996; discussed in Seale, 1999, pp. 79–80).

Most relatives reported that a relative dying alone was an unwelcome event and that they would have wanted to be present at the death if they had been able. Seale argued that such accounts worked to display a relative's moral adequacy.

However, in a small minority of cases, people said they had not wanted to be present at such a death. Rather than treat these examples as statistically insignificant, Seale examined them in greater detail to see if his overall argument needed to be modified.

In all these deviant cases, it turned out that respondents offered legitimations for their position. For instance, in one case, a son said that his father's dementia meant that he would have been "oblivious" if his son had been present. In another case, a husband referred to his own potential distress at being present at the death of his wife. He also added that it "didn't make any difference as she was in a coma" (Seale, 1999, p. 79).

Seale concluded that, in his five deviant cases, respondents did not depart from displays of moral adequacy but rather

successfully demonstrated their moral adequacy by alternative means. In doing this, they showed an orientation towards the event [i.e., not being present at the death of a loved one] as deviant from normal behaviour, requiring explanation, so strengthening the general case that accompaniment of dying people is perceived as a generally desirable social norm. (1999, p. 80)

The second example of deviant-case analysis is drawn from David's ethnographic research on pediatric clinics (Silverman, 1987). In this research, David compared the heart clinic discussed in Chapter 12 with a clinic treating children born with cleft lips and/or cleft palates. The latter is another congenital defect but, unlike cardiac anomalies, is self-evident and treatable by routine, low-risk cosmetic surgery usually carried out when the patient is in the teens. In both clinics, David observed and tape recorded what was said. Transcription was for ethnographic purposes and this meant that its level of detail did not follow all the conventions used in CA.

The rationale for delaying cosmetic surgery in the cleft-palate clinic is that, because appearance is a matter of personal judgment, it is best left until somebody is of an age when he or she can decide for him- or herself rather than be influenced by the surgeon or by the parents. In practice, this reasonable assumption meant that the doctor (D) would ask the young person concerned a question in this general format:

D: What do you think about your looks Barry?

       (3.0)

B: I don't know

D: You heh heh doesn't worry you a lot. (Silverman, 1987, p. 165)

Barry's answer was common at the clinic. Short of a later self-correction or a persuasive parental intervention (both difficult to engineer), it meant that many such patients did not get cosmetic surgery.

Drawing upon evidence of this kind, David argued that questioning such young people about their looks set up the consultation as a psychological interrogation likely to lead to nonintervention. This was strengthened by the fact that, later in the consultation, it became clear that Barry, after all, did want cosmetic surgery. Barry's case and that of others showed that these adolescent patients had far less difficulty when they were simply asked whether they wanted an operation.

However, a visit to a clinic in Brisbane, Australia, provided David with the deviant case shown in this extract:

D: Do you worry at all about your appearance?

S: Oh I really notice it but I um if it could be improved, I'd like to get it done. I really worry about it. (Silverman, 1987, p. 182)

In one leap, Simon seems to have overcome the communication difficulties that a question about your appearance usually generates. He freely admits that he "notices" and "worries" about his looks and, consequently, would "like to get it done." What are we to make of this apparently deviant case?

The first thing to report is that, at 18 years of age, Simon is considerably older than Barry and the other children seen in the English clinic. So reticence to discuss one's appearance may be age related and different medical strategies may be applied to different age groups.

However, there was something more interesting about Simon's case. This was how his reports about his worries were treated by doctors in his clinic. The extract below is a continuation of the last:

S: I really worry about it.

D: Really?

D: Not really but *really*?

S: But *really* yes. (Silverman, 1987, p. 183)

What is going on in this extract? Why is Simon's apparently straightforward response subject to further questioning? To answer these questions, David noted comments made by a doctor before Simon had entered the room. These are shown here:

D: He's er (0.5) it's a matter of deciding whether he should have an opera-
        tion. And, er, what we are concerned about is his degree of maturity
        which it will be very interesting for you [D turns toward David] to make
        a judgment on when he comes in. (Silverman, 1987, p. 180)

We see from this extract that, even before Simon enters the room, his "degree of maturity" will be an issue. We are advised that Simon's answers should not stand alone as expression of his wishes but should be judged as mature or immature and, perhaps, discarded or reinterpreted.

After Simon leaves, this doctor worries some more about what Simon's answers "really" mean:

D: It's very difficult to assess isn't it? Because he's pretty sophisticated in
        some of his comments and it's er (1.0) it's just the, you know, continu-
        ously sunny nature that's troubling me a little bit about the problem as
        to whether it should be done. (Silverman, 1987, p. 186)

Eventually, this doctor concludes that Simon's relaxed manner is merely "a cover-up" for his self-consciousness about his appearance. Although this is rather an odd conclusion as Simon has freely admitted that he is concerned about his appearance, it generates general consent and all the doctors present agree that Simon is "motivated" and should have his operation.

This deviant case considerably added to David's understanding of the mechanics of decision making in the cleft-palate clinic. The English data had suggested that asking young people about their appearance tended to present problems that could lead away from the cosmetic surgery they might want. The Australian data showed that, even when a patient confidently reported his concern about his appearance, this created a further complication. In this case, the doctors worried about how someone so concerned could present himself in such a confident (or "sunny") manner.

A catch-22 situation was now revealed. The doctors' practical reasoning unintentionally resulted in the following impasse:

1. To get surgery, you needed to complain about your appearance.

2. Those who were most troubled about their appearance would often be the least able to complain, so they would not get surgery.

3. Patients who did complain would be viewed as self-confident. Hence their underlying troubles were open to doubt and they too might not get surgery.

The impasse derived from the coupling of the doctors' understandable desire to elicit their patients' own views with psychological versions of the meaning of what their patients actually said.

These two studies show how the identification and further analysis of **deviant cases** can strengthen the **validity** of research. As implied here, it is important to underline the fact that such identification needs to stem from a theoretical approach to the data. Seale's work derived from a way of treating interview responses as moral **narratives**. David's own research was based on an ethnographic interest in the "ceremonial order" of the clinic (Strong, 1979).

So pieces of data are never intrinsically deviant but rather become so in relation to the approach used. This theoretically defined approach to analysis should also properly apply to the compilation and inspection of data in tabulated form.

Using Appropriate Tabulations

A very nice example of how simple tabulations can improve the quality of data analysis is provided by Koppel, Cohen, and Abaluck (2003). Their earlier ethnographic research had revealed that hospital computer-ordering systems were often associated with errors when doctors prescribed patients' medications. A quantitative survey showed that over 75 percent of doctors had used the computer system incorrectly.

It turned out that the computer display tended to convey a false sense of accuracy to many doctors. For example, by focusing solely on the electronic medication chart, doctors would tend to miss crucial paper stickers attached to the hard-copy case notes. Various features of the computer software also seemed to be associated with these errors. For instance, the display on the screen would show amounts of a medication appropriate for warehousing needs and purchasing decisions. Yet this level might be clinically inappropriate. In addition, it was possible for a doctor to add a new medication without canceling an existing prescription for something very similar.

Koppel et al.'s survey increased the validity and generalizability of their qualitative study. Using both sets of data, they were able to argue more convincingly about how the computer software could be improved.

However, it is usually mistaken to count simply for the sake of counting. Without a theoretical rationale behind the tabulated categories, counting only gives a spurious validity to research. For instance, in the observation of classroom behavior, Mehan (1979) suggests that many kinds of quantification have only limited value:

> The quantitative approach to classroom observation is useful for certain purposes, namely, for providing the frequency of teacher talk by comparison with student talk. . . . However, this approach minimizes the contribution of students, neglects the inter-relationship of verbal to non-verbal behavior, obscures the contingent nature of interaction, and ignores the (often multiple) functions of language. (1979, p. 14)

We do not attempt here to defend quantitative or **positivistic** research *per se*. We are not concerned with research designs that center on quantitative methods and/or are indifferent to how participants construct order. Instead, we want to try to demonstrate some uses of quantification in research that is qualitative and interpretive in design.

To some extent, the tabulations David developed in his study of cancer clinics (see Chapter 12, Table 12.3) fell foul of Mehan's criticisms. Although David's comparison of clinics derived from Strong's (1979) discussion of "ceremonial orders," the tabulation was based on dubious, commonsense categories. For instance, it is very problematic to count participants' questions when one's only data is field notes. Without being able to reinspect a tape recording, David's category of "question" has an unknown relation to the participants' orientations.

An alternative is to count members' own categories as used in naturally occurring places. For instance, in David's analysis of cardiac consultations with Down syndrome children (see Chapter 12), he constructed a table, based on a comparison of Down and non-Down consultations, showing the different forms of the doctor's questions to parents and the parents' answers. This tabulation showed a strong tendency with Down children for both the doctor and parents to avoid using the word *well* about the child, and this absence of reference to *wellness* proved to be crucial to understanding the subsequent shape of the clinic consultation.

So there is no reason why qualitative researchers should not, where appropriate, use quantitative measures. Simple counting techniques, theoretically derived and ideally based on members' own categories, can offer a means to survey the whole corpus of data ordinarily lost in intensive, qualitative research. Instead of taking the researcher's word for it, the reader has a chance to gain a sense of the flavor of the data as a whole. In turn, researchers are able to test and to revise their generalizations, removing nagging doubts about the accuracy of their impressions about the data.

As Kirk and Miller remark, "By our pragmatic view, qualitative research does imply a commitment to field activities. It does not imply a commitment to innumeracy" (1986, p. 10).

RELIABILITY

Counting based on members' own categories in the context of comprehensive data treatment is possible because, in principle, the quality of data should be high in qualitative research. By contrast, although quantitative researchers try to claim reliability by using pretested measures and scales, they can end up with highly unreliable tabulations. This is not because survey research questions are ambiguously worded but rather because asking and answering any question can never be separated by mutual interpretations that are inherently local and nonstandardizable (see Antaki & Rapley, 1996).

By contrast with tabulated figures from survey research interviews, tapes and transcripts are open to further inspection by both researchers and readers. However, this opportunity is not always present in qualitative research. There are many observational studies where the reader has to depend on the researcher's depiction of what was going on. Indeed, perhaps the extended immersion in the field, typical of much qualitative research, leads to a certain preciousness about the validity and reliability of the researchers' own interpretations of "their" tribe or set of interview respondents.

As Bryman notes about such studies,

Field notes or extended transcripts are rarely available; these would be very helpful in order to allow the reader to formulate his or her own hunches about the perspective of the people who have been studied. (1988, p. 77)

By implication, Bryman is calling for what Seale (1999) calls **low-inference descriptors**. Although, as Seale notes, no act of observation can be free from the underlying assumptions that guide it (see Chapter 7 of this book), detailed data presentations that make minimal inferences are always preferable to researchers' presentation of their own (high-inference) summaries of their data.

Low-inference descriptors involve "recording observations in terms that are as concrete as possible, including verbatim accounts of what people say . . . rather than researchers' reconstructions of the general sense of what a person said" (Seale, 1999, p. 148).

We would add that low-inference descriptors also mean providing the reader with long data extracts that include, for instance, the question preceding a respondent's comments as well as the interviewer's **continuers** (e.g., "mm hmm"), which encourage a respondent to enlarge a comment (see Rapley, 2004).

Earlier in this book, we have discussed two ways of strengthening the reliability of **field** data: field note conventions and intercoder agreement (referred to in Chapters 11 and 12). In the remaining part of this chapter, we will concretize this discussion of reliability by looking at an example of how reliability was addressed in the context of one ethnographic study. We will then examine practical issues of reliability in a study that worked with tapes and transcripts of **naturally occurring** interaction.

Reliability in One Ethnographic Study

In their ethnographic study of adolescent drug users, first discussed in Chapter 11, Glassner and Loughlin carefully tape-recorded all their interviews. These tapes were then transcribed and coded by "identifying topics, ways of talking, themes, events, actors and so forth. . . . Those lists became a catalogue of codes, consisting of 45 topics, each with up to 99 descriptors" (Glassner & Loughlin, 1987, p. 25).

On the surface, such tabulation appears to involve the counting for the sake of counting found in some quantitative research. However, the authors make clear that their approach to data analysis is different from **positivistic** survey research studies:

In more positivistic research designs, coder reliability is assessed in terms of agreement among coders. In qualitative research one is unconcerned with standardizing interpretation of data. Rather, our goal in developing this complex cataloguing and retrieval system has been to *retain good access to the words of the subjects,* without relying upon the memory of interviewers or data analysts. (1987, p. 27, our emphasis)

By retaining this access to subjects' own categories, Glassner and Loughlin satisfy the theoretical orientation of much qualitative research while simultaneously allowing readers to retain some sort of direct access to raw data.

Moreover, Glassner and Loughlin suggest that their analysis fits conventional criteria of reliability. For instance,

- The coding and data analysis was done "blind"—both the coding staff and the analysts of the data "conducted their research without knowledge of [the] expectations or hypotheses of the project directors" (1987, p. 30).

- The computer-assisted recording and analysis of the data meant that one could be more confident that the patterns reported actually existed throughout the data rather than in favorable examples (see Chapter 12).

Reliability in a Study of Tape-Recorded Interaction

When people's activities are tape recorded and transcribed, the reliability of the interpretation of transcripts may be gravely weakened by a failure to transcribe apparently trivial, but often crucial, pauses and overlaps. For instance, a recent study of medical consultations was concerned to establish whether cancer patients had understood that their condition was fatal.

In this study (Clavarino, Najman, & Silverman, 1995), the researchers attempted to examine the basis upon which interpretive judgments were made about the content of a series of audiotaped doctor-patient interviews between three oncologists and their newly referred cancer patients. It was during this interview that the patients were supposedly informed that their cancer was incurable.

Two independent transcriptions were performed. In the first, an attempt was made to transcribe the talk verbatim (i.e., without grammatical or other "tidying up"). Using the first transcription, three independent coders, who had been trained to be consistent, coded the same material. Intercoder reliability was then estimated. Inconsistencies among the coders may have reflected some ambiguity in the data, some overlap between coding categories, or simple coding errors.

The second transcription was informed by the analytic ideas and transcription symbols of CA. This provided additional information on how the parties organized their talk and, the research team believes, represents a more objective, comprehensive, and therefore more reliable recording of the data because of the level of detail given by this method.

By drawing upon the transcription symbols and concepts of CA, they sought to reveal subtle features in the talk, showing how both doctor and patients produced and received hearable ambiguities in the patient's prognosis. This involved a shift of focus from coders' readings to how participants demonstrably monitor each other's talk. Once one pays attention to such detail, judgments can be made that are more convincingly valid. Inevitably, this leads to a resolution of the problem of intercoder reliability.

For instance, when researchers first listened to tapes of relevant hospital consultations, they sometimes felt that there was no evidence that the patients had picked up their doctors' often guarded statements about their prognosis. However, when the tapes were retranscribed, it was demonstrated that patients used very soft utterances (like "yes" or, more usually, "mm") to mark that they were taking up this information. Equally, doctors would monitor patients' silences and rephrase their prognosis statements.

CONCLUDING REMARKS

Some social researchers argue that a concern for the reliability and validity of observations arises only within the quantitative research tradition. Because what they call the positivist position sees no difference between the natural and social worlds, reliable and valid measures of social life are only needed by such positivists. Conversely, it is argued, once we treat social reality as always in flux, then it makes no sense to worry about whether our research instruments measure accurately (e.g., Marshall & Rossman, 1989).

Such a position would rule out any systematic research because it implies that we cannot assume any stable properties in the social world. However, if we concede the possible existence of such properties, why shouldn't other work replicate these properties?

As Kirk and Miller argue about reliability,

Qualitative researchers can no longer afford to beg the issue of reliability. While the forte of field research will always lie in its capability to sort out the validity of propositions, its results will (reasonably) go ignored minus attention to reliability. For reliability to be calculated, it is incumbent on the scientific investigator to document his or her procedure. (1986, p. 72)

Of course, exactly the same point may be made about the claims to validity, or truth status, of qualitative research studies. So, to underline the point with which this chapter began, unless you can show your audience the procedures you used to ensure that your methods were reliable and your conclusions valid, there is little point in aiming to conclude a research dissertation.

KEY POINTS

Validity is another word for truth. We cannot say that the claims of a research study are valid when

- Only a few exemplary instances are reported
- The criteria or grounds for including certain instances and not others are not provided
- The original form of the materials is unavailable

Five ways of thinking critically about qualitative data analysis in order to aim at more valid findings were discussed:

- The refutability principle
- The constant comparative method
- Comprehensive data treatment
- Deviant-case analysis
- Using appropriate tabulations

Reliability refers to the degree of consistency with which instances are assigned to the same category by different observers or by the same observer on different occasions. For reliability to be calculated, it is incumbent on the scientific investigators to document their procedure and to demonstrate that categories have been used consistently.

FURTHER READING

Clive Seale's book *The Quality of Qualitative Research* (1999) offers an excellent overall treatment of the issues discussed in this chapter. A shorter version of his argument is found in his chapter "Quality in Qualitative Research" in Seale et al.'s edited collection *Inside Qualitative Research* (2004, pp. 409–419). A more specialized treatment is Peräkylä (2004). For a detailed discussion of deviant-case analysis, or "analytic induction," see Becker (1998, pp. 197–212).

Exercise 14.1

This is an exercise designed to help you think about the validity of your data analysis. It is best attempted when you have already written at least one substantial paper on your findings.

1. Choose any paper you have written on your data.

2. Explain on what grounds you chose those particular data extracts to report.

3. To what extent can you claim that the data was typical or representative?

4. To what extent have you investigated and reported deviant cases?

Exercise 14.2

This exercise is meant to accustom you to the advantages and limitations of simple tabulations.

1. Select one data set from your data corpus (e.g., a particular collection of interviews, observations, or transcripts).

2. Count whatever seems to be countable in this data *according to your theoretical orientation.*

3. Assess what this quantitative data tells you about social life in this setting (e.g., what associations can you establish?).

4. Identify deviant cases (i.e., items that do not support the associations that you have established). How might you further analyze these deviant cases, using either quantitative or qualitative techniques? What light might that throw on the associations you have identified?

Exercise 14.3

We reproduce below a quotation from Barry Glassner and Julia Loughlin used earlier in this chapter:

> In more positivistic research designs, coder reliability is assessed in terms of agreement among coders. In qualitative research one is unconcerned with standardizing interpretation of data. Rather, our goal in developing this complex cataloguing and retrieval system has been to *retain good access to the words of the subjects,* without relying upon the memory of interviewers or data analysts. (1987, p. 27, our emphasis)

Now write a short piece (say, 1000 words) explaining how your own data analysis provides the reader with good access to your original data set. Check out this piece with your supervisor and other students. If they think it works, you may be able to use it as part of your final methodology chapter.

CHAPTER 15

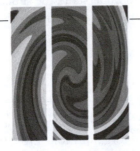

Evaluating Qualitative Research

INTRODUCTION

In Chapter 14, we examined various strategies that can help improve the quality of your research design and data analysis. Knowledge of such strategies also gives you a powerful set of tools through which to evaluate other people's research. Such evaluation skills are crucial in writing effective literature reviews (see Chapter 21). They will also stand you in good stead in preparing papers for publication (see Chapter 27) and in hallmarking your dissertation as the work of a truly professional researcher (see Chapter 5).

In this chapter, we will review evaluation criteria for qualitative research. As ever, we will use multiple case studies to illustrate what these criteria mean in practice.

We start from the assumption that all social science should base itself on a form of inquiry that is self-critical. This means that, if we wish to establish criteria for evaluating qualitative research, we will need to understand the similar issues faced by any systematic attempt at description and explanation, whether quantitative or qualitative.

TWO GUIDES FOR EVALUATING RESEARCH

Researchers are not the only people concerned about the quality of published research. Governments and smaller public and private organizations are currently inundated by research reports that seem to have a bearing on policy. How can they assess the quality of such reports?

A very detailed list of evaluative criteria has recently been devised by a team of researchers commissioned by the British Cabinet Office (Spencer, Ritchie, Lewis, & Dillon, 2003). An adapted version of these criteria is set out in Table 15.1.

Another useful set of evaluative criteria is provided in Table 15.2. Like Table 15.1, it can be employed when you are evaluating research publications. It also, of course, suggests a number of tricky questions that you should also address in your own work!

You should now attempt Exercise 15.1.

Table 15.1   Criteria for Assessing Qualitative Research

Appraisal Question	Quality Indicators
Appropriate research design?	Convincing argument for different features of research design?
Reliable data?	Recording methods? Field note or transcription conventions?
Clear theoretical assumptions?	Discussion of models employed?
Adequate documentation of research process?	Discussion of strengths and weaknesses of data and methods? Documentation of changes made to the research design?
How credible are the findings?	Are the findings supported by data? Clarity of links between data, interpretation, and conclusions?
Can the findings be generalized?	Evidence for wider inference?

SOURCE: Adapted from Spencer et al. (2003), pp. 9–15.

Table 15.2   Criteria for the Evaluation of Research

1. Are the methods of research appropriate to the nature of the question being asked?

2. Is the connection to an existing body of knowledge or theory clear?

3. Are there clear accounts of the criteria used for the selection of cases for study, and of the data collection and analysis?

4. Does the sensitivity of the methods match the needs of the research question? Was the data collection and record keeping systematic?

5. Is reference made to accepted procedures for analysis?

6. How systematic is the analysis?

7. Is there adequate discussion of how themes, concepts, and categories were derived from the data?

8. Is there adequate discussion of the evidence for and against the researcher's arguments?

9. Is a clear distinction made between the data and its interpretation?

SOURCE: Adapted from criteria agreed and adopted by the British Sociological Association Medical Sociology Group, September 1996.

FOUR QUALITY CRITERIA

Although Tables 15.1 and 15.2 set out a very rigorous set of criteria, they focus on purely methodological issues. By now you will be aware that, in this book, we have been arguing for a more broadly based set of criteria for evaluating qualitative research that weds methodological, theoretical, and practical issues. To simplify matters, we limit the discussion to the four aspects of quality set out in Table 15.3.

Using classic case studies, we will now illustrate each of the four quality criteria set out in Table 15.3. Our case studies are taken from sociology and anthropology. For a fascinating attempt to apply these criteria to media studies, see Barker (2003).

Building Useful Theories

The case study here is Douglas's (1975) work on a Central African tribe, the Lele. As this study has already been discussed in Chapter 7, we can be brief.

Table 15.3   Four Criteria for Assessing Research Quality

1. How far can we demonstrate that our research has mobilized the conceptual apparatus of our social science disciplines and, thereby, helped to build useful social theories?

2. How far can our data, methods, and findings be based on a self-critical approach or, put more crudely, counter the cynic who comments, "Sez you"?

3. To what extent do our preferred research methods reflect careful weighing of the alternatives or simple responses to time and resource constraints or even an unthinking adoption of the current fashions?

4. How can valid, reliable, and conceptually defined qualitative studies contribute to practice and policy by revealing something new to practitioners, clients, and/or policymakers?

People in most **cultures** find certain things anomalous. For us, it may be a celebrity who refuses to "reveal all," rejecting invitations to talk shows and eschewing public performances. For the Lele, it was an animal that seemed to be anomalous.

An anteater, called a pangolin by Western zoology, was seen by the Lele to combine apparently opposite characteristics. The Lele were puzzled by how this pangolin seemed to have some human features—for instance, it tended to have only one offspring at a time. Moreover, although most animals were either land or water creatures, it was both.

Douglas noted how most cultures tend to reject anomalous entities. Because anomaly seems to cast doubt on how we classify the world, it would appear to be dangerous to take it too seriously. However, the Lele are an exception. They celebrate their anomalous pangolin, and this suggests that there may be no *universal* propensity to frown upon anomaly.

Douglas moves from this observation to an examination of the forms of social organization that may encourage different responses to perceived anomalies. In particular, she argues convincingly that successful exchange across borders with other groups may be associated with favorable responses to entities that match such border crossing. As successful relations with other groups may not be all that common, it is hardly surprising that, in many cultures, anomaly is not tolerated.

Building on an **ethnography** of an obscure tribe, Douglas has developed an important theory about the relation between cultural categories and social organization. In doing so, she reveals how a simple qualitative case study can build social theory.

Using a Self-Critical Approach

Dalton (1959) carried out an early case study of an American factory. He was particularly interested in eliciting the perspectives of middle managers.

He reports that he was very pleased that, in the early stages of his research, he was approached by several managers prepared to tell him their stories. However, he then started to reflect on what these early informants shared in common and compared it with the background information he could gather on other managers. It turned out that the keen informants tended to be managers whose position and prospects within the firm were the most marginal. In brief, they were keen to talk to Dalton because nobody else wanted to hear their stories!

Dalton used this insight to study the resources that gave different managers **leverage** at the firm. He began to see that power worked through a clique structure in which groups of managers with similar access to resources used collective tactics to oppose (or bring about) particular changes that favored their own clique.

Dalton's study reveals the benefits of a self-critical approach. Rather than treat the accounts of willing informants as "inside dope" on what was really going on at the firm, Dalton reflected on their motivation and, as a consequence, obtained a much broader understanding of the links between control over resources and managers' behavior. In doing so, like Douglas, he made a theoretical contribution (in Dalton's case, a theory about how cliques work within management).

Thinking About Appropriate Research Methods

Like Douglas, Moerman is an anthropologist interested in how a people categorized their world. Moerman (1974) studied the Lue tribe of Northern Thailand.

First, Moerman learned the local language and then he started to interview Lue people. Like many Western ethnographers, he was interested in how his people saw themselves and how they distinguished themselves from other peoples. As a result of his interviews, Moerman assembled a set of traits that seemed to describe the Lue.

At this stage, like Dalton, he thought critically about the status of his data. Put in its simplest terms, what does it mean when you answer the questions of a visiting ethnographer? Imagine someone coming to your town and asking you to identify your "group." You could certainly do it, but it would be an unusual activity of self-reflection. Surely most of the time we manage to live our lives without unduly worrying about our identities? As Moerman put it, "To the extent that answering an ethnographer's question is an unusual situation for natives, one cannot reason from a native's answer to his *normal* categories or ascriptions" (1974, p. 66, our emphasis).

Moerman now started to see that perhaps he had been asking the wrong kinds of questions. He had been using interviews to answer the question, "Who are the Lue?" But a more interesting question was when, if at all, the people being studied actually invoke ethnic identities.

So Moerman changed his research question to, "When are the Lue?" This meant abandoning interviews and using observation and audio recording of the people in question engaged in ordinary events like going to market. In such **naturally occurring** contexts, one could observe when (and with what consequences) people living in these Thai villages actually invoked ethnic identification labels.

By thinking critically about the relation between his research methods and research problems, Moerman rightly moved away from a conventional ethnographic research design.

Making a Practical Contribution

Unlike the three earlier studies, Suchman (1987) gathered data through a VCR. However, like Moerman, her method was entirely appropriate to her research problem.

Suchman was interested in the highly practical issue of how people use photocopying machines. Her video recordings revealed that most people's behavior bore little relation to the user's manual provided by the manufacturer. This was seen most clearly in the troubles that many users had in effectively responding when an order to the machine had produced an unexpected response and the user wanted to abort or repair an activity in which the machine had engaged. People's behavior could exhibit a variety of actions that, from the user's perspective, turned out to be ineffective. However, from a design point of view, the machine was acting quite properly.

Suchman's study has clear practical implications. It suggests the constructive role of users' troubles in system design. As she notes, based on this kind of research, expert systems may seek not to eliminate users' errors but "to make them accessible to the user, and therefore instructive" (Suchman, 1987, p. 184).

Having cited a number of classic studies, we now want to present a more critical evaluation of some more recent research. As before, however, our evaluation will be based on the four criteria set out in Table 15.3.

APPLYING QUALITY CRITERIA

For convenience, we have simply selected the four articles reporting research studies in the last two 1996 issues of the U.S. journal *Qualitative Health Research* (QHR). The Editor of QHR, Janice Morse, has a nursing background, and many of its contributors are in university nursing departments. This nursing focus distinguishes QHR from other journals like *Sociology of Health and Illness* and *Social Science & Medicine*, although its explicit concern with practice has a parallel with *Social Sciences in Health*.

The contents of these articles can, therefore, only offer a taste of the kind of work that counts as qualitative health research, let alone qualitative research in general. Furthermore, such a "taste" does not allow inspection of the deviant cases that we recommend as a feature of good research practice. However, these papers allow us to develop a coherent focus with implications that extend well beyond health research.

Women's Process of Recovery From Depression

Schreiber (1996) describes an interview study with a snowball sample of 21 women who identified themselves as having recovered from depression. She sets out to establish an account of the depression experience, which, she claims, is "grounded in the real world of the participant" (1996, p. 471). This "real world," we are told, contains six "phases" of "(re)defining the self," each with between three and five "properties" or "dimensions."

Schreiber's discussion of her methodology shows some concern for the quality of her research. Like many researchers with an academic appointment in nursing, she holds up Glaser and Strauss's (1967) account of **grounded theory** as a *sine qua non* of good qualitative research (see Chapter 7). Indeed, three of the four articles we are considering here mentioned grounded theory at some point—usually as a central reference.

Following the logic of grounded theory, Schreiber searched her data for subjects' categories and only stopped when her analysis became "saturated" because no new information about the emerging theory was forthcoming (1996, p. 472). These findings were then fed back to the participants and revised accordingly.

However, in our view, a number of problems remain with what we are told about this research, and we set these out in the following:

1. This was a retrospective study. This problem is recognized by the researcher, who comments that the first phase ("My Self Before") "is only seen upon reflection" (Schreiber, 1996, p. 474). Such recognition

might have led her to abandon her claim to access the depression experience.[1] But instead Schreiber is satisfied with the rather glib assertion that "there is merit in hearing the women's understandings of the people they were at the time" (p. 474). What merit, we might ask? Moreover, despite the fragile status of her data, she has no hesitation in setting out to search for external causes of these accounts (1996, p. 489).

2. Schreiber presents extracts from her data. But, in place of analysis, we are simply presented with a commonsense precis of what each respondent said followed by an apparently arbitrary label. This gives the paper an anecdotal feel and makes these reviewers wonder why one needs social science skills to write this kind of report.

3. Of course, it is not difficult to find instances that fit a given set of categories. Despite this, this paper does not report deviant cases although such reporting and subsequent analysis is a central feature of grounded theory.

4. We are uncertain from where Schreiber is claiming her categories (phases and dimensions) derive. It is unclear whether these are the women's categories ("the recovery process was described by the women in this study as . . ." (1996, p. 473) or the researcher's. If the latter, the author gives no hint of the relevant social science theories from which her categories might derive (e.g., a theory of self-definition). If the former, then one wonders at the lack of analytic nerve that treats research as simply reporting what respondents tell you (see our comments in Chapter 4 on "going beyond a list" and Gilbert & Mulkay, 1983).

Urban Healers

Engebretson (1996) reports a participant observation and interview study of three groups of healers who heal through the laying on of hands. She locates her findings in terms of three "dimensions" (setting, interaction, and cognitive process) and finds, unsurprisingly, that such healing differed from biomedicine on each of these dimensions.

Although she mentions no explicit theory and, unlike Schreiber, has no explicit quality controls, Engebretson does strengthen the **reliability** of her account by detailed ethnographic description. Through it, we learn about the setting, how healing was organized, and how the sessions were opened and closed. All of this description has at least the potential to suggest practical relevance. However, three problems remain with the observational data presented:

1. No data extracts are given (presumably what occurred was not taped and, for some reason, the researcher's field notes are not made available). This means that the reader has no basis to contest the researcher's account.

2. No mention is made of the system used for recording field notes and its impact on the reliability of her data (see Chapter 14).

3. Like Schreiber's study, the account of the data is presented just as a simple description. Without a discussion of the analytic basis for the researcher's account, her report once more can only have a journalistic status.[2]

Again, like Schreiber, Engebretson groups her interview respondents' accounts into a number of categories (in this case, physical sensations, emotional experiences, and visual images). But there is nothing to suggest that these are anything but ad hoc labels without a clear analytical basis (see the discussion in Chapter 13 of using categories in **CAQDAS**). Again, the chosen extracts simply illustrate her argument and no deviant cases are provided or explored.

Quality Care in the Hospital

Irurita (1996) describes semistructured interviews with a sample of ten patients (1–2 weeks after discharge) and ten nurses from the same hospital wards. Respondents were asked about what they saw as the nature and causes of "quality care."

According to the author, patients saw themselves as "vulnerable" and described what they and the nurses did to preserve patient "integrity." Nurses described the time and resource constraints that limited them in providing such care.

Like Schreiber, Irurita locates her research within the approach of grounded theory, particularly through her attempt at the constant comparative method. Like many interview researchers, she reports the use of a qualitative software program (in her case Ethnograph). Moreover, she argues that an important quality control was the separation of the studies of nurses and patients and because theory was built as "an ongoing process" (Irurita, 1996, p. 346). Nonetheless, in our view, three serious quality problems remain:

1. Is "quality care" a normative or a participants' category? Irurita's account of her research findings is unclear about this, but her abstract implies that she accepts a normative category without question.[3]

2. The interview protocol is not provided and, unlike Schreiber, no extracts from the interviews are given. Hence the reader is in no position to

know how "quality care" was investigated or how the researchers analyzed data.

3. No analytic basis behind the researcher's selection of categories is given (e.g., "preserving integrity" is presented as a simple description of what respondents said, not, for instance, in relation to Goffman's [1961] account of identity in total institutions). Hence the findings appear, once more, to be journalistic.

Perinatal Cocaine Crack Users

Pursley-Crotteau and Stern (1996) report a longitudinal interview study with nine female crack users during and after their pregnancies. The longitudinal research design allows a solution to the problem of retrospective accounts not found in Schreiber's study.

Moreover, these researchers make a real attempt to establish an analytic framework (based on "four dimensions of temperance"; see Figure 15.1) with which to make sense of how such women struggle with addiction. Thus, unlike the other three studies, this paper does not simply offer lists of (commonsense) categories but combines them into an analytic scheme that holds

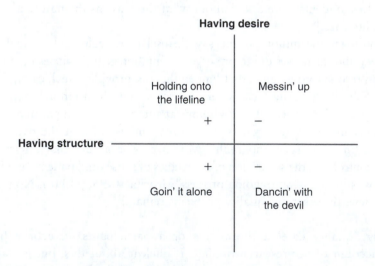

Figure 15.1   Four Dimensions of Temperance

SOURCE: Adapted from Pursley-Crotteau and Stern (1996), p. 360.

out the possibility of generating **formal theories** of the kind that Glaser and Strauss (1967) recommend and that may well have practical relevance.

Unfortunately, Pursley-Crotteau and Stern (1996) do not, in our view, avoid some of the defects of the other studies. In particular,

1. Data extracts are treated as having a self-evident meaning, and no deviant cases are discussed (see Chapter 14).

2. The question(s) which provoked the interviewee's response are not given.

3. An atheoretical reading of grounded theory is offered. For instance, the researchers suggest that grounded theory "is used to discover the problem from the point of view of the actors" (1996, p. 352). But if this is all that research does, how is it different from human interest journalism or, indeed, Oprah Winfrey?

Obviously, from our own perspective, we have found many defects, as well as some good points, in these examples of qualitative research. Table 15.4 summarizes our criticisms.

Having given these examples of the failings (and successes) of several qualitative research studies, the rest of this chapter will contain some positive proposals about each of the four "quality" issues identified earlier.

Table 15.4   Some Defects in Selected Qualitative Studies

They tend to be atheoretical:

- Categories are usually participants' own or are ad hoc and commonsensical (i.e., journalistic)
- Normative concepts are sometimes accepted unproblematically

They use unreliable data:

- Only tidied-up data extracts are given (no interviewers' questions, no indication of how far a particular answer had to be extracted from a respondent, e.g., after a pause or a monosyllabic initial response)
- Data extracts are sometimes replaced by researchers' summaries

The analysis can be of doubtful validity:

- No deviant cases
- Some accounts are retrospective

FOUR QUALITY ISSUES REVISITED

Analytic Depth

How far can we demonstrate that our research has mobilized the conceptual apparatus of our social science disciplines and, thereby, helped to build useful social theories?

A continuing theme of our critiques was that these researchers tended to describe their data in terms of sets of categories that either reproduced participants' categories or put a commonsense gloss upon them. Although it is arguable that this is a proper first-stage procedure within grounded theory, Glaser and Strauss (1967) make it clear that such description cannot itself build theories. To do so, we need to move beyond ad hoc labels and redefine our data within a well-articulated analytic scheme.

As we saw previously, one of the strengths of Pursley-Crotteau and Stern's (1996) account of pregnant crack users is precisely that it attempts to establish an analytic framework (based on "four dimensions of temperance") with which to make sense of how such women struggle with addiction. In this way, categories are combined into an analytic scheme in order to generate what Glaser and Strauss (1967) would call a "formal" theory.

As we argue in Chapter 7, a theory is best understood as a set of concepts used to define and/or explain some phenomenon. A criterion for adopting a theory is its usefulness.

The following examples illustrate this sense of theory in sociology and anthropology:

- Using an interactionist theory concerned with labeling, awareness of dying is related to a set of "awareness contexts" (Glaser & Strauss, 1968).

- Using a **structuralist** theory of the nature of binary oppositions, an African tribe's favorable response to an anteater is used to build a theory about the relation between perceived anomalies and the experience of crossing boundaries (Douglas, 1975).

- Using a **discourse analytic** theory of the active use of language, scientists' accounts of their work are shown to function in local contexts (Gilbert & Mulkay, 1983).

- Using an **ethnomethodological** theory of accounting practices, the "cause" of "suicide" is to be found in the commonsense judgments of coroners (Atkinson, 1978).

Without the active employment of these and other theories, we are bound to lapse into ad hoc use of commonsense interpretations and may, like Irurita's (1996) appeal to the label "quality care," even smuggle **normative** concepts into our data analysis. However, like many other people researching issues that affect our daily lives, health researchers may have two particular difficulties in thinking theoretically. First, their preference for the study of people rather than, say, **variables** may lead to the pursuit of a kind of empathy which does not permit sufficient distance. Second, if you research an area like health, which generates so many pressing social problems, it may sometimes be difficult to look beyond what your commonsense knowledge tells you about the meaning of social situations.

How, then, can we aid our sluggish imaginations to think theoretically about data? In Chapter 6, we discussed how social science theory building can benefit from four types of sensitivity: historical, cultural, political, and contextual. We shall return to the question of whether such theoretically guided research can have a greater practical relevance as well as building a better social science. For the moment, we will turn to our second "quality" issue.

Why Should We Believe Qualitative Research?

How far can our data, methods, and findings satisfy the criteria of reliability and validity or, put more crudely, counter the cynic who comments, "Sez you"?

If we argue for the preeminence of analytic issues in research, the implication might follow that the sole requirement for any research study is analytic integrity. This would mean that the **validity** of a piece of qualitative research could be settled simply by asserting its pristine, theoretical roots.

Along these lines, it is sometimes suggested that the assessment of the quality of qualitative data should transcend the conventional methodological approaches. The quality of qualitative research, it is argued,

> cannot be determined by following prescribed formulas. Rather its quality lies in the power of its language to display a picture of the world in which we discover something about ourselves and our common humanity. (Buchanan, 1992, p. 133)

If Buchanan is saying that the main question in field research is the quality of the analysis rather than the recruitment of the sample or, say, the format of the interview, then we would agree (see Mitchell, 1983). However, Buchanan's opposition to "prescribed formulas" can amount to something that might be called "methodological anarchy" (see Clavarino et al., 1995).

How far do you want to go with such anarchism? First, does it make sense to argue that all knowledge and feelings are of equal weight and value? Even in everyday life, we readily sort fact from fancy. Why, therefore, should science be any different? Second, methodological anarchy offers a clearly negative message to research-funding agencies: that is, don't fund qualitative research because even its proponents have given up claims to reliability and validity. Moreover, in such an environment, can we wonder that qualitative research's potential audiences (e.g., the medical professions, corporations, trade unions) take its findings less than seriously?

The reliability of our data should be a central concern of any research. Attempts to bypass this issue by appealing to the different philosophical position of qualitative research (e.g., Marshall & Rossman, 1989) are unconvincing. As others have recently pointed out,

> Qualitative researchers can no longer afford to beg the issue of reliability. While the forte of field research will always lie in its capability to sort out the validity of propositions, its results will (reasonably) go ignored minus attention to reliability. For reliability to be calculated, it is incumbent on the scientific investigator to document his or her procedure. (Kirk & Miller, 1986, p. 72)

In Chapter 14, we examined in detail methods for improving the validity, reliability, and generalizability of qualitative research. We now turn to our third "quality" issue.

Only Interviews?

To what extent do our preferred research methods reflect careful weighing of the alternatives or simple responses to time and resource constraints or even an unthinking adoption of the current fashions?

In 1996, while writing a paper for a methodology conference, David did a crude survey of recently published research-based articles that used qualitative methods. In his own subspecialty, the sociology of health, the preference for the open-ended interview was overwhelming. Table 15.5 is based on articles in the journal *Qualitative Health Research*.

Table 15.5 is consistent with the four nonrandomly selected health research articles discussed previously, all of which used interviews as their sole (or main) method. The skewing toward qualitative interviews in *Qualitative Health Research* probably reflects the fact, already noted, that many of the authors are

Table 15.5   Type of Research Method (*Qualitative Health Research*)

	Articles	
	Number	*% of Total*
Qualitative interviews	65	71
Other methods	26	29

SOURCE: Qualitative data articles in *Qualitative Health Research*, 1991–1996; N = 91.

in nursing, where the open-ended interview is regarded as both an appropriate research technique and a preferred model of communicating with the patient.

Of course, we should not make too much of findings based on such a tiny and perhaps unrepresentative data set. Nonetheless, Table 15.5 may not be strikingly out of line with the preference for interview-based qualitative research found in the articles published in the more mainstream journals.

To test out this hypothesis, we turned to the journal of the British Sociological Association called *Sociology*. The findings are set out in Table 15.6.

Table 15.6 shows a preference for the use of the interview method in qualitative papers published in *Sociology*. Although the proportion is only 55 to 45 percent, given that the category "other methods" lumps together every other non-interview-based qualitative method, the interview method clearly predominates as the single most preferred method.

Other social sciences may vary in the extent of use made of the interview method. Anthropologists, for instance, may pay relatively more attention to observational methods (but see our foregoing discussion of Moerman's). However, we suspect that the choice of the open-ended interview as the gold standard of qualitative research is pretty widely spread. For example, information systems (IS) is a discipline that studies the human consequences of information technology. In preparing a recent talk to an IS conference, David surveyed the methodologies chosen in research articles published in a number

Table 15.6   Type of Research Method (*Sociology*)

	Articles	
	Number	*% of Total*
Qualitative interviews	27	55
Other methods	22	45

SOURCE: Qualitative data articles in *Sociology*, 1991–1996; N = 49

of recent IS journals. Of the six qualitative research articles, five were derived from interviews.

David has discussed elsewhere the possible cultural roots of this phenomenon in the context of an **interview society** (Atkinson & Silverman, 1997). At the present, we are more concerned with its methodological impact.

In interviews, as Heritage puts it, the mistake is to treat the verbal formulations of subjects "as an appropriate substitute for the observation of actual behaviour" (1984, p. 236). Drew and Heritage (1992) show how this has a direct impact on the kind of data we think are relevant. Most qualitative researchers use such data as interviews, focus groups, and diaries. They thus attempt "to get inside the 'black box' of social institutions to gain access to their interior processes and practices" (1992, p. 5). However, such studies may suffer from two problems:

- The assumption of a stable reality or context (e.g., the "organization") to which people respond

- The gap between beliefs and action and between what people say and what they do (Gilbert & Mulkay, 1983; Webb & Stimson, 1976)

Qualitative researchers' preference for interview studies ironically respects a division of labor preferred by quantitative researchers. According to this division, although quantitative research focuses on objective structures, it falls to qualitative researchers to give "insight" into people's subjective states.

The unfortunate consequence of this division of labor is that *both* approaches neglect a great deal about how people interact. Put more strongly, both kinds of research are fundamentally concerned with the environment around the phenomenon rather than the phenomenon itself.

Moreover, we need to question the argument that observational or other naturally occurring data is unavailable in the supposedly private sphere of human interaction (e.g., in domestic life).

As Gubrium and Holstein have noted,

The formulations of domestic order that we hear outside households are treated as authentic as are those heard within them. . . . As a practical matter, this means that the analyst would treat private and public as experiential categories—constructed and oriented to by interacting persons—not actual geographic or social locations. . . . [This implies that] methodologically, we should not take for granted that privacy implies privileged access—that those occupying the private sphere are taken to be experts on its description, the final arbiters of its meaning. (Gubrium & Holstein, 1995, p. 205)

Such a situation suggests that we need to look twice at the unthinking identification of the open-ended interview as the gold standard of qualitative research (see our discussion of naturally occurring data in Chapter 8). Note that this is not to reject each and every interview study. We merely suggest that the choice of any research instrument needs to be defended and that the pursuit of people's experience by no means constitutes an adequate defense for the use of the open-ended interview.

We now turn to our final "quality" point.

Research and Practitioners

How can valid, reliable, and conceptually defined studies of health care processes contribute to practice and policy by revealing something new to practitioners, clients, and/or policymakers?

Research instruments, like interviews, focus groups, and questionnaires, which ask respondents to provide facts, attitudes, or experiences, have an important part to play in areas like health care, which affect us all. In particular, they can give policymakers a reasonable sense of how, at one moment of time, their clients are responding to a particular service (see Chapters 17 and 28). Moreover, unlike observational or **conversation analytic** studies, interview studies can be completed relatively quickly and, in this sense, can give rapid answers.

Unfortunately, as we have already suggested, some qualitative interview studies may lack the analytic imagination to provide anything more than anecdotal insights. When there are also legitimate doubts about the rigor of the data analysis, then we suggest that policymakers and practitioners should doubt the quality of the answers such research provides.

One response might be to return to purely quantitative research, given the serious attention it usually pays to issues of reliability and validity. Indeed, if the only alternative were *impressionistic* qualitative research, we would certainly always back quantitative studies such as well-designed questionnaires or randomized controlled trials.

However, this is not the only alternative. As already suggested, both the "in-depth" accounts apparently provided by the open-ended interview and the seemingly unequivocal measures of information retention, attitude, and behavior that we obtain via laboratory or questionnaire methods have a tenuous basis in what people may be saying and doing in everyday contexts.

Take the case of general practice consultations. In an interview study of patients involved in 50 British general practice consultations, Webb and

Stimson (1976) noted how doctors were routinely portrayed as acting insensitively or with poor judgment. By contrast, patients presented themselves as having acted rationally and sensibly.

As Webb and Stimson (1976) imply, we only get into difficulties if we treat patients' responses as standing in a one-to-one account with what happened in the actual consultation. This is not to suggest that these patients were lying. Rather, by "telling stories," Webb and Stimson suggest that patients were able to give vent to thoughts that had gone unvoiced at the time of the consultation, to redress a real or perceived inequality between doctor and patient, and to highlight the teller's own rationality. Equally, atrocity stories have a dramatic form that captures the hearer's attention—a point of which qualitative researchers become aware when asked to give brief accounts of their findings.

As David has commented elsewhere,

> Stimson and Webb are rejecting the assumption that lay accounts can do the work of sociological explanations. [They do not] want to take the actor's point of view as an explanation because this would be to equate commonsense with sociology—a recipe for the lazy field researcher. Only when such a researcher moves beyond the gaze of the tourist, bemused with a sense of bizarre cultural practices ("Goodness, you do things differently here"), do the interesting analytic questions begin. (Silverman, 2001, p. 289)

To underline David's earlier point, this is not to suggest that interview studies of patient satisfaction have *no* place in health research. Rather, it implies that such studies must be supplemented by data on what actually happens in the consultation itself. Fortunately, from the pioneering work of Byrne and Long (1976) through to Heath's (2004) precise analysis of videos of the consultation, this is what we now possess. Because of this work, practitioners and clients can be informed of interactional skills they did not know they possessed and of communication dilemmas of which they may have been unaware (see also Chapter 8 in Silverman, 1987). Moreover, policy makers can make decisions on far fuller evidence than that provided by simple records of respondents' "opinions" or "attitudes."

A further bonus of studying communication *in situ* is that both findings and raw data can be valuable resources in training practitioners. Although the researcher cannot tell practitioners how they should behave, understanding the intended and unintended consequences of actions can provide the basis for a fruitful dialogue.

CONCLUDING REMARKS

The ability to evaluate published research is a key skill that will help you to locate gaps in the field that can inspire your own research and to write your literature review (see Chapter 21). In this chapter, we have critically assessed four published qualitative research articles using four criteria of "quality":

1. How far can we demonstrate that our research has mobilized the conceptual apparatus of our social science disciplines and, thereby, helped to build useful social theories?

2. How far can our data, methods, and findings satisfy the criteria of reliability and validity or, put more crudely, counter the cynic who comments, "Sez you"?

3. To what extent do our preferred research methods reflect careful weighing of the alternatives or simple responses to time and resource constraints or even an unthinking adoption of the current fashions?

4. How can valid, reliable, and conceptually defined studies of health care processes contribute to practice and policy by revealing something new to practitioners, clients, and/or policymakers?

KEY POINTS

Good-quality research satisfies the following criteria:

- It thinks theoretically through and with data.

- It develops empirically sound, reliable, and valid findings.

- It uses methods that are demonstrably appropriate to the research problem.

- Where possible, it contributes to practice and policy.

NOTES

1. Abandoning the claim that interview accounts directly represent "experience" need not be disastrous to interview research, as David shows elsewhere (Silverman, 2001, pp. 110–114). As Gubrium and Holstein (1997) point out, we can say analytically and practically interesting things about interviews analyzed as locally structured narrative forms.

2. This is not to criticize journalism which, at its best, can be highly illuminating. It is simply intended to distinguish between journalism and social science.

3. Note that how "quality care" gets defined is not treated as problematic in the following sentence: "The delivery of quality care, although acknowledged as being vital to health care systems, is a complex, poorly understood phenomenon" (Irurita, 1996, p. 331).

FURTHER READING

State-of-the-art accounts of qualitative research that fit the criteria discussed in this chapter are to be found in David Silverman's (Ed.) *Qualitative Research: Theory, Method and Practice* (2004). Martin Barker's recent article "Assessing the 'Quality' in Qualitative Research: The Case of Text-Audience Relations" (2003, pp. 315–335) applies the criteria set out in Table 15.3 to research in cultural studies. Good treatments of theoretically inspired but rigorous qualitative research are Pertti Alasuutari's *Researching Culture: Qualitative Method and Cultural Studies* (1995), Jennifer Mason's *Qualitative Researching* (1996), Amanda Coffey and Paul Atkinson's *Making Sense of Qualitative Data* (1996), and Anselm Strauss and Juliet Corbin's *Basics of Qualitative Research* (1990). The various theoretical traditions that are part of qualitative research are skillfully dissected in Jaber Gubrium and James Holstein's *The New Language of Qualitative Method* (1997). Gary Marx's article "Of Methods and Manners for Aspiring Sociologists: 37 Moral Imperatives" (1997, pp. 102–125) is a lively and extremely helpful short guide for the apprentice researcher.

EXERCISE 15.1

Select a qualitative research study in your own area. Now go through the following steps:

1. Review the study in terms of the quality criteria set out in Table 15.3 (if you prefer, you may use the criteria in Table 15.1 or 15.2).

2. If the study fails to satisfy all these criteria, consider how it could have been improved to satisfy them.

3. Consider to what extent these criteria are appropriate to your area. Are there additional or different criteria you would choose?

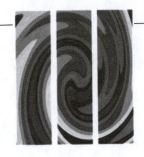

PART IV

Keeping in Touch

CHAPTER 16

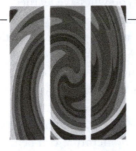

Keeping a Record

INTRODUCTION

Record keeping seems like a very dull activity. It may conjure up a picture of boring account books or even of Dickensian clerks with wing collars poring over ledgers in a gloomy 19th-century office.

In this short chapter, we will try to convince you that good record keeping is not a dull and lonely activity but a fruitful, even enjoyable, way of establishing a dialogue with other people. It should be noted that these other people include yourself and your thoughts as they were a few years, months, or even days ago.

The two principal areas of record keeping discussed in the next section are

- A record of your reading

- A research diary

RECORDING YOUR READING

By the time you begin a research degree, it is likely that you will have learned the habit of keeping your reading notes in a word-processed file, organized in terms of (emerging) topics. I stress "reading notes" because it is important from the start that you do *not* simply collate books or photocopies of articles for "later" reading but read as you go. Equally, your notes should not just consist of chunks of written or scanned extracts from the original sources but represent your ideas on the *relevance* of what you are reading for your (emerging) research problem.

So read critically. Don't just copy chunks of material. Strauss and Corbin (1990, pp. 50–53, adapted here) suggest that the existing literature can be used for five purposes in qualitative research:

1. To stimulate theoretical sensitivity "providing concepts and relationships that (can be) checked out against (your) actual data"

2. *To provide secondary sources of data* to be used for initial trial runs of your own concepts and topics

3. To stimulate questions during data gathering and data analysis

4. *To direct theoretical sampling* to "give you ideas about where you might go to uncover phenomena important to the development of your theory"

5. *To be used as supplementary validation* to explain why your findings support or differ from the existing literature

Following Strauss and Corbin, you should always approach any publication with a set of questions, for instance:

- What are the relevant findings?
- What are the relevant methodologies?
- What are the relevant theories?
- What are the relevant hypotheses?
- What are the relevant samples?
- What is the relevance to how I now see my research problem?
- What possible new directions for my research are implied?

Exercise 16.1 gives you an opportunity to test your skills in using the existing literature to help you in your own research. It emphasizes that we should never read such literature without having formulated some prior set of questions.

It goes without saying that you should use a consistent system for referencing authors and other details of the material you are reading. The American Psychological Association (APA) method of referencing was used in this book. This involves entering an author's surname, followed by the year of publication, for citations in your text. If you are quoting directly from an author, add the number of the page on which the quotation appeared.

[Sentence in text, then:] (Abrams, 1984; Agar, 1986).

["Quotation in text, then":] (Richardson, 2005, p. 135).

By using this method, you can save footnotes for substantial asides rather than for (boring) references. Detailed references are then appended in a reference list in the following form:

Abrams, P. (1984). Evaluating soft findings: Some problems of measuring informal care. *Research Policy and Planning, 2*(2), 1–8.
Agar, M. (1986). *Speaking of ethnography. Qualitative Research Methods Series, Vol. 2.* London: Sage.

In Chapter 21, we discuss how such records of your reading can be integrated into the literature review chapter of your thesis. When you come to write that chapter, ideally toward the *end* of your research, you will have all the relevant material on file. But, just as important, you will also have a record of your changing thoughts about the literature and its relevance to your emerging research topic.

RESEARCH DIARIES

We commonly find the sense of the past in the present. Such **rewriting of history** (Garfinkel, 1967) means that, unless you are careful, you may forget important aspects of your early thinking about your research that may be crucial to your readers' understanding. One way to ensure that you spell out your reasoning is to keep a research diary.

This will avoid presenting the reader with an apparently "seamless web" of ideas that conceals the development of your thinking with all its setbacks and dead ends. In this way, "the text can be like a detective story, where one presents these kinds of 'false leads' until they are revealed to be dead-ends" (Alasuutari, 1995, p. 192).

Another danger with the "seamless web" picture of research is that it can conceal various tricks, sleights of hand, and simple mistakes through which you reach your conclusions. Keeping proper records, including a research diary, helps make your reasoning transparent—to yourself as well as to your readers. In this spirit, Huberman and Miles call for "careful retention, in easily retrievable form, of all study materials, from raw field notes through data displays and final report text" (1994, p. 419).

Keeping such careful records means that you will be amassing material that can form a substantial part of the methodology chapter of your thesis (see Chapter 22). It also implies an open-minded and critical approach to your research. This is what Huberman and Miles mean by "a reflexive stance." It involves "regular, ongoing, self-conscious documentation—of successive versions of coding schemes, of conceptual arguments of analysis . . . episodes—both successful ones and dead ends" (1994, p. 419).

In Table 16.1, we summarize the uses of a research diary.

As an example of the kind of material that can be put into a research diary, here is an extract from the diary of Vicki Taylor, who completed her PhD under David's supervision.

Table 16.1   Why Keep a Research Diary?

1. To show the reader the development of your thinking

2. As an aid to reflection

3. To help improve your time management

4. To provide ideas for the future direction of your work

5. To use in the methodology chapter of your thesis

SOURCE: Adapted in part from Cryer (1996, p. 73).

VICKI'S RESEARCH DIARY

January–May 96

Solid progress
    Continued transcribing extracts. Also wrote chapter on natural history of the research process (to date), chapter on HIV counselling, chapter on offers sent to DS for comments.

May 96

Disaster
    Hard disc crashed—lost 2 chapters and some data files that were not backed up!! Also lost draft chapter prepared on offers.

July 1–5 96

Conference

Went to 4th international social science methodology conference at Essex university. Set out framework for overall PhD and timetable.

September 19–21 96

Workshop

Went to CA weekend data workshop organized by Sarah Collins. This was a good experience for me. I came away feeling very confident about my data and the direction of my research.

October 96

Despair

Time spent trying to recover data and get transcript back to where had been 6 months previously—disheartened!!

October 96–January 97

Time out

I felt I had achieved next to nothing since my hard disk crashed in May. I took time out and went to Australia to visit my sick brother.

January–May 97

Starting up again

Transcribed new data—transcripts 10/14/15 and identified other transcripts for transcription and identified extracts within these. Became interested in how doctors' clients responded to the offer to see the health adviser. Key themes: offers of screening tests for other STDs; offers to see the Health Advisor and offers by doctors/health advisors.

This extract from Vicki's diary covers most of what a research diary should contain. That is (adapted in part from Cryer, 1996, p. 74),

- Your research activities with dates
- Your reading (see the following)
- Details of data collected
- Directions of data analysis, including "special achievements, dead-ends and surprises"

- Your own personal reactions

- Your supervisor's reactions and suggestions

It is also possible to write a research diary in a more structured form. For instance, in ethnographic research, it may make sense to distinguish data analysis from the data itself, using square brackets for analytic observations (Hammersley & Atkinson, 1983, p. 164).

In a still more formalized approach, following Glaser and Strauss (1967), Richardson (2000, pp. 923–949) has suggested that you organize your notes into four different categories:

1. *Observation notes (ON):* "fairly accurate renditions of what I see, hear, feel, taste, and so on"

2. *Methodological notes (MN):* "messages to myself regarding how to collect data"

3. *Theoretical notes (TN):* "hunches, hypotheses, critiques of what I am doing/thinking/seeing."

4. *Personal notes (PN):* "feeling statements about the research, the people I am talking to, my doubts, my anxieties, my pleasures." (2000, p. 941)

The truism that "there is no one right method" applies to the keeping of research diaries as to so many other aspects of research. Whether you use a more or less structured method of diary keeping, the most important thing about keeping a research diary is that it will encourage you to be *meticulous* in record keeping and *reflective* about your data. As Hammersley and Atkinson comment,

The construction of such notes . . . constitutes precisely the sort of internal dialogue, or thinking aloud, that is the essence of reflexive ethnography. . . . Rather than coming to take one's understanding on trust, one is forced to question what one knows, how such knowledge has been acquired, the degree of certainty of such knowledge, and what further lines of inquiry are implied. (1983, p. 165)

CONCLUDING REMARKS

Keeping a record should involve both making an ordered record of your reading and keeping a research diary. In a research diary, you can show your readers the development of your thinking, help your own reflection, improve your time management, and provide ideas for the future direction of your work. As we see in Chapter 22, by keeping a research diary, you also can produce a substantial part of the methodology chapter of your thesis.

KEY POINTS

- Making notes on your reading should be an active and critical process.

- Always keep a research diary because what happens to you in the field is a vital source of data.

FURTHER READING

On keeping a record of your reading, see Anselm Strauss and Juliet Corbin's *Basics of Qualitative Research* (1990), Chapter 4. Pat Cryer's *The Research Student's Guide to Success* (1996), Chapter 7, is a useful account of why and how to keep a research diary. On keeping more specialized notes about your data, see Richardson (2000) and Strauss and Corbin, Chapter 12.

EXERCISE 16.1

Below is an extract of around 300 words from David's book *Discourses of Counselling: HIV Counselling as Social Interaction* (1997).

1. Read the passage and make notes from it (no more than 200 words) appropriate to a thesis on the nature of professional–client communication.

2. Now repeat the process on the assumption that your thesis topic is "effective AIDS counseling."

3. What relevance, if any, does the following extract have to your own research? Note that such relevance can be methodological and theoretical as well as substantive. This means that a reading can be useful even if your substantive topic is very different.

Three major points have emerged from this discussion of a small number of post-test counselling interviews. First, following Peräkylä (1995), "cautiousness" is seen, once more, to be a major feature of HIV counselling. This is true of the activities of both counsellors and clients. Thus, these counsellors seek to align their clients to the disclosure of their test-result, while clients, to whom the character of counselling is presumably "opaque," often demur at taking any action which might demand an immediate telling of their test-result (or indeed, many other activities, like directly demanding clarification of the validity of HIV-tests) even when, as here, given the right to decide the agenda of their counselling interview. However, these agenda-offers, unlike the alignment strategies discussed by Maynard (1991) and Bergmann (1992), are being used in an environment where the upcoming diagnosis is likely to be heard as "good."

Second, we have seen how, when clients respond to agenda-offers by introducing other topics than the test-result (e.g., volunteering statements about themselves or asking, usually indirectly, about the validity of the HIV-test), they seem to "kick in" standard counselling responses (e.g., information and requests for specification). While such responses are consonant with normative standards of good counselling practice, they are, once again, produced in an environment in which their positioning (prior to the telling of the test-result) may be problematic.

Finally, we have demonstrated that, for at least one client, this delay in telling is problematic. As Ex 7 (and its continuations) showed, this client analysed the delay in the delivery of his test-result as implying that C was about to deliver a "positive" result—by referring to "support groups" for HIV-positive people.

This apparent lack of fit between a delayed delivery of the test-result and its content (i.e., as HIV-negative) leads directly into some fairly clear practical implications. (Silverman, 1997, p. 106)

CHAPTER 17

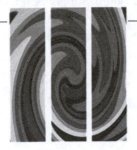

Relations in the Field

CHAPTER OBJECTIVES

By the end of this chapter, you will be able to

- Understand the issues involved in getting access to a field setting

- Address the issue of informed consent and other ethical matters

- Think clearly about your relationships in the field as sources of both troubles and data

- Understand the nature and role of feedback to field subjects

INTRODUCTION

Qualitative researchers prefer to get close to the people and situations they are studying. What should you make of the weeks and months you spend in the field? How should you respond to the challenges you will find there—are they just irritating troubles or can they be valuable sources of data?

In trying to answer these questions, we find ourselves, somewhat surprisingly, deep in a theoretical minefield. The very meaning of "relations in the field" will vary according to the model of social research with which you are operating. For instance, as Gubrium and Holstein (1997) point out, whereas **naturalists** seek to understand the field as "it really is," postmodernists would argue that the field is itself a **narrative** construction, produced by various ways of writing (see Turner, 1989).

The obvious implication is that relations in the field cannot simply be a technical issue to be resolved by technical means. Nevertheless, for ease of presentation, we will begin with some more practical questions, returning to the crucial analytic issues at the end of this chapter.

The following four practical questions are often asked about field research:

- What is involved in obtaining access to a field site?

- What ethical issues lie in wait for me?

- Is feedback to research subjects necessary and/or useful?

- Can I learn anything from relations with subjects in the field?

We discuss each of these questions in the following sections. Each question will lead on to the discussion of possible "solutions," and several case studies will be used for illustration.

SETTINGS AND ACCESS

Textbook chapters (e.g., Hornsby-Smith, 1993, p. 53; Walsh, 1998, p. 225) usually distinguish two kinds of research setting:

1. *Closed* or *private* settings (organizations, deviant groups), where access is controlled by gatekeepers

2. *Open* or *public* settings (e.g., vulnerable minorities, public records or settings), where access is freely available but not always without difficulty either practical (e.g., finding a role for the researcher in a public setting) or ethical (e.g., should we be intruding on vulnerable minorities?).

Depending on the contingencies of the setting (and the research problem chosen) two kinds of research access may be obtained:

- *Covert* access without subjects' knowledge

- *Overt* access based on informing subjects and getting their agreement, often through gatekeepers

The impression you give may be very important in deciding whether you get overt access:

Whether or not people have knowledge of social research, they are often more concerned with what kind of person the researcher is than with the research itself. They will try to gauge how far he or she can be trusted, what he or she might be able to offer as an acquaintance or a friend, and perhaps also how easily he or she could be manipulated or exploited. (Hammersley & Atkinson, 1983, p. 78)

Five ways of securing and maintaining overt access have been noted, as follows.

Impression Management

Impression management is to do with the fronts that we present to others (see Goffman, 1959). It involves avoiding giving an impression that might pose an obstacle to access, while more positively conveying an impression appropriate to the situation (see Hammersley & Atkinson, 1983, pp. 78–88). For instance, David failed to gain access, despite initial expressions of interest, in two settings. In a pediatric clinic in the early 1980s, a very conservatively dressed physician, spotting David's leather jacket, said he was being "disrespectful of his patients" and threw him out! Fifteen years before that, as a novice researcher, he let slip over lunch that he was thinking of moving from the UK to North America when he had completed his PhD. This attitude was apparently viewed as improperly "instrumental" by David's host organization, and the promised access was subsequently refused. The implication of this latter incident is that there is no "time out" in field relations and that the most apparently informal occasions are times when you will often be judged.

Obtaining Bottom-Up Access

This can sometimes be forgotten at great cost. For instance, in the early 1970s, the access granted by the head of personnel at a large local government organization was put in danger by the fact that David had not explained his aims properly to the head of personnel's subordinates. This underlines the point that access should not be regarded as a once-and-for-all situation.

Being Nonjudgmental

Being nonjudgmental is often a key to acceptance in many settings, including informal subcultures and with practitioners of a particular trade or profession. Although the **relativist** tendencies of many social sciences may allow the researcher sincerely to profess nonjudgmentality of particular groups' values and practices, this is not always the case when you are studying certain forms of professional practice. Indeed, to the researchers who think they know something about "professional dominance" or even just basic communication skills, it is very easy to appear judgmental. However, this not only endangers field relations but also espouses a dangerous orthodoxy.

The *divine* orthodoxy is that people are "dopes" (see Silverman, 1997, pp. 23–26). Interview respondents' knowledge is assumed to be imperfect; indeed, they may even lie to us. In the same way, practitioners (like doctors or counselors) are assumed always to depart from normative standards of good practice.

Under the remit of the divine orthodoxy, the social scientist is transformed into a philosopher-king (or queen) who can always see through people's claims and know better than they do. Of course, this assumption of superiority to others usually guarantees that access will not be obtained or, if obtained, will be unsuccessful!

Offering Feedback

Some research subjects will actually want your judgments—providing they are of an acceptable kind. For instance, business organizations will expect some "payoff" from giving you access. We discuss what this might involve shortly.

Establishing a Contract

Establishing a contract with the people researched may vary from an information sheet, read and agreed by an individual, to a full-blown contract (but see Punch, 1986, on postcontract problems).

We have so far avoided discussing covert access (i.e., access obtained without subjects' knowledge). We should not assume that covert access always involves possible offense. For instance, in a course David used to teach, students were asked to observe people exchanging glances in an everyday setting (see Sacks, 1992, Vol. 1, pp. 81–94). Providing the students are reasonably sensitive about this and refrain from staring at others, we do not envisage any problems arising.

However, in other cases, covert observation can lead to severe ethical problems as well as physical danger to the researcher. For instance, Fielding (1982) obtained permission to research a far-right British political party but still felt it necessary to supplement official access with covert observation (see also Back, 2004). In this new situation, he put himself at some potential risk as well as creating ethical dilemmas relating to how much he revealed to his subjects and to outside authorities. It is such ethical issues that we will discuss in the next section.

ETHICS IN QUALITATIVE RESEARCH

As the German sociologist Weber (1946) pointed out nearly a century ago, all research is contaminated to some extent by the values of the researcher. Only through those values do certain problems get identified and studied in particular ways. Even the commitment to scientific (or rigorous) method is itself, as Weber emphasizes, a value. Finally, the conclusions and implications to be drawn from a study are, Weber stresses, largely grounded in the moral and political beliefs of the researcher.

From an ethical point of view, Weber was fortunate in that much of his empirical research was based on documents and texts that were already in the public sphere. In many other kinds of social science research, ethical issues are much more to the fore. For instance, both qualitative and quantitative researchers studying human subjects ponder the dilemma of wanting to give full information to subjects but not "contaminating" their research by informing subjects too specifically about the research question to be studied.

Moreover, when you are studying people's behavior or asking them questions, not only the values of the researcher but also the researcher's responsibilities to those studied have to be faced.

Mason (1996, pp. 166–167) discusses two ways in which such ethical issues impinge upon the qualitative researcher:

1. The rich and detailed character of much qualitative research can mean intimate engagement with the public and private lives of individuals.

2. The changing directions of interest and access during a qualitative study mean that new and unexpected ethical dilemmas are likely to arise during the course of your research.

Mason suggests that one way to confront these problems is to try to clarify your intentions while you are formulating your research problem. Three ways of doing this are to

1. Decide what is the purpose(s) of your research (e.g., self-advancement, political advocacy, etc.)

2. Examine which individuals or groups might be interested or affected by your research topic

3. Consider what are the implications for these parties of framing your research topic in the way you have done (Mason, 1996, pp. 29–30)

Ethical procedures can also be clarified by consulting the ethical guidelines of one's professional association. All such guidelines stress the importance of informed consent where possible (see Punch, 1994, pp. 88–94). The nature of informed consent is set out in Table 17.1.

However, initial consent may not be enough, particularly where you are making a recording. In such cases, it often is proper to obtain further consent to how the data may be used (see Table 17.2).

We have now responded to two of the five questions with which we began, namely:

- What is involved in obtaining access to a field site?

- What ethical issues lie in wait for me?

Table 17.1   What Is Informed Consent?

- Giving information about the research that is relevant to subjects' decisions about whether to participate

- Making sure subjects understand that information (e.g., by providing information sheets written in subjects' language)

- Ensuring that participation is voluntary (e.g., by requiring written consent)

- Where subjects are not competent to agree (e.g., small children), obtaining consent by proxy (e.g., from their parents)

SOURCE: Adapted from Kent (1996), pp. 19–20.

Table 17.2   A Sample Consent Form for Studies of Language Use

As part of this project, we have made a photographic, audio, and/or video recording of you. We would like you to indicate below what uses of these records you are willing to consent to. This is completely up to you. We will only use the records in ways that you agree to. In any use of these records, names will not be identified.

1. The records can be studied by the research team for use in the research project.

2. The records can be used for scientific publications and/or meetings.

3. The written transcript and/or records can be used by other researchers.

4. The records can be shown in public presentations to nonscientific groups.

5. The records can be used on television or radio.

SOURCE: Adapted from ten Have (1998, Appendix C) based on a form developed by Susan Ervin-Tripp, Psychology Department, University of California at Berkeley.

However, so far, we have provided fairly general answers to these questions. We now want to slow the pace down and give an example of a case study. We hope this will flesh out the bare bones of these important issues.

CASE STUDY I

This case study is drawn from David's work on HIV counseling (Silverman, 1997, pp. 226–228). It illustrates the changing trajectory of one qualitative research project according to the nature and kind of access and funding and his relations with people in the field.

In 1987, he was given permission to sit in at a weekly clinic held at the Genito-Urinary Department of an English inner-city hospital (Silverman, 1989). The clinic's purpose was to monitor the progress of HIV-positive patients who were taking the drug AZT (Retrovir). AZT, which seems able to slow down the rate at which the virus reproduces itself, was then at an experimental stage of its development.

Like any observational study, the aim was to gather firsthand information about social processes in a **naturally occurring** context. No attempt was made to interview the individuals concerned because the focus was on what they actually did in the clinic rather than on what they thought about what they did. The researcher was present in the consulting room at a side angle to both doctors and patient.

Next, we set out some of the things that happened during this research using indicative headings.

Making Concessions

Patients' consent for the researcher's presence was obtained by the senior doctor, who preferred to do it this way (this was effective but was it ethical?). Given the presumed sensitivity of the occasion, tape recording was not attempted. Instead, detailed handwritten notes were kept, using a separate sheet for each consultation. Because observational methods were rare in this area, the study was essentially exploratory.

Giving Feedback

Along the way, David also discovered how an ethos of "positive thinking" was central to many patients' accounts and how doctors systematically concentrated on the bodies rather than the minds of their patients. This led to some practical questions about the division of labor between doctors and counselors.

(Continued)

(Continued)

Good Luck

About the time David was writing up this research, Kaye Wellings, who then was working for the publicly funded Health Education Authority (HEA), approached him about the possibility of extending his research to HIV counseling. Until that time, the HEA had been funding research on the effectiveness of "safer sex" messages carried in the mass media. In the light of the explosion in the number of HIV tests in the UK in the late 1980s, Kaye thought it might be useful to take a longer look at the effectiveness of the health promotion messages being delivered in counseling people around the HIV antibody test.

David was interested in such a study for two reasons. First, it was the logical development of his study of medical interviews with AIDS patients. Second, it offered the opportunity to pursue his interest in looking at how communication between professionals and their clients worked out in practice—as opposed to the injunctions of textbooks and training manuals. Consequently, David submitted a research proposal and received funding from the HEA for 30 months beginning in late 1988.

Troubles With Access

As it turned out, receiving the funding was only the first part of what became a battle to recruit HIV-testing centers for the research. It must be remembered that the late 1980s was a time when AIDS health workers were being flooded with patients and by requests from researchers anxious to study AIDS care. Apart from such overload, two other factors complicated access. First, obviously, there were the multiple ethical issues involved in studying consultations where patients were asked to reveal the most intimate aspects of their behavior. Second, extra patients and government worries about the AIDS "pandemic" had brought sudden huge increases in resources to the previously Cinderella branch of medicine treating patients with sexually transmitted diseases. Following the usual pattern, these resource changes produced turf battles between different professions and different centers involved in the AIDS field (see Silverman, 1990).

All this meant that many months were taken in obtaining research access. One leading British center turned David down, offering the understandable reason that it was already overloaded with researchers. At another such center, a doctor gave him access but the counselors subsequently proved very resistant to his observing or tape-recording their HIV consultations. Eventually, a compromise was reached whereby David himself was required to request patients to agree to participate in the research. Predictably, very few agreed in these circumstances.

More Luck

Just as David thought that he had been funded for a study that he could never carry out, his luck began to turn. Riva Miller and Robert Bor agreed to offer him access to their counseling work with, respectively, hemophiliacs and the general population at the Royal Free Hospital (RFH) in London. This was a major breakthrough in two respects. First, Miller and Bor had just produced a major book (Miller & Bor, 1988) on using a *systemic* method in AIDS counseling. Second, Miller and Bor had a video archive of the work of their clinics going back to the early 1980s.

On the basis of David's access at the RFH, a major pharmaceuticals company, Glaxo Holdings plc (now GSK) agreed to fund a 2-year study (subsequently increased to 3 years) of the video archive. David was then lucky enough to recruit Anssi Peräkylä from Finland as Glaxo Research Fellow to work on this archive. Anssi had already conducted distinguished ethnographic work in hospital settings. Following his appointment, he more or less taught himself **conversation analysis (CA)** and had finished his PhD on the RFH data in 3 years, as well as publishing many articles both jointly with David and/or Bor and on his own. Gradually, other centers joined the project, and data was also obtained directly from centers in the United States and Trinidad, as well as from Douglas Maynard's U.S. HIV-counseling materials.

Ethical Issues Again

As the research started to take off, great attention had to be paid to the ethical issues involved. The researchers ended up with a method of recruitment whereby counselors themselves explained the research to patients (often with the aid of written materials) and invited them to participate. Consent was sought on the understanding that the anonymity of all patients would be strictly protected by concealing their names (and other identifying information) in reports or publications. In addition, only Peräkylä, David, and a limited number of trained researchers and transcribers would have access to the audiotapes. The RFH videotapes were given additional protection—Peräkylä himself transcribed them, so access to them was limited to the two of them, and the videos were never to be publicly shown or indeed to leave the premises of the RFH.

The Contingency of Methodology

In a multiple center study, David could not, as in his earlier work, be physically present as all the data was gathered. Instead, the audiotapes were simply sent to him by each of the centers for analysis. Soon they were inundated by data to be passed on to their main transcriber, Dr David Greatbatch, himself a distinguished CA researcher.

(Continued)

(Continued)

However, given the high quality of transcription required and their limited resources, it became totally impractical to transcribe all the tapes. Instead, a few interviews were transcribed from each center. On this basis, what they could best call "candidate hypotheses" were developed about particular features in the talk, for instance how health advice was delivered and received. Peräkylä and David would then transcribe multiple instances from many more interviews where relevant phenomena seemed to occur.

In this way, the initial hypotheses were refined and subject to the test of **deviant cases**, which they actively sought out in their data. Overall, their method had much in common with the method of deviant-case analysis commonly used by anthropologists and ethnographers (see Chapter 13).

Let us now return to the two remaining questions:

- Is feedback to research subjects necessary and/or useful?
- Can I learn anything from relations with subjects in the field?

As we shall see, David's case study bears on both these questions.

FEEDBACK IN CASE STUDIES

The bottom line for practitioners is always, "So what?" A qualitative researcher's efforts to convey nonjudgmental objectivity is likely to be perceived instead as a typical academic cop-out. (Wolcott, 1990, p. 59)

In order to address practitioners' "So what?" question, during and after the research described previously, David held many workshops for AIDS counselors—including many who had not participated in the study. To give some idea of the extent of this "feedback," between 1989 and 1994 David ran four workshops on the research for counselors in London (two at hospitals, one at Goldsmiths College, and one at The Royal Society of Medicine), as well as three workshops in Australian centers, three in Trinidad and Tobago, and one each in the United States, Finland, and Sweden. In addition, each participating center was given a detailed report of the findings.

At these workshops, the researchers did not shield themselves behind a posture of scientific neutrality. But neither did they seek to instruct counselors about their presumed failings. Instead, they spoke about the ways in which their data showed that all communication formats and techniques had mixed consequences. They then invited their audience to discuss, in the light of their own priorities and resources, the implications for their practice. Moreover, when asked, the researchers were not afraid to suggest possible practical options.

In David's judgment, these meetings were successful, not least because their detailed transcripts showed features of counseling of which the practitioners themselves were often unaware. Often such features revealed how these people were cleverer than they had realized in following their own theoretical precepts and achieving their desired goals.

However, less experienced researchers may be more hesitant to offer feedback to practitioners and organizations. In this case, Wolcott (1990) offers three ideas set out in Table 17.3.

Of course, not all qualitative research is concerned with service providers such as organizations or professional practitioners. What kind of feedback is possible when you are studying non-work-related activities?

It is important that you try to offer feedback to all parties that are under study. So, if your target is, say, the activities of counselors or doctors, then you have not finished your task without offering some degree of feedback to their clients or patients. One way to do this is to utilize already-existing networks (e.g., patients' or community groups). So during David's work on pediatric clinics in the early 1980s, he spoke to parents' groups at heart and diabetic clinics. For instance, he used his clinic data to show mothers of diabetic adolescents that their feelings of inadequacy were common and probably inevitable given the guilt-provoking character of diabetic control and the usual rebelliousness of teenagers.

Table 17.3   Giving Feedback to Service Providers

1. Ask for the kind of additional information required for you to make a recommendation (e.g., what exactly is the organization trying to accomplish?)

2. Identify seeming paradoxes in the pursuit of goals (e.g., doctors who encourage their patients to communicate and to make choices may be the most autocratic—see below)

3. Identify alternatives to current practices and offer to assess these

SOURCE: Wolcott (1990), p. 60.

Where it is difficult to find such community groups, you may well find that participants in a study welcome receiving their own transcript of relevant data. For instance, a transcript of your own medical interview may work as a useful reminder of what the doctor said. And a transcript of a life-history interview may give a respondent a tangible autobiographical record.

We now want to move from ethical and practical matters to the methodological issue suggested by our final question:

- Can I learn anything from relations with subjects in the field?

One way of answering this question is to think through how your own identity was viewed by the participants. As the earlier case study showed, David's identity and aims as a researcher were viewed differently, in various contexts, by different professionals such as counselors and doctors and by research funding bodies. However, this was viewed not just as a "trouble" for the smooth running of the research but also as a source of data about how organizations worked (see also Peräkylä, 1989).

We now want to use the example of gender to examine further what we can learn from our relationships with our subjects. Following some general observations, we will offer a second case study.

GENDER IN CASE STUDY RESEARCH

Almost all the classics of the Chicago School were written by men, as were those researchers who rose up the academic hierarchy to become full professors (see Warren, 1988, p. 11). Increasingly, the gender of fieldworkers themselves was seen to play a crucial factor in observational research. Informants were shown to say different things to male and female researchers. For instance, in a study of a nude beach, when approached by someone of a different gender, people emphasized their interest in "freedom and naturalism." Conversely, where the researcher was the same gender as the informant, people were far more likely to discuss their sexual interests (Warren & Rasmussen, 1977, reported by Warren, 1988).

In studies that involved extended stays in the field, people have also been shown to make assumptions based on the gender of the researcher. For instance, particularly in rural communities, young, single women may be precluded from participating in many activities or asking many questions. Conversely, female gender may sometimes accord privileged access. For instance, Oboler (1986) reports that her pregnancy increased her rapport with her Kenyan informants, whereas Warren (1988, p. 18) suggests that women fieldworkers can make use of the sexist assumption that only men engage in "important business" by treating their "invisibility" as a resource. Equally, male fieldworkers may be excluded or exclude themselves from contact with female respondents in certain kinds of situations (see McKeganey & Bloor, 1991).

One danger in all this, particularly in the past, was that fieldworkers failed to report or reflect upon the influence of gender in their fieldwork. For instance, in a study of a large local government organization, David and his colleagues discussed but did not report the different kinds of situations to which the male and female researchers gained easy access (Silverman & Jones, 1976). Moreover, even as the role of doing fieldwork as a woman has become more addressed, hardly any attention has been paid by researchers to questions of male gender (McKeganey & Bloor, 1991, p. 198).

Nonetheless, as fashions change, it is possible to swing too far and accord gender issues too much importance. As McKeganey and Bloor (1991, pp. 195–196) argue, there are two important issues relevant to the significance of gender in fieldwork. First, the influence of gender may be negotiable with respondents and not simply ascribed. Second, we should resist "the tendency to employ gender as an explanatory catch-all" (1991, p. 196).

For instance, McKeganey and Bloor suggest that variables other than gender, like age and social class, may also be important in fieldwork. Equally, we would argue, following Schegloff (1991), that we need to demonstrate that participants are actually attending to gender in what they are doing, rather than just work with our intuitions or even with statistical correlations. None of this should imply that it would be correct to swing full circle and, like an earlier generation, ignore gender issues in research. It is incumbent upon fieldworkers to reflect on the basis and status of their observations. Clearly, how the researcher and the community studied respond to their gender can provide crucial insights into field realities. Indeed, we would do well to become conscious that even taken-for-granted assumptions might be culturally and historically specific. For instance, Warren suggests, "The focal gender *myth* of field research is the greater communicative skills and less threatening nature of the female fieldworker" (1988, p. 64, our emphasis). As Warren notes, the important thing is to resist treating such assumptions as "revealed truths" rather than as "accounts" that are historically situated.

The second case study provides one example of how gender can be relevant to field research.

CASE STUDY II: GENDER IN EAST AFRICAN FIELDWORK

Using observation coupled with face-to-face and e-mail interviews, Ryen (2004) has been doing fieldwork on East African businesses. In part, she is interested in the activities and identities of entrepreneurs of Asian origin.

Ryen's work involves crossing boundaries in three senses:

- Doing fieldwork in different cultures and countries

- Studying entrepreneurs whose freewheeling activities do not fit within a Western organizational model

- Working as a female researcher with male businessmen who regularly seek to test the boundaries of the relationship

The following extract from Ryen's field notes shows how delicate issues can arise in such a context:

[We ended a day by a three hour talk in my informant's office. Here is an extract from our conversation.]

Mahid: I have some American Rotarian visitors here. We are going out for dinner tonight. May I invite you to the dinner?

Anne: Thank you that would be very nice.

Mahid: Let me pick you up at your hotel.

Anne: Thanks but we have a car and a driver.

[At dinner, Anne finds herself seated next to Mahid. He leans toward her and says softly,]

Mahid: Can I invite you out to the disco tomorrow?

Anne: Oh, I have never been to a disco in this region. That would be fun but unfortunately we are leaving tomorrow afternoon.

Ryen reports that such invitations are much more frequent when she is doing fieldwork in East Africa than when studying Western businessmen. Considered purely instrumentally, they represent great opportunities for further ethnographic data and so she is reluctant to dismiss them. At the same time, with the kind of quick footwork seen in Extract 17.1, she establishes clear boundaries, finding "good" reasons not to accept activities that might categorize a meeting as a date.

When such invitations move toward more explicit flirting, matters can become still more delicate, as this extract, from an interview with an Asian businessman (Patel), suggests:

Patel: You are like a Sony radio. You know Sony radio?

A: Yes, we had one years back

Patel: I still have it, and you turn it on, and I get turned on (6.0) and then it comes to fine tuning, ohhhhh (4.0) that is exceptionally good (8.0)

A: that is a compliment

Patel: that is exceptionally good

A: even when I am interviewing, eh? (3.0)

Patel: yeah. The fault does not lie with the other party whom you are interviewing. The fault lies in you

A: Oh really? Tell me more

Patel: no, it is not that you do it deliberately. Ah I find you very attractive (3.0)

Patel: all right?

A: thank you. You made my day

Patel: that's my style. These guys who have probably seen women different ways, they look at you, they probably consider you the goddess

A: (smiling) so you think I should charge them?

Patel: you could actually

A: yes, that's a good idea

Ryen (2004) characterizes what is going on here as "a light hearted flirt." By cooperating with Patel's flirtation, Anne turns it into a playful game of mutual responses in rhythm with each other. In doing so, she argues that she can maintain her relationship with her informant in a relaxed, joyful, and mutually interesting way.

Ryen's data shows how the researcher needs to work at balancing the closeness and distance present in ethnographic fieldwork. In a sense, she is engaged in "emotion work." Such work may not produce better data but may give more data if the result is to prolong the relationship and also give access to data collection in a wider variety of contexts. So this second case study shows how gender may help you learn something from relations with subjects in the field.

Another way in which researchers have attempted to use field relations as data is by seeking and responding to comments made by participants about research conducted upon them. Returning to an issue we first raised in Chapter 14, can responses to feedback be used as a means of validating your research findings?

FEEDBACK AS A VALIDATION EXERCISE?

Reason and Rowan (1981) criticize researchers who are fearful of "contaminating their data with the experience of the subject." On the contrary, they argue, good research goes back to the subjects with the tentative results, and refines them in the light of the subjects' reactions.

This is just what Bloor (1978, 1983) attempted in his research on doctors' decision making. Bloor (1978) discusses three procedures that attempt respondent validation:

1. The researcher seeks to predict members' classifications in actual situations of their use (see Frake, 1964).

2. The researcher prepares hypothetical cases and predicts respondents' responses to them (see also Frake, 1964).

3. The researcher provides respondents with a research report and records their reactions to it.

In his study of doctors' decision making in tonsillectomy cases, Bloor used method 3. However, he had reservations about his surgeons' reactions to his report. It was not clear that they were very interested in findings that were not focused on their day-to-day concerns. Bloor's worries have been very effectively taken up by Fielding and Fielding (1986) (respondent validation is also criticized by Bryman, 1988, pp. 78–79). The Fieldings concede that subjects being studied may have additional knowledge, especially about the context of their actions. However,

> there is no reason to assume that members have privileged status as commentators on their actions . . . such feedback cannot be taken as direct validation or refutation of the observer's inferences. Rather such processes of so-called "validation" should be treated as yet another source of data and insight. (1986, p. 43)

We can only add that, if feedback is a highly problematic part of validating research, this does *not* mean that it should be ignored as a way of maintaining contact with subjects in the field. However, this issue should not be *confused* with the validation of research findings.

Moreover, as Bloor points out, the problematic research status of this activity need not mean that attempts at respondents' validation have *no* value. They do generate further data, which, while not validating the research report, often suggest interesting paths for further analysis (Bloor, 1983, p. 172).

CONCLUDING REMARKS

By referring to the function of respondent accounts, we are implying a **constructionist** model of how social reality operates. By contrast, **positivists** would be more concerned with how far any account was biased, whereas **emotionalists** might treat such feedback as adding to the authenticity of the research's findings. This is because, as noted at the outset of this chapter, the issue of relations in the field is riddled with theoretical assumptions.

So the message of this chapter is to treat your forays into the field as a rare opportunity to come to analytic grips with the nitty-gritty of human interaction. This is not merely an exciting (or boring) escape from the rhythms of academic life but a crucial opportunity to discover if your years of education can offer a useful prism through which to re-view what the rest of the world is up to.

KEY POINTS

In this chapter, we discussed how to respond to four practical questions in doing fieldwork:

- What is involved in obtaining access to a field site?

- What ethical issues lie in wait for you?

- What can you learn from relations in the field?

- Is feedback to research subjects necessary and/or useful?

Throughout, we emphasized that relations in the field are theoretically saturated. This cannot, therefore, be simply a technical issue to be resolved by technical means.

FURTHER READING

Hammersley and Atkinson (1983, pp. 54–76) provide a useful discussion of the practicalities of obtaining access to individuals, groups, and organizations. A more introductory account of these issues, appropriate to the undergraduate researcher, is found in Walsh (1988) Fielding (1982), Ryen (2004), and Back (2004) provide very interesting accounts of the perils of field research in tricky settings. Issues of ethics in qualitative research are well discussed in Jennifer Mason's *Qualitative Researching* (1996), Chapters 2, 4, and 8. Peräkylä

(1989) and McKeganey and Bloor (1991) provide revealing accounts of the negotiation of identity in fieldwork. Before you contemplate taking your findings back to your subjects, you should read Bloor (1978, 1983).

EXERCISE 17.1

Consult your research notes on your contacts in the field. Now answer the following questions:

1. What successes and troubles have occurred during your fieldwork?

2. How can you treat such events as data?

3. What theoretical ideas can you use to help you (if you need help, consult McKeganey & Bloor, 1991; Peräkylä, 1989; or Ryen, 2004)?

EXERCISE 17.2

Make a list of the ethical problems that you have detected in your research. Now explain how you have resolved them.

Then give your account, together with your research diary, to your supervisor or a fellow student. Ask the recipient whether he or she is satisfied with how you have (a) identified and (b) handled ethical issues.

CHAPTER 18

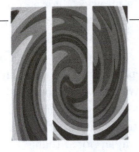

Working With Your Chair/Mentor

CHAPTER OBJECTIVES

In this chapter, you will

- Learn to recognize the differing expectations in the student–mentor relationship

- Know the different roles a mentor can occupy

- Know how to select a chair for your doctoral committee

- Learn how to effectively work with your chair

INTRODUCTION

PhD students at U.S. universities are supervised by a doctoral committee made up of five faculty members (four from their department and one from an outside, but related, field). The committee is headed by a chair, who acts as the student's primary supervisor. It is in consultation with the chair that the student selects the other members of his or her committee. Given the primary role of a committee chair, in this chapter we focus on how to work effectively with this faculty supervisor. While other members of your doctoral committee can play an important role in your academic career, your chair is expected to be your key adviser and thus deserves special attention.

HORROR STORIES AND EXPECTATIONS

As the central figure in your doctoral education, your committee chair is sometimes referred to as your *mentor*, a word that hints at many expectations but explains nothing in and of itself. In August 1998, Jason D. Altom, a 27-year-old PhD candidate in chemistry at Harvard, committed suicide. In his suicide note (a letter addressed to the chair of his department), Altom wrote, "This event could have been avoided. . . . Professors here have too much power over the lives of their grad students" (Schneider, 1998). This event inspired a national discussion about how graduate students are treated by their mentors. A piece in the *Chronicle of Higher Education*, for example, noted that

> good jobs, prestigious grants, even tenure depend on strong letters of recommendation. For many students, the only letter they have is from their adviser. That leaves many of them feeling that their fate hinges on the whims of a single person. (Schneider, 1998)

Perhaps due to its sympathetic tone, this piece generated a good deal of responses from current or former graduate students, who posted their own horror stories on the *Chronicle*'s Weblog. Here are two examples (for a full list of these comments, visit http://chronicle.com/colloquy/98/suicide/re.htm).

> Academia reminds me of a child's pet turtle race.
> Would you work for someone who is accountable to no one?
> Moreover, would you invest years of your time and work for an uncertain compensation at the end of uncertain time, by uncertain rules, at the whim and behest of someone who is accountable to no one?
> Of course not.
> Then why are you in graduate school?
> Here is a parable. A certain professor deliberately starts two graduate students off on the same thesis. . . . The two students are therefore set up to race against each other, like pet turtles. The turtles slowly complete their race course in seven, eight, or more years before the turtle master decides to either toss one out, or merely place one of them back to the starting line. (Marc Adelman, 1998)

> Thank you for opening up this great debate! My seven years in grad school were at least four years longer than necessary and became more emotionally distressful as I moved through the process. The "mind games" began when professors would limit admissions to gateway programs. I left the

Ed Psych program after watching other grad students get pummeled in an endless barrage of requirements and useless information. We called it the "indentured servitude program" since no one got out before seven years, you couldn't work for real money and the University paid $600.00 a month to its TAs. After finally getting my Chair to agree to a topic (a mere three years and countless possibilities), another professor refused the methodology, and later canceled my defense three days prior to its scheduled date. It took years and lots of support to overcome the anger and frustration. The worst thing is that it has nothing to do with scholarship and everything about power! (Michal Rosenberger, PhD, Educational Consultant, 1998)

Horrifying tales of PhD advisers mistreating their protégés are the academic equivalent of urban legends—everyone who hears them suspects that it is not possible for a faculty member to abuse a graduate student to that extent; yet, there is enough truth there for the stories to cause fear. Additionally, a mentor–protégé story is inherently appealing to many listeners because it has all the makings of a good drama (i.e., a person's future is at stake in a close but unequal relationship) or tragedy (much could go wrong here, and sadly sometimes does). Indeed, the student–mentor relationship has been dramatized in Hollywood films for years (e.g., *My Fair Lady* with Audrey Hepburn and Rex Harrison, *Educating Rita* with Michael Caine, *Wonder Boys* with Michael Douglas, and *Finding Forrester* with Sean Connery).

The drama and comedy of graduate school aside, horror stories are exceptions to the norm, and we hope they will not accord with the average student's actual experiences. If you are just starting out, let us reassure you that such happenings are exceptional not least because faculty advisers are usually better trained and are monitored by their departments. Such stories do, however, underline the significance of the mentor–protégé relationship. When writing a dissertation, a bad outcome usually indicates bad supervision. As a graduate student, you have limited time and financial resources. You cannot afford to waste months, if not years, on a dead-end dissertation and a bad mentor.

Our goal in this chapter is to assist you with making the most of your relationship with your mentor and spare you the time and agony of learning from direct experience. To this end, we have organized this chapter along the following central issues:

- Outline of student and faculty expectations

- Definitions of the many roles of a mentor

- Suggestions regarding how to select an ideal mentor

- Consideration of how to be an "ideal" protégé

- Discussion of specific challenges of a qualitative dissertation

Our overall aim is to untangle the precise meaning and various dimensions of student-mentor relationship.

OVERVIEW OF STUDENT AND FACULTY EXPECTATIONS

Estelle Phillips wrote her dissertation on the PhD as a learning process. Some of her findings are reported in Phillips and Pugh (1994). Although her data was obtained in the UK, what she says is equally relevant for North American students. Table 18.1 sets out Phillips' findings about the expectations of PhD students.

All the student expectations shown in Table 18.1 seem quite reasonable. If you do not feel that your PhD adviser is meeting such expectations, it is worth raising your concerns at an early stage.

However, you should also know that your advisers will have certain expectations about you. A good guide to how the land lies in this area is found in Table 18.2.

We suspect that Table 18.2 will contain some items that you may never have thought about. But, yes, it is true that supervisors expect you to be fun to be with, or to use a formal term, they expect you to be *collegial*. Most want to be stimulated by, and, indeed, to learn from, their students. Indeed, graduate students often forget that the mentor–protégé interactions are mutually

Table 18.1   Students' Expectations for Supervisors

- To supervise

- To read their work well in advance

- To be available when needed

- To be friendly, open, and supportive

- To be constructively critical

- To have a good knowledge of their research area

- To be interested/excited by their topic

- To help them get a good job afterward

SOURCE: Adapted from Phillips and Pugh (1994, Chap. 11).

Table 18.2   Doctoral Advisers' Expectations for Students

- The student will work independently.
- First drafts will not usually be submitted.
- The student will be available for "regular" meetings.
- He or she will be honest about his or her progress.
- He or she will follow advice.
- He or she will be excited about his or her work.
- The student will be able to surprise the adviser(s).
- He or she will be fun to be with.

SOURCE: Phillips and Pugh (1994, Chap. 8).

beneficial. Your faculty advisers have scholarly aspirations of their own, and in an ideal student, they find a potential colleague who could advance their research agenda.

In short, like all other meaningful social interactions, your relationship with your faculty adviser will revolve around certain expectations. Problems typically arise from a failure of one or both parties to define and fulfill these expectations.

As you will see throughout this chapter, mentors serve many functions and occupy many roles in a PhD student's life. The full recognition of these variations will help you define and select your ideal mentor.

CHAIR AS THE ACADEMIC ADVISER

The most basic and essential role of a dissertation chair is to advise the student on purely academic matters. Your faculty chairs are formally responsible for assisting you with academic progress in three areas: selecting courses, selecting committee members, and writing the dissertation.

Coursework

Faculty chairs are expected to advise their students with selection of graduate courses that help develop the student's area of specialization within a particular discipline. For example, with the advice of his mentor, for his PhD in sociology, in addition to fulfilling the requirements of his department, Amir also took courses in continental philosophy, anthropology, and German language.

The idea was that such courses could advance Amir's interest in interpretive and qualitative sociology. A good adviser recognizes the students' goals (even if they are poorly articulated at first) and works with him or her to develop a plan for an area of specialization within the practical boundaries of the university and the student's chosen profession.

Selection of Committee Members

In his or her capacity as an academic adviser, your chair will also assist you with selecting faculty members who could serve on your dissertation committee. It is critical to consult your chair about other committee members early in the process of your dissertation work. Your worst nightmare is a doctoral committee made up of people who are personally and professionally incompatible. Attention to the composition of the committee is particularly important for qualitative dissertations. You want to avoid the problem of having a committee that fights over methodological choices at every step of the process. A common source of contention with qualitative dissertations is that quantitatively trained committee members grill the student on issues that are not of direct relevance to a qualitative dissertation. So, for example, a student who has completed an ethnography of a health clinic has to explain why his 20 in-depth interviews are not suitable for logistic regression analysis.

Now, familiarity with statistical analysis is useful and it may be your best choice in some research scenarios (e.g., analyzing the relationship between support for capital punishment and religiosity). Indeed, you should not dismiss questions about causality, sample size, and generalizability simply because they sound positivistic. These are all relevant questions with sometimes surprisingly similar answers (see Flyvbjerg, 2004).

However, your committee meetings should not be used as an occasion for debating these matters *ad infinitum* while what you need is enough feedback to advance to the next phase of your career. Once you complete your PhD, you will have the rest of your academic career to contemplate the pros and cons of positivism. So particularly with a qualitative dissertation, the chair plays a crucial role in minimizing internal conflict in the doctoral committee.

Assistance With the Dissertation

For a dissertation, you can choose from an endless list of topics. Some students start their graduate education with a specific substantive area they want to study (e.g., gender, race, crime). Others have a less clear research agenda. Your chair, based on his or her own specialization and interests, can assist with narrowing down your choices. He or she, for example, might recommend that you join his or her ongoing research on conflict resolution in formal organizations. This kind of assistance is invaluable and a necessary part of your graduate education. Few things are more frustrating than pursuing one dead-end topic after another. Indeed, we suspect this is a primary reason why so many ABDs (graduate students who have completed *all* requirements *but* their dissertation) never finish. Unfortunately, it is all too easy to get lost in the forest of possible dissertation topics and aimlessly wander there for years.

Similarly, your chair should be well versed in your chosen research methodology. This is especially important for qualitative PhD dissertations. It seems that many faculty claim interest or expertise in qualitative methods when few actually have published anything in a qualitative journal. We suggest that you select an adviser whose publication record is commensurate with his or her desire to serve on your committee; otherwise, you end up in the unenviable position of educating your chair, as indicated in the following excerpt from a PhD student:

> I spend as much time teaching my dissertation chairperson as I spend writing my dissertation. At one point, I was so desperate that I seriously considered writing the criteria for evaluating a qualitative study right into my methodology. Of course, my chairperson cut all of that, as well as my reflexive statement—that is, how I became interested in this topic and how my background as an African-American woman would influence my interpretations. (Miller, Nelson, & Moore 1998, p. 389)

You should be able to rely on your chair for guidance through every phase of the dissertation process. That dissertation chairs occasionally have to be critical of their students' writing does not mean they can arbitrarily obstruct their students' progress. Additionally, a good chair should not use your dissertation as a test case for learning about a new methodology. If your dissertation adviser is not helping you in these areas, find another chair.

The academic role of a PhD adviser is well established in universities and in most cases formally stated in graduate handbooks and other documents. If you are not familiar with your particular institution's policies, ask for them. However, in addition to the institutionalized academic role, an adviser is in a position to advance a student's career in many other ways. Let us now consider the less formal roles of a PhD adviser.

CHAIR AS THE CONFIDANT/PROTECTOR

It is not uncommon for graduate students to develop a close relationship with their advisers. Many graduate students have been saved from the depths of despair by motivational speech, or "pep talks," from their caring mentors. Often graduate students develop a close bond with their mentors. Your advisers could become people you look up to, trust, and in some ways idolize. Having said that, do not expect every faculty adviser to be involved in your progress and personal turmoil to the same degree. Some are better at playing social worker than others. Remember that your relationship with your adviser in theory is not a personal one but a contractual agreement between two professionals—you as a student agree to do x, y, and z, and the adviser agrees to perform a narrowly defined set of duties in return. PhD advisers are not trained mental health counselors and many detest being confused with one. So having a close relationship with a faculty adviser is a fringe benefit, not an entitlement.

As a graduate student, you may not be familiar with the history and internal politics of a department. As Charles Crothers (1991, p. 334) notes, academic departments are highly stratified organizations made up of several groups (e.g., administrators, faculty, staff, graduate students, and undergraduate students). Each group has its own status and interests within the hierarchical structure of your university. Graduate students exist in a limbo where they are expected to invest in the institution's long-term goals, but they are also expected to finish their degree within a reasonable period of time and obtain gainful employment elsewhere (as a general rule, most departments do not hire their own graduates). So you are expected to at once be vocal and involved and recognized as a productive member of the department and yet not become so entrenched in departmental politics that you forget that your goal is to move on. Balancing these two, sometimes conflicting, roles can become very challenging.

This is where a good mentor can save you from yourself, as it were. What seems like an innocent comment to you could be viewed as heresy by a senior professor in your department, and the offense might haunt you for the rest of your career there. A good adviser could share the departmental "scoop" with you over a cup of coffee and save you from unknowingly committing egregious offenses. At the same time, your adviser could act as your advocate in closed departmental meetings, where, for example, you and your research are the topic of the latest round of griping about frivolous graduate students. A few words of praise from your adviser could go a long way in establishing your name as a serious graduate student. Most important, a good adviser can tell you when it is time to disengage from a particular issue or fringe departmental skirmish and return your attention to the work of writing your dissertation.

CHAIR AS A COLLEAGUE

Finally, your chair is a potential colleague. The most successful graduate students have coauthored publications before completing their PhD and getting on the job market. The most likely avenue for predissertation publications is collaborations with your chair. Some chairs are so devoted as to edit and comment on their students' work ("shepherd their papers") without even asking to be a coauthor. Indeed, from a purely professional perspective, this is one of the most important sources of support you can receive from your mentor. In the competitive academic world of "publish or perish," nothing ensures your job prospects better than a few publications in refereed journals.

Similarly, your chair's reputation and his or her contacts are essential to your finding and being considered for academic employment. Your chair is the person whose letters of recommendation are most carefully read by search committees when you apply for a job. A weak letter of reference from your chair is the kiss of death on the job market. In some cases, your chair is contacted by his or her colleagues in the field and asked if he or she could recommend a recent graduate for a particular academic position. This kind of referral almost guarantees that you will move to the top of a short list. Finally, even after you receive your PhD and get a job, your contacts with your chair will help you be considered for publications and grants.

WHO IS THE "IDEAL" MENTOR?

After the foregoing discussion about the different roles of a mentor, it is tempting to say that the ideal mentor is someone who embodies all these characteristics (i.e., an academic adviser, a friend, and a colleague). Indeed, a few graduate students have the good fortune of having such mentors. For example, Sylvia Ansay (personal correspondence) referred to her mentor, Jay Gubrium, as "100% helpful." Specifically, she states,

My adviser encouraged and supported me through every phase of the research and defense. He stood up for me against the good folks at NIH [National Institutes of Health] and helped me put together a committee that would support me as well. He relied on me to schedule meetings with him and my committee members any time I had questions. When I asked for direction, he provided numerous examples of possibilities. He was a motivator rather than a dictator. Because we checked in with each other regularly, there were no last minute surprises.

Similarly, Darin Weinberg (personal correspondence) describes his mentor, Mel Pollner, in this way:

My adviser was a great help with respect to many dimensions of the dissertation ranging from relevant literature, to relevant thematic foci, to structuring the dissertation, to writing style, to pragmatic job prospects issues, to advice on publishing outlets, to plain old encouragement. Though Mel sometimes gave me feedback and advice I didn't really want to hear about my work, this was to my mind much appreciated candour and not in any way insulting or disrespectful. I didn't have any difficulties with him, and sought out his guidance as much as I could get it. We formally met perhaps every four to six weeks and once in awhile informally as well.

Darin and Sylvia's experiences are somewhat exceptional. Most graduate students do not have the good fortune of finding such exemplary mentors. Indeed, to some extent, the notion of an "ideal mentor" is a fiction, a mythical creature like the unicorn or Santa. Students are not entirely to blame for the lofty expectation for a perfect mentor. As Edward Tenner (2004) notes, the problem is that the word *mentor* has come to mean someone who is inherently "good." In his words,

The ideal of the mentor has been extolled in business, academe, government, the military, and the professions for decades. I see merit in it, too. But I'm also disturbed that it nearly always is presented as a good in its own right; too rarely are its origins and ethical ambiguities examined. (Tenner, 2004)

Your faculty advisers are no more perfect than members of your immediate family. They have their own particular eccentricities and weaknesses. If you are looking for perfection in your adviser, you are very likely to be disappointed. Several years ago, after complaining about a particular policy, Amir was told by a university administrator, "We cannot be all things to all people." Obviously, the statement fell well short of a satisfactory resolution of the problem, but it does, nonetheless, contain its own wisdom. Few mentors are all these things to all their students. Such a state would require a level of dedication and concern with a student's life that frankly may not be professionally or personally healthy for everyone involved.

Define your ideal mentor based on your particular interests and needs. A handful of students are fortunate enough to receive everything on their wish list. Sometimes PhD students go to a department where they have found their ideal mentor and program. In these cases, the choice of a mentor precedes the selection of a department. For the average applicant, however, family and financial considerations tend to play a larger part in their choice of a graduate program. The norm is to apply to several schools and go where you have the best of all circumstances (financial, personal, etc.).

Thus, for their choice of a mentor or a chair, most PhD students have to make do with the faculty in their particular program. In other words, you have to choose from who is available and willing to work with you, and that essentially means you will have to settle for someone other than your ideal mentor. In short, an ideal mentor is no more realistic than an ideal romantic partner. A student–mentor relationship starts with some fundamentals (e.g., trust and interest) and grows over time (or in some unfortunate cases, deteriorates over time).

Another option is *pluralistic* mentoring. Unlike the world of marital relations, with mentoring there are no monogamy laws. Few faculty mentors demand your undivided attention. Therefore, there is no need to commit to one person when you can learn more from your contacts with many. In the following, Edward Tenner makes a strong argument for pluralistic mentoring:

> Mentoring of the pluralistic kind . . . has become and has remained a great force in my life. I was able to enter science publishing and succeed in it thanks in part to another of my graduate teachers in the early 1970s who offered me a position as a research assistant on a project on the history of disease. From my first employer in publishing, I learned the art of tactful business letters, of which he was the greatest master I have ever known. A science magazine editor told me her private system for finding authors of great popular-science articles before they started publishing in other magazines; I was able to apply her methods to the book world. One of the authors I sponsored, an Israeli historian of science, encouraged me to develop a new scholarly identity through my writing on the history of technology. And all the while an undergraduate adviser's criticisms of my college papers and the example of his playful but vigorous writing and lecturing styles have continued to inspire me. (Tenner, 2004)

In sum, do your homework before settling on a mentor. There is no substitute for an informed choice. Before committing yourself to a particular mentor, consider some of the points we have highlighted throughout this chapter.

WHO IS THE "IDEAL" PROTÉGÉ?

In the interest of fairness and a spirit of reciprocity, this is a very apt question. What should you do to be a worthy protégé? Table 18.3 has some suggestions.

For a more humorous take on the same etiquette standards for dealing with your professor, consider the list from William Nish in Table 18.4.

Humor aside, you will do well to remember that you are being chosen by faculty as much as you are choosing them as your chair or committee members—to say the least, the process is reciprocal. First, the faculty are not obligated to

Table 18.3   Ideal Protégé

- *Clarity*: In your verbal and written communications with your adviser, be clear about what you want. It is rude and impractical to assume people know your aspirations despite your failure to clearly communicate them.

- *Reliability*: Not showing up for meetings, missing deadlines, and constantly changing your mind about your research are big no-no's.

- *Boundary Maintenance*: Do not overwhelm your adviser. Be respectful of his or her time and privacy.

- *Recognize Strengths and Weaknesses*: Know the limitations of your adviser. Do not expect, or worse, pressure him or her to perform beyond his or her personal and professional capabilities.

Table 18.4   Things One Should Not Do If One Expects a Good Recommendation Letter

- Be quick to apply such meaningful and concise labels as "busywork," "irrelevant," and "boring" to anything which you do not like or understand.

- Always be ready with reasons why you are an exception to the rules.

- Avoid taking examinations at the same time and under the same conditions as the rest of the class.

- Be very casual about class attendance. When you see your professor, be sure to ask, "Did I miss anything important in class today?"

- Be consistently late for class and other appointments.

- Do not read your assignments in advance of class lecture and discussion. This actually allows you to study more efficiently, for you can take up class time asking about things that are explained in the reading. To be sure that you get the important information, you can adopt a look of pained confusion when the professor refers to points made in the readings; this will prompt him or her to go over them again.

- Avoid using the professor's office hours for appointments. Instead, show up when he or she is trying to finish a lecture before the next class hour . . . and say, as you enter the office, "Are you busy?"

SOURCE: Adapted from William Nish (2007).

serve on your committee; they can and occasionally do turn students down. But more important, as a graduate student you are under observation even before you are officially admitted into the program. In an interesting article titled "The Protestant Ethic and the Spirit of Academia," Eric Plutzer argues that some graduate students are seen by their professors as "predestined to succeed" (1991, p. 302). According to Plutzer, even the seemingly objective criteria for being selected as a student "who has what it takes" are not entirely empirical or scientific. For example, about the use of standardized scores (e.g., GREs) as an admission criterion, Plutzer notes,

> On a graduate admissions committee, I observed that major emphasis was placed on scores by professors who had taught me in methods classes that such scores were biased, were unreliable, and did not predict academic success. (1991, p. 303)

Similarly, Plutzer suggests that letters of recommendation matter in the admission process primarily if they come from the elite who also belong to the "predestined" class. After you are admitted to the program, additional factors continue to influence your designation as a worthy graduate student. For example, what Plutzer calls "seminar performance," especially in the form of "verbal and written articulateness, as well as a flair for aggressive [masculine] debate" (p. 304) is often viewed by the faculty as a sign of predestination. Another dimension of your perceived worthiness as a protégé is your dissertation topic. As Plutzer puts it, you are damned if your professors respond to your proposed dissertation with "Where is the sociology in all this?" (p. 304).

Some graduate students choose to ignore these realities and press on with little or no regard for how they are perceived by the faculty. Indeed, some of these PhD candidates successfully complete the requirements of their degree and finish their dissertations. However, as Plutzer notes, success in academia is not entirely based on the completion of your degree and even being published. Your long-term employment potential and ability to become a significant player in your field largely depend on whether or not you were perceived as a member of the elect or the predestined. If you are one of the chosen, the recognition and support you receive internally while finishing your dissertation will be augmented with external connections and a network of professors who will nourish your academic career for many years to come. Conversely, you can join the ranks of part-time or unemployed PhDs if you do not have this kind of support.

On the one hand, we acknowledge that the predestination doctrine, as outlined by Plutzer, is unfair and should be changed to a system that enables every graduate student in a PhD program to succeed. Yet, as social scientists, we know that the realities of social institutions do not change overnight. Therefore, we encourage you at least to be aware of your faculty's expectations of you. In that spirit, in the following section, we offer practical advice for how you can increase your chances of being perceived as a student predestined for academic greatness. Specifically, we turn our attention to how the differing expectations of mentors and students can be converted into (good) practice. The next section is divided into three chronological stages that roughly correspond to a typical graduate student's progress in a doctoral program.

THE EARLY STAGES

The first few months of working toward a PhD are crucial. If you fail to make a good start, it may be very difficult to retrieve the situation at a later point. Here are some points to think about:

- *Choosing a mentor*: Ideally you should choose someone whose approach and interests gel with your own. This may be someone whose work you have read or, better still, whose courses you have taken. Alternatively, try to get a look at completed dissertations supervised by this person. Try to avoid simply being assigned to an adviser. Also try to establish beforehand whether your potential adviser is planning any long trips abroad or other career moves that might disrupt your progress.

- *Do you need joint supervision?* Where your work covers more than one area, it can make sense to have two mentors. However, tread warily! Not infrequently, joint supervision means that each adviser will assume that the other is taking care of you. Conversely, joint mentoring could result in unproductive competition and turf wars between your professors. So make sure that there is planning so that you do not fall between the cracks.

- *Combining the PhD with an RA (research assistantship) or TA (teaching assistantship)*: Most graduate students in the United States receive some kind of departmental funding to help cover their tuition costs. This usually comes in the form of teaching or research assistantships. If possible, arrange for this work done for or under the supervision of your mentor. The advantage is that you will have frequent contact with your mentor. However, before signing for any assistantships, make sure that you understand the terms of your contract and can handle the workload.

- *Getting early direction*: In the early stages, you should expect a lot of support. You should not be blown off with a reading list and the promise of an appointment in 3 months' time! Instead, you might expect weekly meetings, based on small tasks, to build your confidence and give you a sense of direction.

- *Being informed*: Right from the start of your studies, you should expect to be properly inducted with regard to your department's research training program and to your rights and responsibilities as a student (this is usually done through first-year-student orientation seminars and graduate handbooks).

THE LATER STAGES

After the first crucial 3 to 6 months, your PhD adviser should gradually wean you from total dependence. As you become more confident and independent, your adviser should encourage you to believe that you know more about your topic than he or she does. At these later stages, the following issues become important:

- *Shaping your writing in a professional manner*: Your PhD adviser should help you move your style of writing to the kind expected in journals in your field. For instance, this may mean encouraging you to cut down the kind of tedious literature reviews you wrote as an undergraduate and to use concepts economically. A few concepts (even just one) applied to your data are generally much more productive than data analysis that is all over the place.

- *Encouraging self-confidence*: To be economical in this way, you need self-confidence, and this is what your adviser should provide. Where appropriate, you should also be told that your work is up to standard for the degree you are seeking.

- *Setting deadlines*: Deadlines and targets can be a source of neurosis for students. However, without them, we guarantee you will be lost. Therefore, at the end of each semester or quarter (or every several months), you should expect to set a reasonable target and agree to a date by which it can be reached.

- *Working with other students*: You should not be confined to your relationship with your adviser. Expect to be advised about relevant conferences and Web sites. You will also meet other students during your research training. Find out which ones have similar topics to yours or are working with similar concepts and/or data. Then organize discussions with them. Even better, ask your mentor to set up data sessions or group discussions with other students that he or she is supervising.

- *Learning tricks*: Based on a long career of supervision, the notable sociologist Howard Becker has suggested a number of useful tricks that advisers can employ for your benefit. As he puts it, "a trick is a specific operation that shows a way around some common difficulty, suggests a procedure that solves relatively easily what would otherwise seem an intractable and persistent problem" (Becker, 1998, p. 4 [for some of these tricks, try Exercise 18.1]).

• *Advising on publications*: Toward the later stages of your work, your mentor should be a good source of advice about which journals are appropriate for submission of some of your work and about how to organize your presentations and seminar papers for such a setting (see Chapter 27).

• *Giving you a mock dissertation defense*: Finally, ask your adviser, a few faculty members, and fellow graduate students to participate in a practice dry run for the oral defense of your dissertation (see Chapter 25).

Much of the support that your adviser can give you should be facilitated by an institutional structure within your department that encourages good practice. We conclude this chapter by discussing such practice.

STANDARDS OF GOOD PRACTICE

As a research student, you have a right to expect the following institutional structures. Although different formats will apply in different disciplines and countries, what follows seems to us to be minimum requirements.

• Orientation seminars in which departmental research and teaching training, as well as funding resources are explained and you get to meet the faculty and some of the senior graduate students.

• A doctoral committee with an identified and accessible chairperson.

• A graduate handbook that explains departmental policies and expectations for the supervision and training of graduate students. This handbook should set out training requirements and the rights and responsibilities of graduate students. It should also explain procedures for changing advisers and filing grievances if you have an intractable problem that you cannot sort out between you.

• Written memos or e-mails from your adviser outlining expectations and deadlines.

Of course, we are not suggesting that you present your adviser with a copy of this book and demand that he or she strictly adhere to these points. However, if your graduate program seems to lack such structures and policies, you have reason to be alarmed.

CONCLUDING REMARKS

The number of students enrolled in doctoral programs seems to be on the rise. One good consequence of this has been that supervision has increasingly become recognized as a professional skill that requires proper training and monitoring. In addition to committee chairs, most departments have a faculty member who serves as a graduate adviser who is responsible for informing new students about policies, updating them about deadlines, and assisting them with filling out and submitting required forms.

Of course, getting a PhD, or even an MA, should never be achieved via any methods resembling factory mass production. We hope that there will always be a place for inspiration and lateral thinking. But such features of intellectual achievement should not be a substitute for an institutional structure that offers proper student support and guidance. Students doing qualitative and field research need to be particularly cautious about potential dangers posed by lack of structure and regular supervision. You do not want to spend months or years in the field only to realize that you do not have enough of the right material for a defensible dissertation. Take the initiative to consult with your adviser frequently about your progress. Above all, as you advance in your career in academia or other professional fields, you will learn that there is no substitute for self-discipline.

A CAUTIONARY TALE

The following parable about choosing a PhD adviser is widely circulated on the Web with no citation or reference for the original author. This particular version was retrieved March 27, 2007, from http://ifaq.wap.org/society/rabbitfoxwolf.html. Although the story might be overstating the case for the importance of a PhD adviser, the "moral of the story," as stated in the last few lines, is not without merit.

The Rabbit, the Fox, and the Wolf: A Fable

One sunny day, a rabbit came out of her hole in the ground to enjoy the weather. The day was so nice that the rabbit became careless, so a fox sneaked up to her and caught her.
"I am going to eat you for lunch!" said the fox.
"Wait!" replied the rabbit, "You should at least wait a few days."
"Oh yeah? Why should I wait?"
"Well, I am just finishing writing my PhD thesis."
"Hah! That's a stupid excuse. What is the title of your thesis anyway?"
"I am writing my thesis on 'The Superiority of Rabbits Over Foxes and Wolves.'"

(Continued)

(Continued)

"Are you crazy? I should eat you up right now! Everybody knows that a fox will always win over a rabbit."

"Not really, not according to my research. If you like, you can come to my hole and read it for yourself. If you are not convinced, you can go ahead and have me for lunch."

"You are really crazy!" But since the fox was curious and had nothing to lose, it went with the rabbit into its hole. The fox never came back out.

A few days later, the rabbit was again taking a break from writing and, sure enough, a wolf came out of the bushes and was ready to eat her.

"Wait!" yelled the rabbit. "You cannot eat me right now."

"And why might that be, you fuzzy appetizer?"

"I am almost finished writing my PhD thesis on 'The Superiority of Rabbits Over Foxes and Wolves.'"

The wolf laughed so hard that it almost lost its hold on the rabbit. "Maybe I shouldn't eat you, you are really sick in your head; you might have something contagious," the wolf opined.

"Come read for yourself; you can eat me after that if you disagree with my conclusions." So the wolf went to the rabbit's hole and never came out.

The rabbit finished writing her thesis and was out celebrating in the lettuce fields. Another rabbit came by and asked, "What's up? You seem to be very happy."

"Yup, I just finished writing up my dissertation."

"Congratulations! What is it about?"

"It is titled 'The Superiority of Rabbits Over Foxes and Wolves.'"

"Are you sure? That doesn't sound right."

"Oh yes, you should come over and read for yourself."

So they went together to the rabbit's hole.

As they went in, the friend saw the typical graduate student abode, albeit a rather messy one after writing a thesis. The computer with the controversial dissertation was in one corner, on the right there was a pile of fox bones, on the left was a pile of wolf bones, and in the middle was a lion.

The moral of the story is: The title of your dissertation doesn't matter. All that matters is who your thesis adviser is.

KEY POINTS

1. Some students have terrible experiences of supervision. By understanding what produced these horror stories, you can try to avoid them happening in your case.

2. It is not unreasonable to have a set of clear expectations about the support and advice that your adviser can offer (and to know what to do if these expectations are not met).

3. Advisers have a set of expectations about you, too. Know what they are and try to meet them.

4. Your department should have structures of training and of monitoring supervision that offer you the support you need.

FURTHER READING

Phillips and Pugh's *How To Get a PhD* (1994) is a gold mine of practical advice. For more American-oriented guides, see Kjell Rudestam and Rae Newton's *Surviving Your Dissertation* (1992) and Robert Peters's *Getting What You Came For: The Smart Student's Guide to Earning a Master's or a PhD* (1997). Howard S. Becker's book *Tricks of the Trade* (1998) is a beautifully written account of a lifetime of helping research students to think critically.

For an in-depth discussion of mentorship, read Edward Tenner's "The Pitfalls of Academic Mentorships" (2004).

For a selected bibliography on doctoral education, visit the following Web site: http://www.grad.washington.edu/envision/project_resources/biblio_alpha .html.

EXERCISE 18.1

To receive concrete help from your dissertation supervisor, ask if he or she could

1. Offer a written summary of your work with an emphasis on the strengths you can build on and the weaknesses that you need to address.

2. Help you do a limited analysis of a particular situation or data segment from your research. The purpose of this exercise is to rein in any excessive theorizing of your work and return your attention to an empirically grounded analysis.

SOURCE: Adapted from Becker (1998).

EXERCISE 18.2

Visit the Web site for Graduate Student Resources (http://www-personal.umich .edu/~danhorn/graduate.html) and see what other graduate students have to say about their experiences.

EXERCISE 18.3

Search the Internet using the words *graduate handbook*. Compare and contrast policies of different universities. Which ones are most supportive of graduate students? Which are least supportive?

CHAPTER 19

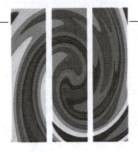

Getting Feedback

CHAPTER OBJECTIVES
By the end of this chapter, you will be able to
• Understand the importance of feedback on your work
• Recognize and organize opportunities for feedback
• Understand the nature and importance of shaping your work with an audience in mind

INTRODUCTION

Analyzing research data and writing up our findings are never solitary activities—although this is certainly how they can seem as we labor in front of our PC screens in the small hours. In practice, researching involves entering a series of social relationships. These include supervisor–supervisee, student–student, student members of the wider academic community, and student researcher–research subjects in the **field**.

As we saw in the previous chapter, such relationships need not just be viewed as potential or real sources of "trouble." Instead, they can and should be treated as important sources of insight into how well we are practicing our research skills. Effective feedback is an essential resource for effective research. As two psychologists have put it,

Adults learn best in situations where they can practise and receive feedback, in a controlled, non-threatening environment. So a good principle to aim for is: no procedure, technique, skill, etc., which is relevant for your thesis project should be exercised by you there for the first time. (Phillips & Pugh, 1994, p. 52)

Nonthreatening feedback can also work if your writing seems to have dried up. Writer's block is something we all experience from time to time. So don't despair. If you can't face feedback, we have found that a complete break for a week or two usually works (for more discussion of writer's block, including solutions, see Ward, 2002, pp. 96–100).

In this chapter, we will discuss two means of obtaining feedback on your research:

- Writing draft papers
- Giving oral presentations

WRITING

Delivering papers on agreed topics at regular intervals to your supervisor is the standard university method of working toward a final piece of assessed research. Constructive feedback from your supervisor can encourage you to scale new heights. By contrast, where that feedback is minimal or even destructive, your whole enterprise may be threatened.

So, if your supervisor is very critical of a paper you have submitted, you should expect to be told how you can improve your work and to be offered practical suggestions rather than woolly generalities. For instance, being told to think "more critically" or to "be more rigorous" is unlikely to be helpful. By contrast, specific advice about a new topic or a different way of pursuing one of your existing topics should give you some useful impetus (see Chapter 18).

But your supervisor is not the only person who can give you useful feedback on your work. Your fellow students, particularly those working in similar areas, should be delighted to provide feedback. In return, they will learn about related work and have the opportunity to test their ideas out on you.

Sometimes you will need to take the initiative to form such a student support group. Sometimes, as David does with his own research students, your supervisor will organize workshops for students working on similar topics or using similar methods to present and discuss their data. In either case, you will gain the opportunity to test out preliminary ideas in a nonthreatening environment.

Writing for your peers or speaking to them is wonderful practice at getting the correct level for your thesis. The great temptation in writing up what may be your first piece of serious research is to try to achieve an exalted level of technical language in order to impress your supervisor. Unfortunately, this attempt often leads to clumsy jargon, which clouds your real line of argument and confuses your readers.

In discussing writing a thesis, Wolcott wisely addresses this issue of the level at which you write:

> Write for your peers. Pitch the level of discussion to an audience of readers who do not know what you are talking about. Write your dissertation with fellow graduate students in mind, not your learned committee members. Address your subsequent studies to the many who do not know, not the few who do. (1990, p. 47)

Contrary to appearances, Wolcott's injunction "write for your peers" is *not* a cop-out. For many researchers, the most difficult thing to do is to write with such clarity that their work can be understood and enjoyed by nonspecialists. Indeed, for some researchers, the hardest thing to grasp is that writing should always be tailored for as big an audience as possible. This means thinking about what that audience may know already and expect from you. Naturally, the same applies to oral presentations.

SPEAKING

Take every opportunity to present your research at any setting that arises, from an informal meeting of fellow students, to interested laypeople, to a scientific conference in your field. Watch out for calls for papers and regularly inspect the sites where they are posted.

When you speak, tailor what you say for your audience. Early in David's academic career, he was invited to talk about his research at a seminar at another university. He had already grasped the need to tailor his remarks to a particular audience and so had prepared two different talks on his research. One was highly specialist; the other was nontechnical. Unfortunately, on that day, he misjudged his audience and brought with him what turned out to be the "wrong" talk. Faced with a heavyweight group of specialists, he was insufficiently experienced to improvise and was forced to present the "Mickey Mouse" version of his research!

He still cringes when he thinks of that experience. However, although he says he "failed embarrassingly" on that occasion, he had at least been partially correct in his method: He had attempted to prepare a talk with an audience in mind (see Cryer, 1996, p. 133). Just as we design our ordinary conversation for particular recipients (children, colleagues, etc.), so **recipient design** should always go into your oral presentations. As Marx comments, "Try to remember who you are talking to, and the differential stake you and your audience have in your topic. Gear your talk to your audience" (1997, p. 107).

Following Marx, you will clearly want to give different kinds of talks to experts in your field, participants in your research, and general but nonspecialist academic audiences. For each audience, you should choose a particular focus (e.g., theory, method, substance) and an appropriate vocabulary (see Strauss & Corbin, 1990, pp. 226–229).

However, such recipient design is insufficient. Many have had the experience of speakers who only have time to get through a small part of their material or who overrun and then use up the time for questions. Good time management is a quality possessed by effective speakers. If you think you will not have the confidence to improvise to beat the clock, then it is wise to try out your talk beforehand with a watch nearby.

The usual experience is that it takes far longer to get through your material than you expect. So take the minimum of material in one file and, if necessary, bring a "security blanket" of additional material in another file to use in the unlikely event that you need it. Bear in mind this wise advice if time runs out:

> If you find that you are running out of time, do not speed up. The best approach is normally to abort the presentation of your findings . . . and move straight to your conclusion. (Watts & White, 2000, p. 445)

Finally, never read out a talk (see Watts & White, 2000, p. 444). We know having your full script is a source of comfort. As Marx puts it,

> The fact that you get only one chance with a live audience may engender anxiety and the written word is a safety net. But it has a pre-determined, even stultifying quality, which denies the fluid and interactive nature of live presentations. (1997, p. 107)

But think back to all those boring talks you have attended in which the speaker had his head buried in his script. Do you really want to inflict that on your audience? More positively: "You will never know what verbal riffs lie buried in your consciousness if you always cling to the security of the page" (Marx, 1997, p. 107). Instead, try to present your points through uncluttered visual aids (e.g., PowerPoint slides, overhead projector transparencies). Where you need to provide extensive material (e.g., long transcripts or tables), then distribute handouts.

Above all, try to grab your audience's attention at the outset. There are many tactics you can use at the start of your talk:

- Begin with a puzzle, as in a detective novel

- Start with an interesting data extract

- Start with a personal anecdote about how you became interested in your topic

- If you are not the first speaker, try to relate what you have to say to what has gone before

- Tell an apposite witty story (but only if this comes naturally!)

Finally, remember that both you and your audience need to get something out of your talk. Avoid the temptation just to give talks based on finished chapters approved by your supervisor. If the chapter is really finished, what will you gain from audience feedback? A much better strategy is to send such a chapter to a journal (see Chapter 27).

Instead, try to use early work or working papers. Here the responses of your audience may well help you see a way ahead. As Watts and White suggest,

> In giving . . . conference papers from your project . . . present incomplete work. In this way, you can seek guidance from your audience and receive stimulus for thinking about the next stage of your work. . . . In your paper you can direct the discussion towards particular issues on which you would like other people's opinions by drawing attention to them. (2000, p. 443)

Let us now illustrate these suggestions by some examples.

THE ART OF PRESENTING RESEARCH

You will have gathered already that, in our view, even the most astounding research can sound dull if not properly presented. Unfortunately, this does not mean that poor research can be rescued if you are a witty and effective speaker, because you will eventually be found out! But effective presentation of good research should be your aim.

To flesh out the bare bones of our argument, we have taken extracts from David's reports on presentations by research students completing their first year in his own department. Naturally, to protect the innocent, he has given these students false names.

Students were allowed up to 15 minutes to make a presentation to their fellow students on their progress during their first year and their plans for further work; 10–15 minutes were allowed for questions.

Just as we tend to preface bad news by good news when giving information in everyday life, let us begin by some reports of good practice. Below are some extracts from David's reports.

Good Practice

• Pat's talk was lively and clear, making good use of overhead transparencies. She responded well to questions. This was a well-focused presentation, lively and interesting. The handouts were helpful and the video data was fascinating.

• Derek gave a lively and relatively clear talk, making good use of his overheads. He spoke with some humor, gave an agenda to his audience, and explained the difficulties of his project.

• This was highly professional with good use of overheads and handouts. She used her limited time well, managing to accommodate her talk to the 15 minutes available. Her answers to questions were most effective, giving me the impression that she is already in control of her topic.

• This was a well-focused presentation, lively and interesting. Sasha's answers to questions were good. Overall, I felt this was an excellent presentation based upon a piece of highly professional research. My views seem to be shared by the students present, one of whom remarked that she hoped her own work would be up to this standard in a year or two's time. Congratulations are due to Sasha and her supervisor.

• This was a well-focused presentation, lively and interesting and improvised rather than read. The audience's attention was held throughout. Ray's answers to questions were thoughtful and helpful. In particular, he was able to establish a dialogue with students from a range of backgrounds and was at home responding to theoretical and practical issues. I especially liked Ray's attempt to derive methodological issues from the data analysis. There were time problems from which Ray will have learned something. Overall, I felt this was an excellent presentation based upon a piece of highly professional research.

Summary

We list below the qualities that impressed David in these presentations:

- Liveliness

- Not reading out a prepared text

- Recipient-design for the audience

- Clarity

- Effective visual aids

- Humor

- Explaining the agenda

- Not minimizing the difficulties

- Good time management

- Good response to questions

Now for the bad news!

Bad Practice

- John was hampered by lack of preparation. His extempore presentation may have confused the audience by introducing too many topics and using too many examples, which were not fully explained. His habit of turning his back on the audience to address the (empty) blackboard was unfortunate and, I am afraid, added to the impression of a non-user-friendly talk. This is disappointing given John's breadth of reading and excellent understanding. I think the only solution is to work harder on trying to relate his concerns to the interests and knowledge of particular audiences.

- This was an interesting presentation. However, Bruce made things a little difficult for his audience by offering no initial agenda, not using overheads, and having only one copy of some data extracts. He also ran into time problems that better planning could have obviated. This presentation will have given him the opportunity in future talks to think through his objectives and to offer more user-friendly methods.

- This was probably too specialized for a mixed audience, although Larry responded clearly to questions. The talk came to life when Larry departed from his script and gave an example (about record production), which brought to life the abstract concepts he was using. I strongly suggest that, in future, for such an audience, he uses more overheads and then talks around them, using helpful examples.

Summary

The following qualities concerned David in this group of presentations:

- Lack of preparation
- Too much material
- Not looking at the audience
- Lack of recipient design
- No agenda
- No visual aids
- Poor time planning

Most presentations fell between these extremes. We will conclude with some mixed examples.

Mixed Practice

- Maurice gave a clear presentation using handouts and overheads. His delivery was good and appropriately recipient designed. My only suggestion is that he should try to type overheads and put less material on each sheet.

- Stan had taken the trouble to prepare handouts. However, it was disappointing that, perhaps because of time limitations, he did not have time to analyze the data provided. I would also have preferred him not to read out a paper. It is important to practice the art of talking using only a few props, like overheads, if you want to keep the audience's attention. Nonetheless, Stan's talk was well organized and timed and he offered interesting responses to questions, showing a pleasing ability to admit when he was unsure about a point.

- As in an earlier talk, this was very professional, combining good overheads with helpful illustrations from video- and audiotape. My only suggestion is that it might be helpful to give more guidance to the audience about the issues to look for before offering data.

- Mary gave a confident, well-prepared talk based on a handout. She responded well to questions. My only suggestion is that, in future, she works more on integrating any handout with her talk so that her audience is not confused about what they should be attending to at any one time.

- Yoko had thoughtfully prepared overheads but these were not as clearly related to her talk as they might have been. Although it is always very difficult to speak in one's second language, it is difficult to keep the audience's attention when a paper is read. In my view, it is worth Yoko practicing at giving presentations simply by talking around her overheads. One way to do this would be to focus on the nice examples of texts and images that she presented and to pull out her analytic and methodological points from them rather than to attempt to read a rather abstract paper.

- Julia gave an engaging, lively presentation, which held her audience throughout. I liked her explanation of the personal reasons behind her research and admired her ability to speak without notes. Her overheads were useful. Some minor suggestions for future talks: remember to avoid turning away from the audience to look at the screen; think about using other information sources as well as overheads (handouts of definitions would have been useful); try out a talk beforehand so as to avoid time problems.

- This was an interesting talk, which carefully explained the issues involved for a nonspecialist audience. Jane's account of how her interest in the topic "coalesced" was very useful as were her overhead transparencies (although, in future, she should note that these can be most effectively used by covering up parts of each slide until she gets to them). She ran into some time difficulties and this is also something to watch in future. Overall, a good account of a fascinating topic.

- Luigi made a good attempt to explain a difficult topic to a nonspecialist audience. I particularly liked his account of his intellectual and personal background. In future, he will need to pay more attention to explaining his concepts and to time constraints.

Summary

The following were the good and bad news about these presentations:

- Using visual aids *but* these are poorly prepared
- Well organized *but* reading out a prepared text
- Giving examples of data *but* not explaining what to look for

- Using handouts *but* not integrating them in the talk

- Explaining the background *but* not explaining the concepts

- Using overheads *but* turning away to look at them or having too much material on the screen

Good and Bad Presentations

Take your oral presentations as seriously as you do your writing. Speak to your audience with clarity, logic, vigour, and examples that will grab them. (Marx, 1997, p. 107)

In Table 19.1, we set out what we have learned about making an effective oral presentation of your research.

Table 19.1   Giving a Talk: Problems and Solutions

Problem	Solution
Losing your audience	Recipient design
Overrunning	Don't prepare too much material
Boring your audience	Use visual aids—don't read out a talk

CONCLUDING REMARKS

Why does feedback matter? There are two reasons why student researchers write papers and give talks:

- To pass some internal assessment

- To get feedback on their work

Unfortunately, in our assessment-obsessed university culture, students tend to forget that feedback from peers and advanced scholars serves both normative and instrumental ends.

In a normative sense, offering material for feedback recognizes the community of scholars to which scientific work aspires. Instrumentally, such feedback will undoubtedly help improve your thesis. If you have long-term academic ambitions, it will also help you to improve your teaching skills and, perhaps, to plant the seeds of future journal articles!

So never think of this as "mere" presentation or the "boring" bit that has to be got through in order to get your degree. If we cannot use our research to engage others in dialogue, maybe we are in the wrong business!

KEY POINTS

Effective feedback is an essential resource for effective research. This chapter has discussed two means of obtaining feedback on your research:

- By writing draft papers

- By giving oral presentations

Writing should always be tailored for as big an audience as possible, and this means thinking about what that audience may know already and expect from you. So get feedback from fellow students as well as your supervisor.

Attempt to give a talk on your research before you write a final version for your thesis. In this talk, avoid losing your audience (recipient-design your presentation); set a time limit and never overrun; and use visual aids to avoid boring your audience.

FURTHER READING

Harry Wolcott's little book *Writing Up Qualitative Research* (1990) covers feedback as well as many other practical matters. Pat Cryer's *The Research Student's Guide to Success* (1996), Chapter 13, and the chapter by Watts and White in Burton's edited book *Research Training for Social Scientists* (2000, pp. 437–455) discuss giving presentations on your work. Gary Marx's article "Of Methods and Manners for Aspiring Sociologists: 37 Moral Imperatives" (1997, pp. 102–125) is a lively and extremely helpful guide for the apprentice researcher.

EXERCISE 19.1

Select two articles in your area of research from two different journals or books. Work out the audience(s) at which the journal or book is aimed by reading the journal's

"Instructions to Contributors" or the book's introductory editorial chapter. Then go through the steps below:

1. In what way does each article attempt to reach its appropriate audience(s)?

2. How successful is it in doing so?

3. How could it be improved to appeal more to its target audience(s)?

Exercise 19.2

Get invited to give a talk on your research and make sure that somebody attends who is prepared to give you good feedback. Plan the talk to reach the audience (e.g., students, staff, laypeople, or a mixture). Having given your talk, ask the attending person for feedback on the success of your talk. Then consider how you could have improved the talk to appeal more to its target audience.

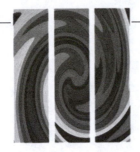

PART V

Writing Up

Alasuutari describes writing a thesis as rather like learning to ride a bicycle through gradually adjusting your balance:

> Writing is first and foremost analyzing, revising and polishing the text. The idea that one can produce ready-made text right away is just about as senseless as the cyclist who has never had to restore his or her balance. (1995, p. 178)

Alasuutari reminds us that writing up should never be something left to the end of your research. Instead, writing should be a continuous process, learning as you go from your supervisor, your peers, and from your own mistakes.

In the following five chapters, we will examine how this writing up can be accomplished efficiently if rarely painlessly. The five chapters address the following topics: how to begin your research report, how to write an effective literature review and methodology chapters, how to write up your data chapters, and what to put in your concluding chapter.

CHAPTER 20

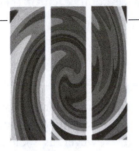

The First Few Pages

CHAPTER OBJECTIVES

By the end of this chapter, you will be able to

- Recognize why the first few pages of your thesis are very important
- Construct a title, abstract, list of contents, and introduction that are appropriate, informative, and attention grabbing

INTRODUCTION

Nearly all dissertations begin with four elements:

- A title

- An abstract

- A list of contents

- An introduction

If you follow our advice and devote most attention to your data-analysis chapters, then you may tend to treat these beginnings as routine matters, speedily disposed of. However, the impression you create at the start of your dissertation is very important, and the writing of the first few pages should never be regarded as busywork, that is, as a triviality.

In this short chapter, we offer some practical advice about each of these beginning sections of your dissertation.

THE TITLE

In the early stages, you will probably be asked to give a short title to your research for administrative purposes. You will almost certainly change this title before long, so do not attach too much importance to it. However, as Wolcott suggests, it is a good idea to be thinking about an effective final title and to keep notes about your ideas (1990, pp. 70–71).

Titles should catch the readers' attention while properly informing them about the main focus of your research. David's preference is for a two-part title: a snappy main title often using a present participle to indicate activity. The subtitle can then be more descriptive. For illustration, two of David's books were titled

Reading Castaneda: A Prologue to the Social Sciences

Interpreting Qualitative Data: Methods for Analysing Talk, Text and Interaction

Among his articles, you will find the following titles:

"Describing Sexual Activities in HIV Counselling: The Co-Operative Management of the Moral Order"

"Unfixing the Subject: Viewing 'Bad Timing'"

"Policing the Lying Patient: Surveillance and Self-Regulation in Consultations With Adolescent Diabetics"

Of course, using a present participle in the main title is merely David's preference, intended to stress the *active* nature of your research as well as the fact that he studies people's *activities*. Nor does he always follow his own rule. For instance, his 1997 book on AIDS counseling was titled *Discourses of Counselling: HIV Counselling as Social Interaction*.

But titles do matter and need careful thought, as any marketing person will tell you. So give this matter thought and discuss it with your supervisor. Then try Exercise 20.1.

THE ABSTRACT

This should succinctly cover the following:

- Your research problem

- Why that problem is important and worth studying

- Your data and methods

- Your main findings

- Their implications in the light of other research

There is usually a word limit for abstracts (100 words is common). So, as Punch points out, "Abstract writing is the skill of saying as much as possible in as few words as possible" (1998, p. 276). Within the word limitations, try to make your abstract as lively and informative as possible.

Read the abstracts of other dissertations in your area and try out drafts on other students and see if they find your abstract clear and pithy. Know what your audience is likely to be most interested in and "emphasize your problem and content, not your fieldwork techniques" (Wolcott, 1990, p. 81).

Wolcott also nicely sums up what makes a good abstract:

An abstract can offer a valuable opportunity to inform a wide audience, to capture potential readers, and to expand your own interactive professional network. Whether others will pursue their reading may depend largely on their assessment of your abstract, including its style. (1990, p. 81)

THE LIST OF CONTENTS

You may think this is a very trivial matter. Not so! A scrappy or uninformative table of contents (or, worse still, none at all) will create a terrible impression.

For your list to be user-friendly, you will need to recipient-design it to achieve two ends:

1. To demonstrate that you are a logical thinker, able to write a dissertation with a transparently clear organization

2. To allow your readers to see this at once, to find their way easily between different parts of the dissertation and to pinpoint matters in which they have most interest

One useful device that helps to achieve these two things is to use a double numbering system. So, for instance, a review of the literature chapter may be listed as

Chapter 3: Review of the Literature

3.1. The Background Studies

3.2. The Core Readings

3.3. The Study Closest to My Own

Of course, this is only an illustration. More detailed discussion of what a literature review should contain is provided in the next chapter of this volume.

THE INTRODUCTION

Murcott (1997, p. 1) says that the point of an introduction is to answer the question, What is this thesis about? She suggests that you answer this question in four ways by explaining

1. Why you have chosen this topic rather than any other (e.g., either because it has been neglected or because it is much discussed but not properly or fully)

2. Why this topic interests you

3. The kind of research approach or academic discipline you will utilize

4. Your research questions or problems

Like this chapter, there is no reason why your introduction should be any longer than two or three pages, particularly if your methodology chapter covers the natural history of your research (see Chapter 22). The role of the introduction, like your abstract, is to orient your readers. This is best done clearly and succinctly.

CONCLUDING REMARKS

The impression you create at the start of your dissertation is very important. Your title should catch the readers' attention while properly informing them about the main focus of your research.

An abstract should describe your research problem, why that problem is important and worth studying, your data and methods, your main findings, and their implications in the light of other research.

Your list of contents should allow your readers to find their way easily between different parts of the dissertation and to pinpoint matters in which they have most interest. Your introduction should explain why you have chosen this topic rather than any other, why this topic interests you, the kind of research approach or academic discipline you will utilize, and your research questions or problems.

KEY POINTS

- The first few pages of your thesis are very important.

- Your title, abstract, list of contents, and introduction should be appropriate, informative, and attention grabbing.

FURTHER READING

Harry Wolcott's *Writing Up Qualitative Research* (1990, pp. 70–82) has an excellent discussion of how to present student dissertations. A further useful source is Pat Cryer's *The Research Student's Guide to Success* (1996), Chapter 12.

EXERCISE 20.1

This is an exercise to encourage you to find a good title and abstract for your dissertation.

1. Make a list of three or four possible titles for your dissertation. Try to make the main title intriguing and the subtitle descriptive.

2. Now reverse the order, putting the subtitle first. Which works best? Why?

3. Try out your titles on students working in similar areas or using similar methods or data. Which do they think works best? Why?

4. Now try out two different abstracts in the same way.

EXERCISE 20.2

Show the introduction to your dissertation to a range of fellow students. Encourage them to tell you whether they feel tempted to read more. If not, why not? If so, why?

Now use their response to revise your introduction.

CHAPTER 21

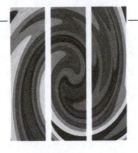

The Literature Review Chapter

CHAPTER OBJECTIVES

By the end of this chapter, you will be able to

- Understand what a literature review should contain

- Know the principles underlying a good literature review

- Think about when is the most appropriate time to write a literature chapter

- Consider the alternatives to having such a chapter

INTRODUCTION

There are four common misconceptions of the literature review chapter:

- It is done just to display that "you know the area."

- It is easier to do than your data analysis chapters.

- It is boring to read (and to write).

- It is best "got out of the way" at the start of your research.

Later in this chapter, all these assertions will be questioned. By contrast, we will argue that a literature review

- Should combine knowledge with critical thought

- Involves hard work but can be exciting to read

- Should mainly be written *after* you have completed your data analysis

We will begin, however, by trying to answer some practical questions about writing a literature review: What should it contain? Where will you find what you need to read? How should you read?

PRACTICAL QUESTIONS

What Should a Literature Review Contain?

In part, a literature review should be used to display your scholarly skills and credentials. In this sense, you should use it "to demonstrate skills in library searching; to show command of the subject area and understanding of the problem; to justify the research topic, design and methodology" (Hart, 1998, p. 13).

Such justification also means, as we remarked in Chapter 6, that any literature review connected with a piece of research has as much to do with the issue of **generalizability** as with displaying your academic credentials. This involves addressing the questions set out in Table 21.1.

Once you start to see your literature review as dialogic rather than a mere replication of other people's writing, you are going in the right direction. Conceived as an answer to a set of questions, your reading can immediately become more directed and your writing more engaging and relevant.

Table 21.1   Contents of a Literature Review

- What do we already know about the topic?
- What do you have to say critically about what is already known?
- Has anyone else ever done anything exactly the same?
- Has anyone else done anything that is related?
- Where does your work fit in with what has gone before?
- Why is your research worth doing in the light of what has already been done?

SOURCE: Adapted from Murcott (1997).

Preparing a Literature Search

As Hart (2001, p. 24) points out, it helps to do some preliminary thinking about what you are doing before you begin the search itself. The following are some issues to think about (drawn from Hart, 2001, p. 24):

- What discipline(s) relate to my main topic?

- How can I focus my topic to make my search more precise?

- What are the main indexes and abstracts relevant to my topic?

- What means of recording will be most efficient for many tasks such as cross-referencing? (Hart points out that index cards are useful.)

Where Will I Find the Literature?

Once you are prepared, it is time to review the many potential sources of information about what literature you need to read and where to find it:

- Your supervisor

- The subject librarian in your university library

- Bibliographies in the literature you read

- Online searches on the World Wide Web

- The social sciences citation index

- Newsgroups on the Internet

- Your fellow students (past and present)

There is no need to worry about admitting your lack of knowledge. Indeed, the American sociologist Gary Marx recommends taking "short cuts": "learn how to use computer searches, encyclopedias, review articles. Ask experts for help" (1997, p. 106).

Once you start looking, you will speedily find that you do not have the problem of too little literature but of too much! Getting away from the books and toward your data is a leap that most of us need to make as early as possible. As Marx cautions, "Don't become a bibliophile unless it suits you" (1997, p. 106).

There's So Much; How Will I Find the Time?

Before you panic, you need to remember that you would not have reached this stage of your academic career without learning the tricks of the reading trade. These tricks go beyond the skills of speed-reading (although these help) but also mean that your aim is usually to "fillet" a publication in terms of your own agenda (not the author's!).

Again, Marx makes the point well:

Sample! Learn how to read by skimming, attending to the first and last sentence, paragraph or chapter. Read conclusions first, then decide if you want the rest. Most social science books probably shouldn't be books; they have only a few main (or at least original) ideas. (1997, p. 106)

If these are some answers to the usual nuts-and-bolts questions, we still need to tackle the underlying principles behind a literature review. As our earlier discussion of misconceptions suggested, these principles are not always obvious or clear-cut.

PRINCIPLES

This is how the best recent book on the topic defines a literature review:

The selection of available documents (both published and unpublished) on the topic, which contain information, ideas, data and evidence written from a particular standpoint to fulfil certain aims or express certain views on the nature of the topic and how it is to be investigated, and the effective evaluation of these documents in relation to the research being proposed. (Hart, 1998, p. 13)

Hart's term "effective evaluation" means, we believe, attending to the following principles.

Show Respect for the Literature

Your single-minded pursuit of your (ideally) narrow research topic should not lead you to show disrespect for earlier research or to disconnect your work from the wider debate in which it figures. Your dissertation will be assessed in terms of its scholarship, and being scholarly means showing respect as well as striking out on your own. In Marx's words,

Even producers of literature must know the literature, and a major criterion for evaluating work is whether or not it is put in a context of prior scholarship. We are not only creators of new knowledge, but protectors and transmitters of old knowledge. Our inheritance is the astounding richness of the work of prior scholars. Beyond that, one has a strategic interest in the peer reciprocity inherent in the citing system. (1997, p. 106)

Be Focused and Critical

Respect can only get you so far. Scholarship also means advancing knowledge—although the level of that advance required will vary according to the degree at which you are aiming. Such advance involves a strict focus and a critical perspective on what you read:

After some initial grovelling, know what you are looking for. Approach the literature with questions and remember that your goal is to advance it, not simply to marvel at its wonders. Seek an appropriate balance between appreciation and advancement of the literature. (Marx, 1997, p. 106)

Avoid Mere Description

Any academic has horror stories of literature reviews that were tediously and irrelevantly descriptive. Rudestam and Newton characterize well such failing reviews: "[they consist of] a laundry list of previous studies, with sentences or paragraphs beginning with the words, 'Smith found . . . ,' 'Jones concluded . . . ,' 'Anderson stated . . . ,' and so on" (1992, p. 46).

In this vein, Marx recommends avoiding writing "a literature summary without an incisive critique that will help your peers to view the world differently" (1997, p. 106). Instead, you need to focus on those studies that are relevant for defining *your* research problem. By the end of the literature review, "the reader should be able to conclude that, 'Yes, of course, this is the exact study that needs to be done at this time to move knowledge in this field a little further along'" (Rudestam & Newton, 1992, p. 47).

This entails giving different amounts of attention to what you read according to how central they are to your topic. Background literature can be described in a sentence. By contrast, the most relevant studies "need to be critiqued rather than reported" (1992, p. 49). Such critique can focus on failings of theory or method (see Chapter 15).

Write Up After Your Other Chapters

The common version of a student research trajectory suggests that a major early aim is to complete a literature review. This version is supported in the "Time Checklist" provided by British Research Councils for PhD students. This includes the following recommendation: "First year . . . student to complete a literature survey" (British Research Councils, 1996). Elsewhere the same publication gives less dogmatic advice:

> In some subjects a literature survey forms an important starting portion of the work, and this should be carried out in the early stages. Before the end of the first year, the student should have a good idea of relevant work carried out by others, but it will be necessary to keep up with new literature throughout the period, so that the thesis takes account of the latest developments in its subject area.

This more considered advice hints at the problems of completing your literature review at an early stage. These problems may include

- Completing the literature survey in year 1 and writing it up can mean a lot of wasted effort—until you have done your data analysis, you do not know what stuff will be relevant.

- You may be tempted to regard the literature review as a relatively easy task. Since it tests skills you have already learned in your undergraduate career, it may become potential busywork. If so, it only will delay getting down to the data analysis on which you should be judged.

- As we asked in Chapter 6, can you ever get out of the library in order to write your thesis? One book will surely have a list of further "crucial" references and so on, ad infinitum. Anybody who thinks a library PhD is a quick fix would be well advised to ponder whether he or she has the willpower to stop reading.

These considerations mean that the bulk of your reading is usually best done in and around your data collection and analysis. In the end, this will save you the time involved in drafting your literature review chapter before you can know which literature will be most relevant to your treatment of your topic. It will also force you out of the library. As Marx comments, "Searching the literature must not become an end in itself or a convenient way to avoid the blank page" (1997, p. 106).

So: read as you do the analyses. By all means write notes on your reading, but don't attempt to write your literature review chapter early on in your research.

However, as researchers, we should be critical and innovative. In this regard, how far is the literature review chapter simply an unthought relic of an out-of-date version of scholarship? Do you need such a chapter?

DO YOU NEED A LITERATURE REVIEW CHAPTER?

The major unorthodox figure here is the American ethnographer Harry Wolcott. He argues that student researchers often mistakenly assume a need to defend qualitative research in general as well as the particular approach or method they are using. But, as he suggests, after a century of qualitative research (and several decades of more specific qualitative approaches),

> There is no longer a call for each researcher to discover and defend [qualitative methods] anew, nor a need to provide an exhaustive review of the literature about such standard procedures as participant observation or interviewing. Instead of having to describe and defend qualitative approaches, as we once felt obligated to do, it is often difficult to say anything new or startling about them. Neophyte researchers who only recently have experienced these approaches firsthand need to recognize that their audiences probably do not share a comparable sense of excitement about hearing them described once again. (1990, p. 26)

Wolcott also points to some positive gains of avoiding the statutory review chapter. As he puts it,

> I expect my students to know the relevant literature, but I do not want them to lump (dump?) it all into a chapter that remains unconnected to the rest of the study. I want them to draw upon the literature selectively and appropriately as needed in the telling of their story. (1990, p. 17)

This means that you can bring in appropriate literature as you need it, not in a separate chapter but in the course of your data analysis:

> Ordinarily this calls for introducing related research toward the end of a study rather than at the beginning, except for the necessary "nesting" of the problem in the introduction. (1990, p. 17)

Wolcott's radical suggestion is, no doubt, too radical for most students (and their supervisors!). Nevertheless, even if you decide to write the conventional literature review chapter, what he has to say is a salutary reminder that, in writing a research dissertation, you should cite other literature only in order to connect your narrow research topic to the directly relevant concerns of the broader research community. Making wider links should properly be left to your final chapter (see Chapter 24).

CONCLUDING REMARKS

In this chapter, we have argued that a literature review should combine knowledge with critical thought. It should involve hard work but be exciting to read and should mainly be written *after* you have completed your data analysis.

KEY POINTS

A literature review should contain answers to the following questions:

- What do we already know about the topic?

- What do you have to say critically about what is already known?

- Has anyone else ever done anything exactly the same?

- Has anyone else done anything that is related?

- Where does your work fit in with what has gone before?

- Why is your research worth doing in the light of what has already been done?

FURTHER READING

The essential book on this topic is Chris Hart's *Doing a Literature Review: Releasing the Social Science Imagination* (1998). This covers in detail all the issues discussed in this brief chapter as well as addressing the different requirements of literature reviews for BA, MA, and PhD dissertations. Hart's later book *Doing a Literature Search* (2001) is a helpful guide to planning and executing a literature search. For shorter, lively discussions, see Harry Wolcott's *Writing Up Qualitative Research* (1990) and Gary Marx's article

"Of Methods and Manners for Aspiring Sociologists: 37 Moral Imperatives" (*The American Sociologist*, Spring 1997, pp. 102–125).

EXERCISE 21.1

Select what you regard as the two or three most relevant pieces of literature. Now,

1. Make notes on each, attempting to use each one to answer the questions found in Table 21.1.

2. Incorporate these notes into a short literature review chapter, which only refers to these two or three works.

3. Discuss this review with your supervisor.

EXERCISE 21.2

When you complete each data-analysis chapter, look back over the literature you have discussed. Now ask yourself these questions:

1. Is there sufficient discussion of each reference to render further discussion (in a literature review chapter) redundant?

2. If not, practice writing about these references in a way that adds to how you have described them in your data-analysis chapters. Again, you may use Table 21.1 as a guide.

CHAPTER 22

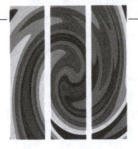

The Methodology Chapter

INTRODUCTION

We can distinguish three different kinds of student dissertation: theoretical, methodological, and empirical. Each of these demands different discussion of methods.

1. *Theoretical*: Here you claim to develop some theoretical insights by means of a critical review of a body of literature. In the theoretical dissertation, your methodology chapter will need to discuss your rationale for selecting your corpus of literature and any illustrative examples. It will also need to show how you have attempted to produce a systematic analysis, for example, by considering the arguments for positions you reject.

375

2. *Methodological:* Here you may be mainly concerned to develop a method (e.g., focus groups or textual analysis) or to compare and contrast the use of several different methods. Here the whole thesis may be devoted to methodological matters and so a separate chapter called "Methodology" may be redundant or simply devoted to explaining why you have chosen certain methods to compare and/or which data you choose to use for this exercise.

3. *Empirical:* In this, the most common form of research report or dissertation, you will analyze some body of data. Here you will be expected to show that you understand the strengths and weaknesses of your research strategy, design, and methods.

This chapter focuses on empirically based research reports. It argues for openness and clarity about what actually happened during your research. It argues that a bland account in the passive voice is an entirely inappropriate format for your methodology chapter.

Qualitative researchers are often interested in the narratives or stories that people tell one another (and researchers). Indeed, our data-analysis chapters tell (structured) stories about our data. It is only natural, then, that our readers should expect to be told how we gathered our data, what data we ended up with, and how we analyzed it.

This is why all research reports seem to have a methodology chapter or at least a section devoted to data and methods. Within that rubric, however, as we show later in this chapter, there are many different (nonbland) formats we can use to give an account of our data and methods. First, however, we need to clear the ground about the issues you need to cover in your methods chapter.

WHAT SHOULD THE METHODOLOGY CHAPTER CONTAIN?

In a quantitative study, there is a simple answer to this question. You will have a chapter usually titled "Data and Methods." As Table 22.1 shows, this chapter will typically contain four elements.

Table 22.1   The Methods Chapter in a Quantitative Thesis

1. Subjects studied

2. Research instruments used

3. Procedures used in applying these instruments to these subjects

4. Statistical analysis

SOURCE: Adapted from Rudestam and Newton (1992), p. 61.

The straightforward character of a quantitative methods chapter unfortunately does not spill over into qualitative research reports. At first sight, this simply is a matter of different language. So, in reporting qualitative studies, typically we do not talk about statistical analysis or research instruments. These linguistic differences also reflect broader practical and theoretical differences between quantitative and qualitative research.

More particularly, in writing up qualitative research, we need to recognize

- The (contested) theoretical underpinnings of methodologies

- The (often) contingent nature of the data chosen

- The (likely) nonrandom character of cases studied

- The reasons why the research took the path it did (both analytic and chance factors)

Each of these four features raises issues which should not be concealed or generate guilt. Your research training courses and your reading should have made you aware of the theories on which your methods rest. So the rule in writing your methods chapter is simply this: *spell out your theoretical assumptions.*

Everybody realizes that contingent events related to personal interest, access, or even simply being in the right (wrong) place at the right (wrong) time often determine which data you are able to work on. So be straightforward: *spell out the (sometimes contingent) factors that made you choose to work with your particular data.*

Finally, everybody knows that qualitative researchers can work fruitfully with very small bodies of data that have not been randomly assembled. If this is the case, *explain how you can still generalize from your analysis.* For example, in Chapter 9, we discussed four different but positive answers to this question of how we can obtain generalizability:

- Combining qualitative research with quantitative measures of populations

- Purposive sampling guided by time and resources

- Theoretical sampling

- Using an analytic model that assumes that generalizability is present in the existence of *any* case

So, when writing your methodology chapter, avoid overdefensiveness. Many great researchers will have used similar methods with few qualms. So draw from their strength.

On the other hand, self-confidence should not mean lack of appropriate self-criticism. Your literature review chapter will already have considered other studies in terms of "the strengths and limitations of different research designs and techniques of data collection, handling and analysis" (Murcott, 1997, p. 2).

Treat your methodology chapter in the same way—as a set of cautious answers to questions that another researcher might have asked you about your work (e.g., why did you use these methods; how did you come to these conclusions?). This means that your methods chapter should aim to *document* the rationale behind your research design and data analysis.

Spencer et al. (2003) argue that this documentation process requires transparency about your methods. In other words, you should anticipate and answer reasonable questions about your research. Table 22.2 sets out the issues involved here.

Another way of putting these kinds of matters has been suggested by Murcott (1997). Table 22.3 shows how we can use our methods chapter to answer a set of questions.

To answer the questions in Table 22.3 will usually mean describing the following:

- The data you have studied

- How you obtained that data (e.g., issues of access and consent)

Table 22.2   How to Document Your Research Transparently

- Give an honest account of the conduct of the research.

- Provide full descriptions of what was actually done in regard to choosing your case(s) to study, choosing your method(s), collecting and analyzing data.

- Explain and justify each of your decisions.

- Discuss the strengths and weaknesses of what you did.

- Be open about what helped you and held you back.

SOURCE: Adapted from Spencer et al. (2003), p. 76.

Table 22.3   Questions for a Qualitative Methods Chapter

1. How did you go about your research?

2. What overall strategy did you adopt and why?

3. What design and techniques did you use?

4. Why these and not others?

SOURCE: Murcott (1997).

- What claims you are making about the data (e.g., as representative of some population or as a single case study)

- The methods you have used to gather the data

- Why you have chosen these methods

- How you have analyzed your data

- The advantages and limitations of using your method of data analysis

A NATURAL HISTORY CHAPTER?

To answer Murcott's four questions in Table 22.3, in the context of our preceding elaborations, may now look to be a pretty tall order, particularly if you feel you have to devote a long section to each of these issues.

However, the methodology chapter of a qualitative study can be a much more lively, interesting affair than this suggests. In this context, there are three issues to bear in mind. First, a highly formal chapter can be dull to read as well as to write. Many is the time one of us has ploughed through a desperately boring methodology chapter, usually written in the passive voice. We often get the feeling that the chapter is there for purely formal purposes. In the words of a British war song, "because we're here, because we're here, because we're here"! In such cases, we can hardly wait to get on to the (more lively) heart of the study.

Second, *methodology* has a more flexible meaning in qualitative research than its quantitative sister. In Chapter 7, we defined *methodology* as "a general approach to studying research topics." As such, your readers will be more interested in a methodological discussion in which you explain the actual course of your decision making rather than a series of blunt assertions in the passive voice (e.g., "the method chosen was. . . .").

Third, a research study submitted for a university degree, even up to the PhD level, is principally evaluated in terms of how far you can demonstrate that you have the makings of a competent researcher. Hence your examiners will be interested to know something about the history of your research, including your response to the various difficulties and dead ends that we all experience.

As Alasuutari argues, false leads and dead ends are just as worth reporting as the method eventually chosen:

It is precisely for this reason that taking "field notes" about the development of one's thinking is needed. . . . The text can be like a detective story, where one presents these "false leads" until they are revealed to be dead-ends. (1995, p. 192)

Alasuutari's version of the history of research as a "detective story" is incompatible with a formal methodology chapter in the passive voice. Instead of a formal, impersonal chapter, one offers the reader "field notes about the development of one's thinking." One way to do this is to rename the methodology chapter "The Natural History of My Research."

In Chapter 3, we saw how some of David's research students used their field diaries to write lively natural histories. These informed the reader, among other things, about

- The personal context of the students' research topic

- The reasons for their research design

- How they developed their research through trial and error

- The methodological lessons they learned

Examples of how these topics can be treated in your "natural history" chapter are set out in Table 22.4.

The more informal, natural history style of methodology chapter that we recommend should not be taken to mean that anything goes. On the contrary, by asking readers to engage with your thinking *in process*, they are in a far better position to assess the degree to which you were self-critical. Moreover, an autobiographical style is only appropriate to the extent that it allows you to address properly the kind of crucial methodological questions set out in Tables 22.2 and 22.3. Clearly, your readers will not want to hear needlessly and endlessly about how your personal life impinged upon the process of obtaining your degree!

CONCLUDING REMARKS

Some universities (like some academic journals) still have a pretty fixed idea of what a methodology chapter (or section) should contain. Therefore, it is probably worth discussing with your teachers whether a natural history format is appropriate to describe the methodology that you have chosen. But even if you do not write your chapter in this way, you will still gain by keeping dated field notes about the trajectory of your project.

However, if you do write a natural history chapter, it is much more likely that you will avoid boring your readers (and yourself). It is also more likely that you will overcome the common problem of failing to explicate to the reader what is now "obvious" to you. As Alasuutari puts it: "Researchers always become more or less blind to their texts and thoughts, so that they do not notice

Table 22.4   Topics for a Natural History Chapter

The Personal Context

By the end of my period of undergraduate study, I was greatly vexed by issues surrounding the tendency within the various schools of sociology toward using "social structure" too loosely as a way of accounting for data. (Simon)

The microanalysis of social interaction seemed to me to be a valuable way of understanding some of the health issues and problems I had encountered in my experience working in clinical health settings as a psychiatric nurse and as a research nurse. Many of these problems appeared to hinge on the interactive practices and skills of the various parties involved. (Moira)

Like Silverman's (1987) experience of gaining access to the field of paediatric cardiology, my entry to the field of mental health casework was a chance happening. I met up with a former colleague in a local supermarket. After recounting my difficulty in negotiating access to an inpatient area, he invited me to meet the community team with whom he worked. (Sally)

Reasons for Research Design

I chose to collect data in the way that I did because it was appropriate to the study of situated action. Audiotapes provide detailed recorded talk that field notes alone cannot provide, while preparing transcripts is itself a research activity. (Sally)

Many qualitative research studies set out clear aims and objectives at the start of a project. These may often refer to collecting and analyzing data on a particular topic, such as describing the views of patients about a particular type of illness experience. The aims of ethnomethodological studies such as this one tend to be quite general, centering on the examination of some data. Decisions therefore need to be made about objectives for particular pieces of analysis at each stage. (Moira)

Developing Through Trial and Error

I had initially intended to undertake separate analyses of instances of criticisms of self and of the dead spouse. However, I decided a more constructive tack would be to conduct a closer analysis of members' practices in producing the accounts. This would involve taking a step back in order to take a closer look. (Moira)

To undertake a case study of "single homelessness" in the context of full-time employment makes heavy demands on the researcher in terms of personal resources and operational constraints. The field is so vast and the nature of subjects' lives so dispersed that I elected to observe professional caseworkers rather than service users. For practical reasons, then, I became a participant-observer at weekly case conferences. (Sally)

(Continued)

Table 22.4 (Continued)

Methodological Lessons I Have Learned

> I was attempting to describe something that I knew was going on but could not see at the start. The need to refrain from introducing my own categorizations before producing the description of members' practices that I was aiming for has not been easy. However, I believe that the fine-grained analysis of the practices adopted by interview participants has enabled me to contribute new insights to the sociology of health and illness. (Moira)

> With hindsight, I might use more conventional transcription devices if I were to do the transcripts again. This would save the "creative" work of devising my own. (Sally)

> How, then, should this research be seen in terms of both sampling variety and external validity? I believe the answer lies in seeing this research not as an attempt to provide categorical "truths" about all parents' evenings in general, but as an attempt to raise questions about such meetings by looking at a single case in detail. This study can therefore be seen as being exploratory rather than definitive, examining the achievement of routine by a single individual in a specific setting in such a way that further analytical possibilities are opened up. (Simon)

that they have failed in spelling out certain premises or starting points without which an outsider has a hard time understanding the text" (1995, p. 192). A natural history chapter, based on contemporary field notes, will be more likely to make your readers "insiders" and avoid making you an "outsider" in relation to your own text.

KEY POINTS

All research reports have a methodology chapter or at least a section devoted to data and methods. In it, you will be expected to show that you understand the strengths and weaknesses of your research strategy, design, and methods. In this chapter you should explain

- Your theoretical assumptions
- The factors that made you choose to work with your particular data
- How you can generalize from your analysis

However, a highly formal methodology chapter can be dull to read as well as to write. Instead, it is often right to offer the reader field notes about the developments of one's thinking called "The Natural History of My Research."

FURTHER READING

The most helpful comments on writing a methodology chapter are to be found in Pertti Alasuutari's *Researching Culture: Qualitative Method and Cultural Studies* (1995), Chapters 13 and 14.

EXERCISE 22.1

Assemble the various memos you have written during your research. Now write 500 words on each of the following topics related to your research:

1. The main things that have helped you finish and the main things that have held you back.

2. What you have learned about your research topic.

3. How you have improved your knowledge of (a) methodology and (b) theory.

4. What lessons your research has for other students at your level.

NOTE: If you have not finished your research yet, do Exercise 2.1 instead.

CHAPTER 23

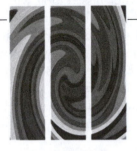

Writing Your Data Chapters

INTRODUCTION

As we have already seen, many supervisors and funding bodies suggest that doing a research study falls into three equal phases. These phases are commonly defined as

- Reviewing the literature

- Gathering your data

- Analyzing your data

Faced with this convention, it may be necessary to restate the obvious. Assuming that you are writing an empirically based study, your data-analysis chapters are (or should be) the key basis on which your dissertation will be judged. Unlike coursework essays, where knowledge of the literature and an ability to analyze it critically will stand you in good stead, dissertations that involve research count as nothing without good data analysis. Moreover, as we have said several times already, there are usually no brownie points awarded for successfully gathering your data. Whether or not such data gathering involves discomfort, danger, or the need to learn another language is, ultimately, neither here nor there. In the final assessment, everything comes down to what you *do* with your data.

This situation implies two clear messages. First, as we have stressed throughout this book, you cannot begin too early in your data analysis. Second, when you write up data, you need to develop the skills to present your analysis clearly and cogently to your readers.

This is why, as Jay Gubrium (personal correspondence) has commented, students need advice on the actual writing up of their data analysis. They need to understand "what to say first, next, where to place things, how to introduce extracts and what to say in relation to them, how to draw conclusions." In this chapter, we offer advice addressed to the issues that Gubrium raises.

It will be useful to make a distinction at once between how you write up your analysis of particular sets of data and how you craft your overall argument. Alasuutari (1995) calls the former area the "microstructure" of a thesis and the latter its "macrostructure." This is how he explains the difference between the two levels:

> The difference between the two could be compared to different dimensions of the architecture of a house. At the macrolevel one thinks how the rooms and different activities are placed in relation to each other, whereas at the microlevel one considers the furnishing and interior decoration of different rooms. (Alasuutari, 1995, p. 179)

This is a helpful distinction because, as Alasuutari suggests, different issues arise in relation to the organization of individual chapters (the microstructure) and the overall organization of your thesis (the macrostructure). In the rest of this chapter, we will consider each structure separately and then go on to explain how to make a final check that everything is in place before you tighten up the structure (Wolcott, 1990, p. 47).

THE MACROSTRUCTURE

The macrostructure is how the investigation proceeds from one chapter to another so that it forms a logical and sound whole. (Alasuutari, 1995, p. 179)

How do you ensure that your data-analysis chapters form "a logical and sound whole"? We discuss next two answers to this question:

- Plan your table of contents at an early stage and continually revise it.

- In the final write-up, decide the form of the "story" you want to tell about your research.

Early Planning of Table of Contents

Plan what you may put into your data chapters as early as you can and then keep revising your list. As Wolcott suggests, projecting a table of contents provides for

an orderly progression, a clear identification of major points and subordinate ones, and an overview . . . to assess whether the structure I have designed accommodates the data to be presented and provides an appropriate sequence for the presentation. (1990, p. 18)

By such early planning of the structure of your thesis, you can help to clarify your research design and identify upcoming problems: "Insurmountable problems in finding a sound macrostructure may be a sign of weaknesses in the research design: problems which have to be sorted out first" (Alasuutari, 1995, p. 179).

Alasuutari gives the example of a set of chapters that veer unpredictably between different themes—a good indication of an unclear research design. This means that, if you have difficulty in working out your table of contents, then you are exhibiting symptoms of a confused research design.

To show you how tables of contents can be projected, in the following we set out examples from two of David's research students, Sally Hunt and Kay Fensom. In each case, these research students started to project a table of contents at an early stage.

Sally gathered audio recordings of case conferences of a community health team seeking to house mentally ill, homeless people. Her work, which was discussed in Chapter 2, is ethnographic in focus. The following example shows the draft table of contents she prepared while she was still writing her data chapters.

Sally's Draft Table of Contents

Producing Single Homelessness: Descriptive Practice in Community Mental Casework

1. Introduction: aims of the study
2. Natural history of the research
3. Literature used in the analysis
4.–6. The ethnographic context
7. Constructing the case
8. Constructing the client
9. Gender as an interpretive framework
10. Constructing the mental health team
11. Conclusion: limitations and implications

In the final version of her thesis, Sally reorganized most of her thesis into two parts: an introduction (which included Chapters 1–3) and data analysis (Chapters 7–10). Sally recognized that her projected chapters on the ethnographic context were peripheral to her main argument. So her draft Chapters 4–6 were vastly shortened and incorporated into her introduction.

Kay analyzed crime stories in local newspapers in London and Northern Ireland. To do this, she used Harvey Sacks's **membership categorization device** analysis (see Chapter 11, in relation to the story about the navy pilot). The next example shows her early ideas about the organization of her thesis.

Kay's Draft Table of Contents

Locating Newsworthiness in Newspaper Headlines: Reading Inference and "Motive"

1. Natural history: stages, directions, and influences
2. Theoretical framework
3. The media, "newsworthiness," and the activity of reading
4.–7. Data chapters (each on a separate crime headline)
8. Dealing with critiques of MCD analysis
9. Conclusions: what has the analysis achieved?

By the time Kay submitted her PhD, she had one extra data chapter. She now felt that two of her draft chapters were based on literature reviews, which were not distinctively original. So Chapters 3 and 8 disappeared from the final version of her thesis, although parts of each were used elsewhere. Kay's title also changed to "Crime, Locality and Morality: Membership Categorization and 'Newsworthiness' in Local Newspapers." This improved title nicely reflected (what had turned out to be) Kay's key concepts and database.

Sally and Kay's redrafting carries three important implications about how you should think about the structure of your thesis:

- Work out what main message and findings you want your data chapters to contain.

- Ensure that the structure of your thesis underlines that message.

- Strip out or minimize draft chapters that are peripheral to your argument.

Deleting or shortening chapters over which you have toiled requires a degree of ruthlessness on your part. Seek the guidance of your supervisor about whether such chapters might find a better home in, say, a conference paper or journal article (see Chapter 27).

More than a year before Sally and Kay finished their dissertations, they were already planning a draft table of contents. Planning is important because your research dissertation will probably be the longest piece of writing you have ever done. BA or MA research essays are commonly 10,000 words, and PhDs are usually between 70,000 and 100,000 words long. However, it is important not to focus on your own difficulties at writing at this length, for we guarantee that, in nearly every case, you will find you have too *little* space.

Instead, think of how the reader needs a guide to follow a long story. Provide that guide at the start and repeat it, as appropriate, in every chapter (see Alasuutari, 1995, p. 180). This will mean giving regular "signposts" to help the reader understand what you are going to do (or have done) and how these relate to your overall theme. It also means planning the form of the story you wish to tell.

Planning Your Story

There are at least three models to choose from in working out the macrostructure of your thesis:

- The hypothesis story
- The analytic story
- The mystery story

Each is discussed briefly in the following.[1]

The Hypothesis Story

This is how many journals require you to organize your paper. It follows a standard three-part way of writing up research reports derived from quantitative studies:

1. State your hypotheses.

2. Test them.

3. Discuss the implications.

As Alasuutari (1995, p. 181) points out, there are two reasons why you are unlikely to want to use this model for writing up your qualitative dissertation. First, you may well be proceeding inductively, developing and testing hypotheses in the course of your data analysis. If so, then clearly you cannot state a prior hypothesis. Second, however, there are reasons to be suspicious of the hypothesis story because, even in quantitative studies, it often represents not the actual logic of the research but a reconstructed logic fitted to how your cross-tabulations of variables actually worked out (see Alasuutari, 1995, pp. 181–183).

The Analytic Story

The hypothesis story usually demands a passive voice format (e.g., "it was hypothesized that . . . " or "the findings were . . . "), which can be difficult to write and still more painful to read! Telling an analytic story is a more conversational way of writing. It involves deciding "the main analytic story line that you wish to tell" (Strauss & Corbin, 1990, p. 230). As they put it,

> Think intently about the analytic logic that informs the story. Every research monograph, indeed every research paper, will have such a logic. . . . In a sense the entire thesis or monograph will represent a spelling out of this analytic story. (p. 230)

To write this story, you need to ask yourself questions like

- What are the key concepts that I have used in this study?

- How do my findings shed light on these concepts and, through them, on the substantive topics I studied?

- What, therefore, has become of my original research problem and the literature regarding it?

Rather than hope that the reader will eventually find out these matters, telling an analytic story lays everything out on a plate at the outset.

There is much to be said for this model, for it helps the readers to settle back, knowing what they will find in the rest of your thesis. Some readers, however, may actually want to be surprised. Such surprises can be planned rather than being the mere outcome of sloppy design. This is where the mystery story comes in.

The Mystery Story

Alasuutari refers to an approach to writing that "proceeds by pointing out mysteries and by gradually developing questions and answers." In this approach, one "starts directly from **empirical** examples, develops the questions by discussing them, and gradually leads the reader to interpretations of the material and to more general implications of the results" (Alasuutari, 1995, p. 183, bold added).

Beginning one's data analysis in the form of a mystery story has at least two advantages. First, it may well capture your readers' attention as, like the readers of detective stories, they want to stay with you in order to find "whodunit." Second, it more accurately mirrors the inductive form of much qualitative research where findings (and even topics) are only gradually revealed.

Set against this, you must remember that writing a mystery story requires many craft skills. Should you fail, you will certainly lose your readers' interest. So, in practice, many writers of good qualitative dissertations follow Strauss and Corbin's idea of telling an analytic story to lead their readers through the data-analysis chapters.

In a sense, whichever story form you choose can be safely left to personal choice. More important is whether you are telling *some* coherent story. For, despite their differences, all three models share one important feature in common: they give the study focus and point. This means that the structure of your thesis should only rarely flow from the chronological order in which you happened to find things. As Cryer puts it, "The final version of the thesis should be written, with hindsight, knowing where one has been" (1996, p. 178).

So, if you remember just one lesson from this chapter, it is this: *avoid telling your story in the order in which you found things out or wrote them up.* Such a story is only appropriate for a natural history chapter (see Chapter 22). If the overall structure of your thesis just reflects the order in which you discovered things, then your examiners are unlikely to praise you for your verisimilitude. They are much more likely to criticize you for being too lazy to work out a coherent structure for your argument.

As Alasuutari puts it, returning to the motif of a mystery story:

> A good investigation is indeed like a murder mystery in that it does not contain much irrelevant text: themes or details that have nothing to do with the solution revealed in the end. . . . One could talk about the *economy principle* of a study: everything included must be related and tied in with the argumentation developed and presented in the investigation. (1995, p. 186, our emphasis)

Now attempt Exercise 23.1.

THE MICROSTRUCTURE

With a clear macrostructure, you are well set up to write well-organized and well-argued data chapters. Whether it is a matter of setting out an overall argument (the macrostructure) or developing an analysis of a particular topic (the microstructure), you should always write in a way that helps the reader. As Jay Gubrium (personal communication) notes, this is not always something that comes easily to inexperienced researchers: Many students, he said,

> don't take their readers into account; they don't know how to "teach" their readers what they should be reading into the empirical material present. Many just throw stuff into the text and expect the reader to get the point.

Thinking about your reader(s) turns out to be an excellent way of answering perennial problems that arise when you first write up a qualitative study. For instance, you may ask yourself: how much depth is needed in my data analysis? How much is enough?

Strauss and Corbin suggest a good way of answering such questions:

> The answer is first that you must know what your main analytic message will be. Then you must give enough conceptual detail to convey this to readers. The actual form of your central chapters should be consonant with the analytic message and its components. (1990, pp. 232–233)

So the answer to these questions is found in how you have depicted the main message of your thesis (the macrostructure). The point here is this: know your message and stick to it!

Normally, each data-analysis chapter will have three sections:

- An introduction, in which you explain what you are going to do in advance

- The main section, in which you work through your data in terms of what you have already said

- A conclusion, in which you summarize what you have shown and connect to the next chapter

We set out in the following some suggestions for writing each of these sections with an audience in mind.

The Introduction

Never spring anything on your readers. Even if you have decided to tell a mystery story (see preceding), your audience should always know what the mystery is about and what kind of "clues" they should be looking for. As Becker has cautioned,

> Many social scientists . . . think they are actually doing a good thing by beginning evasively. They reveal items of evidence one at a time, like clues in a detective story, expecting readers to keep everything straight until they produce the dramatic concluding paragraph. . . .
>
> I often suggest to these would-be Conan Doyles that they simply put their last triumphant paragraph first, telling readers where the argument is going and what all this material will finally demonstrate. (1986, pp. 51–52)

So at the outset, preface each data-analysis chapter with an explanation of how its topic relates to your thesis as a whole and how the chapter will be organized. As a broad rule, no subheading should ever appear in a chapter without it having received a prior explanation of its nature and logical place in your argument.

Along these lines, Pat Cryer suggests four components of a good introduction to a chapter. These are set out in Table 23.1.

The Main Section

Now that your readers know the areas that this chapter will discuss, it is important that you initially pull apart these areas and discuss each one separately. The golden rule for writing data analysis is

- Make one point at a time

Table 23.1   Components of a Data Chapter Introduction

1. Scene-setting for the chapter (i.e. explaining the general area[s] that the chapter considers)

2. Locating the gap in knowledge that the chapter addresses

3. Explaining how the chapter fills that gap

4. Providing a brief overview of what is in the chapter

SOURCE: Adapted from Cryer (1996), p. 182.

So, if you find yourself veering off in another direction, cut out the offending material and put it in another section. Sometimes this will mean returning to the same data but from a different perspective. Sometimes it will mean getting rid of some data altogether.

Your readers will find their lives much easier if they are not distracted by too many different arguments. And it is also much more likely that you will be able to recognize holes in your argument if it is stripped to the bone.

If you are making just one point at a time, it is, of course, crucial that your readers should immediately grasp what that point is. Therefore, a second rule is

- "Top and tail" each data extract

This means writing a sentence or two before every extract to context it in your argument. This way your readers will know what to look for while they read it.

Follow that up with a more detailed analysis of the extract in terms of the single point you are using it to make. If the extract is inconclusive, then admit to it. So, a third rule is

- Always show that you understand the limitations of both your data and your analysis of it

A fourth rule is

- Convince the reader

Not only must your readers be able to see why you interpreted your data in the way you did, but also they must be convinced by your interpretation. As Murcott suggests, "The basis for saying that the data say "x" rather than "y" has to be made apparent" (1997, p. 2).

Murcott also suggests that the way to display that your analysis has this kind of critical component is to "discuss candidate interpretations and make the case for judging, and so discarding, alternatives as inferior or inadequate" (1997, p. 2).[2]

The Conclusion

When you reach the end of a tight piece of data analysis, you may feel that nothing further needs to be done. Not so! You owe it to your readers to tie the whole chapter together again. Not only will this remind them of what you (and they) have learned in the preceding pages, but it will also prepare them for the chapter(s) to follow.

Table 23.2 sets out what the conclusion of a data chapter might contain.

Table 23.2   Components of a Data Chapter Conclusion

1. Explain what the chapter has done

2. Describe the new questions the chapter has identified

3. Explain where these questions will be addressed (e.g., in the next chapter or in the overall conclusions)

SOURCE: Adapted from Cryer (1996), p. 183.

It is worth remembering that it is unlikely that you will achieve a well-argued, reader-friendly thesis at one go. We conclude this chapter, therefore, with some suggestions about moving to a final draft, or what Wolcott calls "tightening up" (1990, p. 47).

TIGHTENING UP

Make sure all parts are properly in place before tightening. (directions for assembling a new wheelbarrow, reported by Wolcott, 1990, p. 47)

Wolcott's analogy of assembling a wheelbarrow reminds us that no subtle change of detail will work if the macrostructure of your thesis is not properly in place. As he puts it,

Before you start tightening, take a look at how the whole thing is coming together. Do you have everything you need? (And do you need everything you have? Remember, you're only supposed to be tightening up that wheelbarrow, not filling it!). (1990, p. 48)

You are likely to be too close to your work to tell easily whether everything is properly in place. As Cryer suggests, the author of a thesis will know it inside and out and back to front. So the link between its components may be clear to you, while not being as clear to those who have met your work only recently. (1996, p. 186)

There are two ways of giving yourself the critical distance necessary to see whether all the parts of your thesis are in place. First, if time allows, put it to one side for a while. After a time on the back burner, Wolcott notes,

I do a better job of strengthening the interpretation, spotting discrepancies and repetitions, locating irregularities in sequence or logic, and discovering overworked words, phrases, and patterns after periods of benign neglect. (1990, p. 52)

Locating what Wolcott calls "irregularities" can mean deleting particular points to which you may have become attached but which detract from your overall argument (Clive Seale, personal correspondence).

A second strategy to obtain distance is to give a talk on your research during the writing-up stage or to find "someone new to your work who will listen to you explaining it or will read the draft thesis and tell you where they have trouble following" (Cryer, 1996, p. 186).

Once the macrostructure is in place, it is time to tighten up the microstructure. Among the things to look at here are

- Unclear or infelicitous language

- Overlarge claims about your data or analysis

- Needless repetition

- Insufficient detail (see Wolcott, 1990, pp. 49–50)

When you have done all of these things, you must recognize that the tightening-up period is nearly over. Certainly, you can ask yourself, "Have I really got the last details in? Got them right?" (Strauss & Corbin, 1990, p. 235).

To check this out, you can ask your supervisor and/or fellow students to have one final read and then respond to their comments. But remember: the revision process is potentially endless! The real cop-out is not submitting a less-than-perfect thesis but being stuck in a process of endless revisions: "Part of an increasing maturity as a research-writer is to understand that no manuscript is ever finished" (Strauss & Corbin, 1990, p. 235).

Just as parents eventually realize that their children have become adults and will leave home, now is the time to make the break with your manuscript. Like "empty nest" parents, you should be ready to strike out in new directions. But first you must let go.

CONCLUDING REMARKS

Your data-analysis chapters are (or should be) the key basis on which your dissertation will be judged. However, different issues arise in relation to the organization of individual chapters (the microstructure) and the overall organization of your thesis (the macrostructure).

Good overall organization is based on planning your table of contents at an early stage and continually revising it. You also need to decide the form of the story you want to tell about your research and structure your data chapters accordingly. Each data chapter should have a microstructure based on three sections: an introduction in which you explain what you are going to do in advance; the main section in which you work through your data in terms of what you have already said; and, finally, a conclusion in which you summarize what you have shown and connect to the next chapter.

KEY POINTS

In planning the overall (macro)structure of your thesis,

- Work out what main message and findings you want your data chapters to contain.

- Ensure that the structure of your thesis underlines that message.

- Strip out or minimize draft chapters that are peripheral to your argument.

When writing data chapters, it is wise to consider the following instructions:

- Make one point at a time.

- Context each data extract in your argument.

- Show that you understand the limitations of your analysis.

- Always number your data extracts.

- Realize that the reader will need to be convinced and that what is obvious to you will not always be so clear to others.

NOTES

1. As we shall see, the idea of the hypothesis story and the mystery story derives from Alasuutari (1995).

2. See Chapter 14 for a discussion of these issues in terms of validity and reliability and Chapter 12 for an explanation of how diagrams and charts may illustrate your rigorous thinking. On this latter point, see also Mason (1996, pp. 131–133) and Strauss and Corbin (1990, pp. 131–137).

FURTHER READING

Harry Wolcott's *Writing Up Qualitative Research* (1990) is a marvelous account of how to write up data. Useful, shorter treatments are Pat Cryer's *The Research Student's Guide to Success* (1996), Chapter 18; Pertti Alasuutari's *Researching Culture: Qualitative Method and Cultural Studies* (1995), Chapter 14; and Anselm Strauss and Juliet Corbin's *Basics of Qualitative Research* (1990), Chapter 13.

EXERCISE 23.1

Try organizing your data analysis into two chapters. Don't do this arbitrarily but find a logical way to do it. Now try reordering this material into five shorter chapters with a different logic. Consider which format works best and why.

EXERCISE 23.2

Select a coherent piece of your data analysis that might become a chapter. Give the chapter a title that fits what you are trying to do there. Using Tables 23.1 and 23.2, now

1. Write an introduction for this chapter.

2. Write a conclusion.

3. Add in your data analysis and show the whole chapter to a colleague. Ask him or her to what extent your introduction and conclusion helped him or her see what you were getting at. If so, why? If not, why not?

4. Now revise and repeat the process.

CHAPTER 24

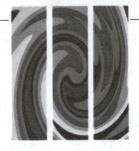

The Final Chapter

INTRODUCTION

In the previous chapter, we concluded with the recommendation to "let go." However, because all research reports (including dissertations) seem to end with a set of conclusions, you cannot finally let go until your concluding chapter is written. Having cycled painfully to the top of the hill, the great temptation at this point is to relax and freewheel down to the finish. In practice, such relaxation of effort is reflected in the all-too-common summaries found in the final chapter of dissertations.

Although summaries are often quite useful devices at the end of data-analysis chapters, we suggest that you should never write a summary as your concluding chapter. If your readers need a summary at this point, then your *macrostructure* (Alasuutari's concept discussed in the previous chapter) is not in place. If it is in place, then what you have said should already be crystal clear. So resist the temptations of a final downhill freewheel.

But does this mean that you even need a concluding chapter? Cannot your thesis stop after you have finished your data analysis?

Take a musical example. Classical symphonies typically end with a fast movement marked *allegro* or *presto*. Rather than merely recapitulating earlier themes, they take them up and develop them still more. As such, they seem designed to provide listeners with some of the most stimulating material in the composition. So your final chapter is, indeed, necessary. But it should function to stimulate your readers by demonstrating how your research has stimulated you.

This chapter begins by showing you the interesting and liberating functions of a concluding chapter. It then provides some practical suggestions about what this chapter should contain and reviews the balance between confessing to your errors and proclaiming your achievements. We go on to show how your concluding chapter should reconnect your data analysis to the basic analytic questions that have inspired you and should think through what your research can offer to a range of different audiences. Finally, we demonstrate why writing your final chapter can be fun.

The Final Chapter as Mutual Stimulation

Your final chapter should be stimulating for you to write. If this is the case, it is likely to stimulate your readers. Part of that stimulation arises in linking the particularities of your own research back to the more general issues that arise within (your part of) your discipline. As the authors of the standard British text on PhDs comment,

> You are not doing some research for its own sake; you are doing it in order to demonstrate that you are a fully professional researcher, with a good grasp of what is happening in your field and capable of evaluating the impact of new contributions to it—your own as well as others. (Phillips & Pugh, 1994, p. 60)

Your contribution is what you must set out to demonstrate in your final chapter:

It is here that you underline the significance [to your discipline] of your analysis, point out the limitations in your material, suggest what new work is appropriate, and so on. (1994, p. 59)

Phillips and Pugh's remarks suggest part of the answer to the practical question, what exactly should your final chapter contain?

WHAT EXACTLY SHOULD YOUR FINAL CHAPTER CONTAIN?

In the most general terms it [your final chapter] is a discussion as to why and in what way . . . the theory that you started with [is] now different as a result of your research work. Thus your successors (who include, of course, yourself) now face a different situation when determining what their research work should be since they now have to take account of your work. (Phillips & Pugh, 1994, pp. 59–60)

A helpful way of looking at this is in terms of Murcott's question: "What does the candidate want the reader to make of all this?" (1997, p. 3). As Table 24.1 shows, the final chapter offers you the opportunity to give your own twist to the wider implications of your research. Such implications must, of course, reflect your own critical sense of what is good and not so good in your own research. Always remember: unless you define your own sense of the limitations (and implications) of your work, your readers will do it for you!

You can, however, go too far in focusing solely on the limitations of your work. Research reports should not just be confessions! In the next section, we discuss the balance between owning up to where you feel you went wrong and blowing your own trumpet about your achievements.

Table 24.1   Suggested Contents for Your Final Chapter

- The relation between the work done, the original research questions, previous work discussed in the literature review chapter, and any new work appearing since the study began
- Some answer to the classic examiner's question, If you were doing this study all over again is there anything you would do differently? Why so? (i.e., the lessons to be learned from the conduct of the study)
- Any implications for policy and practice
- Further research that might follow from your findings, methods, or concepts used

SOURCE: Adapted from Murcott (1997), p. 3.

CONFESSIONS AND TRUMPETS

As Wolcott notes, in assessing your thesis, your examiners will recognize that chance happenings as well as your research design have limited (as well as improved) your research. Be upfront about these matters. So, in your final chapter, write

> a broad disclaimer in which (you) make quite clear (your) recognition of all the limitations of the study (e.g., that it occurred in a particular place, at a particular time, and under particular circumstances; that certain factors render the study atypical; that limited generalization is warranted; etc). (1990, p. 30)

However, what Wolcott calls "this litany of limitations" should be coupled with a stress on what you believe you have achieved. So, as in life, be realistic but don't undersell yourself! This can be in the form of "a conservative closing statement that reviews succinctly what has been attempted, what has been learned, and what new questions have been raised" (1990, p. 56).

Wolcott's helpful suggestion is, in our view, somewhat undermined by his use of the adjective "conservative." Beware of employing so much caution that you bore the reader! If you can effectively show why you have been stimulated, then you are much more likely to stimulate your audience.

Stimulation requires an active imagination. And, in science, it is theory that feeds the imagination.

Theory has been extensively discussed in the first three parts of this volume. Here, we want to suggest a practical sense of theorizing that can help in writing an effective final chapter.

THEORIZING AS THINKING THROUGH DATA

An imaginative conclusion will move on from the careful description and analysis of your earlier chapters to a stimulating but critical view of the overall implications of your research. Without this, your research may amount to no more than a set of descriptions of data achieved by some mechanical use of a method.

Because much qualitative research works inductively, generating and testing hypotheses during data analysis, your final chapter is often the best place to present theoretical linkages and speculations. As Alasuutari comments, in qualitative data analysis, one preferably starts directly from empirical examples, develops the questions by discussing them, and gradually leads the reader into interpretations of the material and to more general implications of the results. If one feels like discussing and constructing them, the best position for grand theoretical models is *in the final pages*. (1995, p. 183, my emphasis)

Grounded theory is a term used to describe a way of inducing theoretically based generalizations from qualitative data. However, it is crucial that, if grounded theory is your "thing," you use it imaginatively rather than as a label to dress up a largely pedestrian study.

As we argue in Chapter 15, some grounded theory studies fall short of imagination. This possibility is recognized in a leading text on grounded theory:

It is entirely possible to complete a grounded theory study, or any study, yet not produce findings that are significant. If the researcher simply follows the grounded theory procedures/canons without imagination or insight into what the data are reflecting—because he or she fails to see what they are really saying except in terms of trivial or well-known phenomena—then the published findings can be judged as failing on this criterion [i.e., of being significant]. (Strauss & Corbin, 1990, p. 256)

The final chapter is likely to be the place where your examiners will discover whether your theoretical pretensions are, as implied by Strauss and Corbin, merely mechanical. But, if theory must never be mere window dressing, this does not mean that theory is ultimately more important than research. Theory without data is empty; data without theory says nothing. This reciprocal relationship between theory and data is well captured by Coffey and Atkinson. As they put it,

Data are there to think with and to think about. . . . We should bring to them the full range of intellectual resources, derived from theoretical perspectives, substantive traditions, research literature and other sources . . . [this means] that methods of data collection and data analysis do not make sense when treated in an intellectual vacuum and divorced from more general and fundamental disciplinary frameworks. (1996, p. 153)

The problem is that you may become so immersed in your highly specific research topic that you are ill-prepared to step back and to think about what Coffey and Atkinson call "more general and fundamental disciplinary frameworks." You can give your research this broader perspective by forcing yourself to think about how what you have discovered may relate to broader issues than your original research topic. In this way, a very narrow topic may be related to much broader social processes. As we saw in Chapter 15, this was how Mary Douglas's anthropological study of an African tribe took us from a very narrow issue (how the Lele perceive the pangolin) to a very broad social process (how societies respond to anomalous entities). In this way, argue Coffey and Atkinson,

> qualitative data, analyzed with close attention to detail, understood in terms of their internal patterns and forms, should be used to develop theoretical ideas about social processes and cultural forms that have relevance *beyond these data themselves.* (1996, p. 163, our emphasis)

WRITING FOR AUDIENCES

A continuing message of this book is that, like any form of writing, writing a research report should always be framed for particular audiences. Drawing on this insight, many of David's PhD students have organized their concluding chapters in terms of the different audiences who might be interested in their research.

Take the case of Moira Kelly's research on how her respondents describe the death of a spouse (discussed in Chapter 3). Her concluding chapter describes what her findings imply for four different audiences: methodologists, theorists, people with a substantive interest in the sociology of health and illness, and health policymakers.

One useful exercise to get you thinking about how to proceed in this way is simply to list all the possible audiences for your research. When David used this exercise recently with students doing business PhDs at the Helsinki School of Economics, the following audiences were noted:

- Disciplinary (e.g., management, organization studies, marketing)

- Methodological (e.g., case study researchers, interviewers, etc.)

- Practitioners (e.g., managers, entrepreneurs, marketers, etc.)

- The general public (clients, consumers, politicians, etc.)

Such a list of your likely audiences should give you a good idea of how you could structure an effective concluding chapter. But don't just guess what will most interest your audiences! Show your findings to groups drawn from each audience and find out what is relevant to them (see Chapter 28 for further discussion of audiences for research).

WHY YOUR FINAL CHAPTER CAN BE FUN

It may surprise you to think that writing your concluding chapter can be fun. Having struggled to reach the end of your data chapters, you may already be exhausted and tempted to try to get away with a short concluding summary. After all, you feel, what more can you add?

We have good news for you! Until your final chapter, you have had to be highly disciplined. Not only have you had to stick to the point, you also (we hope) have had to stick closely to your data. Your only respite has been your footnotes. Used properly, footnotes are the place for asides and barbed comments (never the place for references).

But, if footnotes can be fun, so can your concluding chapter. For this is the place where caution temporarily should go out the window and lateral thinking should rule. Here is the place to make broader links, eschewing the narrow focus found in the rest of your thesis. Here off-the-wall comments ("from left field," as they say in baseball) are not only allowable but welcome. At last, perhaps, here is a space for you to reveal your true colors—providing that you recognize that such self-expression has always to be recipient-designed for an audience.

CONCLUDING REMARKS

Let me make an obvious point: when you have finished your final chapter, it is time to submit your thesis. Yes, we know research reports can always be improved and the beauty of word processing is that the mechanical aspects of revision are quite simple. But how long do you want to stay a student? Providing your supervisor is supportive, isn't it better to submit right now? Even if your examiners require changes, at least your rewrites will have a pragmatic focus.

Being a perfectionist sounds like a nice identity. As Becker has commented,

Getting it out the door is not the only thing people value. A lot of important work in a lot of fields has been done with little regard for whether it ever got out the door. Scholars and artists, especially, believe that if they wait long enough they may find a more comprehensive and logical way to say what they think. (1986, p. 123)

However, Becker also makes us aware that rewriting can also be the alibi for the persistent waverer. By contrast, he tells us,

I like to get it out the door. Although I like to rewrite and tinker with organization and wording, I soon either put work aside as not ready to be written or get it into a form to go out the door. (1986, p. 124)

After a long period of study, do you really want to "put work aside"? Follow your supervisor's advice (providing the supervisor is not a ditherer!) and get your work "out the door"!

KEY POINTS

You should never write a summary as your concluding chapter. Instead, your final chapter must help the reader to decide what to make of your dissertation. This should explain

- The relation between the work done, the original research questions, previous work discussed in the literature review chapter, and any new work appearing since the study began

- Anything you would do differently now

- Implications for policy and practice

- Further research that might follow from your findings, methods, or concepts used

- The limitations of your own study

Above all, your final chapter should stimulate your readers by

- Showing how theories have helped you think through your data

- Addressing each of the audiences who might be interested in your work

FURTHER READING

Estelle Phillips and Derek Pugh's *How To Get a PhD* (1994), Chapter 6, is the best British account of the practical issues involved in concluding a research dissertation. On using theory to develop your conclusions, see Pertti Alasuutari's *Researching Culture: Qualitative Method and Cultural Studies* (1995), Chapter 13; Anselm Strauss and Juliet Corbin's *Basics of Qualitative Research* (1990), Chapters 1–4; Jennifer Mason's *Qualitative Researching*

(1996), Chapter 7; and Amanda Coffey and Paul Atkinson's *Making Sense of Qualitative Data* (1996), Chapter 6.

Get into the habit of keeping files on each of the issues below (taken from Table 24.1):

- The relation between your present work and your original research questions
- Anything you would do differently now
- Implications for policy and practice
- Further research that might follow from your findings, methods, or concepts
- The limitations of your own study

At regular intervals, attempt to write a summary of what you can currently say about each of these issues.

As this chapter has argued,

> Data are there to think with and to think about ... [this means] that methods of data collection and data analysis do not make sense when treated in an intellectual vacuum and divorced from more general and fundamental disciplinary frameworks. (Coffey & Atkinson, 1996, p. 153)

Find one or two recent journal articles you think are important and, following Coffey and Atkinson, show why your dissertation does not exist "in an intellectual vacuum."

Make a list of the different audiences who might be interested in your research (e.g., disciplinary, methodological, practitioners, general public).

Now work out how you could write a chapter that framed the contribution of your research for each of these audiences.

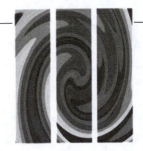

PART VI

The PhD Examination

For PhD students, their qualifying exams and proposal and dissertation defense are crucial and much-feared parts of the process. These may seem to be shrouded in mystery, like some weird secret society or fraternity hazing ritual! Part VI attempts to demystify these PhD rites of passage.

CHAPTER 25

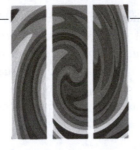

Surviving PhD Exams

CHAPTER OBJECTIVES

By the end of this chapter, you will be able to

- Identify the different types of PhD exams

- Recognize that truly horrific PhD orals are very rare

- Take practical steps to prepare for your oral exams

- Know how to function effectively at the oral exams

INTRODUCTION

For an undergraduate education in the United States, in most cases you can receive your bachelor's degree by simply completing a series of courses. In a PhD program, however, the courses are primarily intended to prepare you for the more important and ultimate task of writing a dissertation (a book-length treatise based on firsthand research) that is evaluated in terms of its original contribution to your discipline by a committee of five professors (four from your own department and an external member from a related discipline). The doctoral student is responsible for forming the committee in consultation with his or her chair, a committee professor who plays a role in mentoring the student throughout the process of writing, defending, and eventually publishing a dissertation (please also see Chapter 18 for advice on how your advisor can help you).

The process of evaluating a PhD candidate and her or his dissertation is divided into three stages and spread over a number of years (at least 2). These stages are respectively (a) coursework, (b) dissertation proposal (prospectus), and (c) dissertation. Advancement through each stage is contingent on your successful completion of written and/or oral exams (oral defenses). In this chapter, we discuss each of these three phases of PhD work with particular emphasis on the last part, the dissertation defense.

QUALIFYING EXAMS

The qualifying exams evaluate a graduate student's ability to proceed to the next phase of his or her progress in a PhD program. The exams are based on your written answers to a series of questions and an oral test when you are asked to elaborate on your written answers. The written exams generally cover three topics (theory, methods, and a specialization area within your discipline) and can be take-home or in-house exams. With a take-home, you pick up the questions at a certain time and deliver your answers within 48 hours (depending on your program, you may be given more or less time than this). In contrast, in-house exams are proctored and you do not have the opportunity to consult books or library material; instead, you are required to answer all the questions on the same day. The length of the answers is typically about five double-spaced pages, and you can be given as many as 20 questions.

For the oral component of your "quals," as they are sometimes called, a meeting will be scheduled after all your committee members have read your answers. The committee members typically ask PhD candidates to elaborate on a particular portion of their answer. In some cases, they might ask additional questions that were not part of the original test. The ostensible goal of the quals is to ensure that a given candidate has a good grasp of his or her discipline and is prepared to conduct firsthand research.

Following is list of suggestions to consider before you schedule your qualifying exams.

The final evaluation of your performance during the qualifying exams is at least in part based on your poise and professionalism. Avoid direct confrontations with your advisors, even if they are baiting you to do so. Alicia Isaac offers particularly good advice in this regard:

Table 25.1   Suggestions for Qualifying Exams

- Schedule your exams when you and your chair feel that you are prepared.
  It is relatively rare for a candidate to fail these exams, but it does happen
  and it is generally because the candidate was not prepared. How do you know
  that you are prepared? If you have completed all your course requirements
  and have established a good rapport with your chair and the other
  committee members, you can simply ask them if the time is right to move to
  the next phase.

- As you prepare for your exams, consult with your fellow graduate students who
  have successfully completed their quals. They can tell you what type of questions
  to expect.

- For the oral qualifying exams, be careful not to give the impression that you
  know more than you actually do. Your committee members are your mentors.
  They know the limits of your knowledge about the field and they also know that
  you are a novice social scientist. Show your mastery of the basics and convince
  your faculty advisors that you are eager to learn more.

- Above all, do not make up answers in your haste to seem intelligent. Nothing
  makes you seem more foolish than making false statements. Honesty and
  composure are the best policies here.

- Show your enthusiasm for every question. That means you have to be
  conscious of your impressions. Your faculty advisors have spent a good deal
  of time developing their questions. The oral exam is their opportunity to shine as
  much as it is yours. Be careful not to frown or appear irritated by a particular
  question. That kind of reaction, however subconscious it may be, only invites a
  confrontation with the committee member. Your unintentional grimace might be
  read as hostility and cause the faculty member to make you "squirm," as the
  saying goes.

- Although prefacing every comment with "That is a great question! Thank you for
  asking that!" could seem phony, it is not a bad idea to maintain eye contact and
  nod, even if you feel you are being grilled.

What should you do if a committee member becomes fixated on a line of
questioning that is going nowhere?

Attempt to answer the question and at first available opportunity shift
the focus to another point in your response by encouraging another committee member to express his or her views on your point. If this doesn't
work, give your major professor "the eye" signaling him or her to jump
in. . . . If your major professor is the one asking the questions, give him or
her the "you are dead" signal or feign seizure. (1998, p. 106)

Similarly, regarding an appropriate strategy for answering seemingly stupid questions, Isaac offers this advice:

Act as if the question is as important as any question you've ever heard and answer it as if your response is vital to world peace. Then, get home and tell all your friends and especially your doctoral colleagues what kinds of buffoons already have doctorates and have the nerve to try to give you a hard time. (1998, p. 106)

Again, to the extent possible, demonstrate mastery of your discipline without arrogance. Be scholarly and tentative about your answers. Start your answers with modest qualifiers like, "As I understand it," "One way to answer this question is . . . ," "My reading of the text is. . . ."

PROPOSAL DEFENSE

As discussed in Chapter 10, before proceeding with data collection and writing for your dissertation, your PhD advisory committee will ask you to present them with a preliminary outline of your plans. In most cases, the dissertation proposal, or prospectus, has to be defended orally several weeks after written copies are submitted to the committee. The oral defense of the dissertation proposal basically centers on the candidate's ability to show that his or her research project is relevant and doable. Here the faculty advisors are not testing the candidate as much as they are helping the candidate develop the proposal. Ideally, the proposal defense is a consultation between you and your committee. Although you are expected to make a convincing case for your project, you have to be careful not to seem overly committed to it. Remember that you are just proposing to undertake a project and, as such, should be flexible. A good practice is to share a draft of your proposal with your committee chair before circulating it to other members. With your chair's help, you can fine-tune the document and fill in any large gaps before you have to defend it.

DISSERTATION DEFENSE

The dissertation defense is the final step in the hazing ceremony that culminates in the conferring of a doctoral degree upon a PhD candidate. The dissertation defense goes by different names in different countries. There is also some variation across different universities, disciplines, and committees, in the way the dissertation defense proceeds. The character of the dialogue between the dissertation committee members and the PhD candidate ranges from a polite conversation to a heated, passionate, or sometimes humiliating exchange for the candidate. As Rudestam and Newton note,

> The defense ranges from a congenial ritual in which the student publicly presents his or her findings to an assemblage of receptive "colleagues," to a more excruciating examination of the quality of the dissertation and grilling of the candidate by an unsympathetic faculty committee. (1992, p. 142)

The dissertation defense sometimes involves surprises. Dissertation committee members who were cordial and supportive before suddenly seem more demanding and strict. As the case of Jennifer de Coste demonstrates in the following, graduate students sometimes feel pressured to make uncomfortable compromises just to "get through" the defense.

> Throughout my PhD work, I have been encouraged to use my background in theatre and music to share my research. In my coursework, I have been able to explore performance-based methods. I have developed performance pieces in response to current events, collaborated with others to create a visual art–based response to classroom readings, and even encouraged my own students to work in alternative media, like film and video, when presenting final projects. However, I have quickly learned that this utopian vision of learning is not what is embraced in the realities of defending a dissertation or publishing. My professors, who were so quick to encourage and support me performing my works, who now sit on my committee, have altered their perspectives. My goal has always been to incorporate my voice throughout my qualitative dissertation, to utilize my feminist research methodologies by placing myself in my research, and to ultimately have a portion of my defense be a performance piece alongside my written work. As the time of defense draws nearer, however, I have been told that the defense may not be the most appropriate place for a performance piece, that dissertations are a process to "get through" by whatever means necessary. I have found myself removing me from my work, slowly but surely, and contradicting all I have strived for, in an effort to "get through."

In the remainder of this chapter, we set out to prepare you for a PhD oral examination, reviewing the mechanics of the oral and its possible outcomes (including the subsequent revisions to your dissertation that your examiners may require). Our goal is to offer sensible reassurance and guidance. As we will later demonstrate, the oral defense is not usually quite as awful as it is made out to be. However, to prepare you for the worst, let us begin with some "horror stories."

Dissertation Defense Horror Stories

One student reported a common fear about an impending defense: "When I went into that room, I was scared—what if they ask me something I do not know, what if they said, this is a PhD, you have got to be joking." Such fears are normal; terrible experiences are much rarer. Rowena Murray (2003, p. 2) provides four examples of pretty nasty defenses:

- A 9-hour viva [a commonly used British word for dissertation defense]

- Aggressive examiners who seem to want to break down the candidate

- The candidate forgetting everything she knew ("blank mind syndrome")

- Examiner(s) deciding that the candidate has made a serious error; but this is based on a misunderstanding about what he has said and he doesn't have the confidence to correct them

What does it feel like to go through a bad dissertation defense? Consider Alicia Isaac's story of her own defense from her book *The African American Student's Guide to Surviving Graduate School*:

> I can imagine what the witnesses must have felt like in the O. J. Simpson trial. The questions were relentless, directive, and intended to test not only my academic competence but my stamina and courage. It was clear that few members on the committee were out to see what I was made of. . . . One professor had six pages back and forth of written comments and questions that neither my major professor nor I had any clue were coming. . . . Though I passed and my committee members congratulated me on an excellent defense, I left there feeling wounded and mangled. I had friends waiting to celebrate but I just couldn't show up. I don't think you should have to break somebody down just to see if he or she can win. (1998, pp. 98–99)

David has his own horror story to add. Back in the 1960s, he felt confident about submitting and defending his dissertation because of the praise it had received from his PhD supervisors. He was totally unprepared when the "external examiner" (the outside member of his committee) was very critical of his work. Indeed, David later learned that it was only his strong defense at his viva that saved him from being failed! Fortunately, the outside member gave David several pages of suggestions and he managed to put together a revised version, which was passed 12 months later.

Preparing for Your Defense

Your dissertation committee needs time to read your dissertation. They also have busy schedules. So you will probably have 1 to 2 months between submission of your dissertation and your oral examination. How should you spend this time?

In the immediate weeks after submission, with the oral defense some time away, you might want to reward yourself with a short break. Take some time off and smell the roses, as it were. Socialize with friends, call your relatives, and generally distance yourself from the dissertation for a short time so that you can return to it with a fresh perspective.

When you are ready to start preparing for your defense (at least about a week before that actual date), consider the preparation listed in Table 25.2:

In addition to the points listed in Table 25.2, we also suggest that you become familiar with your committee members' research, especially if they are related to your dissertation topic. Ideally, you should have cited their research in your dissertation, but at least you should know that the work exists. In the academic world, it is considered an insult to accept the services of a scholar (as in asking them to serve on your dissertation committee) and not bother to read their work. Reading their latest papers may well inform you about the likely

Table 25.2   Preparing for a PhD Defense

- Read your dissertation. You wrote it over months and years and may have forgotten some of the details.

- Update your knowledge of the most up-to-date research about your topic by reading recent journal articles.

- Discuss how you should approach the defense with your committee chair. Air out any misgivings or criticisms your chair has of your dissertation *before* the defense.

- Attend your fellow graduate students' defenses if possible to familiarize yourself with the process.

- Prepare a 30- to 45-minute summary of your dissertation and rehearse this presentation several times.

- Consult fellow graduate students about questions that they have encountered at dissertation defenses (e.g., "What are the policy implications of your research?" or "If you had unlimited time and resources, how would you do this research differently?").

- Stop preparing about 24 hours before the defense and get plenty of rest.

SOURCE: Adapted from Alicia Isaac (1998), pp. 96–100.

slant of their questions and, perhaps, allow you to look for any links between your work and theirs—although you should first consult your chair about whether this is appropriate.

Doing the Defense

Remember that, as a result of your research, you are now a specialist. This probably means that you now know more about your topic than your committee members. As Kjell Rudestam and Rae Newton put it,

> In the best of cases, the oral defense is an opportunity to think about and articulate the implications of your study [for] your own discipline and to be challenged by your committee to claim your right to sit among them as an acknowledged expert in your field of study. (1992, p. 142)

Being "an acknowledged expert" is not a license to wallow in jargon. By contrast, part of one's expertise is the ability to explain your work in a straightforward way and to make links with the work of others.

So, at the defense, be ready to summarize your main research problem, the contribution of your research, and how you would do anything differently. Remember that the oral examination is not a test of memory. So you will be allowed to refer to the text of your dissertation or your notes as necessary.

In order to add more substance to these points, appended at the end of this chapter you will find some details of a Swedish PhD dissertation that David examined in September 1998. Although the questions he asked, as "Opponent," were, of course, tied to that particular dissertation, they nonetheless give you some flavor of the kinds of concerns, both specific and general, that dissertation committees raise at PhD defenses.

As Clive Seale (personal correspondence with David) has pointed out, the skills you need at an oral defense are not dissimilar to those you need at a job interview (see Chapter 29). In both situations, it helps to be fairly assertive while respecting the knowledge and experience of your interviewer. Table 25.3 offers some tips for your oral along these lines.

As indicated by these oral defense tips, successfully defending your proposal, qualifying-exam written answers, or your dissertation requires skilled impression management. As rites of passage, orals test your professionalism and psychological makeup as much as they do your substantive knowledge. As Sally Kuhlenschmidt (1992) notes, graduate students' worst enemy during oral examinations is anxiety, and thus learning to manage it will improve your performance dramatically. In her class on preparing for oral examinations,

Table 25.3   Tips for the Oral Defense

- Always ask for more clarification if you have not understood a question.

- Avoid one-word/one-sentence answers even if the question is a "closed" one. Use the questions as opportunities to get your point across by making links between the questions and the things you want to say.

- Avoid overlong answers that drift very far from the original question.

- Ask if you are on the right track and if your committee wants to know more.

- Refer to the list of points you want to get across when your committee asks whether there is anything they have not covered.

- Ask your chair to make notes of questions and answers. This will be of considerable use if the committee requires that you revise your dissertation or you want to publish any of it.

SOURCE: Adapted in part from Seale (personal correspondence).

Kuhlenschmidt helps graduate students reduce their anxiety by (a) learning more about the process (i.e., the different stages of the examination), (b) speaking with confidence and clarity even if they are nervous, and (c) understanding that critical questions are a routine part of oral examinations and should not be taken personally. If your graduate school offers a similar class, consider taking it. If not, ask your graduate school coordinator to offer a workshop on the topic.

Outcomes

In North American universities, there are basically four possible outcomes after a dissertation defense. These are listed in Table 25.4.

As Isaac's list of possible outcomes indicates, in the worst possible scenario, a PhD candidate would have to significantly revise his or her dissertation in order to receive a doctorate. The more typical outcome is passing without any revisions or with only minor revisions. The high rate of successful dissertation defenses in U.S. universities can be attributed to three factors. First, before advancing to a doctoral program, most graduate students have to write a master's thesis (although some programs allow a nonthesis option). The master's thesis in many ways can be considered a mini-dissertation. Second, the qualifying exams and the proposal defense further polish the doctoral candidate's plan for her or his dissertation. Finally, as a general rule, a committee chair does not allow a dissertation to be defended unless he or she feels the work is ready. In most cases, students work closely with their chair as they write their dissertation;

Table 25.4   Dissertation Defense Outcomes

- *Pass without revisions:* You passed the dissertation and the defense and they all signed it on the spot. There's nothing else for you to worry about except technicalities of printing, binding, and so forth.

- *Pass with revisions:* The committee generally felt good about your work but has suggested some changes to be made in the final draft. Usually they will sign it but expect your major professor to ensure that the changes are made. Some committees will want to wait until the corrections are made before they will sign it. The most important thing here is that you don't have to go through another defense.

- *Fail:* The committee feels that there is still major work to be done on the dissertation. After suitable revisions, another defense is scheduled.

- *Fail the Defense:* In a few rare instances, a student may have done a good job on the dissertation but totally bombed the defense. A second, less formal defense usually is scheduled.

SOURCE: Isaac (1998), pp. 108–109.

some are even so fortunate as to have chairs who read the dissertation chapters as they are written and provide feedback as the work develops. Therefore, by the time of the defense, there are no surprises.

That is the good news. The bad news is that the hard work of publishing, getting a job, and becoming tenured still lies ahead. Some of our colleagues have suggested that writing a dissertation pales in comparison to the harrowing experience of receiving tenure, a 5- to 6-year process that involves preparing dossiers for annual reviews, publishing about one journal article per year, teaching two to four courses per semester, advising undergraduate and/or graduate students, writing grants for external funding, serving on university committees, and performing community service. So if you are done with the dissertation, go out and celebrate for a while. Then come back and try to get a head start on the rat race. Ask your committee members for advice about what parts of your dissertation might be publishable, how you should revise or shorten them, and which journals might be the best place to submit them.

REVISING YOUR DISSERTATION AFTER THE ORAL

As noted earlier, dissertation committees sometimes ask that the dissertation be revised. After discussion with your major professor, they will allow you a certain period to undertake such revision.

Following Seale (personal correspondence with David), we suggest in the following some tips for revising a dissertation.

- Make a list of the main criticisms

- Make sure your revisions address all of these criticisms

- If major revisions were requested, resubmit your dissertation together with a separate sheet of paper identifying what you understand the criticisms to have been, how you have addressed them, and the page numbers where this has been done

DOCTORAL STUDENTS' COMMENTS ON THE DISSERTATION DEFENSE

The average doctoral student views the dissertation defense as the most critical part of graduate work. Much is at stake in this final event; however, as we have noted throughout this chapter, you have little reason to fear a defense. To further illustrate this point, consider what these recent PhDs have to say about the experiences.

Karyn McKinney

The oral defense was free of controversy. It was much easier than I expected it to be, and less challenging than my qualifying exams. Most of the questions I was asked allowed me to explain the research further, and were not critical in tone. My committee members all got along, and said afterward that they enjoyed the oral defense. Strangely enough, in some ways the oral defense was a bit anticlimactic, perhaps because I had been working so hard for so long on the project, and really wanted to have to "prove" myself.

Sara Crawley

As it turns out, I thoroughly enjoyed my oral defense because I had picked committee members who would "get my back" for various issues. When I took one position, one member would support me. When I took another, another member would support me. It turned out to be a very collegial debate—exactly as I had hoped based on the expertise of each member. I felt well prepared for my defense and I think I prepared my committee well for what I hoped they would support. There were no surprises by design. Hence, my defense is memorable to me as an enjoyable event, not a painful fistfight.

Michael Arter

The final defense went extremely well. I remember the words of a professor who I came to know very well and highly respect. He stated, "No one knows your research better than you." As I presented my findings and discussion, I was reassured by those words in that I felt in complete control of the defense.

One question from the committee did cause me concern. I was asked which other theories may have applicability for my research and that threw me completely off balance. I was so focused on defending the use of a theoretical model in qualitative research that I went blank when faced with that question. After stumbling for a few seconds, I realized I had addressed other theories in my study and answered the member's question with those theories. Afterward, I realized that perhaps I may have been overfocused on "my" theory, and may have missed (or dismissed) other theoretical models.

Lara Foley

My oral defense was awesome! It was possibly the first time I felt confident about my work (something I still struggle with). I was nervous because I had gone to some friends' defenses and at times it seemed like the professors were really enjoying "messing with" people. But I knew my data so well, they couldn't trip me up. My qualifying exam defense was much more nerve-wracking for me than the dissertation defense.

Chris Faircloth

My oral defense went fine. Be prepared to answer questions that are quite difficult and have seemingly nothing to do with your dissertation. A good chair is there to protect you from the committee if they get out of your hand. I have long described oral defenses as "academic hazing." Do a darn good dissertation, let the committee have its fun, leave the room, and then get their signatures.

As these testimonials show, oral defenses should not be feared. Most of our colleagues report that their defense was collegial and moved along "smoothly." However, on rare occasions, complications do arise, as in the following story.

Sylvia Ansay

Although I felt well prepared, I froze at my defense and could hardly remember my own name. I couldn't respond to even basic questions from the committee. That's when my advisor came to my rescue. Because I had been in several of his seminars and had kept him well informed on my research, he had confidence in my ability and the research at hand. Several times, he reframed a committee member's question in terms of the work we had done together and I was able to collect my thoughts, respond, and take it from there.

Even in these slightly more complicated cases, all is not lost. Remember that no one on your dissertation committee has a vested interest in seeing you fail. On the contrary, your faculty advisors would very much like to see you succeed and move on to the next phase of your career. If occasional problems do present themselves, as Sylvia and Sharon note, you should rely on your committee chair to come to your rescue and get things back on track.

To help you become even more familiar with an oral defense, in the next section David describes the process from a faculty advisor's perspective.

A CASE STUDY FROM DAVID

Vesa Leppanen completed his dissertation at the Department of Sociology at Lund University in Sweden. I was appointed his opponent because Vesa's work was related to mine analytically (we both use conversation analysis—CA) and substantively (we both had studied communication between health care professionals and patients).

A Brief Summary of the Dissertation

Vesa had researched encounters between Swedish district nurses and their elderly patients. These encounters may take place in the patient's home or at a clinic. Their primary clinical purpose is to perform routine tasks like measuring blood pressure or giving injections. Naturally, in the course of these encounters, other matters arise—from the patient raising a problem to the nurse giving advice. A sample of 32 consultations provided just over 10 hours of videotaped and transcribed nurse–patient interaction—half at primary care centers, half in patients' homes. Standard CA notation was used on the audio. Nonverbal activities were reported by descriptions placed immediately above the place in the transcript where they occurred.

Four principal topics were studied:

- The interactional achievement of tests and treatments
- Patients' presentations of their concerns
- The delivery of test results to patients
- Advice-giving about health behaviors

The dissertation concludes with a summary of the research findings, a practical recommendation that such data is highly appropriate in training nurses (and many other practitioners), and some general implications for future research. Its call for the study of apparently nonproblematic research settings and data is a useful reminder of Harvey Sacks's (1992) call, three decades ago, to discover the extraordinary in the ordinary.

My Questions

What do you see as the main contribution of your research?

Would you do anything differently now?

Chapter 4 on tests and treatments reads as very "descriptive" based on one extended case. Would you agree?

On page 88, you explain that this chapter serves as a background to the other three data chapters. But can you say anything more, for example, do you ever meet resistance to tests? Do nurses ever have to work at getting permission?

[Several detailed questions on the data analysis follow. Now come some more general points.]

Your data is equally drawn from home and clinic. Why did you decide not to systematically compare these different environments? Don't clinic and home provide very different resources? [I mention one of my past PhDs, by Maura Hunt, who had looked at the problems that community nurses may face in beginning their work in the patient's home as well as the work of Anssi Peräkylä on doctors' use of X-rays and scans in the clinic to "prove" diagnoses to patients].

Your use of the video material: I remember us talking about your video data on nurses touching patients when I visited Lund in March 1996. Yet the only detailed treatment is on pages 213–218, where you use the video to show how the nurse underlines advice by abandoning other tasks, gazing at the patient and waving a pill bottle. Why is there relatively little use of the video data elsewhere? [I discuss various possible uses of the video data that might have strengthened the dissertation]

Have you never given feedback to the nurses you studied? Why not?

Your only practical conclusion is about the relevance of this kind of detailed research for professional training. I entirely agree about this but isn't there more that you can say?

Your discussion of the analytic implications of your research is not very specific. How does your work advance other well-known [named] studies and findings?

My Concluding Remarks

This is a fascinating, detailed, and orderly study of great analytic interest. I learned a lot from reading it. It is also an exemplary case from which nurses and beginning researchers could learn a great deal about the value of the analytic mentality of CA.

The highlights for me were

1. Various parts of Chapter 5. First, the most detailed treatment on institutional data about the positioning and functioning of the question "how are you?" Second, the discussion in Chapter 5 about how patients achieve recipiency for the statement of their concerns.

2. Parts of Chapter 7. In particular, nurses finding the right position to deliver advice.

3. An unusually lively methods (or procedures) chapter. This provides a nice natural history of your research and a lovely account of the ethnographic work that preceded it.

4. Throughout, I liked your nonpartisan spirit and open-mindedness, particularly toward the judicious combination of CA and ethnography (for example, page 44).

Of course, as you show, bad news is usually delayed. So, in this case too. But I really have only two reservations. First is your somewhat limited use of your video data. Second is your underplaying of the practical relevance of your research.

But, in the context of such a well-crafted dissertation, these are quibbles. I eagerly encourage you to turn parts of this thesis into journal articles. In particular,

- Your excellent summary and critique of much nursing research (pages 21–27) is highly relevant in a field riddled by crude positivism and emotionalism.

- Your account of patients' skills in positioning their statement of their concerns is highly original and publishable (pages 110–128). Perhaps it could be combined with your comparison (pages 130–131) with Jefferson on everyday trouble-telling or perhaps the latter could be a separate article.

- Parts of Chapter 7, where you compare your findings with other [named] research on advice-giving and advice-reception are also highly publishable.

The Outcome

I am pleased to say Vesa was awarded his PhD by his local committee. When I last heard, Dr. Leppanen had a teaching position at a Swedish university and his supervisor, Professor Ann-Mari Sellerberg, had obtained a substantial research grant for the two of them to study telephone counseling by community nurses.

General Implications

1. My two first questions are pretty standard for PhD defenses, namely (a) "What do you see as the main contribution of your research?" and (b) "Would you do anything differently now?" It pays to prepare your answers to such questions!

2. Prepare for constructive criticism of your analysis, for example, "Chapter 4 on tests and treatments reads as very 'descriptive' based on one extended case. Would you agree?" (This is a nice example of a question where a one-word answer would have been inappropriate. The right strategy here might be to agree in part but point to counterevidence elsewhere.)

3. Prepare to defend your methods and selection of cases, for example, "Your data is equally drawn from home and clinic. Why did you decide not to systematically compare these different environments?" (If possible, explain the advantages of not making such a comparison.)

4. Be ready to discuss further the contribution of your research to your discipline and (where relevant) to practitioners and policymakers.

5. Expect your faculty advisors to offer advice about which parts of your dissertation may be publishable (see my concluding remarks).

CONCLUDING REMARKS

Although the prospect of a PhD oral is intimidating, horror stories are actually quite rare. Use your revision period to prepare a list of points you want to get across at the defense. Now is also the time to find out about your committee members' own published work. In addition, try to get some practice with others in a mock defense.

At the dissertation defense, always say if you have not understood a question and, if so, ask for more clarification. Avoid one-word/one-sentence answers even if the question is a "closed" one. Use the questions as opportunities to get your points across by making links between the questions and the things you want to say. But avoid overlong answers that drift very far from the original question. Finally, refer to the list of points you want to get across when your committee asks whether there is anything they have not covered.

It is also a good idea to ask your chair to make notes of questions and answers. This will be of considerable use if you have to revise your thesis and/or intend to publish any of it.

CASE STUDY

By now, you may be thoroughly scared. But take comfort. For better or worse, most dissertation defenses are not that exciting. For example, Amir's defense was surprisingly cordial. After years of writing the dissertation and days of preparation for the oral defense, he expected a good deal of "fireworks" and drama. Instead, what actually went on was quite routine and ordinary. Amir's fear of an all-out brawl and clenched fists pounding on the seminar table did not come to pass—no switchblades or brass knuckles were brandished, no obscenities were shouted, and generally no blood was spilt on that day.

The entire thing took only about an hour. He introduced his work for 20 minutes. After answering several pertinent questions, he was asked to wait outside for the committee's decision. After a few minutes, Amir was invited back into the room where everyone addressed him as "Dr. Marvasti" and congratulated him for earning his doctorate. The truth is that, with few exceptions, a well-prepared candidate will cruise through the defense. When the exceptions do occur and things become somewhat tense, it becomes critically important to maintain one's composure and not become overly defensive.

For example, the oral component of Amir's qualifying exams was moving along smoothly until a committee member asked him a question about George Herbert Mead and his work on the social origins of the self. Evidently, Amir's answer did not satisfy the faculty advisor. At this point, Amir should have clarified or at least acknowledged that there are other possible answers. Unfortunately, at that point in his career Amir lacked such diplomatic tact, so he obstinately insisted that his reading of Mead was correct and proceeded to offer a long and painfully

(Continued)

(Continued)

redundant explanation. The situation became more dramatic when in the midst of Amir's diatribe about Mead, the committee member produced a copy of Mead's *Mind, Self, and Society* from under the table (apparently the book had been sitting on her lap the entire time with the text under dispute marked with yellow stickers). At this point, beads of cold sweat were forming on Amir's forehead. The advisor went on to read the text aloud, showing how a close reading of Mead contradicted Amir's position. Thankfully, the committee chair intervened and saved Amir from his needlessly firm stand on Mead and the exceedingly embarrassing and pointless argument. In retrospect, a far more diplomatic response to the faculty's question would have showcased Amir's knowledge of Mead while allowing for other interpretations.

KEY POINTS

There are many ways to prepare for your oral. You can

- Revise your thesis, particularly the concluding chapter
- Prepare a list of points you want to get across
- Be ready to explain and to defend any changes to your original research question
- Read up on recent work in your field
- Be familiar with your committee members' research
- Practice with others in a mock defense

At the defense itself,

- Always say if you have not understood a question; if so, ask for more clarification.
- Avoid one-word/one-sentence answers even if the question is a "closed" one. Use the questions as opportunities to get your point across by making links between the questions and the things you want to say.
- Avoid overlong answers that drift very far from the original question.
- Ask if you are on the right track and if your committee wants to know more.

FURTHER READING

The most useful guides to preparing for dissertation defenses are Alicia Isaac's *African American Students' Guide to Surviving Graduate School* (1998);

Pat Cryer's *The Research Student's Guide to Success* (1996), Chapter 19; and Estelle Phillips and Derek Pugh's *How To Get a PhD* (1994), Chapter 10. For an American guide, see Kjell Rudestam and Rae Newton's *Surviving Your Dissertation* (1992), Chapter 8. A useful Web link is http://www.cs.man.ac.uk/infobank/broada/cs/cs710/viva.html

EXERCISE 25.1

To find out about your committee members' own published work, read at least one book or journal article by each of them. As you read, make note about the following points:

1. What model of social research (see Chapter 7) is being used? How far does it differ or complement your own? What useful lessons can you learn from these differences or similarities?

2. Are there any theoretical developments, methodological innovations, or substantive findings that relate to your own work? If so, how can you bring these out in the oral? If not, how can you demonstrate respect for your committee member's approach while standing up for your own?

3. Examine the writing style in this material. How different is it from your own? What can you learn from these differences (or similarities)? For example, do these simply reflect the differing demands of (say) a scholarly journal and a research dissertation or are there basic differences of temperament and outlook?

EXERCISE 25.2

When you have completed your revisions, ask your chair or a couple of your fellow students who are familiar with your research to give you a mock oral defense. Following Table 25.3 and using your prepared list of points that you want to get across, try out your skills in answering their questions.

If possible, videotape this rehearsal and view it for distracting body language or irregular or annoying speech patterns. For example, some people start every sentence with "uh" when they are nervous. Your friends or advisor may be too kind to point such things out to you directly. The videotape will be a more impartial witness.

EXERCISE 25.3

Visit http://www.phdcomics.com/proceedings/index.php to see what other students have to say about their experiences with their advisors and graduate school. You may want to search the site using the phrases *dissertation defense* and *oral defense* to narrow your focus. Alternatively, you can click on the "On Academia" link to see an index of different discussion threads.

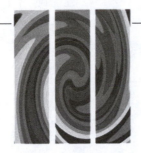

PART VII

Review

This part of the book contains just one chapter. It sums up many of the themes discussed in this work by seeking to describe how to do effective qualitative research.

CHAPTER 26

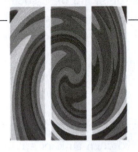

Effective Qualitative Research

CHAPTER OBJECTIVES

This chapter offers an opportunity to revise the main themes of this book.

INTRODUCTION

In this chapter, we want to pull together the different threads that have run through this book. Throughout, we have encouraged you to distinguish relatively easy activities from the really tough ones and to concentrate your efforts on the latter. For instance, writing a literature review should be relatively easy for any graduate student (see Chapter 21). Equally, obtaining your data does not need to be too difficult if you follow some of our suggestions in Chapter 11.

By contrast, the really tough issues tend to concern data analysis. This area is discussed in detail in Part III of this book. In this short chapter, we want to provide a snapshot of the issues involved in the form of four rules to encourage effective qualitative research. Here are the rules:

- Keep it simple.
- Take advantage of using qualitative data.
- Avoid "drowning in data."
- Avoid journalistic questions and answers.

We will now review each rule in turn. But one word of warning: none of us can escape our intellectual biography. We have been influenced in more ways than we can realize by our training and experience as (one kind of) a sociologist. Therefore, if any of our rules look a little odd in the light of your own discipline, please discuss it further with your supervisor. Even if you differ, at least you will have a point of departure!

KEEP IT SIMPLE

In Chapter 6, we identified a kitchen sink mentality. Kitchen-sinkers attempt to study very broad problems, using many concepts and methods as well as large sets of data. Unfortunately, such a wide-ranging approach is unlikely to impress examiners and often will prevent you finishing your study.

In doing student research, simplicity is not a drawback but a necessity. Here are some ways to keep it simple:

- Narrow down your research problem (Chapter 6 offers a number of ways to do this).

- Use one **model** only.

- Use concepts that fit your model.

- Avoid multiple methods or, if you must use them, make sure they fit your model and research problem.

- Analyze a small data set (you can always add comparative data later—if you have time).

- Recognize that the comparative method can be used within a small data set (see Table 12.1).

TAKE ADVANTAGE OF USING QUALITATIVE DATA

Sometimes students elect to use qualitative methods because (they feel) they are not very good at statistics. This is not unreasonable (assuming they are right). However, qualitative methods are not appropriate for every research problem. In Chapter 2, we illustrated this point with one example of a study concerned with how "psychosocial adversity" is related to asthma morbidity and care. We suggested that this study's focus on the relation between a set of **variables** could most effectively be researched using quantitative rather than qualitative methods. The former approach could employ **reliable**, standardized **operational definitions** of the variables studied. It could also work effectively with large data sets to establish correlations between these variables. By contrast, psychosocial adversity is a very slippery concept within most qualitative research models. For instance, we can effectively study whether participants themselves use such a concept, when and how they do so, and with what local consequences. These are interesting research issues, but they take us on a very different path from that envisaged by the original formulation of the research problem.

Considerations of this nature suggest that, if we want to do qualitative research, there is a set of strategies to *avoid*:

- Beginning with variables that you wish to relate

- Beginning with problems that are already defined by members of society (e.g., social or administrative problems)

- Making assumptions about where things take place (e.g., is psychosocial adversity a state of mind, a set of behaviors, or a commonsense category employed in many different ways?)

- Searching for explanations: *why* questions are usually best answered by quantitative methods

- Working with **normative** assumptions (e.g., what is "effective" communication?) and with prior versions of policy outputs

However, we do not need to be entirely negative. Taking advantage of qualitative data means using some or all of the following strategies:

- Asking *how*, *what*, and *when* and delaying (or avoiding) *why* questions

- Wherever possible (and it usually is possible), working with **naturally occurring** data (see Chapter 8)

- Studying the categories actually employed by participants (and when and how they are used—and with what effect)

- Studying what is unremarkable, the routine, and the "ordinary"

- Recognizing the interconnectedness of subjects' categories and of their activities so that we always study how each is laminated upon another (see Chapter 4)

AVOID DROWNING IN DATA

A continuing argument of this book is that, if you delay your data analysis until your final year of study, you are courting disaster. By contrast, we have suggested

- Start data analysis from day 1—if you have no data, then work with other people's data or use other publicly available material, for example, texts of all kinds (see Chapter 11).

- One case is usually enough, providing you use internal comparisons (see Chapter 9); delay other cases and then try to sample theoretically.

- Keep to small targets—recognize that the student researcher is usually an apprentice and that learning from your mistakes is a key to success.

- Write above your PC the following motto: "the point of qualitative research is to say a lot about a little"!

AVOID JOURNALISM

Journalism is a trade that, like any other, has good and bad features. In suggesting that you should avoid journalism, we do not mean to disparage what journalists do but simply to underline that qualitative research should not be the same thing as journalism.

Given the daily nature of most newspapers, journalists tend to focus on unusual, out-of-the-ordinary events that often involve celebrities. When they describe public rather than private issues, the journalistic focus, quite understandably, is on social problems as generally conceived (e.g., the economy, health policy, international relations).

Our message to student researchers is, let journalists get on with what they do best. Your job is somewhat different. Now is the time to display the skills that you have learned through years of training. As an apprentice qualitative researcher, your research will differ from most journalism in the following ways:

- When formulating a problem, you will not begin from a social problem but will often seek to study something that is quite unremarkable, even "obvious" to participants.

- Your data analysis will not rely on identifying gripping or spectacular stories; instead it will reveal the various ways in which apparently "obvious" phenomena are put together

- You will not rush to conclusions even when you have some compelling instances; instead, you will carefully sift all the evidence, actively seeking out **deviant cases**

- You will employ the analytical resources of your discipline, working with your data in the context of a coherent model and set of concepts

- You will unashamedly theorize about situations and events, but this will not serve as mere window-dressing (see Chapter 7); instead you will theorize with your data and build new theories.

CONCLUDING REMARKS

This book has been written to offer you practical ways to cope with some of the doubts that affect most novice qualitative researchers. Apart from what we can offer, we suggest that you turn to your fellow students. If you do so, we guarantee that nearly all of them will have been through many of the same doubts about their research and their capacity to do it.

If you remain worried that you do not have enough data, our message has been that you probably have too much! If you believe that your work is not particularly original, we ask, "whose is?" Just turning to some of the more pedestrian journal articles in your field should convince you of our argument.

As we suggest in Chapter 5, success in student qualitative research can be achieved by demonstrating that you are a professional. We all know that professions contain people with varying capacities. So the bar you face is really quite low. However, we hope you will aspire to something higher!

KEY POINTS

Effective qualitative research can be undertaken on the basis of following these four rules:

- Keep it simple.

- Take advantage of what qualitative data can offer.

- Avoid drowning in data.

- Avoid journalistic questions and answers.

FURTHER READING

A longer version of this chapter is provided in David Silverman's *Interpreting Qualitative Data* (2001), Chapter 10.

EXERCISE 26.1

Select any qualitative research report in your field. Now proceed as follows:

1. Apply to it the four rules discussed in this chapter.

2. Consider how well it stands in relation to each.

3. How could the research be improved?

4. Do any of the rules need to be modified or overturned in the light of your example?

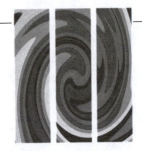

PART VIII

The Aftermath

The three chapters in Part VIII consider the aftermath of a finished piece of research and receiving a PhD. Depending on the level of your work, this may involve the possibility of getting your research published and, perhaps, getting a job. The following three chapters specifically help you with (a) choosing a publication outlet and getting published, (b) writing for the appropriate audience, and (c) searching for and securing an academic position. In these chapters, we approach these practical tasks as encounters between you (the writer or job applicant) and your audience (readers and potential employers). The topics listed in these chapters inform you about interactional choices and possibilities and their consequences for your career. Regardless of your career aspirations, as a good researcher, writer, or job seeker, your work should address a specific audience and be responsive to its expectations.

CHAPTER 27

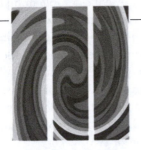

Getting Published

CHAPTER OBJECTIVES

By the end of this chapter, you will be able to

- Recognize the realistic publishing opportunities for your work

- Think about the appropriate place to submit your research

- Work out how to turn your research into something more appropriate for a journal

- Understand how journal editors and reviewers make decisions about which papers to publish

- Treat a decision of "revise and resubmit" as a golden opportunity

WHY PUBLISH?

Publishing your research is work. It will take a good deal of effort, time, and patience. It may take you well over one year to publish a manuscript in a refereed journal. The revisions may at times become tedious and far less exciting than the data collection and writing of initial drafts. Reviewers and editors may ask you to significantly change your work, and by the end, your original idea from the first draft may be barely recognizable in the published manuscript.

Why then, you might ask, should anyone subject himself or herself to this process? There are three ways to answer this question.

The simple answer is that you don't have to publish. A considerable number of PhDs complete their dissertations and never publish anything. However, you have to realize the consequences of this choice. Without publications, your job opportunities will most likely be limited to community colleges and smaller, lesser-known four-year colleges. You will have a heavy teaching load (usually four to five classes per semester) and few opportunities to pursue your research interests. If you find this kind of teaching career rewarding, then publishing is not a priority for you—though in reality even the smaller teaching colleges and universities will certainly appreciate a good publication or two.

In the broader academic job market, most positions require that the candidates have an established or emerging publication track. "Publish or perish" is the injunction that rings true for most of us. Tenure requirements at most universities require about one publication per year. You should keep in mind, however, that this number varies depending on the particular academic institution and its requirements. By the time a junior faculty member reaches the tenure decision (which usually also includes the promotion from the rank of assistant professor to associate professor), he or she is expected to have about five or six publications, mostly or entirely in refereed journals. Therefore, if you aspire to a university career as a teacher/researcher, you need to publish.

Additionally, after you have finished your research, you usually want its readership to extend beyond your supervisor and examiners. Don't expect that any more than a handful of people will check out your dissertation from any university library. So, if you want your work to be disseminated to a wider audience, you must publish it.

There is some discouraging news here. In these competitive times, simply completing an MA or a PhD does not guarantee a university post. Certainly, good references from your committee chair and other advisors will help. And any teaching experience you have gained is also a plus if you are seeking a regular academic post. However, if you have not yet made it into print, compared with applicants with completed dissertations and several publications, you may not even make it on to a short list (see Chapter 29 for a discussion of the job search).

Obviously, your willingness to publish is only the first part of the battle. To secure a successful outcome, one's desires have to be complemented with specific skills, knowledge, and strategies. In this chapter, we begin with an overview of theories of writing and representation. We then discuss possible strategic choices in the world of publishing (books versus journals). We end the chapter with a more focused discussion on what kinds of papers appeal to academic journals and offer suggestions about writing an effective journal article.

THEORIES OF WRITING: REFLECTING ON THE TEXT[1]

The reflexive turn in the social sciences, for the purpose of this chapter, refers to a growing awareness of writing as a constructive process. That is to say, rather than simply representing reality, writing can be viewed as a type of social construction in its own right (see also the discussion of the different languages of qualitative research in Chapter 2). Many figures have contributed to this growing movement, but perhaps the work that is mostly widely cited is James Clifford and George Marcus's seminal book *Writing Culture: The Poetics and Politics of Ethnography* (1986). This collection of readings from different scholars particularly calls for ethnographers to see writing as a craft that involves culture, aesthetics, and politics. As stated in the introduction to their book, "the making of ethnography is artisanal, tied to the worldly work of writing" (p. 6).

Another important work in this area is John Van Maanen's *Tales of the Field* (1988). This book is also concerned with ethnography and its stylistic conventions. In particular, Van Mannen suggests that ethnographies can be organized as realist, confessional, and impressionist writings about culture. He argues there is no single social reality, but that variations in writing create different realities about the empirical world. In his words, "There is no way of seeing, hearing, or representing the world of others that is absolutely, universally, valid or correct" (p. 35).

Of course, some of the greatest contributions to the analysis of writing come from feminist scholars who have raised important questions about the absence of women's voices in the dominant textual paradigms of social science. Feminists have turned our attention to the linguistic nuances and conventions of texts. For example, Laurel Richardson (1990, 2000) shows the prevalence of literary devices (e.g., metaphors) in social science texts. For her, scientific writing is never neutral but is invariably embedded in practices of power and oppression. As she writes, "Power is, always, a sociohistorical construction. No textual staging is ever innocent. We are always inscribing values in our writing. It is unavoidable" (1990, p. 12).

The textual shift in the social sciences is part of a larger movement that questions the value and seemingly benign character of all scientific knowledge. This movement, largely referred to as postmodernism, challenges the very authority of science and its ability to represent "truth." For example, the renowned sociologist and postmodern thinker Norman Denzin (1993) states,

If there is a center to recent critical poststructural thought, it lies in the recurring commitment to strip any text of its external claims to authority. Every text must be taken on its own terms. The desire to produce a valid and authoritarian text is renounced. Any text can be undone in terms of its internal-structural logic. (p. 136)

Although some have dismissed the textual shift as a passing fad, others have embraced it as the new logic of social science and have proposed writing strategies for texts that are sensitive to postmodern sentiments. It is not our purpose in this chapter to assess the validity of these arguments. Suffice it to say, postmodernism (in its various forms) has alerted us to the diversity in writing styles in the social sciences. To illustrate the practical implications of the reflexive turn for writing, in the following section we review two opposing modes of representing reality and their underlying assumptions.

Writing for Truth

The most recognizable goal of scientific writing has been to represent "truth," or reality in its pure, unbiased form. This method of writing is sometimes associated with positivism, or the philosophical assumption that reality can be known positively or without doubt. The basic tenets of positivism are best articulated by Karl Popper in *Conjectures and Refutations: The Growth of Scientific Knowledge* (1963). Popper's main argument is that social sciences should only deal with empirical facts that can be proven to be wrong (i.e., falsifiability). Popper held that we assume that certain things are true until or unless they are shown to be false. As the title of his book suggests, for Popper, scientific knowledge evolves in a loop whereby educated guesses (i.e., conjectures) are initially posed and later refuted (i.e., tested and falsified) and replaced by better guesses (i.e., "truth") and so on.

The essence of Popper's philosophy becomes evident in his critique and dismissal of Karl Marx's revolutionary agenda. Specifically, Popper states,

> For all his acute reasoning and for his attempts to use scientific method, Marx permitted irrational and aesthetic sentiments to usurp, in places, complete control of his thoughts. It was romantic, irrational, and even mystical wishful thinking that led Marx to assume that the collective class unity and class solidarity of the workers would last after a change in the class situation. It is thus wishful thinking, a mystical collectivism, and an irrational reaction to the strain of civilization which leads Marx to prophesy the necessary advent of socialism. (from Popper's *The Open Society and Its Enemies*, page 333, cited in Gorton, 2006, pp. 88–89)

How does the logic of positivism inform writing? According to Popper, as social scientists, we should not write about emotions and beliefs but about facts, because only facts can be empirically tested and falsified. Our personal preferences or biases cannot be tested. Only facts, based on empirical observations, should be allowed in social science writing. Given the tentative nature of scientific knowledge, these facts should be stated in probabilistic terms. This philosophy may help explain the origins of seemingly cold, impersonal positivistic prose like, "The findings of this study show that X is likely to be correlated with Y." While "truth writing," as it were, has been the dominant approach in the social sciences, there are alternatives.

Writing for Politics

Thomas Kuhn's notion of "paradigm shift" as an alternative to the advancement of knowledge has engendered other ways of writing. Unlike Popper, Kuhn believed that the sciences do not necessarily follow an evolutionary path of accumulated tested knowledge but are subjected to "revolutionary" changes (1996). Kuhn departs from Popperian philosophy by approaching scientific knowledge as a human activity that is conditioned by particular sociohistorical forces. Ideas, for Kuhn, do not serendipitously appear and disappear in a social vacuum and in the dispassionate search for truth. The search for knowledge is not exempt from the same social conditions that mediate other human activities.

This way of thinking about knowledge points to relativity of truth. In this context, we can no longer speak of a universal transcendent truth, but instead we have multiple competing truths. The competition between truth claims, then, is rhetorical and purposeful. Here, the epistemological question "How do you know that?" is not limited to whether or not one has followed the proper methodological steps in discovering truth. There are larger, more fundamental issues raised by Kuhn's philosophy. Namely, "Why do we know what we know, for what purpose, and in what social context?" For example, Kuhn would ask, "In what way has the author's social position played a part in advancing or discrediting a particular set of truth claims?"

Kuhn's work made it possible for scientific writing to become explicitly concerned with politics, social justice, oppression, and power (this view of scientific inquiry is also echoed by Michele Foucault's body of work, particularly in his book *The Order of Things*, 1973). The approach to representation in a sense politicizes writing. Consider, for example, the following excerpt in which Norm Denzin suggests that writing is a politically reflexive practice:

I have no desire to reproduce arguments that maintain some distinction between fictional (literary) and nonfictional (nonliterary) texts. . . . These are socially and politically constructed categories. They are too often used to police certain transgressive writing forms. . . . The discourses of postmodern world constantly intermingle literary, poetic, journalistic, fictional, cinematic, documentary, factual, and ethnographic writing and representation. No form is privileged over others. Each simply performs a different function for a writer and an interpretive community. (2000, p. 899)

For social scientists like Denzin, scientific writing is not inherently superior to works of literature. The researcher's decisions about what to report, how, and to what audience involve reflexive political choices. As Denzin puts it, "The age of putative value-free science appears to be over" (1994, p. 501). Scientific research and the writing are thus not exempt from the structures of domination; instead, the focus is on "how power and ideology operate through systems of discourse" embedded in writing (Lincoln & Denzin, 1994, p. 579). From this perspective, the supreme goal of the research enterprise, or "a good text," is to show "how race, class, and gender work their ways in the concrete lives of interacting individuals" (p. 579).

This mode of writing, particularly among qualitative researchers, has spawned numerous subdisciplines. For example, *participatory research* encourages respondents to become fully involved in all facets of scientific investigation, including writing the research report. The goal here is to change and improve the respondents' lives. As Stephen Small notes,

Participatory researchers are openly and explicitly political. Their ideology emphasizes large-scale structural forces, conflicts of interest, and the need to overcome oppression and inequality through transforming the existing social order. The lack of access to useful and valued forms of knowledge by oppressed or disenfranchised people is viewed as a major problem that can be overcome through the research process. (1995, p. 944)

Similarly, critical ethnography encourages the advancement of social justice through research, or, as Soyini Madison puts it,

Critical ethnography begins with an ethical responsibility to address processes of unfairness or injustice within lived domain. By "ethnical responsibility," I mean a compelling sense of duty and commitment based on moral principles of human freedom and well-being, and hence a compassion for the suffering of living beings (2005, p. 5).

For critical ethnographers, writing is emotional, temporal, and situational. Rather than dismissing these conditional factors as sources of bias, critical ethnographers enact time, place, and emotions in their text—the text becomes a performance. In Madison's words, "In performative writing, the reader is not taking disembodied ideas and images from a cognitive word machine or an omniscient knower" (p. 196).

The Continuum of Representation

The two perspectives discussed here (writing for truth versus politics) represent polar opposites on a continuum of thought that contains many in-between positions. For example, instead of hand-wringing worries about the politics of writing, as captured in Howard Becker's famous question "Whose side are we on?" (Becker, 1967, p. 239), David Silverman, drawing on Strauss and Corbin, asks a simpler question: For what purpose do we write? He argues that research is a social practice in its own right, one that emerges in a particular social context and for a particular purpose. David focuses on the practical goals of writing and explains how different types of writing meet the needs of different audiences, such as academics, policymakers, practitioners, and the general public. Indeed, the simplest and most neglected aspect of writing is the audience. We further explore this issue in the next chapter. For now, it is important to remember that writing is ultimately a form of communication that is intended for a specific audience, and the expectations of that audience should in a large measure inform what we write and how we write.

The Basic Skills

Even in its most self-consciously inventive manifestations, writing is a craft that involves endless practice and the mastery of techniques. Indeed, even poets spend hours, if not months, writing and rewriting a short verse to perfect its meaning and impact on their readers. Theory, aesthetics, and technical know-how are not mutually exclusive dimensions of the craft of writing. Without technical skills, the full depth of one's creative and theoretical potential cannot be realized. For example, we sometimes have ideas that appear profound in our minds, but, sadly, we lack the necessary skills to convey them to others. To overcome this problem, we recommend that researchers begin with the basics of writing. For the purpose of the present discussion, this means learning about the challenges that all writers face in representing their ideas, regardless of their topic of analysis or individual writing style. Proofreading, spell-checking, and sentence structure are basic elements that are all too often neglected. Basic how-to guides can be particularly beneficial in this regard. Such books offer sound advice on writing that could help even advanced writers improve their craft. The following are a few suggestions we excerpted from the table of contents of such a book.

- Don't overuse the thesaurus
- Don't underuse the dictionary

- Don't wallow in a sentence straightjacket

- Don't add adverbs and adjectives to prettify your prose

- Don't expect the mail (the editor, that is) to clean up your mess (Noble, 2006)

The Backstage Politics of Publishing

In an ideal world, the peer-refereed system of publishing would allow for scholarly writing to be judged purely on the basis of its merits. And for the most part, that is precisely what happens. Yet it would be naïve not to acknowledge the presence of other extraneous influences in the world of publishing. A good discussion of such factors is offered in Frank E. Hagan's "The Essentials of Research Methods in Criminal Justice and Criminology" (2005, pp. 10–11). Hagan reviews three fascinating, but somewhat disheartening, articles that point to the backstage politics of publishing. The first is Robert Merton's essay on "The Matthew Effect in Science." Merton's use of the term was inspired by the following biblical passage: "For unto everyone that hath shall be given, and he shall have abundance: but from him that hath not shall be taken away that which hath" (Matthew 13: 11–12).

In the context of publishing, the Matthew effect implies that previously published authors, especially those who do not challenge canonical views of their discipline, are more likely to be published again. In Merton's words,

> The Matthew effect consists in the accruing of greater increments of recognition for particular scientific contributions to scientists of considerable repute and the withholding of such recognition from scientists who have not yet made their mark. (Merton, 1986, p. 58)

Hagan notes that the Matthew effect was tested by Michael Mahoney (1977), who asked 75 reviewers of a psychology journal to evaluate five different versions of a fictitious article. The five versions (a) supported pure behaviorism, (b) negated behaviorism, (c) offered no findings, and (d) and e) reported mixed results. Of the five versions, the one that agreed with the basic tenets of behaviorism (i.e., did not challenge an established doctrine) was accepted by all the assigned reviewers. On the other hand, the version challenging behaviorism was rejected and highly criticized for its methodology. According to Hagan, in a similar study by Douglas Peters and Stephen Ceci (1982), the researchers

> took twelve previously published articles and resubmitted them to the same journals where they had appeared two years earlier. The titles were changed and the names of the authors and their universities were altered,

the latter were done to reflect less prestigious institutions. Three of the resubmissions were recognized, but eight of the remaining nine were rejected. While the study itself was published, one of the authors nearly lost tenure because of it. (Hagan, 2005, p. 10)

Though such events may be isolated and your work may very well be judged on its own merits, practicality and realism dictate that novice authors maintain their associations with their senior mentors to the extent possible. Specifically, it is good practice to establish your publication record by coauthoring papers with a senior scholar in your field. Eventually, your work will be recognized by editors on its own terms, but until then, try to bask in someone else's reflected glory. Similarly, institutional affiliation seems to play a role in reviewers' evaluations. Therefore, if you are likely to acquire a job in an institution that is less prestigious than the one from which you will receive your PhD, try to earn your first few publications while you are still at your PhD university. That way, you can use that institution's name for your journal submission.

STRATEGIC CHOICES

The final step in the process of writing is publishing. Publishing is a necessary part of maintaining an academic career; the name of the game is "Publish or perish!" But, as we noted earlier, beyond the necessity of professional survival, publishing allows you to share your ideas with a larger audience. The feedback from the audience can then improve your arguments and essentially help you become a better scientist. So it is not vain or self-serving to try to publish your work; rather, publishing is a very important and effective way of learning more about your field. In this section, we discuss two basic choices (i.e., books and journal articles) for publishing social science research.

As you consider the two choices outlined throughout the remainder of this chapter, keep in mind that book and journal publications are given different weights in the tenure process. For example, in "Books vs. Articles: Two Ways of Publishing Sociology," Alan Wolfe (1990) shows that the balance between book and article production varies considerably across the top 25 sociology departments in the United States. Wolfe's comparison of books-to-articles ratios shows that New York University (NYU), Yale, and the University of Chicago, for example, are "predominantly book oriented." Conversely, the University of Indiana and University of Wisconsin are "predominantly article oriented." Other top 25 schools fall somewhere in between. This analysis also suggests that many other factors shape the two publication strategies and the labor markets associated with them. For example, private institutions tend to be more book oriented than public ones. Note that none of this negates the importance of ref-ereed articles, but it does point out that many top sociology departments give at least equal weight to books.

There is also the fact that for some subdisciplines within sociology, book publishing may be required. Ethnographers and qualitative researchers, for example, are generally expected to publish their fieldwork as a book. Further-more, some of the most important works in sociology have been ethnographic books (e.g., William Foote Whyte's *Street Corner Society* or Elijah Anderson's *A Place on the Corner*). As a whole, we tend to agree with Wolf's conclusion that pluralism in scholarly publications is useful and necessary; books and arti-cles allow for different treatments of topics under analysis and they allow soci-ologists to reach different audiences. With that in mind, let us consider the basic requirements of book and journal publishing.

BOOKS

In the exceedingly competitive and selective publishing market, the chances of publishing your dissertation as a book are slim. Doctoral dissertations are typi-cally written for a small audience—effectively composed of your chair and other committee members. Before even reviewing your submission, publishers usually want to know how you plan to revise your dissertation to reach a wider audience.

Furthermore, publishers in the new millennium are not exactly standing in line to publish (even revised) dissertations. Unless you can find a kind univer-sity press, you will discover that publishers are driven by the commercial need to find books that will sell upwards of 5000 copies. And the sad fact is that even a good research monograph will be unlikely to sell more than 1000—an amount that probably will mean that its publisher will lose money. Most social science publishers rarely publish research monographs—even by established scholars. We encourage you to begin your efforts to publish your dissertation as a book with these facts in mind. You are likely to receive many rejection letters before your dissertation is ready and accepted for publication as a book. Having said that, here are some tips that could help you understand and manage the process.

Select a "Book-Worthy" Topic and Methodology

As noted earlier, the main objective of a publisher is to earn a profit. Acquisition editors are always on the lookout for new authors and topics that will increase their sales. It is not uncommon for them to browse through confer-ence programs and actively solicit an interview with presenters whose work is "book-worthy." To give yourself an edge, first select a dissertation topic that has mass appeal. Second, titles are very important. Avoid esoteric titles. Publishers avoid obtuse titles like the plague for the simple reason that they are not sellable. Finally, give yourself a head start in the game of book publishing by selecting a methodology that is easy to explain for general audiences. In qualitative research, ethnographies have a well-established record of being published as books. Ethnographies sell because they are "exotic," story-like, and easy to understand. Note that book publishers are not interested in representational dilemmas of fieldwork or theoretical dos and don'ts. In fact, they would specifically instruct you to sidestep these discussions or put them in the footnotes. They want a product that sells to the largest possible consumer base.

Write the Dissertation as a Book

You can make the transition from a dissertation to a book manuscript much easier by writing your research manuscript in a readable book format from the start. For example, you can accomplish this by collapsing your methodology and literature review sections into a single chapter or by incorporating them into your introductory chapter. Of course, you have to consult your dissertation chair about your plans and persuade the other committee members to give you some latitude in your writing.

Find a Suitable Publisher

Different publishers specialize in different areas. For example, Sage Publications is known for its *listing* (book inventory) of how-to manuscripts on qualitative research. Begin by finding a press with a record of publishing books like the one you are proposing. You don't have to limit yourself to one publisher. Whereas articles have to be submitted to one journal at a time, book proposals and manuscripts can be sent to more than one publisher. In fact, you can "shop your book idea around" and see who offers you the best deal. Consider, for example, how Eileen O'Brien received her book contract:

I did publish my dissertation as my first book. It was published two years after I graduated. I had one well-known publisher whose name I really wanted on the book, but for some reason that editor totally dragged her feet forever. She sent it for an outside review, and after getting that review back, was kind of lukewarm about my project. But when I looked at the reviewer's comments, I didn't think they were that major, and the revisions were definitely doable. This whole back and forth took an incredibly long time, so in the meantime I had sent it to another publisher, and they wanted it immediately, with no outside review or anything. Once the other editor found out I had sent it somewhere else, she sent me a really nice card, a bunch of free books, and pretty soon a contract.

Sell the Book With a Good Proposal

Editors are inundated with hundreds of requests from aspiring authors. An effective way of getting their attention is by sending them a detailed book proposal that provides (a) a summary of the book idea and its relevance, (b) the intended audience for the book, (c) an explanation of why your book offers an alternative to its competitors or previous texts on the topic, (d) a table of contents with approximate words per chapter, (e) an explanation of why you are particularly qualified to write the book, and (f) a list of potential reviewers for the book and the proposal. In addition to these general points, the process of book publishing involves the following sequential steps.

1. Contact acquisition editors via letters of introduction, which begin with a brief summary of your research topic (an eye-catching abstract) and end with an invitation for the publisher to contact you if they are interested in seeing a book proposal.

2. If an editor contacts you, prepare a book prospectus or proposal and send that along with your best chapters. Do not send the entire manuscript unless it has been "de-dissertationized" (Wolcott, 2001, p. 113).

3. The editor will do an in-house review and/or send out the manuscript or proposal for review by scholars in your field.

4. If you receive favorable reviews, you will be issued a book contract that essentially signals a commitment to publish your book.

5. Review the contract and negotiate the terms before signing it. If possible, discuss the terms of the contract with your mentor or an experienced colleague. First-time authors are offered a small advance, if any. So in reality, the editors know that you are happy to have a contract regardless of the terms.

6. Sign the contract and begin the revisions.

7. Submit the first draft, receive more reviews and suggestions, and do more revisions.

8. Submit the final draft for publication.

9. Receive the proofs and make final copyediting changes.

10. Receive complimentary copies of your book.

As discussed later in this chapter, for most researchers, publishing their dissertation as a book is not a practical option because they either cannot find a publisher or simply don't have enough material for a full-length book. For them, the best strategy is to pick a promising data chapter and rewrite it for a journal. The process of journal article publication is outlined next.

CHOOSING A JOURNAL

The best advice here is to plan ahead. So, if your supervisor likes, say, one of your data chapters, discuss with her or him whether it might not be worth sending it to a journal. You show even more foresight by turning your seminar papers into publishable manuscripts.

Of course, it is important to find the journal that is likely to be most sympathetic to what you have to say because its audience shares your interests and its editorial policy is favorable to your kinds of ideas and/or data. For example, qualitative researchers should be cautious about journals that expect papers to be written in the standard form of Introduction, Methods, Results, and Discussion. As Pertti Alasuutari points out, this format may be unsuitable for nonquantitative, inductive studies (Alasuutari, 1995, pp. 180–181). Again, not all journals have the same policy about what they deem to be adequate data and scientific analysis. For instance, a paper submitted by one of David's students was turned down on the grounds that "it did not have a big enough dataset."

So find the right journal. Seek guidance from established academics and look at recent editions of journals they mention. Pay particular attention to statements of policy printed in most journals and note changes of editor and of editorial policy.

Responding to Editors' Decisions

Once submitted, don't be discouraged by a rejection. Most journal articles are rejected or returned with a request for substantial revision. So treat the outcome as a learning experience. In response to your submission, you are likely to get a set of (often detailed) referees' comments. Treat these as gold dust.

However biased you might think they are, they inform you, in practical detail, of the external audience outside (what may be) your cozy relationship with your advisor.

Usually, the reviews are accompanied with a letter from the editor. If the editor's letter contains the phrase "revise and resubmit" (especially when preceded by the phrase "strongly encourage you to"), that is very good news. In revising your paper, be sure to address the reviewer comments that the editor also raises in his or her letter. In other words, you may ignore some of the reviewers' comments, but it would be a huge mistake to ignore the editor's suggestions. Amir once made that mistake and his revise-and-resubmit very quickly became a rejection. The editor pointedly chastised Amir for not following her suggestions.

The Journal Format

Above all, bear in mind that journal articles (usually around 6000 words) are often much shorter than data chapters from a dissertation. This can make things very difficult for you, because, in a shorter space, you must fill in your audience about the overall orientation of your research. So, in writing a journal article, you must, at one and the same time, be highly focused but also provide a proper context.

Easier said than done! How do you write a paper that is likely to be published? And how do you cope with such strict word limits? Don't you need more rather than fewer words to explain the context of your research?

There are four quick solutions to these dilemmas:

1. Select a topic that will be the most intriguing to readers of this journal.

2. Ensure that this topic can be handled with a limited amount of data extracts.

3. Provide the *appropriate* context for your work—for instance, your audience will not need to be reminded about the basic assumptions of research in their area.

4. Stick rigidly to the point throughout.

The rest of this chapter will expand upon this advice. Shortly, we will discuss how to focus a journal article within the required word length. Such focus requires that you have a good sense of what journal editors are looking for. So now we will look in more detail at the criteria used by academic journals to make their decisions.

What Journals Expect

The policy of academic journals may vary by their focus, discipline, or audience. As noted earlier, many quantitatively oriented journals expect their articles to have a standard format, which assumes that all research has an initial hypothesis and that some form of random sampling will be employed. Equally, journals that seek to appeal to practitioners and other nonspecialists will be particularly interested in looking for papers that set out to have this wider appeal.

Despite this degree of variation, David's experience suggests that there are several criteria that recur in referees' comments in the kind of qualitative journals to which you might submit a paper. These criteria are set out in Table 27.1.

Table 27.1 indicates what to do if you want your submitted piece to have a reasonable chance of success. It, therefore, implies a series of "don'ts":

- Don't cite models or approaches if they are mere window-dressing.

- Don't vary the format; announce a clear structure at the start and stick to it.

- Don't forget that your paper should contribute to an ongoing conversation of scholars in your area.

- Don't defend approaches already familiar to readers of this journal.

Reviewers' Comments

As well as these general points, it is also useful to have advance warning of the specific kinds of criticisms that reviewers make about the submissions they see. As other people may be quite sensitive about showing you the critical reviews they have received, the following are extracts from some of David's (usually anonymous) reviews during the past few years. Naturally, references that might identify the paper or the author have been deleted.

Table 27.1   Evaluation of Qualitative Articles

1. Goodness of fit between the **model** chosen and what is actually delivered
2. Internal coherence
3. Showing something "new" when compared to past work
4. Speaking to the interests of the journal's target audience
5. Clear presentation

SOURCE: Adapted from Loseke and Cahill (2004).

To help you follow these comments, they are grouped as "good news" and "bad news." Each section contains portions of comments about many papers.

Good News

A fascinating topic with some nice data.

This is an interesting paper, using theoretically generated analysis on a practically relevant topic.

This paper deals with an important issue. As presently written, it is highly accessible to practitioners and patients.

The paper is based on an apparently well-transcribed piece of data.

The data chosen is very manageable.

This is a carefully done study and brings out some important practical issues.

This is a highly ambitious methodological paper. Its claim to originality, I take it, is that several different methods can be combined to shed more light on a text than any one alone. There is considerable insight in the way in which these methods are used.

This paper discusses some potentially interesting data. It uses an approach that, I presume, will be relatively unfamiliar to readers of the Journal. Quite correctly, therefore, the author(s) take up a fair bit of space explaining the approach used.

Bad News

These "bad news" comments are grouped under several headings.

Overambition

I think it currently tries to do too much.

Unfortunately, the abstract promises much more than is ever delivered.

There are so many issues that are raised that it is difficult for any to be developed properly. Each would make a separate paper. Given so many issues, it is not surprising that the data analysis is rather thin and not really linked to the literature review.

Overgenerality

The broad brush approach adopted here I found frustrating. There is no attempt to ground the argument in a piece of data.

Unanalytic

For the most part, the observations on the data strike me as commonsensical. To develop this paper further, much more use needs to be made of the vast literature on this subject based on transcripts of this kind.

The final sentence of the abstract is trite and unnewsworthy.

The analysis of data only begins more than halfway through the paper and is very thin.

It hardly analyzes its data at all and should be rejected.

The paper works by assertion. For instance, it simply isn't always the case that [X follows Y].

Unfortunately, the data analysis is very thin indeed, barely rising above descriptions, which are sometimes banal.

Inconsistency

Methodologically, the approach does not fit the issues that the author wants to address.

Methodological Failings

I found the citation of "cases" less than convincing. While space constraints always limit the number of data extracts one can use, the paper fails to give any sense that **deviant cases** were analyzed and that prior assumptions were in any way tested by the data.

Lack of Originality

The paper discusses a contentious methodological issue. It is also an issue that has been discussed in a mountain of publications over the last 10 years. Therefore, it is particularly hard to say anything fresh about the topic.

Lack of Clarity

I am unclear about the relevance of the approach used, the presence of several traditional assumptions which sit uneasily with it, and the issue of practical relevance.

I don't understand the first sentence of the Abstract.

Lack of Recipient Design

The section on theory is, I feel, inappropriate. Readers who know about this already will be bored, and readers who do not will not want to cope with a theoretical discussion before they get to the data. Much better, then, to introduce the required elements of theory in the course of the data analysis.

You may lose your international audience by going straight into issues relating to one small country.

We hope that present readers will not be intimidated by these comments. Please treat them as providing guidance about practices best avoided. After submitting several papers and reading the review, you begin to see a pattern among the reviewers. They fall into five broad categories:

Editor impressers: Their comments are directed at the journal editor rather than the authors. These folks write detailed (sometimes irrelevant) reviews with the hope of being invited to contribute their own manuscript to the journal.

Ego bruisers: These reviewers seem to receive pleasure from attacking the competition in their field. They have elevated their insulting and backhanded comments to an art form (you can almost hear them giggling at their own handiwork in between the lines).

Ego bruised: These reviewers are primarily concerned with the critique of their own work in your paper or the fact that you neglected to cite them. Their comments sometimes include direct references to their own articles.

Shoddy reviewers: These folks (usually well-established scholars in their field) don't really read the papers they are asked to comment on. Their reviews contain comments so brief and perfunctory as if to suggest to the editor, "Don't bother me with this kind of submission again."

Helpful reviewers: This is your ideal reviewer. They actually read the papers carefully, to the point of suggesting copyediting changes (letting you know where you have a missing comma, for example). This kind of reviewer does not lecture you or put you down with condescending comments but instead provides specific suggestions for improving the paper.

Some are undoubtedly more helpful than others, and you have to learn to read them selectively. To borrow a cliché, "Reviewers are people too." They provide their services to editors free of charge. Often they have spent hours reading a paper and writing their comments. While some merely try to impress the editor, for the most part reviewers help the authors improve their work. Even if the reviewer sounds obnoxious or hostile, there may still be very useful tidbits of feedback in their comments. Ironically, sometimes the harsh reviewers are the most helpful ones because they have meticulously read the manuscript and taken its content seriously. For example, a reviewer for this very chapter wrote comments that occasionally bordered on sarcasm (many of them in capitalized letters, to indicate an angry shouting voice). Yet, once we were able to get past the tone, many of his or her comments were helpful in improving this chapter.

Following are some suggestions David (a helpful reviewer) has made to authors.

Suggestions

I would like the paper to be revised to become sharper in focus and to take account of other relevant work.

You need an introduction setting out the *general* themes. Then an early data extract would whet the reader's appetite.

I suggest that you submit your revised draft to a native English speaker. Currently, there are multiple infelicities.

If space allowed, the analysis would also benefit from comparison with one more case.

The present conclusion combines analytic *descriptions* of the findings and practical recommendations. Instead, I would like to see the practical conclusions separated and the paper's analytic *contribution* clarified.

We now turn to the art of writing a short journal article.

HOW TO WRITE A SHORT JOURNAL ARTICLE

As already noted, most journals nowadays cap articles at around 6000 words. Yet, no doubt, you want to context your research but you have so much data and so many findings. How can you present your research in such a small frame?

There are three ways to shorten a paper:

- Stick rigidly to the point (e.g., one topic, one case, one theory, one model, one method).

- If you are working within an existing approach or model, don't waste time defending it (reinventing the wheel).

- Consider whether you need all your footnotes; surely if they are not worthy of being in your main text, you may not need them at all. At this level, you should not need extensive footnotes to demonstrate your academic respectability.

By shortening your paper through such techniques, you can create space to enlarge on what matters. For example,

- Focusing on a topic that will intrigue readers of this journal (e.g., one relating to a recent debate)

- Demonstrating credibility by combining intensive and extensive methods (e.g., short data extracts and simple tabulations)

- Writing a conclusion that displays lateral thinking, for instance by relating your substantive account to a broader area

Finally, if your paper is still too long, consider splitting it up into different topics appropriate for several journals. Working the same material in a number of different ways is what Gary Marx has called **leverage**. Marx's idea is discussed in the next chapter.

CONCLUDING REMARKS

Publications are good for academic careers. They also can provide an outlet for your key data chapters as well as for beloved draft chapters that you decided were too peripheral to be included in the final version of your thesis (see Chapter 24).

Getting published depends on making a number of strategic choices (e.g., Book or journal article? Which journal to select?). There are several ways of improving your chance of getting your paper accepted by a journal. First, "decide on what you wish to focus. What is your theoretical story?" (Strauss & Corbin, 1990, p. 246). Second, you need to ask yourself, "Do I need this detail in order to maximize the clarity of the analytic discussion, and/or to achieve maximum substantive understanding?" (1990, p. 247).

Remember that your audience is both bigger than and very different from the small audience for your thesis. So ruthlessly strip out inappropriate references and material and recontext your work. As Harry Wolcott (2001, p. 113) puts it, when writing a journal article, "de-dissertationize" your work. Don't expect to get your paper accepted as is. Make use of the referees' comments as helpful encouragements to rewrite a better article!

Finally, you should try to write a compelling argument. Jay Gubrium has suggested that much qualitative data is "inherently" interesting (personal communication). Take advantage of this and use the interest that the reader may have in your material to your advantage. Tease, entice, and puzzle your readers.

CASE STUDY[2]

Amir's graduate advisor, Jay Gubrium, was fond of saying, "Writing has a momentum of its own." Amir didn't fully understand what Jay meant until Amir began writing his qualitative dissertation. As he put into writing his many ideas and organized his observations into different chapters, he quickly learned that in the process of moving from vague insights to a coherently articulated text, many new ideas are generated. At the same time, much of what he had previously thought was groundbreaking turned out to be nothing but platitudes. Once he put his ideas in writing, they were much less profound than he originally thought them to be.

For example, at the beginning of Amir's project, he wanted to organize his dissertation around the notion that the homeless are "the postmodern heroes of our time." The idea was inspired by interviews with homeless men who had said things like "It sucks to be a citizen" or "I feel sorry for the poor bastards who are enslaved by their work. I am free to sleep where I want and go where I want." Amir interpreted such statements as clear rejections of the modern, capitalist premise of productive labor. Chatting in coffee shops with fellow students, he would champion the cause of the homeless by quoting their antiwork statements, translating his field notes into political slogans.

Of course, eventually he had to write all of this down into a coherent document. In doing so, he was presented with a serious problem. Namely, he found it impossible to transform a number of catchy statements into a full-length dissertation. Aside from a few banal declarations like "It appears that some homeless people reject conventional notions of work," he had nothing else to write on the topic. Given his data and level of expertise, the notion of the homeless as postmodern heroes was a dead end. On the other hand, as Amir's writing and analysis progressed, he came across another idea that seemed more in synch with the empirical evidence. In particular, he noticed that the very notion of the homeless was problematic. The men and women on the streets and in shelters viewed their circumstances from many different standpoints. Some thought of their situation as a type of personal freedom, whereas others said they were "miserable." This way of analyzing and writing about his fieldwork became the foundation of his research and was further polished as the writing went on. Thus the otherwise unmanageable mass of data started to fit into an orderly framework.

KEY POINTS

There are at least five ways of improving your chances of getting a paper accepted by a journal:

- Find a focus
- Avoid too much detail
- Redefine your audience

- Expect an initial rejection and make use of referees' comments in a second submission

- Make a compelling case

NOTES

1. Portions of this discussion were previously published in *Qualitative Research in Sociology* (Marvasti, 2003a) and in "Alternative Ways of Writing Social Science" in Pertti Alasuutari's *Handbook of Social Science Research* (in press).

2. This section was originally published in Marvasti's *Qualitative Research in Sociology* (2003a).

FURTHER READINGS

The four best sources on this topic are Donna Loseke and Spencer Cahill's chapter "Publishing Qualitative Manuscripts" in Seale, Gobo, Gubrium, and Silverman's (Eds.) *Qualitative Research Practice* (2004); Harry Wolcott's little book *Writing Up Qualitative Research* (1990), Chapter 6; Anselm Strauss and Juliet Corbin's *Basics of Qualitative Research* (1990), Chapter 13; and Nigel Gilbert's chapter "Writing About Social Research" in N. Gilbert's (Ed.) *Researching Social Life* (1993).

For how-to writing references, we recommend the following: William Noble's *Book of Writing Blunders and How to Avoid Them* (2006), James Cochrane's *Between You and I: A Little Book of Bad English* (2004), Ben Yagoda's *When You Catch an Adjective, Kill It* (2007), and Bonnie Neubauer's *The Write-Brain Workbook: 366 Exercises to Liberate Your Writing* (2005).

EXERCISE 27.1

Nigel Gilbert (1993a) suggests choosing a journal article written by someone else and writing a review of it as if you were the referee. If you need guidance on what to look for, use some of the "good news" and "bad news" lines of approach found in this chapter.

Now ask your supervisor to read your review. Use the feedback you get to

1. Think critically about how you might publish your own work

2. Invite your supervisor to ask book review editors to send books to you for review in journals (this is one way to get a first step on the publications ladder!)

EXERCISE 27.2

A good exercise for writing journal articles is to practice writing annotated bibliographies. After reading a journal article that you plan to use for your dissertation or next research paper, visit the University of Wisconsin–Madison Writing Center Web site (http://www.wisc.edu/writing/Handbook/AnnotatedBibliography.html) for information on how to prepare an annotated bibliography.

EXERCISE 27.3

This exercise underlines the importance of familiarizing oneself with a publication before submitting a paper for the editor's consideration. Visit the Web site for several research journals in which you may be interested in publishing your work. See if you can find answers to the following questions.

1. What are their criteria for the content?

2. What are their criteria for format and length?

3. Who are the reviewers?

4. Who is the editor?

5. Are you familiar with their work?

6. Have you cited any of their research in your submission? Should you?

7. Have you read any manuscripts that were published in this journal? How does your work compare with the journal's publication track?

EXERCISE 27.4

For a list of social science and communication journals and their acceptance rates, visit the Iowa Guide at the following Web site: http://fm.iowa.uiowa.edu/fmi/xsl/iowa guide/search.xsl?-db=iowaguide&-lay=plain&-view

Look up several journals that might interest you and compare their review times and acceptance rates.

CHAPTER 28

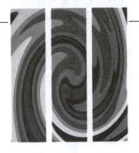

Audiences

INTRODUCTION

As suggested in the previous chapter, getting published is all about designing your writing for a particular audience. Writing should be tailored for the priorities of your audience.

As Amanda Coffey and Paul Atkinson put it,

Reading is an active process, and no text can have a completely fixed meaning . . . when we write—and hence inscribe certain preferred interpretations in our books, dissertations and papers—we do so with an implied audience of readers. (1996, p. 118)

Fellow academics are only one of several potential audiences. Other possible audiences are policymakers, practitioners, and the general public. Each group will only want to hear about your work if it relates to their needs. These four audiences and their likely expectations are set out in Table 28.1.

Table 28.1   Audiences and Their Expectations

Audience	Expectation
Academic colleagues	Theoretical, factual, or methodological insights
Policymakers	Practical information relevant to current policy issues
Practitioners	A theoretical framework for understanding clients better, factual information, practical suggestions for better procedures, reform of existing practices
Lay audiences	New facts, ideas for reform of current practices or policies, guidelines for how to manage better or get better service from practitioners or institutions, assurances that others share their own experience of particular problems in life

SOURCE: Adapted from original citation in Strauss and Corbin (1990), pp. 242–243.

The expectations of academic audiences about both written work and oral presentations have already been discussed at length in this book. As you consider the range of other audiences, as shown in Table 28.1, you may feel overwhelmed by the work required to meet their separate expectations and needs. However, this table contains a simple, easy-to-follow message: good communication requires focus and yet more focus.

The trick is to combine recognition of the expectations and needs of such audiences with your own active shaping of your materials. The good news is that a little practice may make you adept at working the same material in a range of different ways. In this context, Gary Marx's concept of "leverage" is very useful. As he puts it,

> Try to leverage your work. The sociological equivalent of a bases-loaded homerun is to take material prepared for a class lecture, deliver it at a professional meeting, publish it in a refereed journal, have it reprinted in an edited collection, use it in a book you write, publish foreign versions and a more popular version and have the work inform a documentary. (1997, p. 115)

Marx reminds us of the range of audiences that await the qualitative researcher. In the rest of this chapter, we consider the three nonacademic audiences listed in

Table 28.1, policymakers, practitioners, and lay audiences. How do you fashion what Marx calls "a popular version" for such audiences?

THE POLICY-MAKING AUDIENCE

The targeting of policymakers as the primary audience varies depending on one's discipline. The so-called more applied fields tend to be more in tune with policymakers' concerns. For example, in criminal justice, an entire journal, *Public Policy Review*, is devoted to discussion and evaluation of crime policies. The following is an abstract from a study published in this journal:

> The experiences of a group of mothers reentering the community after a period of incarceration are explored. The authors are particularly interested in how incarceration and subsequent reentry influence mothers' family relationships and primary risk and protective factors. . . . [Interviews were] conducted with 28 women probationers who had at least one minor child and had undergone incarceration at least 2 months prior to release. Descriptive analyses reveal that mental health risks characterize many mothers in this study, resource adequacy and parenting stress are significantly related, and family support is an important factor in successful reentry. It also appears that incarceration, even for short periods, is associated with shifts in family configuration on mothers' release by increasing the likelihood of divorce and decreasing the likelihood that mothers will reside with the father of at least one of their biological children. Implications for intervention and directions for future research are discussed. (Arditti & Few, 2006, p. 103)

Another reason for considering policymakers' needs is that lucrative research grants often come from federal and local government agencies that stipulate they only fund research with specific policy implications. For example, Amir is in the process of submitting a grant proposal to a state agency in Pennsylvania to fund his research about the lives of immigrants in rural communities. In the course of preparing his grant proposal, he attended a presentation in which the directors of the agency described what type of research they will support. It was very clear in the course of this presentation that any research without "policy implications" would not be funded. After attending this presentation, Amir revised his original proposal to underline the specific implications of his study. Part of the proposal now reads as follows:

> We aim to develop recommendations and strategies for effective community building based on communication and cooperation between local

residents and new rural immigrants. These recommendations can be promoted, adopted and/or institutionalized by state and local authorities to aid new immigrants in rural areas and at the same time address the concerns of local residents.

Indeed, in the competitive world of external funding (as opposed to "internal funding," which involves your university paying the tab), more and more universities are now encouraging their faculty to attend grant-writing workshops and learn "how to speak the language of policy makers." The central point communicated to faculty at such seminars is that they should present their ideas in a way that suits the needs of the particular grant agency. This is well stated in the following excerpt from a self-proclaimed "grantsmanship presenter":

> It is human nature to feel that we deserve to be funded, but grant agencies want to know what we can do for them—not what we have done for ourselves. The key is not to focus on our program but to demonstrate how our program can further the funding agency's mission. (Himes, 2003, p. 4)

To what extent does your research actually influence policies? This question is a matter of some contention. Although the idea that social research might influence public policy may have been an inspiration for many young social scientists, it is not clear to what extent, if any, things worked in this way.

Qualitative research has rarely had much appeal to civil servants and administrators geared to focus on numbers and the bottom line. The one possible exception, Erving Goffman's (1961) account of the dehumanizing consequences of "total institutions" in his book *Asylums*, appears merely to have legitimated the cost-cutting frenzy known as community care.

Moreover, it is arguable that number-crunching researchers have fared little better. As Roger Hadley (1987, p. 100) has pointed out, "not being heard" is the common experience of social researchers who attempt to influence public policy.

Among the reasons for this, Hadley suggests, is that

- Research is often commissioned to buy time in the face of public scandal or criticism. This means that "the customer's motives for commissioning a research project may not necessarily be directly related to an interest in the topic concerned" (1987, p. 101).

- The time lag between commissioning a study and receiving a report may mean that the customer's interests have shifted (see the discussion in Chapter 17 of the failure of the funding body to implement David's findings about HIV counseling).

- Academic researchers who produce unpalatable conclusions can be written off as "unrealistic" (1987, p. 102).

Of course, fashions change. At the time of this writing, there is some evidence that public bodies may be starting to take qualitative research more seriously. **Focus groups**, in particular, seem to be "the flavor of the month." Focus groups are popular in part because they are relatively cheap and quick and provide nice "sound bites" for politicians and advertisers. However, such changes in fashion do little to affect the natural tendency of policymakers to redefine the meaning of research findings on their own terms.

Another important question is, To what extent *should* university researchers make their services available to policymakers, especially when they are paid to do so? Applied research that specifically targets policymakers' needs is often commissioned by politicians or private stakeholders who screen proposals for "relevance" before any money is disbursed. Opponents of the "research for sale" paradigm are concerned that this emerging model disproportionately represents the interests of the economic and political elite. In the words of one critic,

In recent years, we have all watched the increasing commercialization of the campus. The numerous advertising posters and the golden arches of fast food outlets may be an affront to our aesthetic sensibilities, but they are, arguably, no worse than ugly. Some of the other new features of commercialized campus life do, however, constitute a serious threat to things we rightly revere. "Privatization" and the "business model" are the potential menace.

What do these notions mean? To me, they involve an increased dependence on industry and philanthropy for operating the university; an increased amount of our resources being directed to applied or so-called practical subjects, both in teaching and in research; a proprietary treatment of research results, with the commercial interest in secrecy overriding the public's interest in free, shared knowledge; and an attempt to run the university more like a business that treats industry and students as clients and ourselves as service providers with something to sell. We pay increasing attention to the immediate needs and demands of our "customers" and, as the old saying goes, "the customer is always right." (Brown, 2000, p. 1701)

In addition to concerns about commercialization of research, policy-oriented researchers must be cautious about the politicization of their findings. A good example of this is the research on global warming: For many years, despite the weight of scientific evidence to the contrary, conservatives marshaled their own "scientific evidence" that global warming was a hoax perpetuated by "liberal tree-huggers." For example, the promotional blurb on the back cover of Christopher Horner's (2007) *The Politically Incorrect Guide to Global Warming and Environmentalism* reads, "Finally, someone has written a definitive resource to debunk global warming alarmism" (quote from Senator James Inhofe, Republican, from Oklahoma and former chairman of the U.S. Senate's Environment and Public Works Committee).

Similarly, the theory of biological evolution is not without its "scientific critics," who enjoy the support of some policymakers. For example, the Discovery Institute's Center for Science and Culture (originally named Center for Renewal of Science and Culture) offers generous grants to researchers who are willing to challenge the presumed dogma of evolutionary theory. In the words of one of its founders, the center advocates

> "theistic realism"—or sometimes, "mere creation"—as the defining concept of our movement. That means that we affirm God is objectively real as creator, and the reality of God is tangibly recorded in evidence accessible to science, particularly in biology. We avoid the tangled arguments about how or whether to reconcile the Biblical account with the present state of scientific knowledge, because we think these issues can be much more constructively engaged when we have a scientific picture that is not distorted by naturalistic prejudice. (Phillip E. Johnson, cited in Forrest, 2001, pp. 42–43).

This kind of partisan debate and the use or misuse of scientific research enters the realm of social sciences as well. For example, there is continuing debate about the deterrent effects of the death penalty, mandatory arrests of domestic abuse suspects, or castration of sex offenders (see, for example, Thomas Hickey's *Taking Sides: Clashing Views on Crime and Criminology*). In short, it is naïve to think that social science research is exempt from the world of politics and can be applied by policymakers just as the author wishes it to be. Though we do our best to write accessible research, we need to be aware that our findings sometimes take on a life of their own and become tossed around like political footballs, as it were. The more explicitly you intend for your research to be used by policy-making audiences, the greater the risk that it becomes a pawn in a game of political partisanship.

THE PRACTITIONER AUDIENCE

Whereas policymakers pave the way for new ideas from social science research to be adopted by service providers, it is ultimately up to practitioners to enact those policies or new courses of action. As Michael Bloor notes, policymakers are not the only group that could help put your research into practice. In Bloor's words,

> the real opportunities for sociological influence lie closer to the coalface than they do to head office . . . [they] lie in relations with practitioners, not with the managers of practice. (Bloor, 2004)

Taking the example of the sociology of health and illness, Bloor argues that practitioners rather than policymakers are the most reliable and eager audience for social research:

> Sociologists who have conducted research on sociological aspects of health and medicine . . . have long been aware that there is a role for sociologists as participants in debates on public policy, but that there are also other audiences for social research, notably audiences of patients and practitioners (clinicians, nurses, and other professionals). (1997, p. 223)

Bloor notes that qualitative social researchers have a two-fold advantage in influencing practitioners. First, they can build upon their research relationships with practitioners in order to discuss practical implications. As he puts it,

> In respect of practitioners who are research subjects, qualitative researchers can call upon their pre-existing research relationships with their research subjects as a resource for ensuring an attentive and even sympathetic response to their research findings. A close personal and working relationship, based on lengthy social contact and built up over weeks and months, is likely to ensure that, not only will practitioner research subjects have a particular interest in the findings (because of the identity of the researcher as much as a particular interest in the research topic), but also practitioner research subjects may be willing to devote an unusual amount of time and effort to discussions of the findings. (1997, p. 236)

Second, even if you have no research relationship with them, the detail and transparency of some qualitative data has an appeal to many practitioners:

> The qualitative researcher has the advantage that the research methods allow rich descriptions of everyday practice, which allow practitioner audiences imaginatively to juxtapose their own everyday practices with the research description. There is therefore an opportunity for practitioners to make evaluative judgments about their own practices and experiment with the adoption of new approaches described in the research findings. (1997, p. 236)

Bloor's argument resonates with David's recent experience with AIDS counselors. Like most practitioners, counselors will be suspicious that outside researchers intend to be judgmental. It helps to reassure them that you do not believe in any normative, decontextualized theory of *good* communication. (For further discussion of how to approach such practitioner audiences, please refer back to Chapter 17 and see Silverman, 2001, pp. 294–297.)

The extent to which practitioners are considered legitimate social science audiences differs across disciplines. For example, in the field of social work, considerable attention is given to how research is actually used by so-called front-line workers. By comparison, it is difficult to imagine how the study of history, for example, would involve specific practitioners (unless we are speaking of how the subject is to be taught).

THE LAY AUDIENCE

There are at least four reasons why qualitative researchers may become involved in reporting back to lay audiences:

1. To answer questions asked by your respondents

2. To "check" provisional findings

3. To provide feedback to organizations and relevant groups

4. To provide information for the media

Points 1 and 2 have been considered in Chapter 17. In particular, you should refer to the section titled "Settings and Access," which discusses open and covert access for Point 1, and the section on feedback as a validation exercise for Point 2.

Feedback to lay audiences is usually set up because of your own desire to "give something back" to the general public. The format should vary according to whether your audiences are members of an established organization or simply just a group of people with similar interests or concerns.

As an example, following his research on hospital clinics for children, David gave a talk to the Parents' Association at one of the hospitals he had studied. In this talk, following Table 28.1, he discussed new facts from his research about doctor–parent communication. He also examined the implications of his findings for reform of current hospital practices. Subsequently, David was invited to write a short piece on his research for the newsletter of a British organization called the Patients' Association. In this article, he covered much the same ground as well as adding guidelines for how to manage better or get better service from hospitals that treat sick children. Finally, David spoke at a meeting of parents of children with diabetes. His aim here was to stress what his research had revealed about the painful dilemmas experienced by such parents. In this way, he sought to assure them that others share their own experience and that there is no need for them to reproach themselves.

Similarly, Amir has been writing for local and national papers to inform the general public about his research on Middle Eastern Americans. For example, in an article written for a local Pennsylvania newspaper (*The Altoona Mirror*), he tried to show the adverse effects of ethnic profiling. Here is an excerpt from that piece:

> I began thinking the other day about all the things I don't do anymore because they might appear suspicious in the eyes of my fellow citizens. I compiled a long list of places and people I don't visit anymore. For example, in our family trip to Chicago last August, I had to tell my eleven-year-old daughter that we couldn't go to the Sears Tower because it was too far from our hotel. In reality, I didn't want to go because I feared being humiliated in front of her by peering eyes. My solitary camping trips in the Smokies are also out of the question. Who knows what people might think if they saw a young Middle Eastern man hiking by himself? I don't go to lunch with my Middle Eastern friends anymore either, because someone might think they heard us say something threatening or flippant and our lives will forever change. If we laugh, we might appear disrespectful. If we are too solemn, we could seem stealthy. Of course, the thought of speaking my native tongue, Farsi (not Arabic), in public would not even cross my mind. I am certain the foreign words, regardless of what they mean, will arouse suspicion. However, I didn't finish my list of self-imposed restrictions. It was too self-important. Compared to the thousands of lives that were lost last year, griping about my daily humiliation seemed petty. I don't blame my fellow citizens either. They are told that to be suspicious of people like me is to do their patriotic duty. So perhaps I should do my duty as an American and just shut up about profiling and discrimination. Others have made sacrifices for their country before, this is my turn. Maybe I should welcome the hateful glares, because somehow, in a strange way that I fail to understand, they make my neighbors feel safer. But I think logic (if not morality) dictates otherwise. (Marvasti, 2002)

Here Amir's goal was to make the sociologically distant topic of ethnic profiling more personal and to provide the readers with an insider's perspective.

In Amir's experience, local papers can be surprisingly receptive to social science arguments plainly stated for the masses, especially if they are timely.

It is most unlikely, however, that the complexities and nuances of your research will reach a general audience through the mass media. Nearly all social science goes unreported by such media. Needless to say, this is even more true of student research.

There are times, as in Amir's case, that your research provides you with a story that you want to tell to the general public. How should you go about this? Perhaps a journalist approaches you after a talk you have given. More likely, a media contact will begin after you have studied the kind of topics covered by broadcast programs and by particular journalists and approached the "right" person.

For example, when David's book on communication in hospital clinics was published (Silverman, 1987), he rang the medical correspondent of a national newspaper. He was very interested in some of his findings and, by the next day, David had a reporter at his house.

At this point, David panicked! He started to worry that the reporter might sensationalize his research and, thereby, upset the medical staff who had supported it. To try to avoid this, he got the reporter to agree to let him tape-record her interview and see a draft of the story before it was published. David's cautiousness had an unforeseen and unfortunate consequence. The story that followed ended up being so bland that it was never printed.

This experience highlights the dilemma that researchers have in seeking to get their work more widely known. The cautious way in which researchers are taught to write about their findings runs up against the media's need to pull in the audience with sensational stories. So it is always a question of balance between the media's sense of what is newsworthy and your own desire for an accurate, unsensationalized account of your research.

WRITING AS AUTHOR-AUDIENCE INTERACTION

One way of thinking about different audiences and how they can best be reached is to conceptualize the work of writing and its reception as an ongoing relationship between you and your audience. As such, you can ask what type of relationship do you hope to build with your audience and using what methods? In fact, your interactions with your audience can themselves become topics of research and analysis. Ken Hyland (2002), for example, offers an interesting analysis of the use of *directives* (i.e., words or phrases that instruct the reader to do something) in academic writing. Hyland begins his article by noting that the view that academic writing is an interactive accomplishment is now well established. A writer's development of an appropriate relationship with his or her audience is widely seen as central to effective academic persuasion as writers seek to balance claims for the significance, originality, and correctness of their work against the convictions and expectations of their readers. Utterances must both carry appropriate authority and engage readers in ways that they are likely to find both credible and persuasive. (p. 215)

Hyland then goes on to divide writing directives into three broad categories, as seen in Table 28.2.

Hyland counts the frequency of these directives across three genres of academic writing (textbooks, research articles, and student research reports) as well as across different natural and social science disciplines. As you would expect, directives were most common in textbooks and least common in student papers. According to Hyland, this is because textbooks (like this one) are intended to educate an audience of novices about a particular discipline, and as such they assume greater authority and do not shy away from addressing their readers directly. In Hyland's words,

> [Student] reports are written primarily to gain credit from a supervisor for a research project and so the use of directives may be considered risky here, perhaps claiming an authority which . . . students . . . may not feel and certainly did not wish to display. In textbooks, however, the writer is principally seeking to lead readers to a mastery of new skills and knowledge. Here directives invoke a solid and competent writer in full command

Table 28.2   Categories of Directives

1. Textual Acts
   a. Internal reference (e.g., "see section 1" or "refer to example 2")
   b. External reference (e.g., "see Smith, 1990")

2. Physical Acts
   a. Research focus (e.xg., "the temperature must be set at. . . .")
   b. Real-world focus (e.g., "you should ask your teacher")

3. Cognitive Acts
   a. Rhetorical purpose (e.g., "consider," "suppose," "let's examine")
   b. Elaborative purpose (e.g., "this should be seen as")
   c. Emphatic purpose (e.g., "it should be noted" or "remember")

SOURCE: Adapted from Hyland (2002), p. 218.

of the material. At the same time they help to construct readers as learners and learning as a one-way transfer of knowledge from primary-knower to neophyte. Finally, in research articles directives help writers demonstrate their professional competence, their control of an argument and their understanding of the issues in persuading their peers to accept their claims. (p. 223)

Hyland's analysis also shows that when considering the variation in the use of directives across disciplines, directives are by far more common in the sciences (e.g., engineering) than they are in the social sciences (e.g., sociology). As Hyland notes, this analysis is not a simple enumeration of words, but it evinces different types of writer–reader relationships as constructed through the authority of directives. In fact, you may have noticed frequent uses of words like *should* throughout this textbook. As authors of this text, we have assumed a degree of expertise and thus a particular type of relationship with our audience. The accuracy of this assumption notwithstanding, it is worth noting how it has shaped our writing style throughout this text. Would we have adopted the same tone if we were writing for a mainstream academic journal like the *American Sociological Review*? Most likely not. The textbook format violates the writing conventions of such journals and is very likely to offend its reviewers and readers. The manuscript submission may be summarily dismissed as "condescending" and "sophomoric." Many of us were taught the following axiom in our English composition classes: "Keep it simple, stupid!" Perhaps the axiom should instead read, "Keep it about the audience, stupid!"

CONCLUDING REMARKS

It is appropriate that toward the end of this book we are reflecting on audiences. Too often, qualitative research is written up in an intellectual and social vacuum in which one writes for just oneself or, at best, for one supervisor. Sometimes, this partial approach can succeed in getting you the degree you require. More frequently, in the absence of actual or imagined audiences, it will lead to writer's block and consequent failure to complete.

In the final analysis, if you want to succeed in your research and beyond, you will have to be responsive to the various audiences who might be prepared to listen to what you have to say. If all else fails, try the so-called lowest common denominator approach. As much as possible, avoid jargon. In fact, the holy grail of publishing is to write a book that crosses audience boundaries and appeals to the general public, academics, practitioners, and policymakers alike. If you write in a readable, coherent, and simple way, then your work will most likely appeal to all audiences.

CASE STUDY: KIRSTIN'S NARRATIVE

The following narrative underlines the difficulty of writing across different disciplines (in her case, the world of humanities versus social sciences). As an assistant professor of education, Kirstin Bratt describes how speaking in plain English does not guarantee effective communication in academic circles.

My mother raised me, and certainly I am my mother's daughter. My mother had taught all of the children of the surrounding farms, including her own six children, in a one-room country school. My mother taught high school English, directed the plays, and advised the newspaper. From an early age, I remember her English classrooms. She balanced a love of Shakespeare against the insolence of eighth graders. At family gatherings, we played a card game called "Authors," and my mother's siblings could all recite Edgar Allan Poe's "The Raven." We sang around the piano, and we knew we were a bit different than other families, but we didn't mind.

Children raised in the circus learn to balance a tightrope. The children of English teachers never do. I remember, from early on, a clear distinction between the humanities and the social sciences. Not that one was more or less interesting than the other, but that they were different. The social sciences seemed to make things clear, while literature and the arts shrouded me in mystery.

When I became a researcher, I realized that indeed a wide gulf separates the social scientist from the humanities scholar. These seemingly irreconcilable differences are reflected in writing style manuals like the MLA versus the APA. Sometimes I feel as though trying to climb either bank will just leave me drowning somewhere in the middle.

Think of a word like "research": seems innocuous enough, doesn't it? But a social scientist once spoke scornfully of a colleague who wasn't going to be tenured by saying, "She thinks 'research' means going to the library." It took me a while to figure out exactly what she meant by that. I now realize that my own tenure depends on establishing an active agenda in human science research, outside the library. Or how about "IRB"? My colleagues in English don't know what these three letters stand for. They can write anything they like, short of perjury, without asking permission from an institutional review board, but social scientists face various forms of oversight (or censorship, depending on how you look at it) in trying to begin a research project. There are many other words that cause confusion between social scientists and humanities scholars. Analysis, evidence, interpretation, critique, literature, theory, curriculum, review, statistics. . . . If you think you know what these words mean, ask someone outside of your discipline. You'll likely hear the opposite of what you expect.

No wonder our students feel that they're moving as foreigners in strange lands as they move across the campus from one general education class to the next.

Imagine my identity crisis when after ten years of teaching English in community college, I returned to graduate school in a new field: educational research. My first professor was intimidating. He believed I was a terrible writer, but he couldn't quite convince me. I knew how to construct a metaphor and exploit it. My sentences were interesting, complex, and well-punctuated. I could create a mood and a cast of characters. Well, sure, I think—I could improve my writing: tighten the loose screws here and there, become more evocative and sensual. Of course, that's not what my professor had in mind. He wanted something specific from me. He wanted transparency. He wanted the facts. He wanted brief, specific writing.

(Continued)

(Continued)

I couldn't imagine how to please him. And we all know the rule of survival in academia: Find out what the professor wants and provide it. Years later, and I'm still trying to find a balance between social scientist and humanities scholar. I don't expect to find it, but for now, I find the path worth the effort.

KEY POINTS

Communication should always be designed for a particular audience:

- Academic colleagues will expect theoretical, factual, or methodological insights.

- Policymakers will want practical information relevant to current policy issues.

- Practitioners will expect a theoretical framework for understanding clients better, factual information, practical suggestions for better procedures, and reform of existing practices.

- The general public wants new facts, ideas for reform of current practices or policies, guidelines for how to manage better or get better service from practitioners or institutions, and assurances that others share their own experience of particular problems in life.

- If you want to communicate effectively, you must focus on your audience's concerns and recipient-design your output accordingly.

FURTHER READING

Anselm Strauss and Juliet Corbin's *Basics of Qualitative Research* (1990), Chapter 13, covers both written and oral presentations of your research for different audiences. Gary Marx's article "Of Methods and Manners for Aspiring Sociologists: 37 Moral Imperatives" (*The American Sociologist*, Spring 1997) is a lively and extremely helpful guide for the apprentice researcher desiring to make links with a range of audiences. Roger Hadley's chapter "Publish and Be Ignored: Proselytise and be Damned" in G. C. Wenger's (Ed.) *The Research*

Relationship: Practice and Politics in Social Policy Research (1987) is a lively account of the pitfalls of trying to reach a policy audience. Practitioner audiences are very well discussed in Michael Bloor's chapter "Addressing Social Problems Through Qualitative Research" in D. Silverman's (Ed.) *Qualitative Research: Theory, Method and Practice* (2004).

For more information about applied qualitative research, see Ray C. Rist's "Understanding Social Programs Through Evaluation," Jennifer Greene's "Influencing the Policy Process With Qualitative Research," and Julian Cheek's "An Untold Story: Doing Funded Qualitative Research," all in the second edition of Lincoln and Denzin's *Handbook of Qualitative Research* (2000).

EXERCISE 28.1

Refer back to Gary Marx's comments, cited in this chapter, about leveraging your work. Now take any chapter of your dissertation and outline how you might write it up for as many as possible of the following audiences:

1. A specialist academic journal

2. A nonspecialist social science audience

3. Policymakers

4. Practitioners

5. The general public

Now try out these different versions with their intended audiences.

EXERCISE 28.2

Use an excerpt from one of your interviews or field observations to write a one-page editorial for a local newspaper. Write your essay with the following questions in mind:

1. What is worth knowing here?

2. What is the best rhetorical strategy for communicating the finding to the general public?

3. If there is room for misinterpretation, how could you best prevent it?

CHAPTER 29

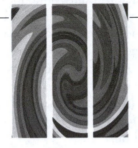

Finding a Job

CHAPTER OBJECTIVES

By the end of this chapter, you will be able to

- Work out ways of getting on a short list

- Devise strategies that improve how you present yourself at job interviews

- Respond appropriately to job offers and rejections

INTRODUCTION

Whereas some have the luxury of learning purely for the sake of learning, most of us find it necessary to turn our academic accomplishments into gainful employment. For the majority of PhDs in the social sciences, this means securing a position at a college or university. The goal of this chapter is to outline the academic job search process from the perspectives of employers and employees. The chapter offers practical advice for effective job search strategies and for avoiding common pitfalls.

SELECTING THE APPROPRIATE JOB AND MARKET

Your job search starts by deciding what type of position you hope to acquire. Basically, you have two choices: academic and nonacademic positions. Academic positions involve a combination of teaching, research, and service, with varying degrees of emphasis placed on each of these three components depending on your place of employment. Nonacademic jobs include working for (a) local, state, or federal government; (b) the private sector; and (c) nonprofit research institutes. Some social science PhDs are employed in the nonacademic job market, but for the majority, the main source of employment is the institutions of higher education. According to data from the American Sociological Association, in 2003, of all social science PhDs in the United States, 65.3 percent were employed in educational institutions (American Sociological Association, 2006a). The remainder of this chapter focuses on strategies for obtaining employment in institutions of higher education.

ECONOMIC REALITIES

You should manage the cost of your graduate training in relation to its expected economic payoff. It has been said that "education can be an expensive hobby." Completing a PhD requires years of work and thousands of dollars in tuition and books. In addition to the known costs, there are many hidden expenses. For example, during your graduate training, your earnings are often too low to allow for significant savings or payroll deductions for pension.

Many graduate students do not receive grants or assistantships and have to obtain government-subsidized loans to cover the cost of their education. The interest rates on these loans vary depending on the private bank that issues the loan. The interest on subsidized loans is paid by the U.S. government during the time you are in school. However, within months of graduation, you are expected to begin making payments on your loans. Students cannot declare bankruptcy and forfeit their loans. On the contrary, in their attempts to collect the debt, U.S. government agents have the authority to garnish your wages, withhold tax returns, and even auction some of your assets.

This grim reality is exacerbated by the fact that some graduate programs recruit students with little or no regard for the students' potential for completing their degrees. Many departments do not provide financial support for all their graduate students. Your chances of being funded depend on your grades, letters of recommendation, and score on a standardized test (e.g., Graduate Record Exam or GRE). Based on these criteria, some students are offered internal funding in the form of assistantships that cover their tuition costs and provide reasonable hourly wages for teaching or research assignments. Additional funding is available through fellowships and grants that require no work or repayment. Depending on the school, all or none of the students may be funded.

Students who are not funded are, nonetheless, allowed to stay in the program and pay full tuition semester after semester. For the departments, high enrollment numbers mean more classes and more new hires. Although you may be reminded that it is time to graduate and "move on," in reality graduate school is a sort of open-ended proposition. Many never complete their degrees, despite being burdened with tens of thousands of dollars in student loans. For example, a study based on data from a large research university (among the top 25 in the U.S.) showed that of a cohort of 24 PhD students in sociology, only 7 completed their degrees, a completion rate of about 30 percent (Valero, 2001). According to this study, completion rates vary depending on one's academic discipline. For example, doctoral candidates in accounting had a completion rate of about 80 percent (from a 15-member cohort, 12 completed their degrees, with a median age of completion of 4.6 years).

As indicated in this study, registering and paying for classes in no way guarantees that one will write a dissertation, successfully defend it, and eventually graduate. An obviously important but difficult-to-find piece of information about a graduate program is this: What is the rate of completion for the doctoral students? Although a low rate does not necessarily mean that the program is a risky investment, it is sufficient cause for asking other questions. For example, is the program lacking in terms of financial and mentoring support for doctoral candidates? Or, are too many students admitted regardless of their potential to graduate? Although such information may be difficult to obtain, from a practical economic standpoint, it makes all the sense in the world to research the school before you spend thousands of dollars and many years of your life there. No one would expect you to do otherwise if you were buying a car or a home; why not do the same with the equally expensive investment of a graduate education?

Admittedly, reducing the search for knowledge to utilitarian cost-benefit analyses may sound crass. Idealistic notions of "serving others," "thirst for knowledge," and sometimes plain chance figure strongly in why we pursue higher education. Nonetheless, as social scientists, we should know better than to exempt ourselves from the economic realities that influence our lives. A competitive labor market is a concrete reality that mediates our career choices and opportunities. Sadly, PhD students are not encouraged to seriously consider their job prospects until they are within a year of completing their dissertation and entering the job market. The prevalent attitude is that one should focus on finishing the dissertation and worry about the job search later. Yet, earlier decisions about which school, which field, which methodology, and which mentor have enormous influence on what happens later in one's professional career.

RELATIVE VALUE AND STATUS OF HIGHER EDUCATION

What economists call "returns to education," or the payoff of education, is not as great as it used to be. The so-called credential inflation means that the same higher degree today produces less financial return than it did in the past. The good news is that the "relative advantage" has increased consistently. Compared to those with no degree or a lower degree, those with higher education continue to earn more (Van de Werfhortz & Andersen, 2005).

You should also be aware of the various hierarchies within higher education. There are at least two important stratification systems at work here. The first is school selectivity or the relative prestige assigned to different schools primarily based on their admission requirements (some are harder to get into than others), and the second is the relative prestige assigned to different disciplines (Davies & Guppy, 1997). Pursuing a degree in sociology, for example, at a less prestigious institution means a lower rate of economic returns than obtaining the same degree from an elite school. Holding the academic institution constant, across different disciplines, the earnings for PhDs in the "hard sciences" tend to be greater than those in the social sciences and humanities. This is irrespective of the fact that the actual cost of a PhD does not vary significantly across disciplines.

Added to these observations is the bleak reality of unemployment, which also varies depending on the school you graduate from (your alma mater) and your chosen field. For example, in 2003, among the social and behavioral science PhDs, sociologists had the highest unemployment rate at 2.9 compared to the lowest at 1.7 for psychology, 1.4 for political science, and 0.9 for economics. The unemployment percentages are based on total numbers in the labor force, which includes "those employed plus those unemployed and seeking work" (American Sociological Association, 2006b).

As if all this was not disheartening enough, qualitative researchers are subjected to a final stratification system that seems to favor quantitative or statistical skills over qualitative research expertise. The relative higher status of quantitative research is reflected in hiring practices and editorial decisions about what is accepted for publication, especially in flagship journals (e.g., *American Sociological Review*). The same is true for the promotion and tenure phase of your career, where, depending on the institution, qualitative articles are ranked lower by tenure committees. To advance from the rank of tenure-track assistant professor to tenured associate professor, new faculty are required to publish a certain number of refereed articles within a fixed amount of time (usually about five articles within 5 years). In this context, sometimes little or no weight is assigned to articles published in qualitative journals, even if they appear in prominent venues like the *Journal of Contemporary Ethnography*. We suspect this is in part due to the misconception that compared to statistical analysis, qualitative research requires little effort and special training (i.e., "it is so easy and descriptive that anyone can do it."). Another consideration may be that qualitative journals, as a whole, are thought to have higher acceptance rates than their more quantitatively oriented counterparts (i.e., it is easier to have a manuscript accepted for publication in a qualitative journal).

Therefore, it is reasonable to suggest that pursuing a qualitative dissertation is a risky choice because it could place you on the lower ranks of your discipline. You should be doubly concerned about your job prospects if you enter the market from a so-called second-tier institution and have no publications. Fortunately, these patterns and misconceptions about qualitative research are changing. However, the exact pace of this change and its final outcome is unknown. For example, in the 2005 December job bulletin for the American Sociological Association, 13 job ads mentioned quantitative research compared to 4 that were explicitly open to hiring a qualitative researcher (three ads mentioned both qualitative and quantitative methods). Of course, there were many job ads that did not mention either methodological orientation. This cursory analysis seems to support the observation that quantitative skills are more likely to be mentioned in job ads than qualitative ones, with the ratio roughly 3 to 1 in favor of quantitative research.

Qualitatively oriented job applicants will serve themselves well by taking a few statistics courses and at least familiarizing themselves with quantitative research and its terminology. Better yet, having one or two quantitative publications will make it clear to any would-be critic that your interest in qualitative methods is not motivated by your inability to comprehend math or statistics.

To summarize,

1. Choose your graduate school carefully (e.g., consider the school's tuition costs relative to its prestige or status in your discipline).

2. Choose a program where you are offered a teaching or research assistantship.

3. Complete your degree in a reasonable time to minimize your costs and maximize your economic returns.

4. Do not shy away from quantitative research and courses; in addition to being analytically useful for some research questions, having quantitative skills will make you a well-rounded candidate.

WHICH SCHOOL?

Your choices of academic employment can be overwhelming. For example, in the field of sociology alone, in 2000–2001 there were 816 institutions that offered baccalaureate degrees (American Sociological Association, 2006a). The following section offers a number of criteria for helping you narrow down your employment choices.

Research Versus Teaching

Institutions of higher learning differ in their emphasis on teaching or research. Typically, schools are referred to as either research or teaching institutions, depending on the amount of their annual expenditure on research and development and their instructors' course load (instructors at research institutions teach fewer courses per academic year but are expected to conduct more research and publish; these expectations are reversed at teaching institutions). Universities and colleges are also ranked by the level of research activities and admission standards. Such rankings are done by organizations like the Carnegie Mellon Foundation for the Advancement of Teaching and the *U.S. News and World Report* (please see the end-of-chapter exercises).

There is no clear division between teaching and research (you are expected to do both effectively). Hiring, promotion, and tenure policies do vary across different institutions depending on which of the two is considered more important. For example, to become tenured at a research institution, you might be expected to publish at least one article per year in highly selective, peer-reviewed, research journals for 5 consecutive years. Journal selectivity is determined based on the journal's prestige and its acceptance rate. For example, publishing in a journal where 25 percent of submissions are accepted counts less toward one's tenure than publishing in a journal with an acceptance rate of 3 percent or less. For the same reason, at research-oriented institutions, book chapters and books tend to weigh less in the promotion and tenure decisions. Failure to publish in select journals will result in the termination of one's employment (thus the saying "publish or perish"). Requirements for promotion and tenure are less stringent at teaching-oriented schools, both in terms of the required number of publications and what is considered an acceptable publication outlet.

Job search committees are unlikely to consider candidates whom they perceive incapable of achieving tenure at their institution. Given the cost of interviewing job candidates and training new hires, the faculty serving on job search committees are risk aversive (i.e., they do not want to be responsible for wasting their school's resources on someone with less-than-certain prospects for tenure). In fact, risk aversion is the guiding principle in many hiring decisions. It makes immanent sense for job candidates to consider to what extent their research and teaching qualifications are a good fit for the institution they hope to work for. In fact, your rationale for this fit becomes the core of your letter of application.

Area of Specialization

Academic departments also vary in terms of their substantive interests. Again the research/teaching distinction has some relevance here. Typically, research schools hire specialists in a narrowly defined segment of the discipline. For example, their job ad might read, "We are especially interested in candidates whose research focus is the sociology of family." By comparison, smaller teaching universities are more likely to look for generalists who can teach introductory or survey courses. How do you know what they are looking for? Read the job ad. In fact, job search committee chairs could get quite irate if an applicant's qualifications do not match the job ad. They might send your application back with a sticky note that says, "Maybe I'm missing something, but how do your qualifications match this job?!"

Future Colleagues

Your job is not just a source of income but an opportunity for growing as a professional in your field. An important part of this process is colleagues who can help you advance your academic training and research interests. Ideally, you should choose a place where you will have the opportunity to collaborate with colleagues and have access to senior faculty who can provide you with mentorship. By the same logic, you should avoid institutions with an apparently hostile working environment where the faculty seem to undermine each other—you do not want to be recruited as a foot solider in an ongoing departmental feud.

Teaching Load

Consider the teaching load, or the number of courses you are expected to cover per semester or per academic quarter. Large teaching loads leave little room for research. Similarly, consider the types of courses you are expected to teach. Do they involve new preparations? If so, do you have the time or the inclination to learn about a new topic in your field? Also, learn about the number of new preparations. For example, a teaching load of three courses per semester may not sound all that time-consuming, but if the courses are in three separate areas and require three new preparations, the work quickly becomes overwhelming.

These considerations essentially come down to how much of your time you are willing to allocate to teaching compared to research. These do not have to be competing interests. Amir, for example, often tries to overlap his teaching with research. For example, when teaching research methods classes, he assigns journal articles that he himself is interested in learning more about. This way, the time Amir spends on preparing for courses also serves as preparation for his research manuscripts. The reality is that even at teaching schools, doing research elevates your status as a faculty member. If nothing else, publishing increases your marketability and thus gives you more leverage in salary negotiations. To have a healthy academic career, it is essential that you find a balance between teaching and research that best suits your particular needs. Do not depend on your future employer to resolve this dilemma for you, but be deliberate and proactive about your career trajectory.

Research Resources

Find out if the schools to which you are applying are committed to offering teaching and research resources. How large are the class sizes; is computer technology widely available on campus; will you have your own computer and the software you need? Regarding research in particular, some schools offer internal start-up grants, grant-writing workshops, and travel funding to assist their faculty with their ongoing projects. On the other hand, some schools neglect research in general and social science research in particular. For example, Amir's first job was at an institution that was just beginning to develop an institutional review board (IRB) office. The problem is that this kind of unexplored research territory sometimes means confusion, lack of support, and indifference about your research. This is especially true for qualitative researchers, who sometimes find themselves in the position of convincing their colleagues and administrators that their work is "real research." In short, consider schools that are supportive of your work.

Where to Look for Answers

There are several sources for finding more information about these topics. The first and most important place to look is the Internet. Almost all universities have

Web sites where they provide detailed descriptions of their academic programs and resources for faculty and students. Where available, look at the specific department's Web site. Many professors have personalized homepages where they post their pictures and vitas. A good deal can be learned about one's potential colleagues, their research interests, and the department's overall standards of tenure and promotion from these homepages. For example, if after browsing tenured professors' homepages, you notice that all their publications are in top-tiered journals, you can be reasonably certain that you would be expected to do likewise in order to get tenured. Another useful source is the job ad itself. Finally, you can always consult the "grapevine." You would be surprised how much you can learn about different departments by attending professional conferences and just chatting with current and former students and faculty—for better or worse, people like to gossip about their jobs and their colleagues.

Cast a Wide Net

The old cliché about not putting all your eggs in one basket certainly applies to academic job searches. Most successful applicants apply for tens of jobs (sometimes upwards of fifty). They then might receive some calls, and make the short list in a handful of places. Finally, the job search might come down to several interviews, and eventually one or two job offers. You can change the odds in your favor by applying to as many jobs as you are qualified for. Be selective but not self-limiting.

Here is how Eileen O'Brien describes this process:

I sent out about 50 applications, got 6 interviews, and one offer (one of the 6 schools, I never found out whether I had gotten the job or not, because I accepted another offer first, but the rest I knew I did not get). In one case they stopped the search and hired no one—big red flag for major politics in that department, which is how I tried to console myself because it was an interdisciplinary college with no letter grades, really cool. In another case, they had an internal candidate they were interviewing, which I did not find out until I was nearly done with the 2-day interview.

Similarly, Karyn McKinney states,

I used the ASA job listings online, and went through them every month to check for new listings in my area of race and ethnicity. I developed a standard letter to send with application materials, as well as standard research and teaching packets, and simply edited the letter for the specifics of the school and sent out a packet every time a new school came up that was looking for someone in my area. I took the advice of most in my department, who said to "cast a wide net," and I basically applied to every school that wanted someone in my area. It was also important for me to be organized about my recommendation letters, giving each reference a list all at one time of all the schools that I needed him/her to write letters for. The lists I gave them included the contact information for the school as well as some details about the position, so that the recommenders could make each letter "fit" the job more easily.

The important lesson here is to think of your job search as a process that essentially becomes a job in its own right ("the job search is itself a job"). You will have to write a different letter of interest for each job, arrange letters of recommendations for each position, and so on. The outcome of the job search is not entirely predictable and within your control. However, there are many things you can do to increase your chances. To begin with, it might be helpful to consider the job search process from the perspective of employers. The next section provides an insider's view of how search committees go about selecting the appropriate candidate for an advertised position.

THE JOB SEARCH FROM THE EMPLOYER'S PERSPECTIVE

The first step in finding the right candidate for an academic job is to form a search committee, which is typically composed of three to five faculty members. The first charge of this committee is to write a job ad for the position. Much consideration goes into the writing of a job ad because it ultimately can determine which applicants are considered for the position and which ones are excluded. Typically, a broadly stated job ad could mean (a) the committee is looking for anyone (i.e., a "generalist") who is qualified to teach a wide range of introductory courses, or (b) it could mean that the academic program is so prestigious and large that they can consider anyone who excels in the field. At the minimum, the job ad contains the name of the department, the mailing address for the department, and the deadline for applications. The job ad is then posted in places like the *Journal of Higher Education* or online employment bulletins for the discipline.

The committee members then begin reviewing the applications, either as they arrive or after the deadline. Applicants are ranked into two basic categories: those excluded from the pool and those worthy of further consideration. It is common for a search committee to receive over a hundred applications for a position. Given that the committee members are faculty with full-time teaching and research responsibilities, there is a tendency to narrow down a large list by simply skimming applications for red flags. Typos, lack of publications, lack of teaching experience, and a degree from a lesser known academic institution are typical justifications for removing names from the list of qualified candidates.

On the other hand, a PhD candidacy from an Ivy League School (e.g., Columbia, Yale, or Harvard) almost guarantees further consideration. The job candidate's institutional affiliation is of huge importance in the hiring process, especially at smaller teaching schools. This is because search committees tend to assume that (a) only exceptional students are admitted into elite schools, and (b) elite-school graduates are superbly trained in their fields. There is also a political or public relations reality at work here. Elite-school graduates allow their employers to bask in their reflected glory, as it were. Universities and colleges often use the accomplishments of their faculty for recruiting students. Statements like the following are standard components of college promotional ads: "Our faculty have received their degrees from some of the finest institutions in the country (e.g., Yale or Columbia)."

For job candidates from so-called tier-two institutions, the practical implication of this observation is that they have to compensate for the lower status of their schools by having stellar publication records; otherwise, they are almost immediately excluded from further consideration.

Of course, many other considerations affect the outcome of a job search. For example, the all-important but vague notion of "collegiality" invariably is brought up during job searches. Committee members try to construct a personality profile using the candidate's letter of application, letters of references, and publications. In a sense, committee members become amateur detectives who glean tone and hidden meanings from the letters: for things that are not said but presumably implied by one's references. For example, a letter of reference that states, "As a graduate student, Jane Doe almost never neglected her duties" may be read with an emphasis on the word *almost*, which implies there were occasions when the candidate was in fact irresponsible.

Concerns about the equity and rationale of the search process notwithstanding, eventually the search committee prepares a list of the top ten (or fewer) candidates for the short list. This list is further narrowed to a group of three to four candidates who are invited to visit the campus. After the job interviews (detailed in the next section), the search committee meets to vote on who should receive an offer. The committee then sends its recommendation to the dean's office. Generally, it is unlikely that the dean will reject the committee's decision, but it is theoretically possible. Finally, the candidate receives a call informing him or her about the offer. If the first choice rejects the offer, the committee may decide to make an offer to the second or third person on the list, or start a new search.

Candidates who are invited for an onsite job interview should know that search committee members are typically restricted from asking certain questions. For example, no one should ask you about your nationality, marital status, family life, or sexual preferences. However, if you volunteer the information, then the committee members are permitted to ask follow-up questions.

THE JOB SEARCH FROM THE CANDIDATE'S PERSPECTIVE

Let us now consider the job search process from the perspective of a typical applicant. In this section, we emphasize the dos and don'ts of a job search and end with a checklist that can help you get organized by breaking down the daunting challenge of finding a job into smaller, more manageable tasks.

Learning About Vacancies

There are two main information channels about jobs: formal and informal. The formal channels consist of job advertisements in the general press and in more specialized, professional publications, as well as the job markets that may be set up at career fairs and meetings of professional associations. For instance, the annual meetings of the American Sociological Association provide a venue for university employers to meet with potential recruits.

The informal channels work through the guidance and information you can get from people on "the inside." Here the most likely contacts will be your supervisor(s) and, perhaps, the academics who examined your thesis.

Whatever channels you use, it is worth making an inventory of the skills you possess and then relating them to the skills demanded by likely employers. This should be done well before you complete your degree so that you can seek to give yourself the best chances on the job market.

Your research should have given you the useful qualities of being able to express yourself clearly, to work independently, and to meet deadlines. It will also have probably provided you with substantive knowledge of a particular area relevant to university and non-university employers.

Other kinds of marketable skills that you can pick up during your university courses are

- Information technology skills

- Knowledge of basic statistical packages

- Teaching experience

- Administrative skills (for instance, gained by serving as a student representative)

So plan for the future: find out where the job openings are and gain the skills that will be most likely to fit you for them.

Getting on a Short List

Of course, before you get a job interview, you have to be short-listed (make the top list of the candidates being considered for the job). David's experience as candidate and selector suggests that there are several things that may tilt the balance in the applicant's favor. For instance,

- Write a curriculum vitae that embodies the capacity for logical, organized thought that your employer will be looking for. Spelling mistakes and hasty corrections are complete "no-no's"! Don't undersell yourself. Recipient-design your curriculum vitae for different employers, having worked out which features are most likely to interest that employer.

- Choose referees that cover the different aspects of your life in which a particular employer is likely to be interested. Try to ensure that you are getting the "right kind" of references for the position. If a possible reference does not seem highly enthusiastic about agreeing to write a letter for you, find somebody else.

- Always write an accompanying letter with your curriculum vitae in which you explain why your experience is right for this job and your provisional thoughts of what fresh ideas you can bring to the tasks involved.

Short-listing committees will generally assess your application in terms of agreed criteria. For instance, many years ago, David was asked to write a report for a university offering a senior academic appointment in the field of medical sociology. He used the following criteria in his assessment of the candidates:

1. Breadth of interests

2. Quality of published work

3. Research productivity

4. International research contacts

5. Overall standing as a sociologist

He then attached a letter grade to these criteria for each candidate.

This gives you an idea of some of the criteria that selectors may use when they scan your curriculum vitae. Of course, how they will use these criteria is an open question. As David's research on selection interviews suggests, such criteria are sometimes retrospectively constructed to rationalize choices already made rather than influencing forthcoming decisions (Silverman & Jones, 1976). In a practical sense, this means that committee decisions and selection criteria are not set in stone. There is an element of flexibility and subjectivity inherent in the process—make it work for you.

Teaching Portfolio

Consider including in your application a detailed account of your teaching experience in the form of a portfolio. Most colleges and universities, especially the smaller four-year liberal arts schools, consider teaching a central part of their institutional mission. A teaching portfolio showcases your skills as a professional educator. In it, you can include (a) a statement of your teaching philosophy, (b) student and peer evaluations, (c) course syllabi, (d) teaching awards and certificates, (e) sample lesson plans and lectures, and (f) examples of your class discussion and participation exercises. A word of caution is necessary here. Do not overwhelm the committee with unnecessary paperwork. Be brief. You don't have to include every syllabi and student evaluation. Provide samples and summaries. If you are not sure if a teaching portfolio will help your application, ask if the committee would like to see one.

The Job Interview

Job selection interviews are one of the most intimidating experiences that we have to go through. Part of the reason for this is that we know that employers will treat our answers as a way of evaluating our qualities. This is, of course, very different from question-answer sequences in ordinary conversation where no such hidden agenda may be present.

For instance, as Graham Button (1992) points out, in ordinary conversation, where an answerer seems to have misunderstood a question, the questioner will repair the understanding. This is shown in the extract below:

Mandy: There should be "bout twuny or so people

Tina: I hope- will Chris be coming?

Mandy: If she can:[: get

Tina: [No you ninny Christo (Button, 1992)

Button (1992) compares this extract with data from a job interview for the post of head of an arts faculty in an English comprehensive (or high) school. The following extract occurs during this interview (IV = interviewer; IE = interviewee):

IV: Huhrm (.) What sort of sty::le do you see (.) yourself as-as a le::ader of- of (.) a- a team of teachers.

        (0.5)

IE: D'you mean how w'd I get other people to do it.

        (1.5)

IE: Well er:: (0.5) I think there are two ways of approaching tea::m teaching (adapted from Button, 1992)

Although, as Button suggests, IV's question is hearable as about person-management, IE chooses to hear it as about a teaching style ("team teaching") and the selectors do not take up the opportunity he gives to correct him. Later, however, the selectors noted that the candidate's answer "does not answer the question."

As Button points out, unlike the Mandy-Tina extract, where Tina corrected Mandy's understanding of her question,

> the interviewers never undertook this sort of correction on occasions where understanding problems may have been possibly relevant. Interviewers not only did not start to speak at first possible places where a transfer of speakership could be co-ordinated [e.g., where the IE begins to speak, above—but note that IV might have nodded at this point], they neither, without request from the candidate, intervened in the course of an answer (Button, 1992, p. 217)

Button's data makes clear that you can expect few favors at job interviews. Amir's own job interviewing experience supports this observation. For example, at the end of a phone interview, Amir was asked if he wanted to keep his job search secret from anyone. Specifically, the interviewer asked him, "Is there anyone you don't want us to contact as we check your references?" Amir responded with, "I have no secrets to hide. My reputation as a scholar and teacher is unimpeachable. . . ." Thinking that the question referred to his professional integrity, Amir launched into a long, self-righteous defense of his record. The interviewer thanked him for his time and informed him that he would be in touch. Several months later, Amir received the letter containing the patented lines, "Thank you for your application. Unfortunately, you were not chosen for this job. . . ." In retrospect, the question may have been about whether or not he wanted his current employer to know he was on the job market. The practical lesson is that if you are not sure about the question, ask for clarification before you try to answer it. You could simply do this by saying something like, "If I understand you correctly, you are asking me whether. . . . Is this correct?"

Some interviewers in fact will go out of their way to ask ambiguous questions to gauge the candidate's ability to "think on her feet." How do you deal with this kind of mind game? First and foremost, stay relaxed. Do not lose your focus and composure; as the saying goes, "Don't let them see you sweat." Second, preparation and planning will help you present yourself in the best light. Some ideas about what such preparation can involve are set out in Table 29.1.

As at your university oral examination, your job interview is the time to sell yourself while respecting the knowledge and experience of your assessors. So refer back to Table 29.1 and follow the tips there about self-presentation.

Table 29.1   Getting Through Job Interviews

- *Research*: Find out what the job entails in order to relate your own experience to the duties involved. Check the employer's Web site and talk to anybody listed on the job advertisement.

- *Rehearsal*: Compose half a dozen sentences to cover how your background fits the job description, why you want to work here, and what you hope to be doing in 5 years time. Practice these out loud so they are easy to say.

- *Interview*: Don't say too much in any answer but ask the panel if you have covered what they wanted. If you are worried about saying too little ("drying up"), use a written note of some key sentences as a prompt.

- *Afterward*: Before accepting a job, negotiate the terms and conditions; if you are turned down, don't take it personally—there is always a lottery element in any appointment and you will have gained experience for your next interview.

SOURCE: Adapted from Bradby (2002).

The Onsite Job Interview Schedule

When you visit a distant campus for a job interview, you will have a tight and grueling schedule. As the following list indicates, you will be introduced to numerous people and will give one or two presentations, sometimes all in the same day.

Table 29.2   Typical Onsite Job Interview Schedule

a. Airport pickup

b. Drive to the hotel

c. Breakfast with faculty the next day

d. Teaching and research presentations

e. Lunch with faculty and students

f. Meeting with college deans and other "hotshots"

g. Faculty dinner

h. Back to the hotel

i. Drive to the airport

For better or worse, the pressure and anxiety are part of the game. You and your potential employers know you are under the spotlight. The question is, how will you perform knowing that your every move is being critiqued? The thinking is, if you can maintain your composure under these circumstances, you will do okay as a colleague on a day-to-day basis. You are being evaluated at every step of the game, even when they tell you you can "let your guard down and relax."

Nowhere is the evaluation more intense than during your research presentation. This is a fascinating and very dynamic event. In larger departments, it is a time where junior faculty could impress the senior faculty by asking tough questions that they spent hours preparing. It is also an occasion where old faculty rivalries become manifest—you may think the questions are directed at you, but the faculty may in fact be taking cheap shots at one another. Be careful not to step into any traps.

Most important, qualitative researchers have to be careful not to overstate the strength of their methodology. It is possible that some of the people interviewing you do not fully understand qualitative research. You do not need to intimidate them with unnecessary jargon. Similarly, there is no need for alarming them by suggesting that qualitative research is superior to quantitative research. Show that you are methodologically tolerant and flexible (i.e., be "collegial"). As a qualitative researcher, you will almost certainly be asked about the validity and generalizability of your findings. Be prepared to answer such questions without appearing defensive. Again, the key to survival here is to be relaxed and prepared.

Overall, job interviews are scripted. Tempting as it may be to violate (breach) the script, your ability to play along is considered a sign of intelligence. As the satirist Dave Barry notes, there are good and bad answers to standard interview questions. Here are some of his humorous examples:

Question:	Why did you leave your last job?
Good Answer:	I felt that I had accomplished all I could and was looking for a more challenging environment where I could make an effective contribution.
Bad Answer:	The arson investigation was getting too close.
Question:	What would you say is your biggest weakness?
Good Answer:	Sometimes I get so involved in my job that I tend to neglect my personal life.
Bad Answer:	Heroin. (Barry, 2006, p. 48)

CHECKLIST FOR AN ACADEMIC JOB SEARCH

Preparations Before Entering the Job Market

- Attend an accredited school
- Develop a good working relationship with your professors
- Complete your degree or be near completion
- Present research manuscripts at professional conferences
- Submit papers to academic journals
- Develop teaching skills (teach a course or work as a teaching assistant)

Selecting Schools

- Narrow your search to places that are a good fit for your training and qualifications
- Decide on teaching, research, or equal emphasis
- Study the job description (course load, types of courses, areas of specialization)
- Consider the location (do you want to live in that area of the country?)

- Look at the school's overall ranking
- Look at the department's ranking

Preparing an Application

- Job letter (explain why you like the job and why they should want you for the job)
- Vita (arrange accomplishments to target their interests)
- Statement of teaching philosophy and evidence of teaching
- Statement of research philosophy
- Transcripts (if required)

The Interview Process

- Did you make the short list? (often you don't know)
- Study the program and the faculty before the onsite interview (use Internet sources; most have Web sites)
- Be prepared for screening phone interviews
- Prepare a "job-talk" research presentation
- Prepare a "job-talk" teaching presentation
- Be collegial during the interview (smile, make eye contact, listen before you speak, and overall be confident but not arrogant)
- Be aware of potential internal conflicts (don't take sides)

Accepting an Offer

- Compare with other offers
- Negotiate salary, benefits, office space, computer equipment, and credit toward tenure
- Sign the contract and Start the New Job

If Not Offered a Position

- Send out more applications

- Improve your vita

- Wait

CONCLUDING REMARKS

Unfortunately, job candidates will never know the exact reasons they were rejected. Typically, if you are not being considered for the job, you will receive a form letter that starts with these words, "Thank you for applying for the position. Unfortunately, . . ." Such letters are common. Do not be disheartened by them and do not spend an excessive amount of time trying to decipher the subtext of rejection letters. If you have a sense of humor, you could start a rejection letter scrapbook. Amir used to joke about how he was rejected by some of the finest institutions in the country.

A good rule of thumb is that if you were not invited for an interview or contacted by phone within a few weeks of the job ad's closing date, you did not make the top-three list. It is possible that your name is still on the short list. This means if the other three or four people are not suitable or they were offered the job but turned it down, you will be considered next.

One way or another, the waiting and anticipation during a job search becomes a great source of anxiety. A good practice is to stay busy with productive activities like polishing the dissertation or preparing manuscripts for submission to research journals. Regular exercise and spending time with friends and relatives are other sources of relief. A bad practice is waiting for the phone call and checking your e-mail twenty times a day. Do your best with preparing the applications, send them off, and then relax.

As with policymakers, selection committees have their own agendas. For instance, in the short-listing example discussed earlier, the appointing committee chose not to follow David's advice. Nonetheless, this is a game that has to be played and that can be played well or badly. Like any other game, this process requires a good deal of flexibility, alertness, and persistence on the part of players. Not everyone is offered their ideal job at the start of their career. As Amir's job search story shows (following), an academic career may take many turns and twists and still be fulfilling.

A CASE STUDY FROM AMIR

I chose the sociology program at the University of Florida in Gainesville mostly because I wanted to be close to my family. It was the only program to which I applied. To make matters worse, my application packet was not that impressive. For example, my letter of intent, which I later learned was used as a sample of my writing ability, was done on an old typewriter the night before the application deadline. This was 1991, long before word-processing computers became common household items. There were many typos, and they were corrected using correction fluid ("White-out"). The finished letter was more impressive for its physical properties than its content. The paper had become unusually heavy and textured—the thing almost looked like a watercolor painting. Despite these shortcomings, I was admitted to the program but not funded. Aside from my oddly distinguished letter, there was the fact that only students with a GRE score of 1200 or higher were funded—mine was barely over 1000. Luckily, my funding status changed in my second year in graduate school when the word got around that I was good at handling large data sets and working with both mainframe and personal computers. Ironically, despite my qualitative interests, managing numerical data was a reliable source of funding for me throughout graduate school.

I met my mentor, Jay Gubrium, in a required qualitative course I took with him in my second year in graduate school. I had been taught in my first-year graduate seminars that "good" research involved testing hypotheses using numerical data. So I was totally confused by Jay's ideas of research, which tended to be about subjectivity, textuality, discourse, and practice. Jay's enthusiasm about his work kept me interested, but I really had no sense of the bigger picture of qualitative research as an alternative paradigm. Occasionally, I would make a comment in class and I could tell from Jay's reaction that I had just said something insightful. Unfortunately, my moments of brilliance were often followed with questions or comments that seemed to puzzle my mentor. For example, I would ask something about random sampling in the context of a discussion about institutional ethnography, not knowing that the question just did not quite fit the model.

Things turned around when I started volunteering at a local homeless shelter as a class project. The assignment was intended to help students learn about qualitative research by doing their own mini-ethnographies. Each week we discussed our field observations in class. Through these class discussions, I realized I enjoyed talking to people much more than crunching numbers. I later asked Jay to serve as the chair of my dissertation committee. He agreed and recommended that I pursue homelessness as a dissertation topic. Several years later my dissertation was done and became my first book, titled *Being Homeless: Textual and Narrative Constructions*.

As the dissertation was wrapping up, I started applying for jobs, but with one publication I was not making it on anyone's short list. My job prospects were beginning to look pretty dim after rejection letters started to roll in. Things were wrapping up at the graduate program and I did not have any job offers. So I started looking for part-time teaching jobs. Luckily, a nearby college, Bethune-Cookman College in Daytona Beach, needed someone to cover three

(Continued)

(Continued)

sociology courses because one of their professors had accepted a new job and notified the college about this decision only weeks before the start of the semester. After a brief phone conversation, I was invited to the campus for an interview. I got to the campus about an hour late because I underestimated the driving distance and partly because I got lost.

At this point, I was sure I had no chance of getting the job. In addition to being late, I didn't think I connected with the faculty and administrators who interviewed me. In every encounter, I went on and on about my research interests, not realizing they were just looking for someone to teach several courses for one semester. To my surprise, I was offered the job. My guess is that with the start of the semester being just days away, there was no time for an extended search. As it turned out, at the end of my adjunct contract, I was offered a full-time assistant professor position at Bethune-Cookman, where I spent the next 2 years before moving to Penn State Altoona in North Central Pennsylvania (about 1000 miles north of Daytona Beach).

My job search story is not unusual. Many recent PhDs start their careers as adjunct or part-time instructors. I have been fortunate to have full-time employment, considering my haphazard career choices. In retrospect, I could have tried to be more actively involved in getting published and been more focused with my research agenda. Now that I serve on job committees where I screen tens of applications to select the top three candidates for onsite interviews, I have become intensely aware of the importance of "building up" one's vita. One of the first things I and my fellow committee members look for is where the candidate received his or her degree and how many articles, book chapters, and reviews he or she has published. Although teaching credentials are important, we are more likely to hire a qualified researcher who can become a good teacher than to hire a qualified teacher with little or no research experience. I imagine this view is more or less shared by the majority of administrators and faculty who serve on job search committees. There is truth in the "publish or perish" cliché. Publications significantly expand one's career opportunities in the academic job market.

KEY POINTS

There are two main information channels about jobs:

- Formal channels (job advertisements and job markets)

- Informal channels, which work through the guidance and information you can get from people on "the inside"

Whatever channels you use, make an inventory of the skills you possess and then relate them to the skills demanded by likely employers.

To improve your chances of getting a job, you should do the following:

- Write a model curriculum vitae showing logical, organized thought.

- Redesign your curriculum vitae for the needs of different employers. Also, list your publications in reverse chronological order, beginning with your most recent (most relevant publications).

- Choose referees that cover the different aspects of your life in which a particular employer is likely to be interested.

- Try to ensure that you are getting the "right kind" of references.

- Always write an accompanying letter with your curriculum vitae geared to what you can bring to this particular opening.

- Prepare yourself for the job interview and check with the selectors before making any one answer very long.

FURTHER READING

For research on job selection interviews, see David Silverman and Jill Jones's *Organizational Work: The Language of Grading/The Grading of Language* (1976) and Graham Button's chapter "Answers as Interactional Products: Two Sequential Practices Used in Job Interviews" in P. Drew and J. C. Heritage's (Eds.) *Talk at Work* (1992, pp. 212–234).

For instruction on how to create a teaching portfolio, see Peter Seldin's *The Teaching Portfolio: A Practical Guide to Improved Performance and Promotion/Tenure Decisions* (2004).

EXERCISE 29.1

If your university is hiring, attend a job presentation. Usually, the candidate's teaching and research presentations are open to graduate students. If possible, ask for a copy of the candidate's application. This material may be distributed in your department prior to the candidate's campus visit. Read the candidate's application letter, vita, and letters of recommendation. How do you compare with the candidate? What and how long will it take for you to become an interview-worthy candidate?

EXERCISE 29.2

Visit the *US News and World Report* Web page (http://www.usnews.com/usnews/edu/grad/rankings/phdhum/phdhumindex_brief.php) to see the rankings of top social science graduate programs in the Untied States. (Please note that top-three lists can be accessed free of charge at this site but the more expanded rankings require a fee).

1. Does your school appear in any of the rankings?

2. What are the rankings based on?

3. Consider what effect, if any, these rankings might have for your job search.

EXERCISE 29.3

Visit the Carnegie Foundation for the Advancement of Teaching Web page (http://www.carnegiefoundation.org/index.asp) to see the rankings of various social science graduate programs in the United States. To look up your institution, (a) select "Classifications," (b) choose "Lookup & Listings," (c) select "Institution Lookup," and (d) enter your school name in the box.

1. How is your institution ranked?

2. What are the rankings based on?

3. Consider what effect, if any, these rankings might have for your job search.

EXERCISE 29.4

Look at the employment bulletins at the American Sociological Association's Web site (www.asanet.org). Access to current job ads is limited to dues-paying members, but you can easily look at older ads free of charge. In reading these ads, consider the following questions:

1. What are the requirements for most jobs?

2. How many jobs do you feel you qualify for?

3. How many of those jobs would you like to have based on the geographical location, the school's reputation, and other development career opportunities?

4. How many job ads specifically require that the applicants be able to teach qualitative research classes? How many require the ability to teach quantitative research?

Appendix

Simplified Transcription Symbols

Symbol	Example	Explanation
[	C2: quite a [while Mo:　　　[yeah	Left brackets indicate the point at which a current speaker's talk is overlapped by another's talk.
=	W: that I'm aware of = C:　= Yes. Would you 　　confirm that?	Equal signs, one at the end of a line and one at the beginning, indicate no gap between the two lines.
(.4)	Yes (.2) yeah	Numbers in parentheses indicate elapsed time in silence in tenths of a second.
(.)	to get (.) treatment	A dot in parentheses indicates a tiny gap, probably no more than one-tenth of a second.
_____	What's up?	Underscoring indicates some form of stress, via pitch and/or amplitude.
::	O::kay?	Colons indicate prolongation of the immediately prior sound. The length of the row of colons indicates the length of the prolongation.
ALL CAPS	I've got ENOUGH TO WORRY ABOUT	Capitals, except at the beginnings of lines, indicate the speaker is speaking in an especially loud voice relative to the surrounding talk.
.hhhh	I feel that (.2) .hhh	A row of h's prefixed by a dot indicates an inbreath; without a dot, an outbreath. The length of the row of h's indicates the length of the in- or outbreath.
(　　)	future risks and (　　) and life (　　)	Empty parentheses indicate the transcriber's inability to hear what was said.
(word)	Would you see (if there's) anything positive to confirm that	Parenthesized words indicate words the recorder may have heard but is not certain of.
((　　))	((continues))	Double parentheses contain author's descriptions rather than transcriptions.
. , ?	What do you think?	These symbols indicate speaker's intonation (. = falling intonation; , = flat or slightly rising intonation).
>	>What do you think?	This indicates data later discussed.

Glossary

Adjacency pairs: Consecutive actions that are grouped in pairs and constrain what the next speaker may do (e.g., questions and answers).

Anecdotalism: Found where research reports appear to tell entertaining stories or anecdotes but fail to convince the reader of their scientific credibility.

CAQDAS: Computer-assisted analysis of qualitative data.

Coding: Putting data into theoretically defined categories in order to analyze it.

Concepts: Clearly specified ideas deriving from a particular model.

Constructionism: A model that encourages researchers to focus on how particular phenomena are put together through the close study of particular behaviors.

Content analysis: Data analysis, usually of texts, using a systematic approach that involves sampling, coding, and quantification.

Continuer: An utterance that signals to a listener that what he or she has just said has been understood and that he or she should now continue.

Control group: A group not given some stimulus provided to another group. A control group is used for comparative purposes.

Conversation analysis (CA): A qualitative approach based on an attempt to describe people's methods for producing orderly talk-in-interaction. It derives from the work of Sacks (1992).

Credibility: The extent to which any research claim has been shown to be based on evidence.

Culture: A common set of beliefs, values, and behaviors.

Deviant-case analysis: In qualitative research, this involves testing provisional hypotheses by "negative," or "discrepant," cases until all the data can be incorporated into your explanation.

Discourse analysis: The study of "the way versions of the world, of society, events, and inner psychological worlds are produced in discourse" (J. Potter, 2004, p. 202).

Emotionalism: A model of social research in which the primary issue is to generate data that gives an authentic insight into people's experiences. Emotionalists tend to favor open-ended interviews (see Gubrium & Holstein, 1997).

Empirical: Based on evidence through trial or experiment.

Empiricism: An approach that believes that evidence about the world does not depend on *models* or *concepts*.

Ethnography: Puts together two different words: *ethno* means "folk," and *graph* derives from "writing." Ethnography refers, then, to social scientific writing about particular folks.

Ethnomethodology: The study of folks'—or *members'*—methods. It seeks to describe methods persons use in doing social life. Ethnomethodology is not a methodology but a theoretical *model*.

Field: The setting or place where *ethnographic* research takes place.

Focus groups: Group discussions usually based upon stimuli (topics, visual aids) provided by the researcher.

Formal theories: Theories that relate findings from one setting to many situations or settings.

Frames: Following Goffman (1974), how people treat what is currently relevant and irrelevant defines the frame through which a setting is constituted.

Gatekeeper: Someone who is able to grant or refuse access to the *field*.

Genealogical: Following Foucault (1977, 1979), the study of the ways in which *discourses* have been structured at different historical points.

Generalizability: The extent to which a finding in one setting can be applied more generally.

Grand theory: A term used by Mills (1959) to describe highly abstract speculation that has little or no use in research.

Grounded theory: A term used by Glaser and Strauss (1967) to describe a way of inducing theoretically based generalizations from qualitative data.

Hermeneutics: An approach concerned with interpretation (originally derived from the study of biblical texts).

Hypotheses: Testable propositions often based on educated guesses.

Idioms: A term used by Gubrium and Holstein (1997) to describe a set of analytical preferences for particular *concepts*, styles of research, and ways of writing (see *model*).

Inductive: Based on the study of particular cases rather than just derived from a theory.

Interactionism: A theory, commonly used in qualitative sociological research, that assumes that our behavior and perceptions derive from processes of interaction with other people.

Intervening variable: A *variable* that is influenced by a prior factor and then goes on to influence another. Commonly used in quantitative research to work out which statistical association may be spurious.

Interview society: A term used by Atkinson and Silverman (1997) to point out the ways in which interviews have become a central medium for understanding who we are.

Leverage: Used by Marx (1997) to describe ways of finding multiple publishing outlets for one piece of research.

Low-inference descriptors: Recording observations "in terms that are as concrete as possible, including verbatim accounts of what people say, for example, rather than researchers' reconstructions of the general sense of what a person said, which would allow researchers' personal perspectives to influence the reporting" (Seale, 1999, p. 148) (see *reliability*).

Member: Used by Garfinkel (1967) to refer to participants in society. It is a shorthand term for "collectivity member" (see *ethnomethodology*).

Membership categorization device: A collection of categories (e.g., baby, mommy, father = family; male, female = gender) and some rules about how to apply these categories.

Methodology: Refers to the choices we make about cases to study, methods of data gathering, forms of data analysis, and so forth, in planning and executing a research study.

Models: Provide an overall framework for how we look at reality. They tell us what reality is like and the basic elements it contains (*ontology*) and what is the nature and status of knowledge (*epistemology*). See also *idioms*.

Narratives: The organization of stories (e.g., beginning, middle, and end; plots; and characters) that makes stories meaningful or coherent in a form appropriate to the needs of a particular occasion.

Naturalism: A model of research that seeks to minimize presuppositions in order to witness subjects' worlds in their own terms (Gubrium & Holstein, 1997).

Naturally occurring data: Data that derives from situations that exist independently of the researcher's intervention.

Normative: Pertaining to a norm or value; prescriptive.

Operational definitions: Working definitions that allow the measurement of some *variable*.

Paradigm: A conceptual framework (see *model*).

Paradigmatic: A term used in structuralism to indicate a polar set of *concepts* or activities where the presence of one denies the existence of the other (e.g., a red traffic light).

Participant observation: A method that assumes that, in order to understand the world firsthand, you must participate yourself rather than just observe at a distance. This method was championed by the early anthropologists but is shared by some *ethnographers*.

Positivism: A model of the research process that treats "social facts" as existing independently of the activities of both participants and researchers.

Postmodernism: An interdisciplinary movement based on the critique of all *concepts* and *paradigms*.

Preference organization: A concept derived from *CA* that suggests that recipients of actions recognize a preference for what they should do next.

Recipient design: Work that is designed for a particular audience (the term derives from *CA*, where it is used to describe how all actions are implicitly designed in this way).

Reflexivity: A term deriving from *ethnomethodology*, where it is used to describe the self-organizing character of all interaction so that any action provides for its own context. Mistakenly used to refer to self-questioning by a researcher.

Relativism: A value position where one resists taking a position because one believes that, because everything is relative to its particular context, it should not be criticized.

Reliability: "The degree of consistency with which instances are assigned to the same category by different observers or by the same observer on different occasions" (Hammersley, 1992, p. 67) (see *validity*).

Rewriting of history: A term used by Garfinkel (1967) to refer to the way in which any account retrospectively finds reasons for any past event.

Sample, sampling: Statistical procedure for finding cases to study. Sampling has two functions: it allows you to feel confident about the representativeness of your sample and such representativeness allows you to make broader inferences.

Semiotics: The study of signs (from speech, to fashion, to Morse code).

Social constructionism: See *constructionism*.

Social structure: A term used in sociology and anthropology to describe the institutional arrangements of a particular society or group (e.g., family and class structures).

Social survey: A quantitative method involving the study of large numbers of people often through the use of questionnaires.

Structuralism: A *model* used in anthropology that aims to show how single cases relate to general social forms. Structural anthropologists draw upon French social and linguistic theory of the early 20th century, notably Ferdinand de Saussure and Emile Durkheim. They view behavior as the expression of a "society" which works as a "hidden hand" constraining and forming human action.

Subculture: A set of beliefs, values, and behaviors shared by a particular group.

Substantive theory: A theory about a particular situation or group. Can be used to develop *formal theory*.

Syntagmatic: A term used within *semiotics* to denote the order in which related elements occur (e.g., how colors follow one another in traffic lights).

Theories: Arranged sets of concepts to define and explain some phenomenon.

Triangulation: The comparison of different kinds of data (e.g., quantitative and qualitative) and different methods (e.g., observation and interviews) to see whether they corroborate one another.

Turn-taking: The sequential organization of speech acts (see *CA*).

Validity: "The extent to which an account accurately represents the social phenomena to which it refers" (Hammersley, 1990, p. 57). Researchers respond to validity concerns by describing "the warrant for their inferences" (Fielding & Fielding, 1986, p. 12) (see *reliability*).

Variables: Factors that are isolated from one another in order to measure their relationship; usually described in quantitative research.

References

Acourt, P. (1997). *Progress, utopia and intellectual practice: Arguments for the resurrection of the future*. Unpublished PhD thesis, University of London, Goldsmiths College.

Alasuutari, P. (1995). *Researching culture: Qualitative method and cultural studies*. London: Sage.

American Sociological Association. (2006a). *Trend data on the profession*. Retrieved January 24, 2006, from http://www.asanet.org/page.ww?section=Profession+Trend+Data&name=Trend+Data+on+the+Profession

American Sociological Association. (2006b). *Unemployment rates for doctorate social and behavioral scientists*. Retrieved January 24, 2006, from http://www.asanet.org/page.ww?section=Profession+Trend+Data&name=Unemployment+Rates+for+Doctorate+Social+and+Behavioral+Scientists%2C+1993+-+2003

Antaki, C., & Rapley, M. (1996). "Quality of life" talk: The liberal paradox of psychological testing. *Discourse and Society, 7*(3), 293–316.

Arber, S. (1993). The research process. In N. Gilbert (Ed.), *Researching social life* (pp. 62–80). London: Sage.

Arditti, J. A., & Few, A. L. (2006). Mothers' reentry into family life following incarceration. *Criminal Justice Policy Review, 17*(1), 103–123.

Armstrong, D., Gosling, A., Weinman, J., & Marteau, T. (1997). The place of interrater reliability in qualitative research: An empirical study. *Sociology, 31*(3), 597–606.

Atkinson, J. M. (1978). *Discovering suicide*. London: Macmillan.

Atkinson, J. M., & Heritage, J. C. (Eds.). (1984). *Structures of social action*. Cambridge: Cambridge University Press.

Atkinson, P. (1992). The ethnography of a medical setting: Reading, writing and rhetoric. *Qualitative Health Research, 2*(4), 451–474.

Atkinson, P., & Coffey, A. (2004). Analysing documentary realities. In D. Silverman (Ed.), *Qualitative research* (2nd ed, pp. 56–75). London: Sage.

Atkinson, P., & Silverman, D. (1997). Kundera's immortality: The interview society and the invention of self. *Qualitative Inquiry, 3*(3), 324–345.

Avis, M., Bond, M., & Arthur, A. (1997). Questioning patient satisfaction: An empirical investigation in two outpatient clinics. *Social Science and Medicine, 44*(1), 85–92.

Back, L. (2004). Politics, research and understanding. In C. Seale, G. Gobo, J. F. Gubrium, & D. Silverman (Eds.), *Qualitative research practice* (pp. 261–275). London: Sage.

Baker, C. (2002). Ethnomethodological analysis of interviews. In J. Gubrium & J. Holstein (Eds.), *Handbook of interview research* (pp. 777–796). Thousand Oaks, CA: Sage.

Baker, C., & Keogh, J. (1995). Accounting for achievement in parent-teacher interviews. *Human Studies, 18*(2/3), 263–300.

Barkan, S. E., & Cohn, S. F. (1994). Racial prejudice and support for the death penalty by whites. *Journal of Research in Crime and Delinquency, 31*(2), 2002–2009.

Barker, M. (2003). Assessing the "quality" in qualitative research: The case of text-audience relations. *European Journal of Communication, 18*(3), 315–335.

Barry, D. (2006). *Dave Barry's money secrets: Like: Why is there a giant eyeball on the dollar?* New York: Crown.

Barthes, R. (1973). *Mythologies.* London: Paladin.

Baruch, G. (1981). Moral tales: Parents' stories of encounters with the health profession. *Social Health and Illness, 3*(3), 275–296.

Becker, H. (1963). *Outsiders: Studies in the sociology of deviance.* New York: Free Press.

Becker, H. (1967). Whose side are we on? *Social Problems, 14*(3), 239–247.

Becker, H. (1986). *Writing for social scientists.* Chicago: University of Chicago Press.

Becker, H. (1998). *Tricks of the trade: How to think about your research while doing it.* Chicago and London: University of Chicago Press.

Becker, H., & Geer, B. (1960). Participant observation: The analysis of qualitative field data. In R. Adams & J. Preiss (Eds.), *Human organization research: Field relation and techniques.* Homewood, IL: Dorsey.

Becker, H. S. (2004). Comment on Kevin D. Haggerty, "Ethics creep: Governing social science research in the name of ethics." *Qualitative Sociology, 27*(4), 415–416.

Bell, J. (1993). *Doing your research project* (2nd ed.). Buckingham: Open University Press.

Berelson, B. (1952). *Content analysis in communicative research.* New York: Free Press.

Bergmann, J. (1992). Veiled morality: Notes on discretion in psychiatry. In P. Drew & J. Heritage (Eds.), *Talk at work* (pp. 137–162). Cambridge: Cambridge University Press.

Blaikie, N. (1993). *Approaches to social enquiry.* Cambridge: Polity.

Bloor, M. (1978). On the analysis of observational data: A discussion of the worth and uses of inductive techniques and respondent validation. *Sociology, 12*(3), 545–557.

Bloor, M. (1983). Notes on member validation. In R. Emerson (Ed.), *Contemporary field research: A collection of readings.* Boston: Little, Brown.

Bloor, M. (1997). Addressing social problems through qualitative research. In D. Silverman (Ed.), *Qualitative research: Theory, method and practice* (pp. 221–238). London: Sage.

Bloor, M. (2004). Addressing social problems through qualitative research. In D. Silverman (Ed.), *Qualitative research: Theory, method and practice* (2nd ed., pp. 304–323). London: Sage.

Blumer, H. (1969). *Symbolic interactionism.* Englewood Cliffs, NJ: Prentice Hall.

Boden, D., & Zimmerman, D. H. (Eds.). (1991). *Talk and social structure: Studies in ethno methodology and conversation analysis* (pp. 44–71). Cambridge: Polity.

Bosk, C. (2004). The ethnographer and the IRB: Comment on Kevin D. Haggerty, "Ethics creep: Governing social science research in the name of ethics." *Qualitative Sociology, 2004, 27, 4, Winter* 27(4): 417–420.

Bosk, C. L., & De Vries, R. G. (2004). Bureaucracies of mass deception: Institutional review boards and the ethics of ethnographic research. *The Annals of the American Academy of Political and Social Science, 595,* 249–263.

Bradbury, M. (1988). *Unsent letters*. London: Andre Deutsch.

Bradby, H. (2002). Getting through employment interviews. *Network, 84,* 20–21.

British Research Councils. (1996). Priorities news Spring. Swindon: ESRC, http://www.pparc.ac.uk/home_old.asp

Brown, J. R. (2000). Privatizing the university. *Science, 290*(5497), 1701.

Brown, P., & Levinson, S. (1987). *Politeness: Some universals in language usage.* Cambridge: Cambridge University Press.

Bryman, A. (1988). *Quantity and quality in social research.* London: Unwin Hyman.

Buchanan, D. R. (1992). An uneasy alliance: Combining qualitative and quantitative research methods. *Health Education & Behavior, 19*(1), 117–135.

Bulmer, M. (1984). *The Chicago School of Sociology.* Chicago: Chicago University Press.

Burton, D. (Ed.). (2000). *Research training for social scientists.* London: Sage.

Button, G. (1992). Answers as interactional products: Two sequential practices used in job interviews. In P. Drew & J. C. Heritage (Eds.), *Talk at work* (pp. 212–234). Cambridge: Cambridge University Press.

Byrne, P., & Long, B. (1976). *Doctors talking to patients.* London: HMSO.

Chapman, G. (1987). *Talk, text and discourse: Nurses' talk in a therapeutic community.* Unpublished PhD thesis, University of London, Goldsmiths College.

Cicourel, A. (1968). *The social organization of juvenile sustice.* New York: Wiley.

Clavarino, A., Najman, J., & Silverman, D. (1995). Assessing the quality of qualitative data. *Qualitative Inquiry, 1*(2), 223–242.

Clifford, J., & Marcus, G. (Eds.). (1986). *Writing culture: The poetics and politics of ethnography.* Berkeley: University of California Press.

Cochrane, J. (2004). *Between you and I: A little book of bad English.* Naperville, IL: Sourcebooks.

Coffey, A., & Atkinson, P. (1996). *Making sense of qualitative data.* London: Sage.

Coffey, A., Holbrook, B., & Atkinson, P. (1996). Qualitative data analysis: Technologies and representations. *Sociological Research Online, 1*(1). Retrieved January 2006 from http://www.soc.surrey.ac.uk/socresonline/1/1/4.html

Cohen, S. (1980). *Folk devils and moral panics: The creation of the mods and rockers.* Oxford: Martin Robertson.

Cohen, S., & Young, J. (1973). *The manufacture of news.* London: Constable.

Cornwell, J. (1981). *Hard earned lives.* London: Tavistock.

Crothers, C. (1991). The internal structure of sociology departments: The role of graduate students and other groups. *Teaching Sociology, 19,* 333–343.

Cryer, P. (1996). *The research student's guide to success.* Buckingham: Open University Press.

Curtis, S., Gesler, W., Smith, G., & Washburn, S. (2000). Approaches to sampling and case selection in qualitative research: Examples in the geography of health. *Social Science and Medicine, 50,* 1000–1014.

Dalton, M. (1959). *Men who manage.* New York: Wiley.

Davies, S., & Guppy, N. (1997). Field of study, school selectivity, and student inequalities in higher education. *Social Forces, 75,* 1417–1438.

Delamont, S., & Atkinson, P. (2001). Doctoring uncertainty: Mastering craft knowledge. *Social Studies of Science, 31*(1): 87–107.

Deming, A. H. (1998). Science and poetry: A view from the divide. *Creative Nonfiction, 11,* 11–29.

Denzin, N. (1994). The art and practice of interpretation. In N. Denzin & Y. Lincoln (Eds.), *Handbook of qualitative research* (pp. 500–515). Thousand Oaks, CA: Sage.

Denzin, N. (1997). *Interpretive ethnography: Ethnographic practices for the 21st century.* Thousand Oaks, CA: Sage.

Denzin, N. (2000). The practice and politics of interpretation. In N. Denzin & Y. S. Lincoln (Eds.), *Handbook of qualitative research* (2nd ed., pp. 897–922). Thousand Oaks, CA: Sage.

Denzin, N., & Lincoln, Y. (Eds.). (1994). *Handbook of qualitative research.* Thousand Oaks, CA: Sage.

Denzin, N., & Lincoln, Y. (Eds.). (2000). *Handbook of qualitative research* (2nd ed.). Thousand Oaks, CA: Sage.

Denzin, N. K. (1993). Rhetoric and society. *The American Sociologist, 24,* 135–146.

Dey, I. (1993). *Qualitative data analysis: A user-friendly guide for social scientists.* London: Routledge.

Dingwall, R., & Murray, T. (1983). Categorization in accident departments: "Good" patients, "bad" patients and children. *Sociology of Health and Illness, 5*(12), 121–148.

Douglas, M. (1975). Self-evidence. In M. Douglas, *Implicit meanings.* London: Routledge.

Drew, P. (2001). Spotlight on the patient. *Text, 21*(1/2), 261–268.

Drew, P., & Heritage, J. C. (1992). Analysing talk at work: An introduction. In P. Drew & J. C. Heritage (Eds.), *Talk at work* (pp. 3–65). Cambridge: Cambridge University Press.

Durkheim, E. (1951). *Suicide.* New York: Free Press.

Durkin, T. (1997). Using computers in strategic qualitative research. In G. Miller & R. Dingwall (Eds.), *Context and method in qualitative research* (pp. 92–105). London: Sage.

Emerson, R. M., Fretz, R. I., & Shaw, L. L. (1995). *Writing ethnographic fieldnotes.* Chicago: University of Chicago Press.

Emmison, M., & Smith, P. (2000). *Researching the visual. Introducing qualitative methods series.* London: Sage.

Engebretson, J. (1996). Urban healers: An experiential description of American healing touch groups. *Qualitative Health Research, 6*(4), 526–541.

Fielding, N. (1982). Observational research on the national front. In M. Bulmer (Ed.), *Social research ethics: An examination of the merits of covert participant observation*. London: Macmillan.

Fielding, N., & Fielding, J. (1986). *Linking data*. London: Sage.

Fielding, N., & Lee, R. (Eds.). (1991). *Using computers in qualitative research*. Newbury Park, CA: Sage.

Fisher, M. (1997). *Qualitative computing: Using software for qualitative data analysis*. Cardiff Papers in Qualitative Research, Aldershot: Ashgate.

Flyvbjerg, B. (2004). Five misunderstandings about case-study research. In C. Seale, G. Gobo, J. Gubrium, & D. Silverman (Eds.), *Qualitative research practice* (pp. 420–434). London: Sage.

Forrest, B. (2001). The wedge at work: How intelligent design creationism is wedging its way into cultural and academic mainstream. In R. T. Penncock (Ed.), *Intelligent design creationism and its critics: Philosophical, theological and scientific perspectives* (pp. 5–53). Cambridge: MIT Press.

Foucault, M. (1973). *The order of things: An archeology of human sciences*. New York: Vintage.

Foucault, M. (1977). *Discipline and punish*. Harmondsworth, UK: Penguin.

Foucault, M. (1979). *The history of sexuality, Vol. 1*. Harmondsworth, UK: Penguin.

Frake, C. (1964). Notes on queries in ethnography. *American Anthropologist, 66*, 132–145.

Fraser, M. (1995). The history of the child: 1905–1989. PhD thesis, University of London, Goldsmiths College.

Frazier, C., Bishop, D., Lanza-Kaduce, L., & Marvasti, A. (1999). Juveniles in criminal court: Past and current research from Florida. *Quinnipiac Law Review, 18*(3), 573–596.

Garfinkel, H. (1967). *Studies in ethnomethodology*. Oxford, England: Polity Press.

Gilbert, N. (1993a). Writing about social research. In N. Gilbert (Ed.), *Researching social life* (pp. 328–344). London: Sage.

Gilbert, N. (Ed.). (1993b). *Researching social life*. London: Sage.

Gilbert, N., & Mulkay, M. (1983). In search of the action. In N. Gilbert & P. Abell (Eds.), *Accounts and action*. Aldershot: Gower.

Glaser, B., & Strauss, A. (1964). The social loss of dying patients. *American Journal of Nursing, 64*(6), 119–121.

Glaser, B., & Strauss, A. (1967). *The discovery of grounded theory*. Chicago: Aldine.

Glaser, B., & Strauss, A. (1968). *Time for dying*. Chicago: Aldine.

Glassner, B., & Loughlin, J. (1987). *Drugs in adolescent worlds: Burnouts to straights*. New York: St Martin's Press.

Goffman, E. (1959). *The presentation of self in everyday life*. New York: Doubleday Anchor.

Goffman, E. (1961). *Asylums*. New York: Doubleday Anchor.

Goffman, E. (1974). *Frame analysis*. New York: Harper and Row.

Gorton, W. A. (2006). *Karl Popper and the social sciences*. New York: SUNY.

Gouldner, A. (1954). *Patterns of industrial bureaucracy*. Glencoe, IL: Free Press.

Gubrium, J. (1988). *Analyzing field reality.* Newbury Park, CA: Sage.

Gubrium, J. (1992). *Out of control: Family therapy and domestic disorder.* London: Sage.

Gubrium, J. (1997). *Living and dying in Murray Manor.* Charlottesville, VA: University Press of Virginia.

Gubrium, J., & Buckholdt, D. (1982). *Describing care: Image and practice in rehabilitation.* Cambridge, MA: Oelschlager, Gunn and Hain.

Gubrium, J., & Holstein, J. (1987). The private image: Experiential location and method in family studies. *Journal of Marriage and the Family, 49,* 773–786.

Gubrium, J., & Holstein, J. (1995). Qualitative inquiry and the deprivatization of experience. *Qualitative Inquiry, 1*(2), 204–222.

Gubrium, J., & Holstein, J. (1997). *The new language of qualitative method.* New York: Oxford University Press.

Hadley, R. (1987). Publish and be ignored: Proselytise and be damned. In G. C. Wenger (Ed.), *The research relationship: Practice and politics in social policy research* (pp. 98–110). London: Allen and Unwin.

Hagan, F. E. (2005). *The essentials of research methods in criminal justice and criminology.* Boston: Pearson Education.

Haggerty, K. D. (2004, Winter). Ethics creep: Governing social science research in the name of ethics. *Qualitative Sociology, 27*(4), 391–414.

Hamburg, P. (2004). The new censorship: Institutional review boards. *Supreme Court Review,* 271–354.

Hammersley, M. (1990). *Reading ethnographic research: A critical guide.* London: Longmans.

Hammersley, M. (1992). *What's wrong with ethnography? Methodological explorations.* London: Routledge.

Hammersley, M., & Atkinson, P. (1983). *Ethnography: Principles in practice.* London: Tavistock.

Handy, C., & Aitken, A. (1994). The organisation of the primary school. In A. Pollard and J. Bourne (Eds.), *Teaching and learning in the primary school* (pp. 239–249). London: Routledge.

Hart, C. (1998). *Doing a literature review: Releasing the social science imagination.* London: Sage.

Hart, C. (2001). *Doing a literature search.* London: Sage.

Heath, C. (2004). Analysing face-to-face interaction: Video and the visual and the material. In D. Silverman (Ed.), *Qualitative research: Theory, method and practice* (2nd ed., pp. 265–281). London: Sage.

Heaton, J. M. (1979). Theory in psychotherapy. In N. Bolton (Ed.), *Philosophical problems in psychology* (pp. 179–198). London: Methuen.

Heise, D. (1988). Computer analysis of cultural structures. *Social Science Computer Review, 6,* 183–196.

Heritage, J. (1984). *Garfinkel and ethnomethodology.* Cambridge: Polity.

Heritage, J., & Sefi, S. (1992). Dilemmas of advice: Aspects of the delivery and reception of advice in interactions between health visitors and first time mothers.

In P. Drew & J. Heritage (Eds.), *Talk at work* (pp. 359–417). Cambridge: Cambridge University Press.

Hesse-Biber, S., & Dupuis, P. (1995). Hypothesis testing in computer-aided qualitative data analysis. In U. Kelle (Ed.), *Computer aided qualitative data analysis: Theory, methods and practice* (pp. 129–135). London: Sage.

Hickey, T. (2005). *Taking sides: Clashing views in crime and criminology.* Columbus, OH: McGraw-Hill.

Hickey, T. (2006). Taking sides: *Clashing views on crime and criminology* (7th ed.). Dubuque, IA: McGraw-Hill.

Hill, C. E. et al. (1988). *Therapist techniques and client outcomes.* London: Sage.

Himes, A. C. (2003). A formula for successful grant writing: Four proven keys. *Academic Leader, 19*(3), 4, 8.

Hindess, B. (1973). *The use of official statistics in sociology.* London: Macmillan.

Holstein, J. A. (1992). Producing people: Descriptive practice in human service work. *Current Research on Occupations and Professions, 7,* 23–29.

Holstein, J., & Gubrium, J. (1995). *The active interview.* Thousand Oaks, CA: Sage.

Horner, C. (2007). *The politically incorrect guide to global warming and environmentalism.* Washington, DC: Regnery.

Hornsby-Smith, M. (1993). Gaining access. In N. Gilbert (Ed.), *Researching social life* (pp. 52–67). London: Sage.

Houtkoop-Steenstra, H. (1991). Opening sequences in Dutch telephone conversations. In D. Boden & D. H. Zimmerman (Eds.), *Talk and social structure: Studies in ethnomethodology and conversation analysis* (pp. 232–250). Cambridge: Polity.

Huber, G. L., & Garcia, C. M. (1991). Computer assistance for testing hypotheses about qualitative data: The software package AQUAD 3.0. *Qualitative Sociology, 14*(4), 325–348.

Huberman, A. M., & Miles, M. B. (1994). Data management and analysis methods. In N. Denzin & Y. Lincoln (Eds.), *Handbook of qualitative research* (pp. 413–427). Thousand Oaks, CA: Sage.

Hughes, E. C. (1984). *The sociological eye.* New Brunswick, NJ: Transaction Books.

Humphreys, L. (1970). *Tearoom trade: Impersonal sex in public places.* Chicago: Aldine.

Hyland, K. (2002). Directives: Arguments and engagements in academic writing. *Applied Linguistics, 23*(2), 215–239.

Irurita, V. (1996). Hidden dimensions revealed: Progressive grounded theory study of quality care in the hospital. *Qualitative Health Research, 6*(3), 331–349.

Isaac, A. (1998). *African American students' guide to surviving graduate school.* Thousand Oaks, CA: Sage.

Jeffery, R. (1979). Normal rubbish: Deviant patients in casualty departments. *Sociology of Health and Illness, 1*(1), 90–107.

Jones, J. H. (1981). *Bad blood.* New York: Free Press.

Kafka, F. (1961). Investigations of a dog. In *Metamorphosis and other stories.* Harmondsworth, UK: Penguin.

Kelle, U. (Ed.). (1995). *Computer aided qualitative data analysis: Theory, methods and practice*. London: Sage.

Kelle, U. (1997). Theory building in qualitative research and computer programs for the management of textual data. *Sociological Research Online, 2*(2). Retrieved January 2006 from http://www.socresonline.org.uk/socresonline/2/2/1.html

Kelle, U. (2004). Computer assisted qualitative data analysis. In C. Seale, G. Gobo, J. F. Gubrium, & D. Silverman (Eds.), *Qualitative research practice* (pp. 473–489). London: Sage.

Kelle, U., & Laurie, H. (1995). Computer use in qualitative research and issues of validity. In U. Kelle (Ed.), *Computer aided qualitative data analysis: Theory, methods and practice* (pp. 12–28). London: Sage.

Kelly, M. (1998). Writing a research proposal. In C. Seale (Ed.), *Researching society and culture* (pp. 111–122). London: Sage.

Kelly, M. (2004). Research design and proposals. In C. Seale (Ed.), *Researching society and culture* (2nd ed., pp. 129–142). London: Sage.

Kendall, G., & Wickham, G. (1998). *Using Foucault's methods*. London: Sage.

Kent, G. (1996). Informed consent. In *The principled researcher* (pp. 18–24). Unpublished manuscript, Social Science Division, the Graduate School, University of Sheffield.

Kirk, J., & Miller, M. (1986). *Reliability and validity in qualitative research*. London: Sage.

Kitzinger, C., & Wilkinson, S. (1997). Validating women's experience? Dilemmas in feminist research. *Feminism and Psychology, 7*(4), 566–574.

Koppel, R., Cohen, A., & Abaluck, B. (2003). *Physicians' perceptions of medication error using differing research methods*. Paper presented at the meeting of the European Sociological Association (Qualitative Methods Group), Murcia, Spain.

Kuhn, T. S. (1970). *The structure of scientific revolutions* (2nd ed.). Chicago: University of Chicago Press.

Kuhn, T. (1996). *The structure of scientific revolutions*. Chicago: University of Chicago Press.

Isaac, A. (1998). *African American students' guide to surviving graduate school*. Thousand Oaks, CA: Sage.

Lee, R. M., & Fielding, N. G. (1995). Users' experiences of qualitative data analysis software. In U. Kelle (Ed.), *Computer aided qualitative data analysis: Theory, methods and practice* (pp. 29–140). London: Sage.

Lincoln, Y., & Guba, E. (2000). Paradigmatic controversies contradictions and emerging influences. In N. Denzin & Y. Lincoln (Eds.), *Handbook of qualitative research* (2nd ed., pp. 162–188). Thousand Oaks, CA: Sage.

Lincoln, Y. S., & Denzin, N. (1994). The fifth moment. In N. Denzin and Y. S. Lincoln (Eds.), *Handbook of qualitative research* (pp. 575–586). Thousand Oaks, CA: Sage.

Lindström, A. (1994). Identification and recognition in Swedish telephone conversation openings. *Language in Society, 23*(2), 231–252.

Lipset, S. M., Trow, M., & Coleman, J. (1962). *Union democracy*. Garden City, NY: Anchor Doubleday.

Livingston, E. (1987). *Making sense of ethnomethodology*. London: Routledge.

Loseke, D. (1989). Creating clients: Social problems' work in a shelter for battered women. *Perspectives on Social Problems, 1*, 173–193.

Loseke, D., & Cahill, S. (2004). Publishing qualitative manuscripts: Lessons learned in C. Seale, G. Gobo, J. F. Gubrium, & D. Silverman (Eds.), *Qualitative research practice* (pp. 576–591). London: Sage.

Lynch, M. (1984). *Art and artifact in laboratory science.* London: Routledge.

Madison, S. (2005). *Critical ethnography: Methods, ethics, and performance.* Thousand Oaks, CA: Sage.

Mahoney, M. J. (1977). Publication prejudices: An experimental study of confirmatory bias in the peer review system. *Cognitive Therapy and Research, 1,* 161–175.

Malinowski, B. (1922). *Argonauts of the Western Pacific.* London: Routledge.

Marsh, C. (1982). *The survey method.* London: Allen and Unwin.

Marshall, C., & Rossman, G. (1989). *Designing qualitative research.* London: Sage.

Marvasti, A. (2002, November 2). Ethnic profiling takes its toll on the innocent [Editorial]. *Altoona Mirror.*

Marvasti, A. (2003a). *Qualitative research in sociology.* London: Sage.

Marvasti, A. (2003b). *Being homeless: Textual and narrative constructions.* Lanham, VA: Lexington Books.

Marvasti, A. (2004). *Qualitative research in sociology.* Thousand Oaks, CA: Sage.

Marx, G. (1997, Spring). Of methods and manners for aspiring sociologists: 37 moral imperatives. *The American Sociologist, 102–125.*

Mason, J. (1996). *Qualitative researching.* London: Sage.

Mason, J. (2002). *Qualitative researching* (2nd ed.). London: Sage.

Maynard, D. W. (1991). Interaction and asymmetry in clinical discourse. *American Journal of Sociology, 97*(2), 448–495.

McKeganey, N., & Bloor, M. (1991). Spotting the invisible man: The influence of male gender on fieldwork relations. *British Journal of Sociology, 42*(2), 195–210.

McLeod, J. (1994). *Doing counselling research.* London: Sage.

Mehan, H. (1979). *Learning lessons: Social organization in the classroom.* Cambridge, MA: Harvard University Press.

Mercer, K. (1990). *Powellism as a political discourse.* Unpublished PhD thesis, University of London, Goldsmiths College.

Mergenthaler, E. (1996). Emotion-abstraction patterns in verbatim protocols: A new way of describing psychotherapeutic process. *Journal of Consulting and Clinical Psychology, 64*(6), 1306–1315.

Merton, R. K. (1968). The Matthew effect in science. *Science, 159,* 56–63.

Miall, D. S. (Ed.) (1990). *Humanities and the computer: New directions.* Oxford: Clarendon.

Miles, M., & Huberman, A. (1984). *Qualitative data analysis.* London: Sage.

Miles, M., & Weitzman, E. (1995). *Computer programs for qualitative data analysis.* Thnousand Oaks, CA: Sage.

Miller, G., & Silverman, D. (1995). Troubles talk and counseling discourse: A comparative study. *The Sociological Quarterly, 36*(4), 725–747.

Miller, J. (1996). *Female gang involvement in the Midwest: A two-city comparison.* Unpublished doctoral dissertation, Department of Sociology, University of Southern California.

Miller, J., & Glassner, B. (1997). The "inside" and the "outside": Finding realities in interviews. In D. Silverman (Ed.), *Qualitative research* (pp. 99–112). London: Sage.

Miller, J., & Glassner, B. (2004). The inside and the outside: Finding realities in interviews. In D. Silverman (Ed.), *Qualitative research: Theory, method and practice* (2nd ed., pp. 125–139). London: Sage.

Miller, R., & Bor, R. (1988). *AIDS: A guide to clinical counselling.* London: Science Press.

Miller, S., Nelson, M., & Moore, M. (1998). Caught in the paradigm gap: Qualitative researchers lived experience and the politics of epistemology. *American Educational Research Journal, 35*(3), 377–416.

Mills, C. W. (1959). *The sociological imagination.* New York: Oxford University Press.

Mitchell, J. C. (1983). Case and situational analysis. *Sociological Review, 31*(2), 187–211.

Moerman, M. (1974). Accomplishing ethnicity. In R. Turner (Ed.), *Ethnomethodology* (pp. 34–68). Harmondsworth, UK: Penguin.

Monk, R. (1991). *Ludwig Wittgenstein: Duty of genius.* Harmondsworth, UK: Penguin.

Morse, J. M. (1994). Designing funded qualitative research. In N. Denzin & Y. Lincoln (Eds.), *Handbook of qualitative research* (pp. 220–235). Thousand Oaks, CA: Sage.

Mulkay, M. (1984). The ultimate compliment: A sociological analysis of ceremonial discourse. *Sociology, 18,* 531–549.

Murcott, A. (1997). *The PhD: Some informal notes.* Unpublished paper, School of Health and Social Care, South Bank University, London.

Murray, R. (2003, September 16). Survive your viva. *Guardian Education.*

Nelson, C. (2003). Can E.T. phone home? The brave new world of university surveillance. *Academe, 89,* 30–35.

Neubauer, B. (2005). *The write-brain workbook: 366 exercises to liberate your writing.* Cincinnati, OH: F & W Publications.

Nish, W. W. (2007). *Professors' pet peeves: How to receive a less than enthusiastic letter of recommendation.* Retrieved November 4, 2007, from Hanover College Psychology Department's Graduate School Planning Web site at http://psych.hanover.edu/gradschoolplanning.html

Noble, W. (2006). *Noble's book of writing blunders and how to avoid them.* Cincinnati, OH: Writer's Digest Books.

O'Brien, M. (1993). Social research and sociology. In N. Gilbert (Ed.), *Researching social life* (pp. 1–17). London: Sage.

Oboler, R. (1986). For better or for worse: Anthropologists and husbands in the field. In T. Whitehead & M. Conway (Eds.), *Self, sex and gender in cross-cultural fieldwork* (pp. 28–51). Urbana: University of Illinois Press.

Penslar, R. L. (2007). *IRB guidebook.* Retrieved October 15, 2007, from the U.S. Department of Health and Human Services at http://www.hhs.gov/ohrp/irb/irb_guidebook.htm.

Peräkylä, A. (1989). Appealing to the experience of the patient in the care of the dying. *Sociology of Health and Illness, 11*(2), 117–134.

Peräkylä, A. (1995). *AIDS counselling.* Cambridge: Cambridge University Press.

Peräkylä, A. (2004). Reliability and validity in research based upon transcripts. In D. Silverman (Ed.), *Qualitative research: Theory, method and practice* (2nd ed., pp. 282–303). London: Sage.

Peters, D. P., & Ceci, S. J. (1982). Peer-review practices of psychological journals: The fate of published articles, submitted again. *The Behavioral and Brain Sciences, 1982,* 187–195.

Peters, R. (1997). *Getting what you came for: The smart student's guide to earning an M.A. or Ph.D.* (rev. ed.). New York: Farrar, Straus, and Giroux.

Phillips, E., & Pugh, D. (1994). *How to get a PhD* (2nd ed.). Buckingham: Open University Press.

Plutzer, E. (1991). The Protestant ethic and the spirit of academia: An essay on graduate education. *Teaching Sociology, 19,* 302–307.

Popper, K. (1959). *The logic of scientific discovery.* New York: Basic Books.

Popper, K. (1963). *Conjectures and refutations: The growth of scientific knowledge.* London: Routledge.

Potter, J. (2002). Two kinds of natural. *Discourse Studies, 4*(4), 539–542.

Potter, J. (2004). Discourse analysis as a way of analysing naturally-occurring talk. In D. Silverman (Ed.), *Qualitative research: Theory, method and practice* (2nd ed., pp. 200–221). London: Sage.

Potter, J., & Wetherell, M. (1987). *Discourse and social psychology: Beyond attitudes and behaviour.* London: Sage.

Potter, J., & Wetherell, M. (1994). Analysing discourse. In A. Bryman & R. G. Burgess (Eds.), *Analysing qualitative data* (pp. 47–66). London: Routledge.

Potter, S. (Ed.). (2002). *Doing postgraduate research.* London: Sage.

Propp, V. I. (1968). *Morphology of the folktale* (2nd rev. ed., L. A. Wagner, Ed.). Austin and London: University of Texas Press.

Psathas, G. (1990). *Interaction competence.* Washington, DC: University Press of America.

Punch, K. (1998). *Introduction to social research: Quantitative and qualitative approaches.* London: Sage.

Punch, K. (2000). *Developing effective research proposals.* London: Sage.

Punch, M. (1986). *The politics and ethics of fieldwork.* Beverly Hills, CA: Sage.

Punch, M. (1994). Politics and ethics in fieldwork. In N. Denzin & Y. Lincoln (Eds.), *Handbook of qualitative research* (pp. 83–97). Thousand Oaks, CA: Sage.

Pursley-Crotteau, S., & Stern, P. (1996). Creating a new life: Dimensions of temperance in perinatal cocaine crack users. *Qualitative Health Research, 6*(3), 350–367.

Radcliffe-Brown, A. R. (1948). *The Andaman Islanders.* Glencoe, IL: Free Press.

Rapley, T. (2004). Interviews. In C. Seale, G. Gobo, J. F. Gubrium, & D. Silverman (Eds.), *Qualitative research practice* (pp. 15–33). London: Sage.

Reason, P., & Rowan, J. (1981). *Human inquiry: A sourcebook of new paradigm research.* Chichester, UK: Wiley.

Reid, A. O. (1992). Computer management strategies for text data. In B. F. Crabtree & W. L. Miller (Eds.), *Doing qualitative research* (pp. 125–145). Newbury Park, CA: Sage.

Richards, L., & Richards, T. (1994). Using computers in qualitative analysis. In N. Denzin & Y. Lincoln (Eds.), *Handbook of qualitative research* (pp. 445–462). Newbury Park, CA: Sage.

Richardson, L. (1990). *Writing strategies: Researching diverse audiences*. Newbury Park, CA: Sage.

Richardson, L. (1992). The consequences of poetic representation. In C. Ellis & M. Flaherty (Eds.), *Investigating subjectivity* (pp. 125–137). Thousand Oaks, CA: Sage.

Richardson, L. (2000). Writing: A method of inquiry. In N. Denzin & Y. Lincoln (Eds.), *Handbook of qualitative research* (2nd ed., pp. 923–948). Thousand Oaks, CA: Sage.

Riessman, C. K. (1993). *Narrative analysis*. Newbury Park, CA: Sage.

Rosenau, P. M. (1992). *Postmodernism and the social sciences: Insights, inroads, and intrusions*. Princeton, N.J.: Princeton University Press.

Rudestam, K., & Newton, R. (1992). *Surviving your dissertation*. Newbury Park, CA: Sage.

Ryen, A. (2004). Ethical issues. In C. Seale, G. Gobo, J. F. Gubrium, & D. Silverman (Eds.), *Qualitative research practice*. London: Sage.

Sacks, H. (1974). On the analysability of stories by children. In R. Turner (Ed.), *Ethnomethodology*. Harmondsworth, UK: Penguin.

Sacks, H. (1984a). On doing "being ordinary." In J. M. Atkinson & J. Heritage (Eds.), *Structures of social action: Studies in conversation analysis* (pp. 513–529). Cambridge: Cambridge University Press.

Sacks, H. (1984b). Notes on methodology. In J. M. Atkinson & J. Heritage (Eds.), *Structures of social action: Studies in conversation analysis* (pp. 21–27). Cambridge: Cambridge University Press.

Sacks, H. (1992). *Lectures on conversation, Vols. 1–2*. Oxford: Blackwell.

Sacks, H., Schegloff, E. A., & Jefferson, G. (1974). A simplest systematics for the organization of turn-taking in conversation. *Language, 50*(4), 696–735.

Schegloff, E. (1986). The routine as achievement. *Human Studies, 9,* 111–151.

Schegloff, E. (1991). Reflections on talk and social structure. In D. Boden & D. Zimmerman (Eds.), *Talk and social structure: Studies in ethnomethodology and conversation analysis* (pp. 44–70). Cambridge: Polity.

Schneider, A. (1998, October 23). Harvard faces the aftermath of a graduate student's suicide. *Chronicle of Higher Education*.

Schreiber, R. (1996). (Re)defining my self: Women's process of recovery from depression. *Qualitative Health Research, 6*(4), 469–491.

Schwartz, H., & Jacobs, J. (1979). *Qualitative sociology: A method to the madness*. New York: Free Press.

Seale, C. (1996). Living alone towards the end of life. *Ageing and Society, 16,* 75–91.

Seale, C. (1999). *The quality of qualitative research*. London: Sage.

Seale, C. (Ed.) (2004). *Researching society and culture* (2nd ed.). London: Sage.

Seale, C., Gobo, G., Gubrium, J. F., & Silverman, D. (Eds.). (2004). *Qualitative research practice*. London: Sage.

Seale, C. F. (2002). Computer-assisted analysis of qualitative interview data. In J. Gubrium & J. Holstein (Eds.), *Handbook of interview research* (pp. 651–670). Thousand Oaks, CA: Sage.

Seldin, P. (2004). *The teaching portfolio: A practical guide to improved performance and promotion/tenure decisions.* Bolton, MA: Ancher.

Sharples, M., Davison, L., Thomas, G., & Rudman, P. (2003). Children as photographers: An analysis of children's photographic behaviour and intentions at three age levels. *Visual Communication, 2*(3), 303–330.

Shea, C. (2000). Don't talk to humans: The crack down on social science research. *Lingua Franca, 10*(6).

Silverman, D. (1981). The child as a social object: Down's syndrome children in a paediatric cardiology clinic. *Sociology of Health and Illness, 3*(3), 254–274.

Silverman, D. (1983). The clinical subject: Adolescents in a cleft palate clinic. *Sociology of Health and Illness, 5*(3), 253–274.

Silverman, D. (1984). Going private: Ceremonial forms in a private oncology clinic. *Sociology, 18,* 191–202.

Silverman, D. (1985). *Qualitative methodology and sociology: Describing the social world.* Aldershot, UK: Gower.

Silverman, D. (1987). *Communication and medical practice: Social relations in the clinic.* London: Sage.

Silverman, D. (1989). Making sense of a precipice: Constituting identity in an HIV clinic. In P. Aggleton, G. Hart, & P. Davies (Eds.), *AIDS: Social representations, social practices.* Lewes, UK: Falmer.

Silverman, D. (1990). The social organization of HIV counselling. In P. Aggleton, G. Hart, & P. Davies (Eds.), *AIDS: Individual, cultural and policy perspectives* (pp. 191–211). Lewes, UK: Falmer.

Silverman, D. (1997). *Discourses of counselling: HIV counselling as social interaction.* London: Sage.

Silverman, D. (1998). *Harvey Sacks: Social science and conversation analysis.* Cambridge: Polity, New York: Oxford University Press.

Silverman, D. (2001). *Interpreting qualitative data: Methods for analysing text, talk and interaction* (2nd ed.). London: Sage.

Silverman, D. (2004a). Analysing conversation. In C. Seale (Ed.), *Researching society and culture* (2nd ed., pp. 261–274) London: Sage.

Silverman, D. (Ed.) (2004b). *Qualitative research: Theory, method and practice* (2nd ed.). London: Sage.

Silverman, D., & Bloor, M. (1989). Patient-centred medicine: Some sociological observations on its constitution, penetration and cultural assonance. In G. L. Albrecht (Ed.), *Advances in medical sociology* (pp. 3–26). Greenwich, CT: JAI Press.

Silverman, D., & Gubrium, J. (1994). Competing strategies for analyzing the contexts of social interaction. *Sociological Inquiry, 64*(2), 179–198.

Silverman, D., & Jones, J. (1976). *Organizational work: The language of grading/the grading of language.* London: Collier-Macmillan.

Silverman, D., Baker, C., & Keogh, J. (1997). Advice-giving and advice-reception in parent-teacher interviews. In I. Hutchby & J. Moran-Ellis (Eds.), *Children and social competence* (pp. 220–240). London: Falmer.

Singleton, R., Straits, B., Straits, M., & McAllister, R. (1988). *Approaches to social research*. Oxford: Oxford University Press.

Small, S. A. (1995). Action-oriented research: Models and methods. *Journal of Marriage and Family, 57*(4), 941–955.

Smith, J. K., & Heshusius, L. (1986). Closing down the conversation: The end of the qualitative-quantitative debate among educational enquirers. *Educational Researcher, 15,* 4–12.

Sontag, S. (1979). *IIIness as metaphor*. Harmondsworth, UK: Penguin.

Speer, S. (2002). "Natural" and "contrived" data: A sustainable distinction? *Discourse Studies, 4*(4), 511–525.

Spencer, L., Ritchie, J., Lewis, J., & Dillon, J. (2003). *Quality in qualitative evaluation: A framework for assessing research evidence*. London: Government Chief Social Researcher's Office.

Spradley, J. P. (1979). *The ethnographic interview*. New York; Holt, Rinehart and Winston.

Stake, R. (2000). Case studies. In N. Denzin & Y. Lincoln (Eds.), *Handbook of qualitative research* (2nd ed., pp. 435–454). Thousand Oaks, CA: Sage.

Stimson, G. (1986). Place and space in sociological fieldwork. *Sociological Review, 34*(3), 641–656.

Strauss, A., & Corbin, J. (1990). *Basics of qualitative research*. Newbury Park, CA: Sage.

Strauss, A., & Corbin, J. (1994). Grounded theory methodology: An overview. In N. Denzin & Y. Lincoln (Eds.), *Handbook of qualitative research* (pp. 262–272). Thousand Oaks, CA: Sage.

Strong, P. (1979). *The ceremonial order of the clinic*. London: Routledge.

Suchman, L. (1987). *Plans and situated actions: The problem of human–machine communication*. Cambridge: Cambridge University Press.

Sudnow, D. (1968a). *Passing n: The social organization of dying*. Englewood Cliffs, NJ: Prentice Hall.

Sudnow, D. (1968b). Normal crimes. In E. Rubington & M. Weinberg (Eds.), *Deviance: The interactionist perspective*. New York: Macmillan.

ten Have, P. (1998). *Doing conversation analysis: A practical guide*. London: Sage.

Tenner, E. (2004). The pitfalls of academic mentorships. *Chronicle Review, 50*(49), B7.

Turner, R. (1989). Deconstructing the field. In J. F. Gubrium & D. Silverman (Eds.), *The politics of field research* (pp. 30–48). London: Sage.

Tyler, S. A. (1986). Post-modern ethnography: From document of the occult to occult document. In J. Clifford and G. Marcus (Eds.), *Writing culture: The poetics and politics of ethnography* (pp. 122–140). Los Angeles: University of California Press.

U.S. Department of Health and Human Services. (2005). Code of federal regulations. Title 45: Public welfare (§46.102d). Retrieved November 4, 2005, from http://www.hhs.gov/ohrp/humansubjects/guidance/45cfr46.htm#46.102

Valero, Y. F. (2001). Departmental factors affecting time-to-degree and completion rates of doctoral students at one land-grant research institution. *Journal of Higher Education, 72*(3), 341–367.

Van de Werfhorst, H. G., & Andersen, R. (2005). Social background, credential inflation, and educational strategies. *Acta Sociologica, 48*(4), 321–340.

Van Maanen, J. (1988). *Tales of the field*. Chicago: University of Chicago Press.

Vandiver, M., Giacopassi, D. J., & Gathje, P. R. (2002). "I hope someone murders your mother!": An exploration of extreme support for the death penalty. *Deviant Behavior: An Interdisciplinary Journal, 23*, 385–415.

Walsh, D. (1998). Doing ethnography. In C. Seale (Ed.), *Researching society and culture* (pp. 225–238). London: Sage.

Ward, A. (2002). The writing process. In S. Potter (Ed.), *Doing postgraduate research* (pp. 71–116). London: Sage.

Warren, A. (1988). *Gender issues in field research*. Newbury Park, CA: Sage.

Warren, A., & Rasmussen, P. (1977). Sex and gender in fieldwork research. *Urban Life, 6*, 359–369.

Watts, H. D., & White, P. (2000). Presentation skills. In D. Burton (Ed.), *Research training for social scientists*. London: Sage.

Webb, B., & Stimson, G. (1976). People's accounts of medical encounters. In M. Wadsworth (Ed.), *Everyday medical life*. London: Martin Robertson.

Weber, M. (1946). Science as a vocation. In H. Gerth & C. W. Mills (Eds.), *From Max Weber*. New York: Oxford University Press.

Weber, M. (1949). *Methodology of the social sciences*. New York: Free Press.

Weinberg, M. S. (1994). The nudist management of respectability. In P. Kollock & J. O'Brien (Eds.), *The production of reality: Essays and readings in social psychology* (pp. 392–401). Thousand Oaks, CA: Pine Forge Press.

Whyte, W. F. (1949). The social structure of the restaurant. *American Journal of Sociology, 54*, 302–310.

Wield, D. (2002). Planning and organizing a research project. In S. Potter (Ed.), *Doing postgraduate research* (pp. 35–70). London: Sage.

Wilkinson, S. (2004). Focus group research. In D. Silverman (Ed.), *Qualitative research: Theory, method and practice* (2nd ed., pp. 177–199). London: Sage.

Wilkinson, S., & Kitzinger, C. (2000). Thinking differently about thinking positive: A discursive approach to cancer patients' talk. *Social Science and Medicine, 50*, 797–811.

Wittgenstein, L. (1980). *Culture and value* (P. Winch, Trans.). Oxford: Basil Blackwell.

Wolcott, H. (1990). *Writing up qualitative research*. Newbury Park, CA: Sage.

Wolcott, H. (2001). *Writing up qualitative research* (2nd ed.). Thousand Oaks, CA: Sage.

Wolfe, A. (1990). Books vs. articles: Two ways of publishing sociology. *Sociological Forum, 5*(3), 477–489.

Yagoda, B. (2007). *When you catch an adjective, kill it: The parts of speech, for better and/or worse*. New York: Broadway Books.

Author Index

Subject Index

About the Authors

David Silverman is Professor Emeritus, Sociology Department, Goldsmiths College, and Visiting Professor, Management Department, King's College, University of London. He is the author and/or editor of many top-selling qualitative books for Sage London, including *Interpreting Qualitative Data* (3rd edition published 2006), *Qualitative Research Practice* (2004), *Qualitative Research* (2nd edition published 2004), and *Doing Qualitative Research* (2nd edition published 2004). His latest book for Sage London is *A Very Short, Fairly Interesting and Reasonably Cheap Book about Qualitative Research* (2007). He is also the editor of the series Introducing Qualitative Methods.

Amir Marvasti is Assistant Professor of Sociology at Pennsylvania State University, Altoona. He received his PhD in sociology from the University of Florida. He has published in the *Quinnipiac Law Review*, *Qualitative Inquiry*, the *Journal of Contemporary Ethnography*, and *Symbolic Interaction*. His research interests include race and ethnicity, deviance, and social theory. He is the author of *Qualitative Research in Sociology* (Sage, 2004) which was published in David Silverman's series Introducing Qualitative Methods. He is also the author of *Being Homeless: Textual and Narrative Constructions*, and *Middle Eastern Lives in America* (with Karyn McKinney, 2004). His current research focuses on the immigration experiences of Middle Eastern Americans.